tree. All these aspirations are directed toward ennobling man's life, lifting it from the sphere of mere physical existence and leading the individual towards freedom."

SCIENCE AND CHRISTIAN FAITH:

THEIR RELATIONSHIP IN THE PAST, PRESENT AND FUTURE

by
Stephen C.Y.Liu

This book is dedicated to:

Zachary; Grace, Emily, Anna; Jeremy, Linus, Talitha, Christopher-Tiffany; Amanda-Peter; Paul M-Rebekah; Grace-Paul; Betty-Theodore; and Christine, my life-partner, fellow-traveler and critic.

美商EHGBooks微出版公司

www.EHGBooks.com

EHG Books 公司出版

Amazon.com 總經銷

2013 年版權美國登記

未經授權不許翻印全文或部分

及翻譯為其他語言或文字

2013 年 EHGBooks 第一版

ISBN-13 : 978-1-62503-072-6

✠ Prof. John Polkinghorne, FRS Former President of Queen's College, University of Cambridge. Canon Theologian; Particle Mathematic physicist; & Stephen Liu.

✠ Prof. Brian Heap Former President of Edmund College, Cambridge Univ. 2009; & Stephen Liu.

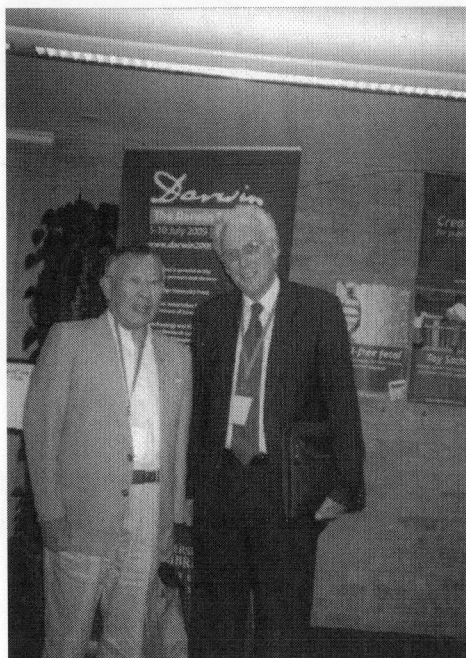

✠ "Apple Tree" in the front yard, King's college. Isaac Newton observed the fall of apple tree. "Universal Gravitation", University Cambridge.

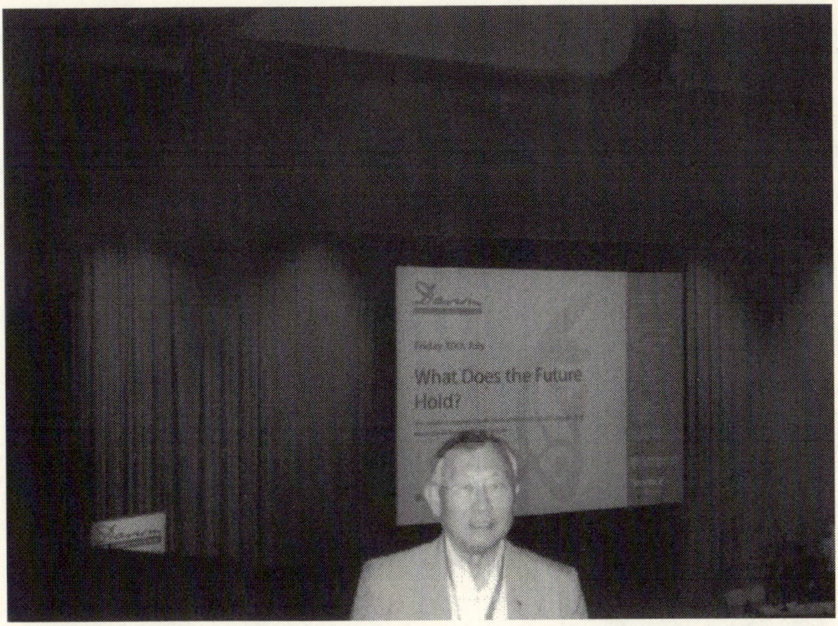

✠ Cavendish Laboratory, Univ. of Cambridge where James D. Watson & Crick worked on DNA molecule & won Nobel Prize in 1953. Many Nobel Prize winners worked in Cavendish.

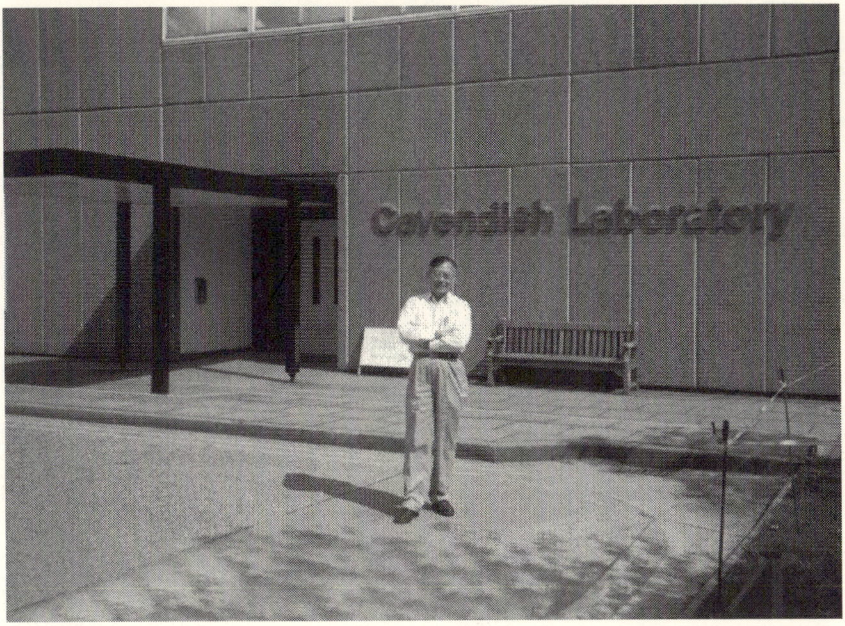

✠ Stephen speaks in "Science & Christian Faith" in a classroom of students at Cambridge, 1998

✠ Stephen & Christine, Ed Kwong at Chinese Christian Church in Cambridge

✠ Stephen & Christine and Pastor Vincent Aun of Chinese Church in London, England

✠ Stephen Liu speaks on "Science & Christian Faith" at Cambridge Chinese Church

✠ Stephen Liu lectures at Bible Institute of Queensland Australia

✠ Stephen Liu lecture on "Science & Faith" on Oxford University campus

✠ Stephen Liu speaks in Chinese Church in Paris, France

✠ Stephen Liu speaks in Chinese Church in Melbourne, Australia

✠ Stephen Liu speaks in Chinese Christian church in Cambridge, England

✠ Stephen Liu lectures at University of Gottingen, Germany

✠ Stephen Liu preaches at Chinese Church in Paris

✠ Stephen & Christine in Brisbane City, Queensland, Bible College

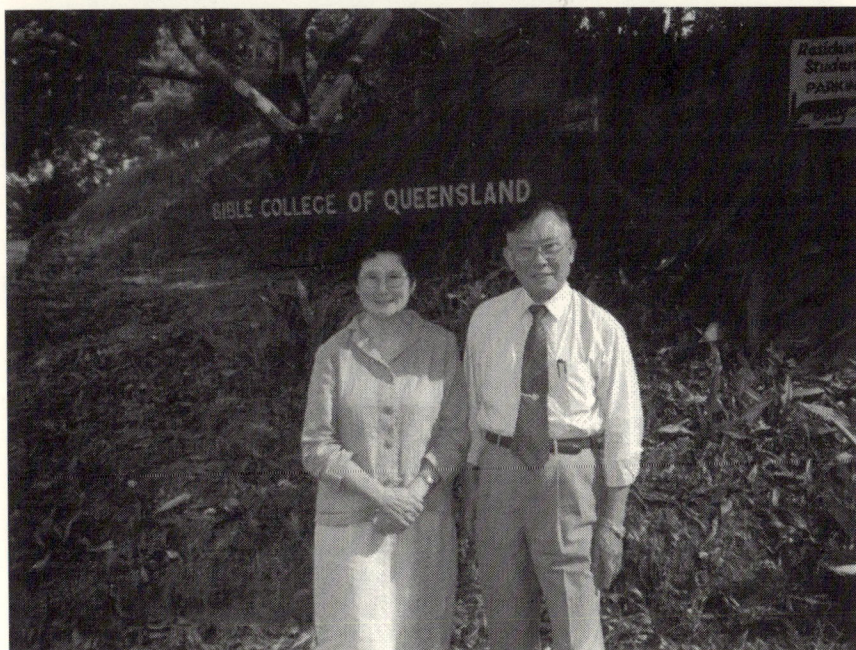

✠ Stephen & Christine Liu visited the Cloned sheep Dolly, 1988, Roslin Institute, Scotland

✠ Stephen & Christine Liu lecture of Singapore Bible College and Seminary

✠ Singapore Bible College's President Chan, Dean Chan and Stephen Liu

✠ Stephen Liu speaks on Christian ethics, at Singapore Bible College

✠ Stephen & Christine Liu visited/lectured at Malaysia Bible Seminary, Kuala Lumpur, Malaysia

✠ Stephen Liu with Rev. & Mrs. James Hudson Taylor. Internet Medical Service in Hong Kong

✠ Stephen preaches on "The Great Commission" at Nanjing Theological Seminary, NanJing China

✠ Stephen preaches on "The Great Commission" at Nanjing Theological Seminary, Nanjing, China

✠ Stephen Liu lectures on "Evolution vs. Creation", at China Theological Seminary, in Taipei, Taiwan, China

✠ Panel on "Evolution vs. Creation", at China Theological Seminary, in Taipei, Taiwan, China

✠ Stephen Liu lectures/explains: "The Five School of Creation Narratives" at Taipei

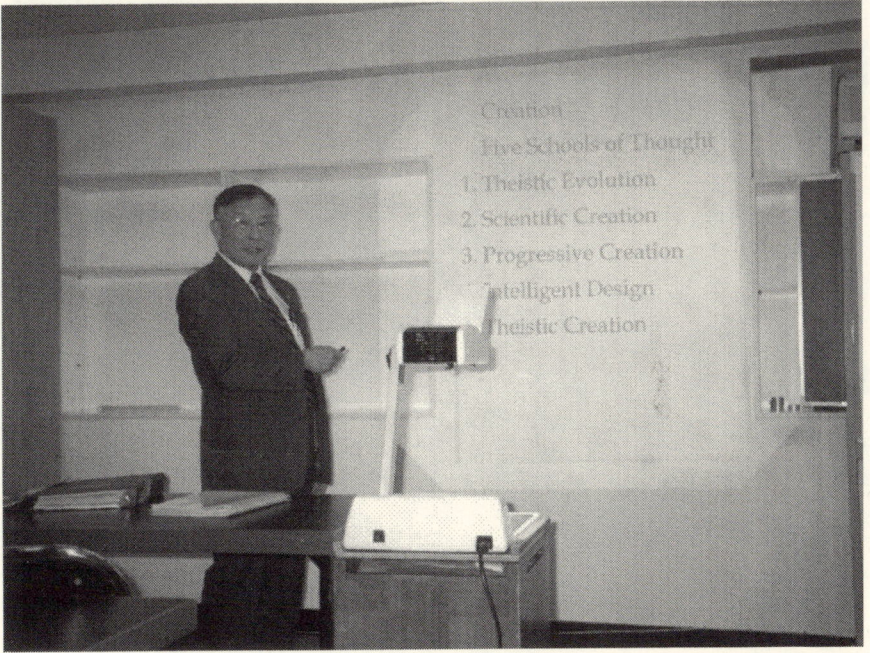

✠ "Genetically Engineered Food & Crops, Perils or Prospects?" – lecture on the platform

✠ "Genetically Engineered Food & Crops, Perils or Prospects?" – speaks to the audience

✠ "Genetically Engineered Food & Crops, Perils or Prospects?" – speaks to the audience, KuaLaLumpur, Malaysia.

✠ Science Forum "Evolution vs. Creation (2)" in Vancouver Canada

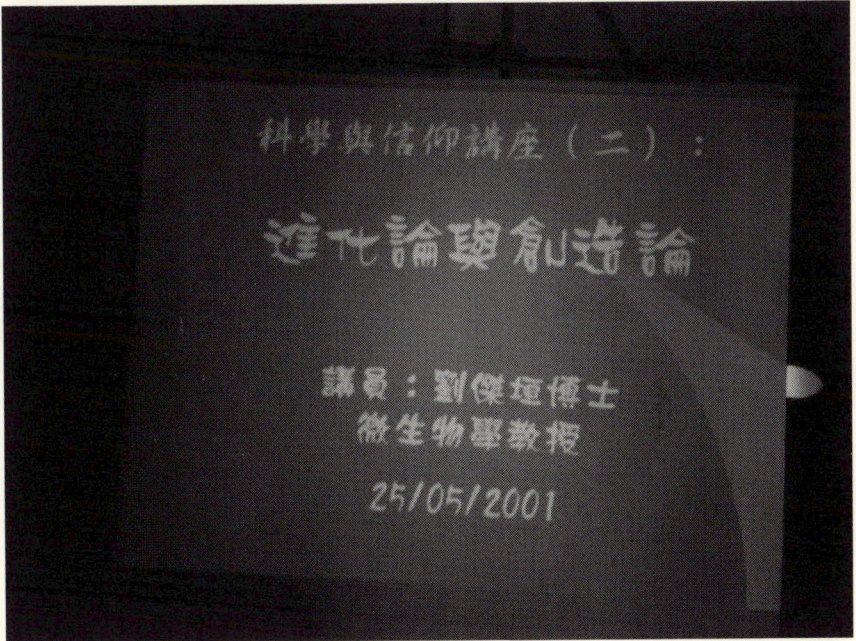

✠ Science Forum "Stem Cells Research & Genetic Cloning Human?" in Vancouver Canada

✠ Visit/lectures at Shanghai Academy of Agriculture "on Animal Vaccines & Vaccination"

✠ Group picture of 62 students on "Molecular Immunology" at Chinese Academy of Agriculture/Graduate school, Beijing, China, 1999

✠ Lecture on "Biotechnology: Principles & Research Endeavor" at Institute of Special Animal/Plant Products", Chinese Academy of Agricultural Sciences, at Chang-Chun, China

✠ Stem Cells & Cloning, Vancouver, Canada

✠ Stephen and Christine Liu Lecture at Zhe Jiang Medical University, Hangzhou, China

✠ Welcomes & students at Advance Molecular Biotechnology in Medical Science
(浙江医大)

✠ Stephen and Christine Liu together with President of Fudan University (复旦大学)
Prof. Xide Xie (谢希德教授)

✠ Stephen Liu lectures at Genetic Research Institute at Fudan University, Shanghai

✠ Stephen Liu lectures at Genetic Research Institute at Fudan University, Shanghai

✠ Stephen Liu speaks to Chinese House Church in Shanghai

✠ Well-known Chinese Evangelist and church pastor Wang Mingdao (王明道与夫人)

✠ Well-known Chinese Evangelist and church pastor Yuan Shao-Cheng

(Rev. & Mrs. Yuan), China（袁相枕與夫人）

✠ By invitation, Stephen Liu leads a group prayer at Presidential Breakfast prayer/Annual Meeting, Washington, D. C.

✠ Stephen & Christine Liu as founders of Chinese Overseas Christians' Church in Suo Paulo, Brazil

✠ Church Elders Group of Chinese Overseas Christians' Church in Suo Paulo, Brazil

✠ Forty year's Anniversary of Chinese Overseas Christians' Church in Suo Paulo, Brazil

Science and Christian Faith

Their Relationships in the Past, Present and Future

Stephen C. Y. Liu, Ph D.

A brief biography of the Author and this book

Stephen C. Y. Liu is a Professor Emeritus of microbiology and molecular biology, concurrently at two state universities in Michigan, (EMU & U/M) 1965-2006, USA. In 2006, after 30 years' teaching-research service, he retired from academic work. Then, he devoted his training, energy and time to Christian ministry worldwide. *This book is a by-product of his university teaching in USA, Brazil and China; and Christian ministry worldwide.*

A. My College and post-graduate education:

I was born in Hunan Province, China. When Imperialistic Japanese Government invaded China which eventually led to the Second World War, I was unable to complete my elementary to high school education. In 1948, I migrated to Taiwan. I received both B. Sc. (1951) and M.Sc. (1954) at National Taiwan University. Then, Stephen pursued further graduate studies at University of Minnesota, Mpls., MN. , receiving his Ph. D. degree (1957) specialized in molecular virology and immunology. Under a Nobel Laureate, Prof. Salvador E. Luria of 1965, at MIT (1967-68), I did my post-doc work, in molecular biology and phage genetics.

B. My University teaching and research overseas:

My first academic appointment as Assistant Professor was at Univ. of Minn. (1957-58). Then, my wife, Christine, and I migrated to Brazil, and became Brazilian citizens. I worked, as Molecular Virologist with Brazilian National Research Council, being assigned to the Institute Biologico in Sao Paulo state, for 3 years. Subsequent to this, Stephen joined Charles Pfizer International, as Virologist and Assistant Manager of an Animal Vaccine Plant, for 4 years. While I and my wife were in Brazil, we concurrently pioneered in Christian church-planting ministry in both Brazil and Argentina. We were instrumental in establishing Chinese Churches in both Brazil and Argentina. On the side, Stephen worked with ABU (Allianca Biblica dos Universitarios) a Brazilian Inter-Varsity group, among college students. Altogether, these activities took seven years, 1958-65.

C. University teaching, again in USA:

In June of 1965, I and my family returned to USA. Then, I accepted an academic appointment as Assistant Professor of microbiology, at Eastern Mich. Univ. (EMU). In 72, Stephen was appointed concurrently, as Adjunct Prof. of Biological Sciences, at Univ. of Michigan, working with Dr. Alfred Sussman (Vice President for Academic Affairs and Dean of Graduate School). In 1975, Dr. and Mrs. Liu, together with their three children became naturalized US citizens. With sabbatical leave, he did his post-doc work, at MIT, under Nobel Laureate/Professor Salvador E. Luria, in the field of molecular biology and phage genetics, in 1967-69. Upon returning to MI, he continued his academic career, teaching courses with research, at graduate level of molecular biology and virology for another 20 some years.

D. Teaching overseas and Christian Ministry worldwide:

In 1980, USA-China's diplomatic relation was normalized. The People's Republic of China (PRC) opened its gate to the outsiders. He undertook his professional work in the land of his birth, mostly in summer months or sabbatical leaves. With a sabbatical leave of six months, he pioneered teaching services at many national universities, and also Chinese Academies. With an official invitation of both Ministries of Education (MOE) and Agriculture (MOA), of China, as Visiting Prof., Stephen taught Molecular Biology of Animal Viruses (1980), at Chinese Academy of Agricultural Sciences (CAAS) in Beijing; and Fudan University in Shanghai. Beginning in 1981. Again and again, Stephen taught Molecular Immunology; and Molecular Biotechnology in 1985. In 1993 to 1999, with invitation by Chinese Academy of Medical Sciences (CAMS), Prof. Liu taught various courses at Union Medical College in Beijing; Zhejiang Medical University; and several other medical schools. With this experience in both research and teaching, he authored four sets of textbooks (two volumes each) for use in university research-teaching. With these services rendered, he was able to elevate the traditional biology to molecular biology level, in PRC. This was his major contribution to the bio-sciences. Under the auspices of CAAS, he and his wife toured a large number of research institutes, literally covering four corners of the nation. Recognizing his meaningful contribution, the MOE conferred on him of Honorary Professorship in Biological Sciences.

E. My Christian journey and ministry:

Writing a book on science and Christian faith and their relationships, I feel that I should share my Christian faith. This paragraph is a summary of my journey, and a life-style. While I was a young boy in my native land, through the instrumentality of two British Methodist missionaries, Messrs A. Griffith and R. Bell, I became a Christian. I was baptized and received into church fellowship. The Chinese-Japanese War in the 1940-50 drove me to southwestern part of China, i.e. Kweichow Prov. While I was in the capital city, Kweiyang, without a high school diploma (so-called equivalency in academic level) I was admitted to

Kweiyang Medical College. In the later part of 1948, The Second World Was ended. The Chinese Government ordered all those students who had come to the hinterland to return to their home provinces. So, Stephen returned to Hunan Prov., being exceedingly rejoicing seeing my parents and the family. Of course, I intended to transfer to Yale in China Medical College in Changsha, the Capital city of my province. Unfortunately, I did not succeed. So, I migrated to Taiwan. I was fortunate enough to get a job, working as a technician with the Provincial Dept. of Public Health for years. Then Stephen was admitted to National Taiwan University, in 1948, majoring in agricultural microbiology and virology. I graduated with a B.Sc. in 1951. Then, my major Japanese Professor Takashi Matsumoto accepted me in the graduate program. Under his tutorship, I received my M.Sc. degree in 1954. While I was at Nat. Taiwan Univ., I was active in Inter-Varsity Christian students' work on campus. During that time, British missionaries, Dr. and Mrs. Donald Dale; and American Rev. Egbert Andrews, labored among college students on campus. With these two missionaries, I worked on various projects. In many ways I was self-taught in Scripture and biblical principles. Stephen led group Bible Study for a number of years while he was in colleges. I spent a great deal of time in equipping myself in Biblical/evangelical theology, prayer, personal discipline and church-planting enterprises. My personal conviction was to follow the Lord Jesus, being a disciple. I took the Scripture seriously. In practice, I intended to follow the Apostle Paul in church-planting and self-supporting, as he had demonstrated in his missionary journeys recorded in the book of Acts   (Chapters13-28).

While I was at University of Minn. (1954-57), once again I was active with Bible Study Class among Chinese students on campus.   In those years, there was a movement for Bible Study Class among Chinese students on university campuses, in both USA and Canada. As a newcomer, I took part at Christian Brethren's Church in the Twin City area. At the same time, Stephen received The Navigators' training in both Bible study and personal discipleship. In 1957, I completed my graduate program, and was conferred with a Ph. D. degree. In 1958, while I was assistant professor at my Alma Mater, concurrently I served as Pastor of Chinese Christian Fellowship Church in Twin Cities. In a way, I was doing two professional jobs at the same time. With the Lord's enabling, I did well with both of them.   While I was on academic work, I felt the Lord's calling for missionary work overseas. With my wife, Christine, I migrated to S. America with two-fold objective. One was to continue in my professional teaching-research, as I had done before in both Taiwan and MN. The other was to engage in Christian pioneering work among Chinese immigrants. In those years, in both USA and Canada, there were only a few Chinese churches. They did not know me well enough. I was neither a professional clergy nor a missionary. In no way, these churches were able to support me in my proposed ministry.

I had to pursue it in other direction. In many ways, I was self-taught in Christian theology, church-planting and expository preaching. I came to the conclusion that I could work as a self-supporting missionary (so-called

"tent-making ministry", cf. Acts, Chapter 18:1-4). I was confident that I could do well with them, if I were given this opportunity. So, with genuine faith in God, The Bible as the Word of God and the various kinds of training I had received, I ventured to launch this dual objective.

The Brazilian Consulate in Chicago granted me a permanent visa on the basis of my post-graduate training and academic teaching. My wife, Christine and young son, Ted. migrated to Brazil, in 1958. The first year while I was in Brazil, I worked as Research Associate in Molecular Virology under the Brazilian Nat. Research Council, being assigned to the Instituto Biologico in Sao Paulo. After three-year's work, I joined the Charles Pfizer Co., International Division, with assignment in producing animal vaccines in Sao Paulo State. I should say that with the Lord's enabling, I did very well in these assignments. So, both my wife and I spent seven years in S. America (1958-65).

While in S. America, we concurrently engaged in Christian missionary work among the Chinese immigrants in Sao Paulo of Brazil and Buenos Aires of Argentine. The Lord granted us of a good measure of success. We were instrumental in establishing two Chinese churches in Brazil, and one in Buenos Aires of Argentina. When we left, we left behind three thriving churches in the two capital cities.

In 1965, I and my wife returned to USA, for another adventure in life. By divine providence, I was able to return to university teaching in Michigan. While teaching-researching, we were working among college students on campuses. In many ways this was indeed our cherished Christian vocation. All these are recorded in my first book in Chinese language, entitled in *"Our Tent-Making Years"* by Cosmic Light Press in Taiwan, in 1985.

F. Again, teaching in USA:

Upon returning to USA, as I described before, I accepted teaching-research faculty position with two state universities in Michigan, viz. **Eastern Michigan. University.**, and **University of Michigan**. We made our home in Ann Arbor where IVF Chapter was active. While teaching-researching at the universities, I was very much involved in Chinese students' ministry on campus. I briefly described it in previous paragraph. Here, I elaborate it in a wee bit more.

At first, we organized a Chinese Bible Study Class, which was evolved to/ as a Christian Fellowship Church. Then, concurrently I undertook again the pastoral ministry on campus for 18 years. The first book, "My Tent-Making Years" (1985, in Chinese) was an autobiography, and also a comprehensive history of the Chinese Churches in both S. Amer. and Mich. I spent 30 solid years in both teaching and research in Mich. (1965-1998). I retired in 1998. In 2006, both my wife, Christine and I relocated in Potomac, MD, a suburban of Washington, D. C.

G. Natural Science and Christian Faith:

While I was at two state universities, in summer months I opted no teaching-research work, I undertook summer trips to elsewhere or overseas. Both my wife and I went to England & Scotland, France, Germany, Holland, Sweden, Switzerland, Poland and Austria, more than a couple of times, ministering mainly in Chinese churches. When opportunities were available, I ministered among college students groups and English-speaking congregations. After my retirement, I managed to travel even more extensively, not only in Europe but also in Australia, New Zealand and SE Asia. In addition, I undertook teaching seminars on "science and Christian faith, their relations in time past, present and future"

The lectures were well-received by the Christian public. The reason was my lectures being historical, biblical and practical. As a rule, I emphatically pointed out that in 16th -17th centuries when *modern experimental sciences* were borne, it was a historical landmark in sciences. It was due two important principles guiding the evangelical Christians. One was the Christian doctrines of creation as given in Genesis narratives. The other was the fact that Christian scholars endeavored to search the Scripture as God's Word, and also explored the created world as God's work. Christian scholars such as *Kepler, Cupernicus and Galileo* did not think that their rational and empirical search would invalidate their Christian faith. On the contrary, they believed that rational research would only confirm what they had believed. Furthermore, the empirical data would assist them to explain what was given in the Scripture. Consequently, their genuine faith and research endeavor brought the birth of modern experimental sciences (Chapter 5). Galileo Galilea coined his famous dictum:

"There are two Books,

i.e. the Book of Scripture and the Book of Nature.

The Former was God's Word, and the latter God's Work.

God is the Author of these Two Books.

Therefore, they could not contradict each other."

Consequently, he was proclaimed as *Father of modern experimental sciences*, by scientific societies around the world. In essence, *these early Christian scholars were passionate believers of eventual unity of knowledge*. In our time, Prof. John Polkinghorne of Cambridge Univ. in his book (Belief in God in An Age of Science, 1998, Yale Univ. Press) said emphatically:

"I am a passionate believe <u>in the unity of knowledge</u>.

I believe that those who are truly seeking an understanding through and

through, and who will not settle for a facile and premature conclusion to that

search, are seeking God, whether they acknowledge that diving quest or not.

Theism is concerned with making total sense of the world. (pp. 24).

Then, Prof. Polkinghorne concluded,

"The unity of knowledge is under-written by the unity of the one true God; the veracity of well-motivated belief is underwritten by the reliability of God."
(pp# 122).

To Prof. Polkinghorne's conviction and worldview, I wholeheartedly subscribe, as I portrayed in "The Integrated Perspectives of Theology and Science", Chapter #2, Fig. #3.

H. The objectives of writing this book:

In recent years, I joined many other Christian scholars in USA and in UK, in pursuing this noble task.   i. e. *the unity of knowledge: academic/ intellectual and Christian religious*.   What we contemplate to do is to engage in both dialogues and in scholarly writing, with materialistic evolutionists/scientists for mutual acceptance and mutual respect.

At the same time, I took part in US national conferences and seminars. With consistent efforts, I produced a book of *Science and Christian faith: their relationship in past, present and future*. It was first published in 2009 (in Chinese simplified script), by China Protestant Church in Mainland China. In less than one year, more than 5,000 copies were sold. That indicated a great need of such a book in that land. The second printing was done in 2011. At the same time I have translated it to English version, for English-speaking audience. I do feel that there is a need of such a book in science and Christian faith, dealing with these two disciplines in historical perspectives and in a parallel fashion.

I. The dichotomy of the two disciplines:

In western civilization, especially in early time, Christianity and her theology occupied a very important position in both society and in education. The Bible was accepted as the Word of God. Christian churches were not only the centers of religious activities but also educational and social centers. Clergymen were highly respected for their learning and sacrificial services. When a new city was built, invariably the church was/occupied the center of the city. Then, legal court, post office and train station were built around in the central square. When you visited cities in Europe, the vestiges of such legacy could still be seen.

Then, in 16th- 17th centuries a number of modern philosophies came to the scene. Gradually, these secular philosophies entered into institutes of higher learning. Over the years, theological educations were gradually replaced by humanistic, secular philosophies. Then, in 19th-20th centuries, the two disciplines, i.e. Christian theology and sciences parted their company. So, there is such a

dichotomy of the two disciplines in western societies. Gradually, this trend has been extended to the other parts of the world.

By late 19th century, the gap between materialistic/atheistic scientists and evangelical Christian Scientists was somehow and regrettably created. To bring these two professional groups together, could be difficult. (Chapters 12th and 13th). In USA, there has been a great deal of debate on evolution theory in public squares and in schools. That creates a great division in the intellectual society, and also public education. The way to resolve this kind of issue is through scholarly writing and seminars expounding the differences, and also the eventual unity of knowledge. Christian scholars, including myself consider this as a "bridge" of mutual understanding and respect to be built.

In Christendom, there are two camps, i.e. evangelical Christians and fundamental Christians. They do differ in the interpretation of the creation narratives, as given in Genesis Chapters 1-3.   Theologically and historically, there are five schools of thought among evangelical Christians. In addition, the two groups also differ in their conviction in public/social service, and attitude toward sciences. Though being less-debated in churches and in public, it is in need of harmonizing them, maintaining Christian unity.

J. The overall objective of this book

is to confirm genuine Christian faith in relation to natural sciences in historical perspectives. It is apologetic in essence and in approach.

This book is a by-product of my teaching-research at universities, and also my worldwide ministry in Christian churches. With my training in life sciences, and global experience in Christian ministry, I feel that I am well qualified to present the subject of sciences and Christian faith to the public. My prayer is that what is said in this book will enlarge readers' vision and reinforce Christian faith. Therefore, I present it to you for your enjoyment of reading, enlarging your horizon of knowledge and your vision.

Preface

"Science and Christian Faith: Their Relationships in the Past, Present and Future" is a book dealing with natural sciences and Christian faith in their historical perspectives. The main objective is to present the inherent nature of science and Christian faith and their relations. It is based on my academic career of many years of college teaching-research on these subjects, and personal Christian experience and understanding of evangelical Christian faith. In this book, I present them to the Christian public as well to the secular world of learning

Students in either high schools or at college level, due to their learning experience in schools, may have the impression that Christian faith or Christianity is something irrational, even anti-scientific. The general public gets this erroneous idea from current/conventional culture. This could be more so in China. If this were case, reading this book, especially after reading the first four chapters, they could discover the fact that they were given the wrong teaching and erroneous conclusion. Their quest for knowledge and truth should encourage them to go further and more than that.

Christianity or Christian faith has its rational basis, and scholarly way of learning. Genuine faith matters. To Christians, *evangelical Christian faith is a matter of heart and head*. Only through studies in depth you will know it. It was, in fact very important and essential. In the western world Christianity played an important role. In early eras, when a city was planned, the first thing on the agenda was the church built at the center of that city. Surrounding the church, there would be legal court, post office and railroad station. That pattern was true almost in any large cities. When you go to visit some relatively old cities, you would see the vestiges of them.

In western civilization and culture, religion and science are two rocks. They were more so in early eras. As a rule, in institutes of higher learning, theology occupied the foremost important place. Clergy was highly respected for their public services. Christians are the pillars of the society. They were the dynamic force for renewal and revival. Nations and governments were established with biblical doctrines and teaching. As a result, people did enjoy more freedom in society. Intellectual standard was much higher. Superstition was abolished or prohibited. The living standard was much higher. All these exerted a great deal of influence in the thinking of scholars and the general public as well. It also contributed greatly in societies and personal life-style. By and large, Christianity is different from scientific discipline and its response to nature. Therefore, their research endeavor and methods are different. Logically, the results and the interpretation are different. In fact, in the 16th to 17th centuries Christian scholars believed the doctrine of God's creation of the cosmic universe. Scholars such as Cupernicus, Kepler and Galileo discovered the sun-centered universe to replace

the geo-centric theory. Consequently, **Galileo Galelei,** was acknowledged as the founder of modern experimental sciences by scientific communities worldwide. He once coined the **dual system of God's Word and God's Work**. In 19th and 20th centuries, morphology and classification of living things and genetics were the result of research work of devoted Christian scholars. In many ways, both Christianity and Christians made great contribution to societies in the past. They continue to do so in the present time.

Both sciences and Christian religious faith are scholarly disciplines. In their inherent nature, they are neutral. They could not come into conflict at all. If they somehow come to conflict, it is due to the science professionals and Christian scholars interpreting their work in different worldviews. **It is in their worldviews, they come into conflict.** Unfortunately, it was seen in our early history. It is also true with radicals and irrationals in our present era. We can not afford to have these two major forces in the world working in such an unpleasant way. Both world Christians and open-minded naturalists seem to agree that we have to resolve this issue. We all know well that the way to resolve such a difference is through genuine dialogues, and mutual understanding and appreciation. **This book is aimed at achieving these objectives**.

In the last 1950-80, we all witnessed the tremendous progress made by sciences and technology. Their applications in technology have made our living and personal life-style much easier, more pleasant and enjoyable. No one could deny this. On the other hand, genuine faith in supernatural deity and applications in our lives has also enriched our personal living and societal relationships. The key issue is how we are to integrate these ways of learning, seeing each other in its own perspective, and also their proper relationships. In our society nowadays, so many well-known and accomplished scientists, scholars, theologians have been contributing their efforts to this task. Yet, we could not deny that there is a small fraction of scientist and people of faith somehow could not arrive at this genuine conclusion. They engage in vain in their struggle against one another. Reading Chapter Four, "**Quotations by well-known scholars**", they would come to this conclusion. It is up to us to extend our hands to them, inviting them to come to join us in this noble undertaking.

Christianity was born when Jesus of Lazarus began his movement in the first century in mid-eastern part of the world. First, it reached the Jewish people. Then, gradually, Christianity advanced to Europe, England and America. Western civilization and history tell us that Christianity exerted a great deal of influence on people's living, and had impact on society for centuries. All these are well recorded in history. While we look at the world today, we realize the fact that Christianity has made a stark difference between different political systems and world of politics. **Christian faith has replaced superstition, enlightened the mind and elevated living standard of the people**. Countries with Christians as majority of their population are more stable and prosperous in many ways. This is a fact. Christianity came to China 200 some years ago. **She is not yet well**

integrated into Chinese culture, therefore her contribution has been relatively limited in scope. No doubt, Christianity will continue to grow and make her contrition in both the world and China.

I am a Chinese-American scholar and university professor. I was born in Mainland China. By way of Taiwan, I came to USA for graduate studies. Receiving my Ph.D. in natural sciences, I and my wife went to Brazil as missionaries. Seven years were spend in church-planting in S. America. Then, we returned to USA. I accepted a teaching position in Mich. I and my wife, Christine became naturalized citizens. I taught at state university, in USA, beginning in 1965. After the normalization of diplomatic relations between China and USA in 1980, by invitation I have returned almost every year to my motherland for lectures and assisting research work for 20 some years. While I was in childhood age in his homeland, I accepted Christ Jesus as Savior. Many years later, i adopted a self-supporting lifestyle in Christian ministry. It is true even today. In my public lectures I advocate positive approach to both natural sciences and Christian faith, as mutually enriching and explaining. This book is a by-product of my university teaching-researching and ministering in Christian church worldwide. The objectives are to provide for your learning enrichment, and enlarging your scope of intellectual understanding.

Table of Contents

Chapter 1
Introduction

"All Religions, sciences and arts are branches of the same tree. All these aspirations are human's endeavors, being directed toward ennobling man's life, lifting it from the sphere of mere physical existence and leading the individual toward freedom."

Albert Einstein

Out of My Later Years, pp# 7, 1950 Ed.

In 1954 I came to University of Minnesota, Mpls.-St. Paul, MN, pursuing my further graduate studies. In campus bookstore, I bought several extracurricular books for my leisure reading. The authors and the titles of these books are as follows:

1. Albert Einstein, 1879-1965

A. The World As I See It, 1934

B.   Out of My Later Years, 1950

2. Albert Schweitzer, 1871-1965

A. The Quest of the Historical Jesus, 1906

B. Reverence for Life, 1915

3. Bernard Ramm, 1954

Christian View of Science and Scripture.

4. Norman Vincent Peale, 1952

The Power of Positive Thinking

Albert Einstein was proclaimed in 1999 as *the greatest Scientist in 20ᵗʰ century*, by both US National Academy of Sciences and American Association for the Advancement of Sciences. These two books were written in his later years of academic career. They described his life-style as a physicist in academic career, personal philosophy and also worldview. These books are very instructive and mind-enlightening for reading, and in scientific career/professional work.

Albert Schweitzer was well-known in western world, as *a jungle medical missionary doctor*, engaging in Christian philanthropic work in Africa. He was a

Christian theologian. He served as President of theological seminary in Germany. Also, he was known as an expert in both Bach's music and organ. Based on his great humanistic work, he was awarded with *Nobel Peace Prize*.

Bernard Ramm was Professor of Theology at Bethel College and Seminary, St. Paul-Mpls., MN. He was *one of outstanding evangelical scholars*. With this book published in 1954, Prof. Ramm endeavored to develop a philosophy of science in general, and of life science in particular. He is the founder of Christian Progressive Creation, one of five schools of thought on creation. His scholarly writings had a profound impact on thinking of Christian professionals and theologians in USA and worldwide.

Norman Vincent Peale was *a Minister* of Manhattan Marble Collegiate Church, New York city. Based on Philippians 4:13, he developed a practical Christian philosophy of *"positive thinking"*, a bestseller that outlines how people can improve and strengthen their lives through dynamic faith. With his wife, Ruth Stafford, they found "Guideposts", an inspiring organization which provided hundred of thousands of free magazines and books to hospitals, nursing homes and relief organizations.

These books were my companions in my graduate student's days, academic career and Christian ministry, anywhere and everywhere I went. Rev. Peale and his philosophy reinforced and rejuvenated my way of living, practically in every area. I personally received a great deal of blessings in applying his positive living philosophy. Dr. Schweitzer and his inspiring work in Africa encouraged me in pioneering missionary work in S. America; with professional services in US and elsewhere. His example inspired me for Christian missionary work, and work among college students. Prof. Ramm taught me how to deal with science and Christian faith in constructive and positive ways. Beginning in 1954 and that year on, I adopted his Progressive Creation as my conviction, and the way to understand the creation narratives. Einstein, though he was not an evangelical Christian, was a deist of Spinoza's type. He considered religions, arts and sciences are mutually explainable and complementary. They are in no way being conflict to one another. His philosophy and worldview are acceptable by us scientists and people of faith. In fact, he was acclaimed as the great scientist of the 20th century. Therefore, in this book (Chapt. 4 and the others) I have quoted the sayings of both Einstein and Ramm more and often, substantiating my premises of parallel model of both science and Christian theology (Chapter #2).

I. The Project of writing this book:

Now, a few paragraphs pertaining to my writing project will be in place. While I was doing teaching-research in two state universities in Michigan in early 1960, I took the advantage of using university libraries, enriching my knowledge and reinforcing my thinking. I found that these efforts in my preparation for Christian ministry well in advance were very profitable and educational. During

summer months in those years, I undertook trips for Christian ministry both in USA and elsewhere. The Chinese Bible Study Classes on university campuses, and churches in cities requested for additional lectures on my academic specialties. I gladly accepted their suggestions. Utilizing educational principles and for more effective impact, I utilized the multi-media services, as additional assistance. The response was enthusiastic and encouraging. With this, I foresaw that in the future, likely I would devote myself to Christian ministry and scholarly writings, in full-time.

In 1995, utilizing the recording facilities of Chinese Christian Mission in Petaluma, Calif., I produced 10 audio tapes. Then, the Campus Christian Fellowship in Taiwan reproduced tapes with 400 sets, being available for /church/public use. In 1996, I intended to transcribe it, and assembly them in a book form, being ready for publication. When I traveled to Shanghai, attending the annual Forum on Diplomatic Relations between China and USA. I brought along a couple of chapters. In a courtesy visit to the headquarters of China Protestant Church (CPC) in Shanghai, I was graciously received by Mr. Gi Chien-Fung, then Chairman of the National Committee. He took a casual glance at the manuscript of Introduction, and many quotations by well-known scholars. Mr. Gi, a church elder, was very much impressed with the high scholastic level of the contents. Then, Elder Gi responded very enthusiastically. He wanted the book to be published by CPC, without any string attached. His conviction was that in China, with such a huge population of students and professionals, *the need was greater than anywhere*. The CPC will undertake the printing project, without any charge to me. They promised that they would not alter any of my original meaning and intention. If needed, they would make the reading easier for readers in Mainland China. In addition, CPC would pay me a token of money for my labor of writing it. I gladly accepted his offer. Of course, that was a great encouragement to me. Upon returning to MD, I worked hard on the manuscript, revising and increasing it to 24 chapters. During the time I was working on the draft, Dr. Wu Ye, a computer specialist working with NIH in Rockville, MD voluntarily offered his assistance in typing the whole manuscript in his spare time. So, the book was completed on time. Then, it was published in Shanghai, in 1999. The first edition was 10,000 copies. To every body's surprise, the 10,000 copies were sold in one year. The second printing was 5,000 copies. As I was told that the sale was relatively good, as compared with other books available in the market.

II. Now, the book is an English version:

After the book was published, then my attention turned to the possibility of having it in English language. I am confident that I could translate it all by myself. As a naturalized citizen living in this country for more than half a century, *I taught both undergraduate and graduate courses of microbiology at state universities in Michigan, for 30 years*. If these students of those years could understand me and my lectures, I am confident that my English language is good enough to communicate to the public, with clarity. In addition, I spoke at both

English and Chinese Christian churches in both USA and England. The people in these churches could understand my preaching well, and expressed their appreciation to me. With all these public appearances and speaking engagement, I am confident that I could communicate well through printed pages.

My major concern is to maintain my fidelity to my evangelical Christian faith. On the other hand, as a Scientist-Biologist *I want to be true to my science.* What has been reported in literature and what has been written in textbooks, even reference books, I shall be true and loyal. In short,, I shall have the best and the most reliable results in this book.. Of course, I would appreciate your feedback once you have completed the reading of this book.

In this respect, I wish to thank my dear daughter, Rebekah Christine Liu, who is a full-fledged lawyer working with SEC in federal government, for her work of love on paging and format. Also, to my son-in-law, Mr. Paul K. Martin, who is a classmate of Rebekah at Georgetown Univ. Law Center. Paul has been with NASA, as Inspector General. My thanks to him for assisting me often in my computer work. Dr. Ye Wu of Rockville, MD, for his assistance in the work of my manuscript , and the color photos.

I admit the fact that the literatures reviewed or the quotations given were mainly taken from western countries. There is very little to almost nothing from China. It is due to the fact that in these western nations Christianity has her long history. Her influence and impact are far-reaching. In these countries, so many scholars have been involved in one way or another in sciences and Christian faith. Literatures are readily available. On the other hand, I do admit that I have no Chinese literature in my personal library. Nowhere else I could turn or consult them.

III. The title of "Science and Christian Faith: Their Relationships in the Past, Present and Future." and its contents:

As the title implied, the book will deal with sciences and Christian faith: their relationships in the past, present and future. Specifically, *I deal only with natural sciences and my personal evangelical faith.* I am in no position of representing the total body of Chinese Christian church, let alone the universal church. It is my personal faith, not the faith of Christian church at large. As a professor of microbiology and molecular biology, I can only deal with natural sciences. It is in those two specific areas I am doing my writing.

The target populations I am aiming at are of three different groups. First, the general Christian population. Those who are mature enough in their faith, and accumulating enough daily working experience, would like to know more in science in relation to their faith. If so, this is the book. There are several chapters dealing with Christian faith in relation to science. Above all, subjects are dealt in a comprehensive way. They may find them interesting enough to read and more

chapters. I have endeavored to write in such a way, making it easier for them. Secondly, the student population, which is very huge. The title begins with a word, "science". I am not hiding anything by myself in my endeavor. I write for those who have had some minimal exposures to sciences, either in high school or in college. They have enough background information so that they could read more, and more chapters in my book. With high school education, they would be interested in reading the book, or buying the book. Reading the book itself would give them answers to a large number of questions they probably have in mind. There are seven to eight subjects, being dealt with in such a way much more than what they had in regular school curriculum. I know well what college professors teach in regular classes. They seldom deal with them in relation to Christian religious faith. Even in Christian theological seminaries, the subjects are seldom dealt with in such a comprehensive way and at elementary level. So, this will be something new, and wider in scope. We all know that self-education is life-long endeavor. It is going to add a new dimension to their education. It is a life-long learning experience.

Thirdly, I am writing with professional people in general, in mind. This is the group I am specifically aiming at it. I know so well that so many schools/colleges/universities do not offer such a course of "The philosophy of sciences". I have it in Chapter 8th. In fact, I personally feel that this chapter is the best-written, and well-integrated. This book may give them an overall, integrated view of science and Christian faith in historical perspectives. My book has a good number of chapters on sciences.

Those three groups are people I have in mind. I shall mention a few felt-questions in the following paragraphs.

How to read this book? For those who are primarily interested in Christian faith in relation to sciences, I suggest that they should read Chapter 11, first. This chapter would help them to understand what Christian faith is, and what impact it would have on personal daily living. Then, go to Chapter 10, this will tell them that there are other ways to knowledge and truth. From there on, they could go to Chapter 2, which would give them an overall view of faith in relation to sciences. Then, they could turn to science subjects more specifically, Chapt.5, 12, and 6.

For those whose interest is primarily science in relation to Christian faith, begin with Chapter 2, an overall view of science in relation to Christian faith. Then, go to Chapter 5, the birth of modern experimental sciences, followed by Chapter 6, science and Christian faith are going in separate ways. Once you have a general grasp of their relationship, then you could go to Chapters 8 and 9, their philosophies. From there on, readers can be on their own choice.

The reasons why I suggest the ways of reading the chapters in a sequence is the complexity of the subjects dealt with in this book. I do admit the depth and width of subjects being dealt with. I do not want to see people being discouraged by reading chapters which are by their inherent nature more complex and

interwoven so much. Readers could be discouraged if they begin reading chapters which are not of their primary interest. They should by all means to avoid this. Interest is something you could acquire as you go on reading, more in depth and in wider in scope.

IV. The bridges of mutual understanding, appreciation and cooperation:

With this book, *I intend to build bridges of mutual understanding and appreciation*. The first bridge to be built is between secular/ materialistic scientists and Christian scientists. While in college or in graduate school, if students did not take a course of "philosophy of sciences", they may not know what science could do, and also science couldn't do. Also, we could draw three overlapping circles, with science as the smallest, then philosophy as the second, then the largest one is worldview. If they do not know that the domain of science is relatively small, there is a danger of trespassing. This is the domain we scientists should remain, especially when we interpret our empirical results. If somehow we scientists trespass to philosophy when we interpret our scientific data, likely such interpretation would be in conflict with the interpretation by other scientist. By all means, we scientists should remain in science domain. Then, philosophy is a larger domain, being larger than that of science. Worldview is even largest domain, being larger than that of philosophy. Knowing these when we draw three circles with increasing size overlapping. Science by nature should be the smallest circle. Then, philosophy is a bigger circle, being bigger than science. The largest circle is worldview. Knowing these domains, their spheres and limitations, scientists should abide by the paradigms (cf. #p170, Fig. (I), (II), (III) and (IV) illustrations, pay more attention to (IV)).

It seems to me that many of young scientists in our time have the tendency of interpreting their empirical results beyond the science domain. Once awhile or quite often, they interpret their empirical results in the domain of philosophies, even in worldviews. What I am implying is this. By inherent nature, science and theology (or faith) are neutral in their nature. They could not come into conflict. Conflict will come when scientists interpret their empirical results or scholarly work in term of their personal philosophy. Then, conflict comes. This is quite common in our scientific literature.

The same is true with Christian theology. In essence, theology is a systematic knowledge of God or of divinity. It is in the domain of philosophy, or greater domain worldview. It is not an empirical science, therefore, it is not in the domain of science. Theology could not be tested experimentally with empirical method. It is a value system. Also, it is a faith system. It takes personal, subjective experience more than objective empirical search. So, when biblical scholars or theologians interpret their scholarly work, they should remain probably first in philosophy, then to worldview. If they interpret their scholarly work as if they were science, then conflict comes. Scientific creationism is a good example. Creationism is theological, not scientific. It is the interpretation that leads to

conflict between the two scholarly disciplines. Let me give you an example to illustrate my point.

In USA, before 1925, Christian doctrine of creation was the one theory taught in biology class of middle schools. Many of us know well what happened in 1925. In that year evolution theory was taught the first time in biology class at Dayton, Tenn. That scenario led to the endless quarrel, first in local scene, then to national controversy. In USA, we have so-called "cultural war". In a matter of 70-80 years, nowadays evolution theory is taught exclusively at middle schools of our nation. What a drastic change it has been taking place in USA. Consequently, we have the so-called "culture warfare" or "equal time movement" going on in USA. There is a huge gap of understanding between secular to materialistic scientists (or naturalists) and Christian scientists. The matter is this. It is the fact that evolution theory (as a bio-science theory) is currently taught as a bio-philosophy (cf. Darwinism, Design and Public Education, Part I, 2003). Then, conflict comes. Therefore, we need to make them crystal clear. In order to achieve this, we need to build a bridge between materialistic/secular scientists and Christian scientists.

By and large, evolutionists have no intention of engaging in dialogue with Christian scholars for mutual understanding, appreciation and cooperation. With this book and in a small way, I endeavor to build "a bridge of mutual understanding and mutual appreciation" between these two groups. Likely, it would take much more efforts in pursuing evolutionists coming to the table for dialogue.

In recent years, there are many Christian scholars such as Profs. John Polkinghorne, Keith Ward and Alister McGrath of UK, and American scholars such as Prof. Ian G. Barbour, Bernard Ramm, Owen Gingerich of Harvard Univ., Prof. William Phillips, Nobel Laureate and Prof. of Astronomy at Univ. of MD, and Prof. Francis Collins of NIH have been genuinely involved in this noble task. In a small way, I join them in their efforts.

The second bridge I intend to build is between so-called Christian fundamentalists and evangelicals. In essence, it is in Christian circle. Somehow, these two groups do have different ways in reading the Holy Scripture and also in interpreting them too. In addition, they also differ in their view of social services to society and attitude to science and scientific discovery. These create disharmony and ruin the Christian unity, as taught in the New Testament. It seems to me that it would take more effort in pursuing fundamentalists for dialoguing and mutual appreciation and respect. At any rate, with my book I intend to build a "small bridge" between these two groups.

V. Christianity and sciences in historical perspectives

Historically, *Christianity was born when Jesus of Nazareus began his movement in Jerusalem of Mid-East*. It was in 1st century when Jewish people

were looking forward to the coming of their Messiah. With miracles, wonder, and teaching, Jesus of Nazareth demonstrated his deity and power. Quickly, the movement spread to the neighboring regions. With his resurrection from death, his disciplines went around to proclaim him as Messiah to the Jews and Savior to the Gentile world. Books of history tell us that Christianity as the rational religion advanced very fast in the West, especially in Germany, Scandinavians and England. With missionaries sent out with the message of salvation in Christ, Christian came to this new continent of North America. From both old counties in Europe, USA and Canada, this movement came to Asia in the 17th to 19 centuries. More than 200 years ago, Christianity was introduced to China mainland. Due to many inherent factors in Chinese culture in society, this movement made a dent only in certain sectors of Chinese society. Therefore, contribution by Christianity to Chinese culture has been relatively restricted.

In the West, before Christian era, Greek philosophy (with science in it as one of the components) was taught in institutes of higher learning. Greek scholars, Socrates, Plato, and Aristotle were well known figures. So, Greek influence in the West was strong and felt anywhere. Modern experimental sciences were born in 16th - 17th centuries. Scholars such as Cupernicus, Kepler, and Galileo, based on their observation and experimentation, proposed *sun-centered universe* to replace the earth-centered theory. Consequently, modern experimental sciences such as astronomy, mathematics, astrophysics and physics were born. Then, Isaac Newton contributed his share in physics and mathematics, above all with his universal gravitation. ***Christianity has so much to do with the birth of these new disciplines.*** Informed scholars could not deny the fact that Christianity had so much to do with the birth of such sciences. It is appropriate to consider ***Christianity as the mother of modern experimental sciences***. Of course, since then sciences have made great stride in the last four centuries in the West as well as in the East.

Did the Greek Aristotlianism in any way stimulate or inhibit this movement? Did the Christian doctrine of creation have anything to do with the birth of modern sciences in 16th-17th centuries? Who were the main players? In what specific areas? Did Christianity and sciences maintain a friendly relations, or otherwise? All these questions should be answered fairly and on historical fact.

In the West, in the last 20-40 years eminent scholars such as Profs. John Polkinghorn of Cambridge Univ. Keith Ward, and Alister McGrath of Oxford, UK; and William Phillip, Bernard Ramm, Ian G. Barbour, Howard Van Till, Robert John Russell, Francis Collins, and Stephen J. Gould in USA; and George Ellis of South Africa Union have contributed their efforts with scholarly writing to promote mutual dialogue, understanding and appreciation between science and Christian faith. The John Templeton Foundation in PA has recognized their contributions with/by granting prize, as an encouragement for others in doing the same. In addition, Templeton has lent financial assistance in sponsoring dialogue and conferences. The conference and forum have been taken place on Cambridge

Univ. Oxford Univ., Harvard Univ. and Univ. of Calif./Berkeley campuses. Personally, I attended some of these meetings. I was inspired by these evangelical scholars. The last conference I attended was on both campuses of Cambridge and Oxford, in 2009. Therefore, I have joined them. In a small way I have written this book with the same objectives. Those of us who are involved in this noble undertaking admit that much remains to be done.

Then, Christianity was introduced to China by western missionaries in the 17th- 19th centuries. Now, what active role has Christianity played in Chinese societies? Could we derive the full benefit and rich blessings both in nation's life and personal living style? What active and positive role we Chinese Christians have to play to promote the cooperation and even integration of these two major forces? In the East, not much has been done as far as I am aware of it. China is a huge country, with students' population larger than anywhere else. To reach this huge population of students, professional and scientists is my objective, at least in my first edition in Chinese simplified script. So, this book in Chinese language was first published in Shanghai, in 2009. The response by both the Christian public and professional circles was very encouraging indeed. Less than a year, 5,000 copies of my book were sold through church stores alone. This remains to be my main focus. My book written in Chinese language, with quotations, could be the first one with such an effort. At any rate and on my part, I do launch this project with such an objective in view.

VI. A short and comprehensive review of contents of each chapter will be given here.

Chapter 1 is an introduction. Chapter 2 presents Christian perspectives of both science and theology, separately and also the two disciplines integrated together, in a parallel model. Also, it is the Christian classic doctrines of both *general revelation and specific revelation*. At the same time, they present our quest for God through rational studies of the cosmic universe and the Christian Scripture. In 16th-17th centuries, Italian scholar, Galileo Galelei used the metaphor of two books. The two books are: one is the God's World whereas the other was God's Word.

Since God is the Author of the two books, they should not and would not conflict into conflict. This is the fundamental principle and philosophy of this book. In a way, it is my personal philosophy and worldview.

I have presented it in a parallel model. It is emphasized as *the central theme*, and it runs through all the chapters of this book.

Chapter 3 presents several additional models, as a comparison. Over these years scholars and scientists have different viewpoints and convictions. They have different ways looking at the relation between the two disciplines. The different

models are given here as a comparison.

Chapter 4 has a large number of quotations or saying by renowned scientists, Bible scholars and theologians, including a large number of Nobel prize winners, are enlisted. These quotations or sayings represent their convictions, viewpoints and worldviews. Indeed, what they said are *inspiring and mind-enlightening*. Take them, digest them and absorb them in our thinking will indeed impart us of a great deal of wisdom and knowledge. They are taken from books, literatures and scientific journals, mostly in western world.

Chapter 5 presents the birth of modern experimental sciences in 16th and 17th centuries. In essence, the birth was due to both Christian doctrine of God's creation and Christian scholars who perceived his deity, wisdom and power as being manifested in the created cosmic world. They thought of their endeavored in studying the cosmic world would eventually reinforce their Christian faith. It was through their painstaking work, modern experimental sciences were borne. **This is something Christians should know it. With that they could derive a great sense of pride and satisfaction.**

Chapter 6 tells us that in 19th and 20th centuries, in western world a number of secular philosophies were emerging and slowly taking their shape. Gradually and slowly, these philosophies penetrated into academic institutions and became influential on scholars' thinking. Eventually, they moved into the central arena of learning, slowly replacing theology as the core curriculum. Unfortunately, two American academicians, with their books introduced "war hypothesis" or "conflict hypothesis" between science and theology. Unfortunately, this hypothesis did have an influence in academic circle. Until recently a large number of university professors of history of science, after their systematic research on literatures, advocated complexity thesis to replace it. That is given in Chapter 7.

Chapter 8 describes *what is the philosophy of sciences*, and Chapter 9th the Christian philosophy of biological sciences. I do suggest that readers should read these two chapters in one setting so that they could grasp well what these two chapters convey. In the last 50-60 years we all have witnessed an explosion of knowledge, especially scientific and its application in technology. No one could deny the fact that science and technology have made our lives and daily living much more enjoyable and comfortable. Their importance is dully recognized and appreciated. But not being aware of it, professionals and students have a tendency to think that science is able to solve all the problems we face. Then, in this way science becomes the only way to knowledge. That becomes scientism. Yes, science and technology could accomplish something, but not everything. In fact, in 2005, American Association for the Advancement of Science (AAAS), celebrating 125th Anniversary, published *in "Science" 125 questions that we scientists do not know or do not have any answers*. Sciences have their domain, scope and limit. Knowing all these would prevent us adopting an attitude of scientism. Chapter 10 reveals to us that there are other ways to acquire knowledge and wisdom. Knowing all these will assist us to have an adequate evaluation and

proper perspective, also enhancing the future progress for human welfare.

Chapter 11 deals with faith or believing, and its importance. *We all have our faith systems*. Without faith or believing, we are unable to manage well our daily living. The only difference is that each one of us has his/her own systems, differing from some one else. People may not realize its importance as an ingredient in our thinking and life-styles. Christian faith has its own rational basis. Faith could be first conceived by/through our feeling or emotion, then being reinforced by intellect, or vice versa. Eventually, it is crowned in the consent of the will. Such a genuine faith will be dully expressed / manifested in our daily conduct and living. That is in essence what Christian faith is, and the teaching of faith and resultant good work of the Christian church.

Chapter 12 presents the *Christian doctrine of creation* by Jehovah God. There are five schools of thought. Over these years Bible scholars and theologians studied diligently the creation narratives as given in Genesis Chapters 1 and 2. Knowing the peculiarity of ancient Hebrew culture and language, against the historical background of polytheisms in those times, also God's deity and wisdom being manifested in cosmic world, scholars came up with five schools of thought. All the schools are orthodox Christians. Under the umbrella of creation, they have secondary and minor differences. Knowing these common denominators, Christians could maintain their unity in faith and in practice.

In Chapter 13, I discuss *the evolution theory at three different levels*. Of the three levels, *the classic organismal evolution*, as the lowest level, with adaptation, struggle for existence and survival of the fitted as mechanisms, as first advocated by Charles Darwin in 1859,. These mechanisms are valid mechanisms. *Mechanisms are not theories. Mechanism and theory are two different categories in sciences.* It is the final conclusion as a *theory which scientists do differ*. Over these years evolution theory has evolved from one single theory to many theories, with various and a large number of mechanisms. By and large, scholars have classified them in three different levels, as we taught them at academic institutions. It is a bio-scientific theory, having its validity in science. Evolution, as defined by materialistic biologists in essence means changes over time, scientifically implying upward improvement. In fact, in nature it is regress or degradation more than anything else. In practices, as we all know that nowadays we have to *save our endangered species*.

The reasons why we have better plants and more productive varieties, are due to the efforts and labor of/by those plant geneticists and breeders have worked on selection, hybridization, new varieties and eventually cultivation. This is a known-fact. For better understanding and critical appraisal, I present evolution as a bioscience theory at three levels, i.e. organismal level (the general evolution theory), biochemical level and molecular level (the specific evolution theory); and from single-celled organisms to multicellular organisms (as proposed by Prof. Christian de Duve, 2002).

Chapters 18 deals with **Creation theory** which is derived from the creation narratives in Chapter 1 of Genesis from the Holy Bible. I have taken the initiative to outline **the creation in five theories**. My concern and conviction are to invite evangelical Christians to maintain unity, as prayed by our Lord Savior. So, the 15th to 18th deal with various current scientific subjects in depth. Such subjects do take a wee bit more of basic and background knowledge and studies. Readers could have a choice in reading of these subjects as they see fit.

Chapter 19 deals with **the subject of biblical exegesis and explanation**. I am in no position to provide them in large scope or in depth. In essence, they are up to Bible theologians and church clergymen. They could do far better job, and far more in depth. In this chapter I deal only with biblical exegesis and explanation in relation to sciences. Even so, the scope and the depth are limited. I present them just for information and for reference. Readers could choose which chapter(s) of interest to them.

Chapter 20 gives a **categorization and summary of Christian theology**. All I have done in this chapter is to list the reference and literature available in my personal library. With that, readers would have a bird's eye view of what Christian theology is.

Chapter 21 reports **the current dialogues between open-minded scientists and world evangelical Christians** (not worldly) on university campuses in recent years. We can not deny the fact that there is a small fraction of people engaging in disputing and arguing, mostly in worldviews. Something positive and constructive has to be done, if we are to avoid unnecessary dispute. It is very encouraging when we know these world citizens have been working for harmonization and integration of the two major disciplines in our society.

Chapter 22 records briefly **my personal itinerant ministry** on university campuses and in Christian churches, in USA and worldwide. These trips were carried out in last 20 some years. My objective is to promote the understanding of inherent nature of both science and Christian faith and their relationships in historical perspectives, and also people's enthusiastic response to my presentations.

Chapter 25 It deals with globalclimatic changes in the last 2 scores of years. The change has been very large and well-manifested everywhere. Well-known scientists call for five measures with international cooperation. If nations ? we people fail to take timely action, it could lead to disaster in global scale. If it were so, this could be our last century.

Chapter 26 shares what I have read in "**God for the 21st century**", a book with articles written by 50 some eminent scholars, in a world-wide circle. On the basis of what are their experience and scholarships, they shared with us/you of their viewpoints, conviction and worldview for 21st century. What they portray is a bright and better future for humanity if we all maintain a constructive and positive

attitude toward sciences and Christianity, the two major forces in the world today. I also present a summary of a book entitled in "*Our Final Century*", and a talk by *Prof. Martin Rees*, a well-known astronomer, in the 150th anniversary celebration of Darwin's "Origin of Species" on campus of Univ. of Cambridge, in 2009, as additional. Then, in Chapter 24th final concluding remarks, in which I quoted Prof Alfred Normal Whitehead and his saying that "*the future course of human history would depend on the decision of this generation as to the proper relationship between science and religion*" as the final remark.

In conclusion, I present this book (when the book was first written in Chinese, in 1999, in simplified script by the China Protestant Church, to my countrymen) to professionals/university faculty, and students in the English-speaking world, for their learning experience. It is my sincere wish that the book would broaden-up their vista and worldview. Reading this book, they could derive some intellectual benefits and a blessing. If that is the case, I have been rewarded richly and more than what I could expect. Also, I dedicate this book to my family members. With their sustaining love and encouragement, especially by my wife, Christine, I was enabled to spend hours of labor in writing this book.

Now, the book is being translated into English language all by myself, as an English version of "Science and Christian Faith: Their Relationships in time of Past, Present and Future". I sincerely present this book to those who are keenly and genuinely interested in these two disciplines in their historical perspectives, for their understanding.

And last, but not least, I wholeheartedly dedicate this book to my Lord Savior Jesus. Over these years I have been serving Him, with dedication and love. May He use this book to enlighten the mind, also as a means to reach others with the saving gospel.   Then, his disciples will stand firm in holy faith, and defend it whenever it is required any where they find themselves, any where they go. So, to the end they enjoy an enriched, meaningful and fruitful life, and   their adoption of   evangelical Christian worldview.

Chapter 2
Christian Perspectives of both Theology and Science (I)

Parallel Model (1)

"Modern man worships in the temple of science.

But, science tells us what is possible, not what is right."

Albert Einstein

"Theology and Science are inter-dependent.
Collaborative interaction ought to Characterize their present relationship
rather than the misunderstanding and Conflict in the past.
Science can purify religion from error and superstition,
religion can purify science from idolatry and false absolutionism."

Pope John Paul II

"I am a passionate believer in the unity of knowledge.
I believe that those who are truly seeking an understanding
through and through, and will not settle for a facile and
premature conclusion to the search, are seeking God,
whether they acknowledge that divine quest or not.
Theism is concerned with making total sense of the world."

Prof. John Polkinghorne, Univ. of Cambridge

Introduction

Reading books of history of science and Christianity, I have come to know scholars holding different viewpoints of the two disciplines and their historical perspectives. Evidences indicate that viewpoints not only determine how they look at the two scholarly disciplines but also influence their attitude toward one another. The consequence is either mutual respect or antagonistic to hostile. In the former case it was beneficial both individually and collectively. In the latter case it is damaging to harmful. The importance of seeing either theology or science in a proper perspective indicates not only your conviction, but determines your lifestyle. Also it plays an important role in our societal and professional life as well.

Reading literatures written by renowned and authoritative scholars, I have derived a great deal of blessings and also enlarging scope of my knowledge. Their scholarly work published reveals how well-advanced and in depth they have achieved. They serve as a source of joyfulness and encouragement to all of us. As a faculty in microbiology, in the following paragraphs I shall present what I consider Christian proper perspectives of science and theology, with diagrams, as crystallization and a scholarly nugget.

I. Christian perspective of theology:

"No one has seen God at any time.

The only begotten Son (Jesus Christ)

who is in the bosom of the Father,

He has declared Him."

John 1:18

"I and the Father are One"

John 10: 20

Anyone who has seen me has seen the Father.

···. Don't   you believe that I am in the Father,

and that the Father, living in me."

John 14:9

Knowing these verses and also the New Testament as a whole, I present the Christian perspective of theology in the following diagram:

The God
- The Creator
- The Sustainer
- Interacting with Humanity
- Continuous Creator

Jesus Christ
- The Incarnated
- Man－God
- The Messiah，the Savior
- Historical Figure

The Bible
- The revealed Word
- God's plan of salvation
- Man's foundation of faith
- Wisdom-imparting & guide in life

Human quest for truth & knowledge
- Man's Faith
- Contemplation
- Search for truth & knowledge
- Rational research

Figure 1. Christian perspective of theology

(from the bottom, move upward) by Stephen C.Y. Liu

In 21st century as well as in the past centuries, man's/ his quest for God is through the Bible, the living Word. The Bible reveals and records the life and the ministry of Jesus Christ. Through this two-step pathway mankind knows God as Creator and Savior of humanity.

Briefly explain it as follows:

- The Bible records the life and the ministry of Jesus Christ,

- He is a historical figure, no one could deny this fact in history,

- He declares Himself as Son of God, authenticating Himself with miracle, healing and teaching,

- God and He as One, seeing him is seeing God,

- God is the Creator of cosmic universe and humanity; He is sustaining the world with his power; and He interacts with humanity,

- In Old Testament time, Moses, Priests and Prophets saw God in vision,

- God cannot be seen in any time and by any human being,

- God appears himself in anthromorphic form to humanity,

- The appearance was true in OT time, in NT time, and in present time, He is incarnated in human form,

- Jesus Christ died as atonement for sin of his people, and then resurrected, and ascended to heaven,

- Jesus Christ as God is the Messiah (to Israelites) and Savior (the people of the world).

- Jesus by himself manifests as God; God-Son is in one,

- Humanity sees Jesus Christ, they see God as well, by perception,

- No man has ever seen God with his/her own eyes, in the past as well in present,

- In conclusion, nowadays Christians see Jesus Christ, through the Scripture and theology,

- When they see Jesus Christ, they see God as well.

II. Christian perspective of science:

> *"For since the creation of this world God's invisible qualities –*
> *his eternal power and divine nature – have been clearly seen,*
> *being understood from what has been made,*
> *so that men are without excuse".*

> *The book of Romans 1:20*

With this verse as well the whole New Testament, I present the Christian perspective of science. Only through the rational studies on what is in the created cosmic universe, humanity comes to see that invisible God, his deity and his power. With this, they could not have any excuse for not knowing him. I shall illustrate this with the following figure/diagram (Christian theistic worldview).

The God

- The Creator，the first, the first cause
- The Sustainer of universe
- He interacts with humanity
- He is the Continual Creator

The Cosmic Universe

- The reality in this universe as evidence of His personality, diety, presence & creation
- The present world/universe, as evidence
  - ✓ The humanity
  - ✓ The biological world
  - ✓ Humanity and society (the social world)
  - ✓ The physical & chemical world, etc
  - ✓ The cosmic world/universe

Human quest for truth & knowledge

- Intellectual or spiritual perception
- Observation
- Rational research
- Laws, principles and theories
- Scientific methods in rational research

Figure 2. Christian perspective of science *

by Stephen C. Y. Liu

*Christian theistic worldview versus

Non-Christian worldviews: naturalistic, materialistic, atheistic

Briefly explain the scientific worldview, as follow:

1) The formulation of scientific knowledge through rational inquiry as follow:

a) Observation: evidence/fact in the present world/universe and collecting data

b) Hypothesis formulated, and then theory.

c) Falsify hypothesis first, and then verify hypothesis through experiments

2) Experimental results analyzed

    d) Conclusion drawn

    e)Elaboration and explanation of results with principles, laws, postulates,

    f)Theories formulated

3) Extension and philosophilization/theory, to worldview

    f) Sciences: principles and methods

    g) continuous search and research

    h) New, renovation and reformulation

4) Sciences: principles and application

5) Worldview; scientific worldview; materialistic worldview, atheistic worldview.

6) Scientists study, by necessity and by limit, this created universe only; not beyond.

    Human societies: sociology, anthropology, paleontology, etc

    Physical world: astronomy, geology , space exploration, physics (the physical world),

    Engineering sciences, etc

    Biological world: microbes, plants, animals and humanity (the biological world)

    Theoretical and pure sciences

7) New principles, new laws, new postulates, etc

8) New frontiers and exploration

9) Philosophical perspective: the visible versus the invisible worlds.

10) Conclusion:

    Scientific perspectives: Christian theistic perspectives (God exists as cardinal premise)

    Scientists perspectives: scientific, materialistic, atheistic

    perspective, secular perspectives

11) worldviews: Christian theistic worldview;

    Scientists' worldviews: secular, materialistic, atheistic worldview.

III. Integrated perspective of theology and science:

Place Figure 1 and Figure 2 together in one figure, we have an integrated perspective of   both theology and science as follow:

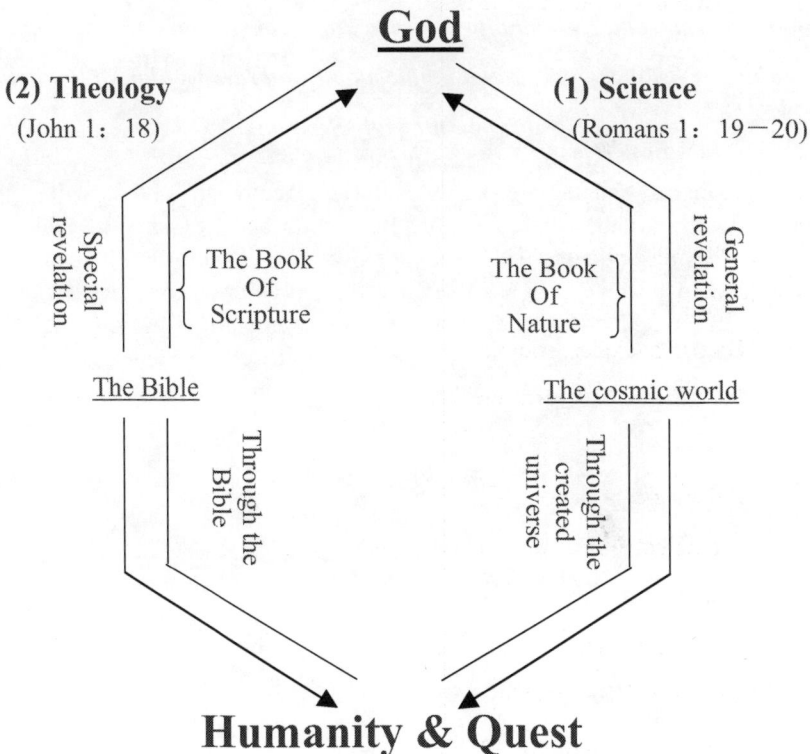

God

(2) Theology
(John 1：18)

(1) Science
(Romans 1：19－20)

Special revelation

{ The Book Of Scripture

The Book Of Nature }

General revelation

The Bible

The cosmic world

Through the Bible

Through the created universe

Humanity & Quest

Figure 3:   The integrated perspective of theology and science

by Stephen C. Y. Liu

Comments/views by well-known scientists and scientific societies worldwide:

Galileo Galilei, an Italian naturalist, astronomer and astrophysics, and who is acclaimed as *the Father of modern experimental sciences (in 16th-17th centuries)*

21

once adopted as his description and conviction of an integrated perspective of both theology   and science as an integrated perspective, with two metaphors of Books: He said:

"The metaphor of Two Books:

The Book of Scripture (the Holy Bible)

and The Book of Nature (the created cosmic universe).

God is the Author of the Two Books. The Two Books should not and could not

contradict each other. Humanity comes to know God through the created cosmic

universe by/ through rational inquiry; and God reveals himself to human

through the Holy Scripture."

In Christian church, over many centuries, theologians and sages taught two classic doctrines : they are a) Special Revelation and b) General Revelation. In essence, they describe that with two ways God reveals himself to humanity. In the former case, God reveals himself through the Holy Scripture by Jesus Christ, the Messiah and the Savior. In the latter case, He reveals himself through the created cosmic world with living things. His deity and power are manifested thereby in this world which is visible. By and with reference humanity knows him who is not visible.

Galileo Galilea adopted the metaphor of the two books that illustrates explicitly well the truth in a parallel model. In conclusion:

"it is an integrated model of both science and theology. "

In 1865, The Royal Society of London, the most prestigious and learned society in those days endorsed this parallel model of both science and theology in their relationships.

Then, in 1887, the British Society of Ordained Scientists, with 300 some members also endorsed this integrated parallel model of science and theology in history of science, literature and arts. The British Royal Society of London was the earliest scholarly society, composed of eminent academicians and scientists. The Society with her members explicitly endorsed this principle and illustration. The Society of Ordained Scientists was composed of members of the Society, at the same time they were ordained church officials.

IV. Evaluation and Comments by renowned scholars:

In 20th and 21st centuries eminent scholars and scientific establishments endorsed the integrated parallel model of both science and theology, describing

their relationships. Their comments and viewpoints are given as follows:

A. British scientists/ scholars:

1. **Prof. William Braggs**, Member of British Royal Society of London, Nobel   Laureate

"Science and theology work with mutually irreducible sets of concepts. They are not in opposition but only they are different.

In fact, I consider the relation between the two disciplines likened unto the cooperation of the thumb and the fingers, whereby one can grasp things and more firmly. Their cooperation is spatial and functional opposition. Only by remaining different are they helpful in grasping a large variety of propositions."

2. **Prof. John Eccles, Nobel Laureate** said:

"Science and religion are very much alike.

Both disciplines are imaginative and creative aspects of the human mind. The appearance of conflict is a result of intellectual ignorance."

3. **Prof. John Polkinghorne, Mathematic Particle Physicist**, former President of Queen's College of Cambridge University, and Cannon Theologian of Liverpool said: "

"Science and theology are intellectual cousins. They both are concerned with interpreted experience, and with quest for truth about the reality. Scientific and theological enquiries are parallel."

4. Prof. Dr. Kenneth A. Koestler, Biologist and Philosopher of science said:

"Sciences, especially natural sciences investigate the created things in the universe with empirical methods.   In essence and by nature, scientists do not attempt to investigate the Creator who is beyond the domain of sciences. Religions, especially Christianity tries to understand and to know the Creator with philosophico-theological contemplations. By necessity and in essence,

Christians appreciate the divine design, purpose and the value of being human. Though science and religion are different in scope and in methods, their final goals are compatible and complementary."

B. US American scientists/scholars:

1) Christian scholars:

1. Prof. Bernard Ramm, Biologist and Professor of Theology, said in his book:

"1) Science needs the light of revelation,

2) revelation needs the perspective of science and

3) both science and theology are fundamental human pursuits."

2. Prof. Howard Van Till, of Astronomy at Calvin College, Michigan, said:

"Scientists un-informed by theology is prone to scientism, the un-warranted elevation of scientific methodology from learning about selected features of reality to the exaggerated status of being considered a superior, perhaps even the exclusive means toward knowledge of reality. Similarly, a community in which theology is un-informed by (misinformed about) the natural sciences is prone toward Biblicalism and the un-warranted elevation of one portrait of the creation's formational history from the realistic status of one artistic biblical portray among to the elevated status of being treated as a normative chronicle that rules out the concept of a full-gifted creation capable of actualizing new creaturely forms by the use of its God-given gifts. In the absence of healthy partnership, both lose. In place of mutually informative dialogue between Christian theology and the natural sciences, there are only turf wars and the non-fruitful shouting matched known as the creation-evolution debate."

3. Prof. Robert John Russell, Director of Center for Theology and Natural Science, Univ. of Calif., at Berkeley, said:

"God not only creates but also guides and directs the evolution of life toward the fulfilling of God's overall purposes. God is the Creator of the universe, without God there would be no universe, nor would the universe exist moment by moment. Granted that God maintains the efficacy of nature, manifest God's faithfulness and rational intelligibility as Creator."

2.) Evolutionists/scholars in USA:

1) **The late Prof. Stephen Jay Gould**, of Paleontology of Harvard University, well-known evolutionist said in his book. In 2000, he died at age 50.

" I join nearly all people of good will in wishing to see the two old and cherished institutions, our two rocks of ages – science and religion – co-existing in peace while each works to make a distinctive patch for the integrated coat of many colors that will celebrate the distinctions of our lives, yet cloak human nakedness in a seamless covering called wisdom."

2) **Prof. Francisco J/ Ayala,** Geneticist of Univ. of Calif., said

"I maintain that science and theology are two complete separate realms of knowledge."

3) **Prof.. Edward O. Wilson** , Socio-Biogist of Harvard Univ., said

"Science and religion are the two most powerful forces in the world today – they need each other."

C. The US National Academy of Sciences, Washington, D. C.

In the front yard of the Academy, where the statue of Prof. Einstein has been erected, and a plague with his saying as follows:

1. *Albert Einstein:*

"All religions, arts and sciences are branches of the same true. All these inspirations are directed toward ennobling man's life, lifting them from the sphere of mere physical existence and leading the individual toward freedom."

2. *The US Academy of Sciences:Washington, D.C.*

In view of the debate going on between scientists in professional organization and Christian religious establishment in USA, for clarifying objective, the US Academy affirms its stand on this issue in 1998, as follows:

"The US National Academy of Sciences clearly endorses the view that science and religion need not to be in conflict. At the root of this apparent conflict between some religion and evolution is the misunderstanding of the critical difference between the religious and scientific ways of knowing. Religion and science answer different questions about the world. Whether there is a purpose to the universe or a purpose of human existence are not questions for science. Religious and scientific knowing have played, and will continue to play significant roles in human history."

3. *Prof. Bruce Albert*, President of US Academy of Sciences, in 1998, while commenting on the book written by Prof. Kenneth R. Miller, said,

"Finding Darwin's God: A Scientist Searching for Common Ground between God and Evolution", " in a very personal and direct way Dr. Miller takes issues with those scientists who claim modern science has disprove the existence of God. He convincingly argues that science and religion offer different, but compatible way of viewing the world. In taking this position, he is supported by leaders of most of the world's major religions. His book should be read by all those who want to understand this central issue."

4. Prof. Francisco Ayala also made comment on Miller's book as follow:

"Can evolution and God co-exist? With powerful and evidence, Ken Miler, a distinguished biologist and a believer, develops an affirmative answer "yes"! "Finding Darwin's God" is artfully constructed argument against both those who deny evolution and those using science to justify a materialistic worldview."

Conclusion

In this Chapter, on the basis of both Gospel of John and the Romans, I present a parallel model of perspectives of science and theology in their relationship. In essence, the two ways of God's revelation to humanity are classic doctrines of special revelation and general revelation.

Galileo Galelei, acclaimed as the Father of modern experimental sciences, used the metaphor of two books conveying the two ways of God's revelation to humanity, and also humanity searching for God through the Scripture and the created cosmic universe. Many eminent British and American scholars and scientists agreed/subscribe to his conviction and worldview

US Academy of Sciences affirms to the public and to the scientific community at large that science and religion need not to be conflict. The world of humankind responds to God (to Christians) to the cosmic world (materialistic) in different ways. Prof. Albert Einstein, his philosophy and worldview are indeed inspiring, and also encouraging the scientific community to see the inherent nature of the two disciples, their differences and ultimate unity in knowledge.

Literature Cited

As given in the text.

Chapter 3
Christian Perspective of Science and Theology (II)

Different Models (2)

i) Conflict, ii) Conversation, iii) Convergence, iv) Complementary and v) Non-Overlapping.

"Science and theology work with mutually irreducible sets of concepts. They are not in opposition but only they are different. In fact, I consider the relation between the two disciplines likened to the cooperation of the thumb and the fingers, whereby one can grasp things. Their cooperation is spatial and functional opposition. Only by remaining different, are they helpful for grasping a large variety of propositions."

William Bragg, (1862-1942), Nobel Laureate

Prof. of Physics, Univ. of Cambridge

In Chapter 2, I present the parallel model of science and theology and their relationships. In 17th century Galileo used the metaphor of Two Books, the Book of Scripture and the Book of nature, with God as the Author of the Two Books. Therefore, they should not and will not come into conflict.

In the last several decades, a number of scholars proposed different models. In some ways, they are somewhat different, in viewpoints and convictions. I present them for comparison, as follows.

1. Dr. Arthur Peacocke, Prof. of Biochemistry and Canon theologian, Cambridge University, England.:

Prof. Peacocke acknowledged that

"By inherent nature, both science and theology (Christianity) are different disciplines, with different objectives in inquiries and different methods of searching. Consequently, their answers are different."

29

Science is, of course, rational research work with empirical methods in lab experiments or field work, obtaining empirical results. They interpret the ways they are trained and experienced in their scholarly fields.

"Often, they extend their results to the domain of their philosophies, which are no longer in science. In literature, sometimes you find that scientists interpret their data even mistakenly with worldviews."

In these two areas, likely they are to have conflict with others not in scientific domain. On the other hand, religion is based on fact, partly seen/known, with reasonable faith they accept what is not seen, as real. Then, they interpret their results in the domain of faith or philosophy. So, we see the

" two disciplines ask for different questions, and use different methods of inquiries. Eventually, they obtain different kinds of results. They could interpret their results differently"

With their results they interpret them in their philosophies and worldviews. We have to realize the inherent nature of both science and faith. We insist on having them in their own fields/domans/worldview. With this, likely professionals and people of faith would avoild coming into conflict.

Prof. Peacocke, as a scientist and a cannon theologian, integrates well these two disciplines. His teaching is indeed inspiring. He will be a good example for young people to follow. In 2002, in a Conference sponsored by AAAS and US Academy of Sciences and some other foundations, being held on Harvard Univ. campus, with more than 400 participants, Prof. Peacocke was the keynote speaker. Both my wife and I had the privilege of attending the conference. We enjoyed a chat with Prof. Peacocke in coffee break and dinner.

2. The late Prof. Stephen Jay Gould of Harvard Univ., 1999

In his book, "Rocks of Ages: Science and Religion in the Fullness of Life", 1999, Prof Gould proposed two non-overlapping magisteria (NOMA). He advocatcd that this would be the best way to harmonize the two disciplines.

"The magisterium of science covers the empirical realm: what is the universe made of (fact) and why does it work this way (theory). The magisterium of religion extends over questions of ultimate meaning and moral value. The two magisterias do not overlap, nor do they encompass all inquiry. To cite the old clichés, "science gets the age of the rocks, and religion the rock of ages. Science studies how the heavens go, religion how to go to heaven."

"I do get discouraged when some of my colleagues tout their private

atheism (their right, of course, and in many ways my own suspicion as well) as a panacea for human progress against an absurd caricature of "religion" erected as a strawman for rhetoric purposes. .... If these colleagues wish to fight against superstition, irrationalism, philistinism, ignorance, dogma and a host of other insults to the human intellect, then God bless them....... But do not call this enemy, religion."

3. **Prof. Ian G. Barbour,** formerly at Kalamazoo College, Kalamazoo, Mich.

In his book "Religion and Science: Historical and Contemporary Issues", (1971)

Prof. Barbour dealt with issues between science and Christianity. In the 60, he encouraged both scientists and Christian scholars to meet together for dialogue for mutual understanding and eventual integration.

He traced to 17th century, totalitarian church authorities exercised too much jurisdiction, and led to a most unfortunate event, i. e. the condemnation and house arrest of Galelio. That left a bad taste in the mouth of scientists. In 18th century, various schools of philosophies arose in Europe. Gradually and eventually, they took over the prime seat of instruction in the institutions of higher learning, including theological seminaries. Science and theology parted their company. In 19th, evolution theory presented a tremendous challenge. The reaction to this challenge varied. Eventually, all these led to the following four kinds of conditions:

a) Conflict: The conflict has been due to **scientific materialism** on one hand, and **biblical literalism** on the other. The former group is represented by scientists such as Richard Dawkins, Jacques Monod, Carl Sagan, Francis Crick, Edward O. Wilson and Daniel Bennett and others. The latter group is by people associated with the Creation Science or Scientific Creationism.

b) Independence: Science and theology differ in inherent character as well as methods of investigation. To avoid conflict even unnecessary debate, it is advisable to have them being independent. They work separately in their domains, and contribute whatsoever to the society with whatsoever they could.

c) Dialogue: I strongly advocate that those professionals in respective fields engage in open and friendly dialogue or in conference so that they could reach mutual understanding and respect. In fact, Prof. Barbour took an active role in the Conference held on Harvard Univ. campus in 2002. In

31

his book, he proposed dialogue in the following aspects: i) Presuppositions and limit questions, ii) Methodological parallels, and iii) Nature-based spirituality.

d) Integration: There are three distinct versions for integration: i) Natural theology, ii) theology of nature, and iii) Systematic synthesis.

Once again, both my wife and I met with Prof. Bardour on Harvard Univ. campus, and enjoyed a conversation around the dinner table.

4. Dr. John F. Haught, Georgetown University, Washington, D. C.

Dr. Haught is a Research Associate in Philosophy and Religion at Georgetown Univ. He subscribes to Theistic Evolution theory of creation. He has written a number of books. He considers that "*reducing life to basically macro-molecules in essence is over-simplification*". One of these is "*Science and Religion: From Conflict to Conversation*", describing four kinds of relationship between science and theology.

a) Conflict: Science and theology differ in essence and in methods of inquiries. The former is based on empirical methods of either falsification or verification of hypothesis, the latter subjective experience and intuition. Each discipline has its own domain and its methods of research, they could not experience any conflict. If somehow the methods are crisscrossed, very likely they would come into conflict. Going to extreme, scientism is what scientists tend to entertain in their thinking whereas biblical literalists overuse their preferred method of searching the Scripture. All these would lead to conflict of the two disciplines.

b) Contrast: Scholars do consider that science and theology are two separate disciplines. Each has its domain and its limits. One should not evaluate theology with scientific method, or religious method for science. They are in different domains. Depending on circumstance, once awhile they could mutually be explanatory and confirmatory, e.g. the Big Bang theory and the creation narratives.

c) Contact: In term of etymology and knowledge, science and theology should not be compartmentalized. Instead, "*scholars in these two*

disciplines should engage in dialogues so that they could reach mutual understanding and appreciation for eventual unity. In western world, Christianity and cultural milieu led to the discovery of natural sciences. Scientific discoveries and knowledge could assist people of faith in better exegesis. *They are mutually supplementary and complementary*.

d) *Confirmation*: Dialogues between scholars of the two groups could lead to exchange of information, and harmony. In 17th century when modern experimental sciences were born it was attributable to devout Christians' efforts to appreciate divine deity and wisdom in creation with rational research. The universe is comprehensible, and it gives us a sense of awe and mystery. That provides the rational for scientific research. In this sense, scientific work is theologico-religious search for ultimate intelligence.

Dr. Haught wholeheartedly supports dialogue and mutual confirmation.

5. Drs. Ted Peters and Gaymon Bennett.

Dr. Peter was Prof. of Systematic Theology at Lutheran Seminary, and **Dr. Bennett** was Information Specialist at Univ. of Calif. They authored this book *"Bridging Science and Religion"*

With grant of Templeton Foundation, in 2001 and 2002 they sponsored conferences with a number of scientists and Christian scholars at the Center for Religion and Natural Sciences at Berkeley, in bridge-building between the two groups. Those who took part acknowledged the inherent differences between the two disciplines. Yet, in reality they are two different and separate routes to knowledge and truth. *For mutual appreciation, bridges between scholars should be built by those who have genuine concern for their harmony*.

6. *Prof. John Polkinghorne*, Particle Mathematic Physicist at Univ. of Cambridge and Cannon theologian of Liverpool. In his book *"Believe in God in An Age of Science"*

Prof. Polkinghorne declared:

"I am a passionate believe in the unity of knowledge. I believe that those who are truly seeking an understanding through, and who will not settle for a facile and premature conclusion to the search, are seeking God, whether they acknowledge that divine quest or not.

Theism is concerned with making total sense of the world. The force of its claims depends upon the degree to which belief in God affords the best explanation of the varieties, not only the religious experience, but of all human experience. "

7. Prof. Stephen C. Y. Liu, of Microbiology and Molecular Biology"

Those of us who are specialized in life sciences emphatically affirm:

" Science is not only our profession but also our Christian vocation. Part of that   vocation is applying scientific knowledge to deepen our understanding of God through the Scripture, and through the Book of Nature. Our calling is Christian steward, and stewardship of God's creation".

Conclusion

This chapter I introduce a number of convictions and viewpoints pertaining to the relationship between science and Christian faith by scholars who differ from what is given in Chapter 2. In a way, they proposed different models. As I stated before, the conviction and the way they consider the relations between the two disciplines not only affords to their own intellectual satisfaction but also the way they look at one another. Mutually acceptable? Mutually exclusive? No

overlapping?

Personally, I wholeheartedly subscribe to the parallel model. Also, I concur with all the convictions and views expressed by these eminent scholars. For a number of years, *I myself have been engaging in building "bridge" between science and Christianity. That is the reasons why I have written this book*. I thought I could do well and better with Chinese scholars and the public. That was the reasons why I wrote this book in Chinese, and published it in China, in 2009. In less than one year, more than 4,000 copies were sold in China alone. That indicates the tremendous need in harmonizing these two disciplines not only in China, but in the world.

Prof. Alfred North Whitehead

Eminent educator at Cambridge and Harvard, and philosopher once wrote in his Book, "Science and the Modern World" in 1949, emphatically said as follows:

"The future course of human history would depend on the decision of his generation as to the proper relation between science and religion; so powerful are the religious symbol through which men and women conferred meaning on their lives, and so powerful the scientific models through which they could manipulate their environment."

Literature Cited

1. Arthur Peacocke, 1981, God's Creation and the World of Science, Bishop William Memorial Lecture, Oxford Univ. Press, UK.

2. Ian Barbour, 1997, Religion and Science: Historical and Contemporary Issues. Harper-Collins Publishing, N.Y.

3. Stephen Jay Gould, 1999, Rocks of Ages: Science and Religion in the Fullness of Life. The Ballantine Publishing Group, N.Y.

4 John F. Haught, 1995, Science and Religion: From Conflict to Conversation. Paulist Press, N. Y.

5 Ted Peters and Gayman Bennett, Ed., 2003, Bridging Science and Religion, Fortress Press, Mpls. MN.

6. John Polkinghorne, 1999.

   Belief in God in An Age of Science, Yale Univ. Press

7. Alfred North Whitehead, 1949.

   Science and the Modern World. Yale Univ. Press.

Chapter 4
Quotations by Renowned Scholars

a. "Imagination is more important than knowledge,

for knowledge is limited while imagination embraces the entire world."

b. "Science can only ascertain what is, not what should be.   Religion, on the

other hand, deals with value and purpose. Though the realms of sciences and

religion are in themselves marked off from each other, nevertheless there exists

reciprocal relationship and dependence."

Albert Einstein

Christianity and Science are the two rocks in western civilization and culture. Science and Christian faith have played important role in western civilization and societal life. They are recognized by scholars as two pathways for searching for wisdom and knowledge, and also for the benefit to human society. Those professionals and workers in these two areas have their varied perceptions, acquisition and applications, ultimately to their worldviews.

As a university professor, by necessity, I have read a great deal of scientific literature by renowned scholars in   sciences.. As a Christian professional, I have also availed myself of a great deal of sound and evangelical writings of the past and the current.. Whenever I have read some inspiring sayings of these scholars in the two disciplines, I copied them down and kept them in my record. Over the years I have accumulated large number of quotations and saying by eminent scholars. They are indeed inspiring, mind-enlightening and soul-nourishing. These literatures in these two fields are indeed my accumulated wealth and precious savings.

In writing this book, I share some of them with you in this chapter, as follows.

1. Gelileo Galilea, 1564-1624, A.D.

Galileo was proclaimed, in 1999, by academic community worldwide as the Father of Modern Experimental Sciences, which was born in the 16-17th century. He was a member of Roman Catholic Church, and a Prof. of astronomy, physics and mathematics, in various universities in Italy. Pertaining to science and theology and their relationship, Galileo first advocated/used the metaphor of two books to portray them.

Galileo said:

"God gives us Two Books: One is the Scripture, God's Word, and the other is the Book of Nature, God's Work. God is the Author of these Two Books. Therefore, These Two should not and could not come into conflict. The Bible tells us how to go to heaven, not how the heavens go."

What an inspiring message Galileo portrayed, not only science and but also Christian theology in parallel relationship. At the same time, he also conveyed the Christian classic special revelation and general revelation to Christians. His view and conviction were unique and historical.

2. Albert Einstein, 1879-1955.

In 1999 both US National Academy of Sciences (ACS) and American Association for the Advancement of Sciences (AAAS) proclaimed Prof. Albert Einstein as the greatest Scientist in the 20th century. In his academic career and scientific research, Prof. Einstein shared his philosophy and worldview in his writings, as follows:

1) *"All religions, arts and sciences are branches of the same tree. All these aspirations are directed toward ennobling man's life, lifting it from the sphere of mere physical existence and leading the individual towards freedom."*

This quotation was engraved in a plaque erected in the front yard where Prof. Albert Einstein's statue stands of US National Academy of Sciences. In a way this saying represents the institution's foundation, philosophy and conviction pertaining to these three academic disciplines.

2) *"Though the realms of science and religion are in themselves marked off from each other, nevertheless there exists reciprocal relationship and Inter-dependence."*

3) *"Modern men worship in the temple of science. But science tells us what is possible, not what is right."*

4) *"Science can only ascertain what is, not what should be. Religion, on the other hand, deals with value and purpose.*

5) *"Science does not deal with questions such as planning and purpose of, nature nor value and meaning of human life.*

6) *"Science without religion is dangerous, religion without science is irrational."*

3. *Professor William Bragg* (1862-1942) of Physics at Cambridge, and

Nobel Laureate:

"Science and theology work with mutually irreducible sets of concepts. They are not in opposition but only they are different. In fact, I consider the relation between the two disciplines likened the cooperation of the thumb and the fingers, whereby one can grasp   things. Their cooperation is spatial and functional opposition. Only by remaining different, are they helpful for grasping a large variety of propositions."

4. *Pope John Paul II,* (1978-2005)

"Theology and science are inter-dependent. Collaborative inter-action ought to characterize their present relationship rather than the misunderstanding and conflict in the past. Science can purify religion from error and superstition, religion can purify science from idolatry and false absolution."

5. *Francis Bacon* (562-1626):

"I maintain that the Bible as the book of God's Word, and nature   as the book of God's work. I encourage students learning as much as possible of both disciplines."

6. *John Eccles:* British neurological science, Nobel Laureate:

"Science and religion are much alike. Both disciplines are imaginative and creative aspects of human mind. The appearance of conflict is a result of intellectual ignorance."

7. *Bernard Ramm,* Prof. of Theology at Bethel College and Seminary,

St.Paul, Minnesota.

"1) Science needs the light of revelation,
2) Revelation needs the perspective of science.

3) Both science and theology are fundamental human pursuits.
We must have a spirit of mutual respect and gratitude.

4)"Theologians and scientists must be keenly aware of the imperfection of human knowledge in both science and theology"

5)"In the main, the task of science is to understand Nature; and the task of theology is the understanding of God. It is the thesis of this Author that the two tasks and two bodies of conclusions. They should exist in a state of harmony."

6) "Ideally, in their mutual pursuits the scientists and the theologian should supplement each other. Their efforts should merge into each other to form one harmonious continuum of reliable knowledge. A positive attitude and relationship must exist between science and theology."

7)" Opposition to Christianity at the level of science is in many instances simply vocalized opposition to Christianity in general. Therefore, anti-Christian man takes pleasure in making the gap between science and Christianity as wide as he can make it, and will heartlessly ridicule any efforts at reconciliation. In this instance, the gap between science and Christianity is in reality the gap between faith and un-belief."

8) The intent of science is to amass all the facts about the universe in its countless facets. It is the function of theology to give these data their purpose and teleological ordering. Through revelation we know that this great system we call universe is from God. Without theology science sets for the vast universe scheme as blind, meaningless, purposeless, never knowing an hour of creation, never knowing of an hour of consummation…. But with the help of theology the vast system which science creates for us takes on meaning and we see it from a credible perspective. It has a personal, meaningful, valuable core. Human life with its hope, joys, tragedies, aspirations, civilizations, intellectual and artistic achievement is now the very center of the universe. ……. Only a

serious intelligent, critical   Biblicism can hope to hold in happy
relationship Christian theology and modern science."

8. **Kenneth A. Koestler,** British Biologist and philosopher

"Sciences, especially natural sciences, investigate the created things in the
universe with empirical methods. In essence and by nature, scientists do
not attempt to investigate the Creator who is beyond the domain of
science. Religion, especially Christianity tried to understand and know
the Creator with philosophico-theological contemplations. By necessity
and in essence, Christians appreciate the divine design, purpose and the
value of human being as created by Him."

9. **John Polkinghorne,** Mathematic Particle Physicist, Cannon Theologian of
Liverpool and Former President of Queen's College, Cambridge University.

"a) Christian faith is not blind. It has its own rationality.

It begins with the existence of an omnipotent God as supreme intelligence.
He is partly seen in the created world as evidence, and partly unseen so
we have to take it by faith To those who believe, the genuine faith has
profound impact on their daily practical living.

b)   Science and Christian theology are "intellectual cousins". They both
are concerned with interpreted experience, and with quest for truth about
the reality.   Scientific and theological inquiries are parallel.

10. **Charles Hummel,** Former President of Barrington College, PA, and former
President of US   Inter-Varsity Christian Fellowship.

"Christianity and science are different responses o nature, they
nevertheless share some vital components, i.e. both are faith community
activities. We should consider them allies rather than enemies.

11. **Keith Ward,** Prof. of Sociology and Philosophy, Univ. of Oxford

a) Belief in God is compatible with modern science.

b) "The scientific view of the universe does lead to one almost inevitably to
think of the wisdom and power of an un-imaginably awesome Creator.
The Christian view of God is one of the breath-taking scope. E It extends
to   the whole created universe, with its million galaxies and its immense

solitude of space. The Biblical view and scientific view together provide an intellectually satisfying and spiritual illuminating account of creation.

12. *Allan R. Sandage,* Professor and renowned Astronomer

"Modern astronomy has enough evidence to support a belief in a Judeo-Christian God? Many scientists would doubtless agree that "you have to answer the question what is sufficient for yourself. The inability of science to provide a basis of meaning, purpose, value and ethics is evidence of the necessity of religion."

13. *David Scott,* Prof. of Physics and former V.P. of Univ. of Calif.

"The true scientists are not afraid to ponder on the larger religious aspects of their work. They found this intellectually engaging. Newton, for example, was fascinated by biblical prophecy. The plants did not occur by chance, and showed an aesthetic sense of the art of a Maker.

14. *Ronald Turner, Prof. of Biological Sciences, Univ. of Calif., Berkeley*
"Religion gives science its purpose; and science gives religion its eyes and its hand."

15. *Freeman Dyson,* renowned Physicist

"Science and Christianity look at the same reality through different windows. It seems to me that life world be rather dull if we only look at it through the window of science."

16. *William Phillips,* Professor of Quantum Physics at Univ. of Maryland, Nobel Laureate of 1997

"Science and Christianity differ in some respects, i.e. verifiability and falsiability of claims, they also have common features, viz. conclusions based on received knowledge, experience and reason." " My religious faith is neither baseless, irrational nor non-scientific. I believe that unlikely science could confirm the personal nature of God. I express this opinion that all these questions are less important than the question of how God expects us to at toward each other in this world, and how we are going to respond to that expectation."

17. Howard Van Till, Professor of physics and astronomy, Calvin College, Mich.

> *"Is it possible that modern evolutionary biology could stimulate an enrichment of Christian theology?   I believe that it is not only possible, but that the partnership   of biology and theology is essential if Christianity is to regain its relevance to the modern university."*

18. Robert John Russell, Director of Center for Theology and Natural Sciences, Univ. of Calif., Berkeley

> *"Christian theology and science are now entering into a new relationship. Rather than undercutting faith, scientific discoveries are offering support for Christian faith, and theology is giving science a sense of spiritual insight and meaning. Many scientists see that there is a design intelligence purpose behind the universe.   Scientists and theologians are meetings in academic conferences on university campuses in USA and England. They endeavor to integrate the two disciplines."*

19. Stephen Jay Gould, the late renowned Evolutionary Biologist and Paleontology, Harvard University

> *"I myself join many others of good wish to see science and religion at peace, working together to enrich our practical and ethical lives…I propose that we encapsulate this central principle of respectful Non-interference, accompanied by intense dialogue between the two distinct subjects, each covering a central facet of human existence."*

20. Edward O. Wilson, Prof. of Evolutionary Socio-Biology at Harvard Univ.

> *"I emphatically say that science and religion are the two most powerful forces in the world to-day – they do need each other."*

21. Fr. Hans Kung, Roman Catholic Theologian and Scholar

> *"Religion and science are not mutually exclusive, but complementary. Confrontation model for the relationship between science and religion is out of date, whether put forward by fundamental believers and theologians or by rationalists and philosophers   At a time when faith and science seem constantly for clash, is it possible   for theologians and*

43

scientists to share common beliefs or at least to develop a kind of truce to allow a meeting of mind. I have little patience for scientists who do not see beyond the limits of their disciplines, or for believers who try to tell experts how things must have been at the beginning. In my writings, while accepting evolution as scientists generally describe it, I still maintain a role of God in founding the laws of nature by which life evolved and in facilitating the advance of creation."

22. **Alfred Norman Whitehead,** world renowned Educator at Cambridge and Harvard, and Philosopher.

"The future course of human history would depend on the decision of this generation as to the proper relationship between science and religion".

Conclusion

The twenty three renowned scholars, theologians and scientists whose quotations I cited in this chapter are indeed accomplished scholars in their own rights. Their ideals, convictions, visions and worldviews are inspiring. What they say is based on what they know well, and what they have experienced in their specific fields. They recognize the two disciplines: sciences and theology and their importance in education and in human civilization.

Let us read their sayings, memorize them, apply them in our own fields of work, and promote the dialogue and ultimate integration of these two disciplines.

Literature Cited

1. John Polkinghorne,   1999
    Belief in God in an Age of Science
    Yale University Press
2.   Bernard Ramm,   1954
    The Christian View of Science and Scripture
    William B. Eerdemans Publishing Co., Mich.
3.   Charles Hummel, 198
    The Galileo Connection
    IVF Press, Ill.
4.   Stephen Jay Gould,   1999
    Rocks of Ages: Science and Religion in the Fullness of Life.
    The Bellantine Publishing Co, N. Y.
5.   Albert Einstein,   1930
    Out of My Mind.
    N.Y. Times,N.Y.
6.   William D. Phillips, 2001
    Ordinary Faith and Ordinary Science
    SSQ Conference. Harvard Univ.Campus, MA
7. Keith Ward,   1999
    God, Faith and New Millennium
    One World Publishing Co., Oxford, UK
8.   Howard Van Till,   2001
    Portray of Creation:Biblical and Scientific Perspectives
    Wm. B. Eerdmanns Publishing Co., MI
9.   Robert John Russell,   2003
    Perspectives on an Evolving Creation
    Wm. Eerdmann Publishing Co, MI
10.   Galileo Galilea,   1632
    Dialogue on the Two World Principal Systems of the World.
    Metaphysics Foundation
11.   Hans Kung, 2008
    The Beginning of All Things.
    Eerdmann Publishing Co, MI.
12.   Alfred North Whitehead, 1949
    Science and the Modern World
    New American Library, N.Y.

Chapter 5
The Birth of Modern Experimental Sciences

"God gives us two books,

they are: The Book of Scripture   and the Book of Nature.

The former is the Word of God, the latter is the Work of God.

God is the Author of the Two Books.

Therefore, they should not contradict each other.

The Bible tells us how to go to heavens,

but not how the heavens go."

Galileo Galilea,   1564-1642

"Galileo sought to keep the church, for its own good, from the mistake of making an article of faith out of any disputed   scientific question. He wanted science to be free from the control of theology as well as philosophy."

Dr. Charles Hummel

The history of world civilization shows that the birth of modern experimental sciences in 16th -17th centuries was attributable to three astronomers-physicists, viz. ***Nicholas Copernicus, Johannes Kepler and Galileo Galilei***. These early Christians and scientists in the true sense of the word, with strong evangelical Christian conviction, engaged in their rational research endeavor. They genuinely believed that this cosmic universe had been created by Jehovah God, demonstrating his deity, wisdom and power. They believed that their searching and researching would strengthen their religious faith, in no way to deny it.   As a result of their endeavor, astronomy, astrophysics and mathematics were borne. In the following century, Isaac Newton contributed his work in physics. The era of modern experimental sciences was thereby borne.

1. Five ancient civilizations of the history of humanity:

A. Chinese civilization.

B. Indian civilization,

C. Egyptian, Babylonian and Persian civilization,

47

D. Greek civilization, and

E. Israeli civilization.

The characteristics of these five civilizations:

A. Chinese civilization:

China has a written history of more than 5,000 years. In early days Chinese invented paper, compass and dynamites. For a long time, the Chinese people derived a great sense of pride. Yet due to the lack of logic reasoning and empirical methods designed, improving qualities and efficiencies, they were left behind. When international trade came in modern time, they were unable to compete with international trade and products. British scholar, Prof. Joseph Needham once indicated in his writing, "*Surveying Science and Civilization in China, 1960*", somehow the inventions did not lead to an industrial revolution in the East." That was true. In Chinese history books, scholars did record their observation of celestial bodies and their related phenomena, with philosophical speculations. Gradually and eventually, they led to religious worship of the created order, becoming a polytheistic religion.

B. Indian civilization:

India is another old civilization, having more than 5,000 years of recorded history. For centuries India was known for her eastern philosophy and religions. Buddhism began in India, and gradually extended to the neighboring countries. Nowadays, in India and in any foreign land where Indians have their colonies and societies established, Buddhist temples are full of idols and images, and religious relics are commonly seen in their communities, becoming a polytheistic religion.

C. Egyptian, Babylonian and Persian civilization:

The Egyptians, Babylonians and Persians were indigenous races in mid-eastern region. They constitute another ancient civilization of the world. The Old Testament recorded their observation of celestial bodies and phenomena. Their emperors and kings treated the Israelites fairly, and granted them limited degree of freedom. With that, the Israelites were able to migrate. Their own history books revealed glorious history with spectacular pyramids and sphinex built. Their sites and relics are great tourists' attractions today. Their sages in the early days had observed celestial bodies, movement and related phenomena. Somehow, their religions and religious observances eventually became polytheistic.

D. Greek civilization:

Greece is another civilization of the world, with more than 5,000 years of recorded history. Greek sages and philosophers such as Plato, Socrates and

Aristotle were known to the world. Their writings are often quoted to-day. They established "Academies" for instruction of younger generations. These academies eventually became "model" or the patterns of higher education in the West. Aristotle and his naturalism or Aristotlianism was the predominant philosophy in higher learning for more than ten centuries in the West, with profound influence. Eventually, in 16th-17th centuries, it was replaced. Seeing their magnificent architectures and statues, we know in Greek culture they emphasized so much on physique of human bodies and exercises. Their religious inclination tended to be more civilized, yet polytheistic in nature and in practices.

E. Israeli civilization:

Israeli was another ancient civilization in Mid-East, with more than 5000 years of history. The Old Testament, a part of authentic Israeli history recorded observation and phenomena of celestial bodies of the universe. From early dates on, the Israelis were quite different from other civilizations. Israeli was the only early civilization that worshipped one God, Jehovah the Lord, the Creator of the cosmic universe. There were no other gods besides Jehovah the Lord. *Their faith stands out as unique, monotheistic, and significant among the world's early civilizations.*

In Israeli holy script, the Psalmist in Old Testament describes "When I look at your heavens, the work of your fingers, the moon and the stars, which you have set in place. What is man that you care for him? Yet you have made him a little lower than the heavenly beings. And crowned him with glory and honor" (Psa. 8:3-5); Also,

"The heavens declares the glory of God,

and the sky above proclaims his handiwork.

Day to day pours out speech, and night to night reveals knowledge.

There is no speech, nor are there words, whose voice is not heard.

Their voice goes out through all the earth,

and their words to the end of the world."

(Psa. 19:1-4)

"By the word of the Lord the heavens were made,

and by the breath of his mouth all their hosts.

He gathers the waters of the sea as a heap;

he puts the deeps in storehouses.

Let all the earth fear the Lord;

let all the inhabitants of the world stand in awe of him." (Psa. 33:6-8).

Reading all these, *we spontaneously responded with a sense of awe of how great is the God, the Creator and the Sustainer* the Israelis had worshiped and proclaimed. The created world with all the living things demonstrate his deity, wisdom and power. He is the only true God, we are his handiwork. Humanity occupies such an important place in his created world. In teachings, their God does not permit his chosen people to worship any others. He commands his people to have a sense of honor and respect that are due to their parents , and high standard of morality in societal and domestic life (Exod. 20:1-17). *In essence, it is monotheistic*. The Israeli's religion, philosophy and teachings have much to do with the birth of modern experimental sciences. (cf. the next paragraph)

2. The Israeli's religious-philosophical perspectives, and Christian doctrines in relation to the birth of modern experimental sciences in 16th – 17th centuries:

A. Doctrinal domain:

1. Monotheistic

2. The cosmic universe, with its living things (plants, animals and humans) are created by Him. He alone possesses this unique authority and ability. He is the continuous Creator and Sustainer, accomplishing his eternal plan.

3. He created humanity in his own image, with endowed value and honor and sense of moral responsibility.

4. The created universe demonstrates his deity, wisdom, glory and almighty.

5. His chosen people worship only the true God, the Creator and Sustainer, absolutely not any of the created of whatsoever kind.

B. Moral and socio-cultural domains:

In western civilization and societies, Christian Church is invested with moral authorities in her teachings, and highly respected by her citizens. Clergymen are respected and honored for their devotion, integrity and scholarship. Churches are not only the centers of worship, and also the educational institutions. *Church fathers, scholars and the saints have so much to do with the birth of modern experimental sciences in 16th and 17th centuries.*

The God who is all-wise and know-all choose to his son, Jesus be incarnated among the Jews in the Israel civilization so that humanity will worship one God, the rules of the universe.

3. *Greek philosophy and Christian doctrines in relation to the birth of modern experimental sciences::*

Greek philosophers such as Plato, Socrates, and the others first established the "Academy" for instruction. Later on, the learning center moved to Macedonia, the Capital. The Academy attracted many students to come from neighboring countries. Aristotle at age 17 entered the Academy, and was one of the outstanding students. He associated with the Academy for 20 some years. When Plato passed away in 347 BC, Aristotle assumed the Master's position. His philosophy was well-known till 16th-17th centuries.

Aristotle (384-322 BC) was considered the founding father of logics. His philosophy (often being referred to "science", with ingredients in astronomy, mathematics and physics) was known as Natural Philosophy or Aristotlianism which remained as influential in western civilization for many centuries. Aristotle's philosophy was consisted of two main parts:

1) Aristotle's view of the world/universe:

    (a) The universe is eternal, without beginning and ending.

    (b) The earth is mad of water, air and fire; the heavens are incorruptible and immutable, being superior to water, air and fire.

    (c) The heavens are incorruptible, and the earth is round and corruptible, and

    (d) The earth is the center of the universe (geocentric) , Jupiter, mars andother stellar bodies circulate around the earth, without beginning and ending with perfect motion.

2) Aristotle's view of philosophy/science: In essence, it is composed of four

causes, working toward the final ending:

    (a) material cause: the earth

    (b) formal cause: blue-print

    (c) efficient cause, and

    (d) final cause.

Aristotle advocated that these principles are universal principles. He first proposed that knowledge was derived from observation, and using reductionism to arrive at universal principle. His logical reasoning was far superior to other philosophers, having something to do with the birth of modern experimental

sciences. At that time, his philosophy was not subject for dispute or discussion. His view was eventually integrated with Claudius Ptolemaeus' astronomy, confirming his earth-centered theory. This theory was well-known and also a dominate philosophy in western world, till 16ᵗʰ-17ᵗʰ centuries it was replaced by heliocentric philosophy (cf. the next section).

Greece with her history also has something to do with the birth of modern experimental sciences. The Greek Empire was subsequently split into 3 states. Then, the Roman Empire came and became the world power. The world's learning center was gradually shifted to Rome. Then, Christianity came, with Jerusalem as her center of influence and extension. Roman Emperor Constantine became a Christian, proclaiming his empire as a Christian Empire. With that Roman Catholic Church came into existence. The Pope   occupied such a unique position worldwide. Royalty and families were in no way could compete with her claim and her power. It was under such a climate modern experimental sciences borne in time, as a "Western Revolution in Sciences".

Three scientists & the birth of modern experimental science:

(1) Nicholas Copernicus (1473-1543):   The Sun and the earth

(2) Johannes Kepler (1571-1630):   Planetary orbits

(3) Galileo Galelei   (1564-1642)   (Helio-centered universe)

These three scientists advocated and demonstrated the "Sun-centered Universe".

Historical background:

In 16ᵗʰ-17ᵗʰ centuries, The Roman Catholic Church was the most powerful religious organization of the world. The Pope enjoyed his unique authority, being based on literal reading and interpretation of Scripture. Matthew Gospel 16:19-20 Jesus said " I will give you the keys of the kingdom of heaven, and whatsoever you bind on earth shall be bound in heaven, and whatever you loose on earth shall be loosed in heaven." With that authority, the Church has the unique authority to determine who goes to heaven, and who goes to hell. No one could challenge it, including the kings and nobilities of those days. The earthly kingdoms should submit themselves to the authority of the Church, being loyal and faithful.

a) *The Roman Catholic Church adopted the geocentric universe* theory as

the valid and authorized theory:

Based on the literal reading and interpretation of two Old Testament Scripture, the Roman Catholic Church accepted the geocentric universe theory as her doctrine. Psalm 93:1-5 "The Lord reigns; he is robed in majesty; he has put on

52

strength as his belt. Yes, the world is established, and it shall never be moved". Joshua 10:12-13, Joshua spoke to the Lord, " Sun, stand still at Gibeon, and the moon, in the valley of Aijalon". And the sun stood still, and the moon stopped, until the nation took vengeance on their enemies." The Roman Catholic Church interpreted the earth is the center, and the sun and moon circulate around the earth. In a way, the Church was sanctified the geocentric universe theory.

b) *The popular observation*: When the common folks, based on their daily experience of seeing the sun coming up from the east and going down in the west, they take it that the earth is the center of the universe.

c) In those days, the institutes of high learning accepted and upheld the Aristotle's philosophy, including the geocentric theory. So, the theory itself was deeply rooted in the mind of scholars and church officials. When the three scholars, on the basis of their observation with telescope and mathematic calculations, advocated the heliocentric universe, they met with vehement opposition from both the Roman Catholic Church and the educated elite.

4. The heliocentric Universe theory as advocated:

A. Nicholas Copernicus, 1473-1543

Nicholas Copernicus was born on Feb. 19, 1473, in Poland, as the youngest son in a wealthy Polish family of four children. In early years on, Nicholas was exposed to the culture of arts, literature, music and probably even philosophy (science). He studied Latin and wrote well. He spoke German, and had a basic knowledge of Polish, being like other students,

Copernicus made his way to Italy, the world center of learning in those days. He entered the University of Bologna, studying law, yet his first love was astronomy. In 1496, the Church bishop had him being elected as cannon, though he never became a priest. In 1497, Copernicus became a friend of Prof. Dominico M. de Novara at Bologna, a confirmed Neo-Platonist. Novara criticized Ptolemy's planetary theory, Copernicus assisted him in measuring the position of stars. Often the two discussed ways the Ptolemy's theory could be improved.

At age of 30, Copernicus acquainted well in mathematics, theology and astronomy. By 1514, Copernicus wrote a beginning outline of new astronomy, known as "Commentarilus", (Brief Treaty) with illustration (Fig. 1). In this Treaty, he criticized the traditional geocentric system with "the center of the earth is not the center of the universe". He also described the mechanism of planetary motion, and gave data for the dimensions of the circles and epicycles. Copernicus and his fame as an astronomer spread to cosmopolitan parts of Europe. He continued to work on mathematic support for the axioms of "Brief Treaty". Then, "De revolutionibus Orbium Caelesticum" (On the Revolutions of Heavenly Spheres) in Latin was published (400 pages long, but less than 500 copies), He did not claim its originality. Knowing this would spark much controversy, he

dedicated it to the Pope Paulo III. It was because the fact the Church not only accepted the earth-centered universe, but also proclaimed it as a church's doctrine.

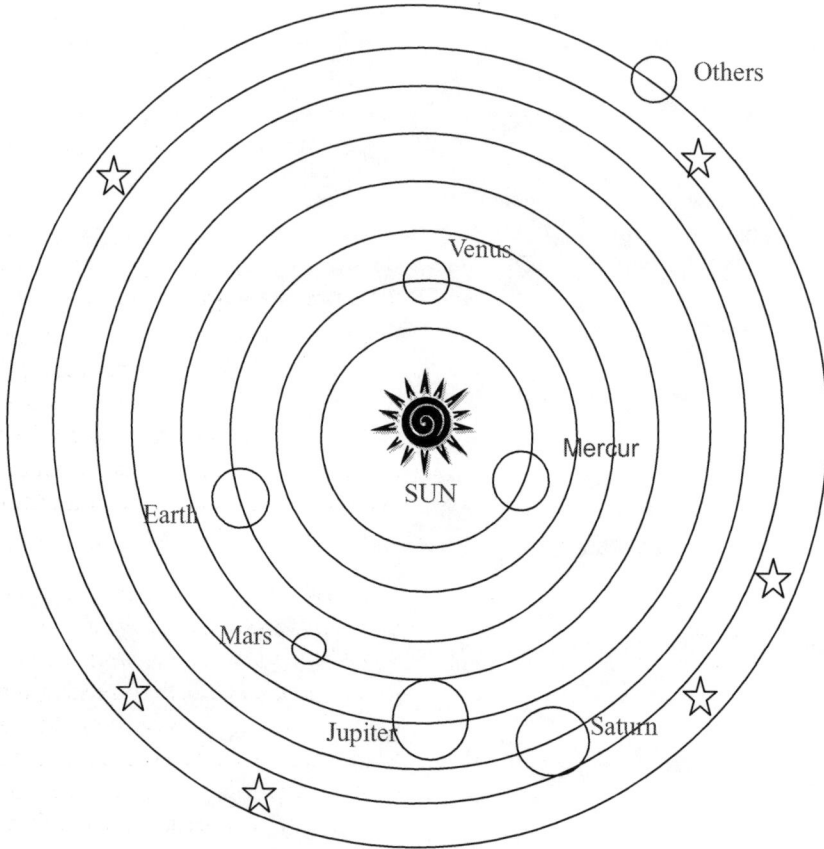

Figure 1. The Copernican Universe

by Stephen C. Y. Liu

In that year, another scholarly contribution was made by Copernicus. The problem of calendar was under intensive discussion. Copernicus suggested that the problem could not be solved until the lengths of the year and month, and the motions of the sun and moon were first measured. His tables paved the way for the calendar reform eventually introduced what we now know as the Gregorian calendar in the west,

In that time, Christian Church Reformation under the leadership of Martin Luther was in early stage in Europe. Copernicus was open to this new movement.

He found it necessary to argue vehemently for his novel sun-centered system. He presented threefold motion of the earth (rotation, revolution and precession), Copernicus was the first one to build a complete mathematical system. By the end of the century, his publications were readily available, and satisfied the requirement. Removing the sun from the category of planets (the earth-center universe) was one of Copernicus' most significant contributions to astronomy. He wrote and professed that "this world has been built for us by the best Workman. With loving duty, I have been seeking the truth in all things of the celestial system, in so far as God as granted that to human reason. Though my views expressed by me were difficult, and quite contrary to the opinion of the multitude. Nevertheless in what follows, we will, with God's help, make them clearer than the day – at least for those are not ignorant of the art of mathematics".

Copernicus's writing (six volumes) were finally published in 1543, the year he died in old-age. He reaffirmed that the goal of astronomy was to explain the movement of heavenly bodies on the basis of uniform circular motion. His writing on sun-center universe, thought being taught as a hypothesis, laid the foundation of studies pursued by both Kepler and Galileo in a later time. His sun-centered system satisfied all the requirements that everything should move uniformly and regularly about their own centers as that law of absolute motion required. The order of movement had firmly established the following order: Mercury, Venus, Earth, Mars, Jupiter and Saturn. The very center of the universe and the distances could be nicely calculated of the earth-sun radius.

Copernicus was an accomplished scholar. He was a churchman, poet, physician, painter and a scholar. He was a genuine believer in the Savior Jesus. His Christian faith was so personal and transparent. During his years as cannon, he had served the church with a genuine sense of "love, and duty" in seeking the truth in all things. He never considered his work would in any way contradict to the church's teaching. In his written work, his mathematic calculation was so accurate and beautiful, no one could deny them. He attributed all his accomplishment to God's grace and divine endowment. In 1542 he suffered from high fever, being afraid that he was unable to complete his scholarly writing. In 1543, he was paralyzed, suffering from brain haemorrhage, and eventually died on May 24. In the last few hours of his life, Copernicus had his book of " De Revolutionibus Orbium Celesti Urn" in his hands, and closed his eyes for eternity.

In the memorial service, Bishop Giese commemorated Copernicus with following words: "We all are his debtors on account of his pure soul, his integrity, and his extensive learning, a friend who has abundantly earned our love and gratitude."

B.   *Johannes Kepler, 1571-1630*

In 1571, Johannes Kepler was bon to a German family. His parents were members of Lutheran Church. In his early childhood on, Johannes became a

Christian, being taught in Scripture and Christian doctrines. Though he suffered from various kinds of illness including smallpox, he was able to concentrate on his studies at well-known Tuebigen University. He demonstrated his scholastic and inquisitive abilities, being ranked high in his classes. At the age of 13, he undertook his concentrated studies on Protestant theology, for several years. Years later, Johannes became keenly interested in astronomy and mathematics.

In 1589, while in Tuebigen, Kepler was under the tutor ship of Prof. Michael Maestlin, a highly regarded scholar in academic circle as an outstanding astronomer and mathematician. Prof. Maestlin was an effective instructor, Kepler was fascinated in what Prof. Maestlin had taught it, and saw this simplified Cupernicus' model being better over the Ptolemic system. He devoted so much time in these two disciplines, and began to collect evidences indicating that Copernicus's theory was correct. Not only he showed such an interest in these subjects, but also undertook them as his career. At the same time, he maintained his interest in Christian theology. In fact, in 1594 he took intensive studies, and later on he wrote that "God had a master's plan when He created this orderly, mathematically perfect world in harmony" in his first book, "Mysterium cosmographicum" (Cosmographic Secret) in 1596. Kepler believed that the sun's centrality was essential to celestial physics; the sun must provide the force to keep the planets moving. He also endeavored to describe mathematically how that force diminished with distance. He firmly established that Kepler as the first astronomer demanded physical explanation for celestial phenomena.

In 1597, Kepler married Barbara Mueller. Their marriage was not a happy one. Kepler was such a genius whose science was his consuming passion, for which his wife did not appreciate. They moved to another city, Graz where he was fortunately to meet a Danish scholar, Tycho Brahe. Their knowledge and specialties complement each other. With Tycho's assistance, Kepler concentrated on working on Mars. After painstaking work for a long time, Kepller discovered that the Mars's orbit might be non-circular. With superimposed of the two orbits, Kepler discovered that the planes move in ellipses with the sun at one focus. For the first time, one single geometric curve and one single speed law were sufficient for predictions of planetary position. It was the first time that the prediction was accurate as what had been observed.

This new model of the solar system was mathematically simple and aesthetically beautiful. Above all, this presented an accurate picture of physical reality.

In 1609, Kepler published his "New Astronomy" (Astronomia nova). It was a landmark in the history of astronomy, breaking away the century-long tradition o perfect circles and uniform angular motion. In the book, Kepler described that the Copernican system could be reconciled with the Holy Bible. One significant contribution was Kepler's calculation of the year in which Jesus was born. At first, he questioned how could Quirinius be governor of Syria when Augustus was Caesar? In searching both Roman and Greek records in comparison with Hebrew

and Bebylonian calendars, Kepler discovered a mistake in the Latin calendar. He re-calculated that Jesus had been born in the year 4 B.C. as given in the Luke's Gospel.

In 1618-1621 while living in the city Linz, Kepler wrote his monumental work "Epitome Astronomiae Coperrnicanae" (Epitome of Copernican Astronomy). It was a complete astronomy, including Kepler's three laws and concept of modern celestial mechanics. One feature which was rather significant was the problem of force which we now call gravity. This book is the theoretical handbook of Kepler's new celestial tables based on his reform of the Copernican system. In fact, he was the first professional who had accepted Copernicus' theory and work.

In addition, he worked out the mathematical detail which could explain the natural phenomena.

Kepler argued that the sun itself was and must provide the driving force to keep the planets moving. All these would give a true picture of the real world. In fact, Kepler went one step further, discovering how God was the architect, and He planned the earth and set it in motion. Kepler's sense of order and harmony was so closely related to his theological understanding of God as the Creator. It must be the "archetypal Laws" in the mind of the Divine Architect. All in all, Kepler played a decisive role in the advancement of modern science. Even when Newton later deduced his law of universal gravity, Newton started with Kepler's laws of motion. When Newton presented his "Principia Mathematica" to the Royal Society of London as a " mathematical demonstration of the Copernican hypothesis as proposed by Kepler.

In Oct. of 1630, Kepler came down with high fever that grew steadily worse. On deathbed, friends asked him where he thought his Christian salvation lays, he answered confidentially, "only and alone on the service and sacrifice of Jesus Christ". In the Savior Jesus, the well-known Astronomer found his eternal refuge and solace. On Nov. 15, Kepler died. He was buried in the cemetery of St. Peter's Church outside the walls of Regensburg. On a simple tombstone, the following verses which Kepler had written were chiseled:

"I used to measure the heavens, now I shall measure the shadows of earth.

Although my soul was from heaven, the shadow of my body lies here."

C. Galileo Galilei, 1564-1642

Galileo, as commonly called, was an Italian, of an old noble Florentine family. His father Vincenzio was a musician. Galileo was born on Feb. 15, 1564, the year of Shakespeare's birth. Galileo in his childhood inherited/derived a love of music and also interest in mathematics. Later on, he became a fine flute

player and organist. Also, he was very fond of poetry and painting. Somehow, he also picked-up his fathers interest in making mechanical devices. All these helped Galileo in his life-style in later time and scientific work. He professed as a Christian being affiliated with Roman Catholic Church in his whole life.

In 1574, his family moved to Florence. Galileo attended the famous Benedictine monastery where he received the current Renaissance education and religious training. Though Galileo showed keen interested in monastic life, his father diverted him from that course. At age of 17, Galileo entered the University of Pisa, studying medicine. In those days, Italy was known as the world's center of learning, with 13 universities (in contrast, both England and Scotland had only 3 such schools). Though in Renaissance time, the academic instruction was given in Latin, and largely authoritarian style, not encouraging creative thinking. The Greek Aristotelianism reigned in both philosophy and science. Universities could maintain a monopoly in these areas.

Galileo, due to his writing and experimental contribution in sciences, he was named as *the Founding Father of Modern Experimental Sciences. His life and academic carrier could be divided into three stages as follows:*

1) 1564-1610:   Studying at Pisa and Padua Univ., then teaching

2) 1610-1616: from Rome, returned to Florence, and published his book "Dialogue", and

3)1616-1643:   Roman Catholic Church ordered/condemned him in house-arrest due to   his provocative writings; physically ill and died, ending his life and career.

....

1) 1564-1610: Galileo's early years:

At Univ. of Pisa, Galileo first studied medicine, and then found his real interest in mathematics. He was gifted in public debate. He demonstrated his caliber as a very good student. In 1585, due to financial difficulties, he discontinued his studies, without a university degree. Returning home, he was under the tutor and his instruction of Prof. Ostilio Ricci, a well-known scholar in those days in Euclide and Archimedes. While he was doing his studies for only one year, Galileo designed and produced an improved hydrostatic balance. Somehow, this new instrument earned him of his first recognition. The new Copernicus and Tychos Brahe did not make their way into curriculum. Galileo developed a love for classics and popular literature.

In 1589, Galileo returned to Pisa. With his scientific success in the passing years, Galileo earned a 3-year's appointment as professor of mathematics at Pisa.

As he studied natural phenomenon, he realized the crucial importance of mechanics. He perceived that the understanding of movement would play a much larger role. Galileo began writing an untitled treatise, "De motu" ("On Motion), being privately circulated. He attacked Aristotle's concept of two classes of motion, i.e. natural and violent. Galileo introduced imaginary rotations of massive spheres and defined "neutral" motions, a concept that led to the inertia in terrestrial physics. His endowed capacity of deriving "thought experiments" with imagining idealized situation such as motion without friction. In his "on Motion", Galileo tried to negate Aristotle's two rules on the speed of falling bodies. He failed to recognize the importance of gravitational acceleration, therefore he was unable to reconcile his conclusion about motion with the observed objects dropping from the top of tower of Pisa. Yet, in later years, with details filed in by others, the experiment was called "the most famous of all experiments."

Galileo somehow had a habit of antagonizing colleagues in his writing and speaking. He thereby made many fellow faculty members as enemies. They in turn made fun in his public lectures. When his appointment at Pisa expired in 1592, Galileo realized the impossibility of renewing his appointment at Pisa. Somehow, he was able to enlist the support of several influential faculty members, he succeeded in having another appointment as professor of mathematics at University of Padua. In those days Padua was known for freedom of thought attracting many good students from all over Europe. They came to Padua in order to study under Galileo during his 18 years at that University.

Galileo continued his work in mathematics and experimental physics at Padua. At the same time he developed his interesting in astronomy. Before long, he accepted Kepler's new astronomy. The years at Padua were years fruitful for Galileo studies of mechanics. Although Galileo had the conviction that the earth moved around the sun, somehow he remained as "a closet Copernican". In 1609, Galileo constructed an instrument which could identify approaching ships two hours before they could be spotted by observers with trained naked. In showing gratitude, the Rulers of Venice granted Galileo the Chair at Padua for life, with double salary, at a level unprecedented for mathematicians. Galileo was able to make telescope, no one else could match the quality he had achieved. With a twenty-power telescope, he scanned the heavens and discovered countless "new worlds". The Milky Way became a gigantic collection of stars. The vast expanse of the universe taught by Copernicus appeared suddenly as plausible. More surprising were several new discoveries closer to earth that flatly contradicted Aristotle's teaching. Galileo could see that the moon was not a perfect sphere shinning with it own light. Rather, it has imperfections, with mountains and valleys, very much like the earth. Galileo was able to calculate the depth of those valleys. He also discovered the planet Venus which has phases like those of the moon. To make things worse, the sun has dark spots that appeared and disappeared; even the sun was not perfect, unchangeable sphere of Aristotle's astronomy. Galileo concluded that either the sun turns on its own axis or the earth

much move around the sun. He also discovered four small bodies moving near Jupiter. Seeing them in different times, Galileo concluded that four bodies were moons revolving around Jupiter. Yet, according to Aristotle, only the earth as the center of the universe could have a moon. Now, Jupitor and its four moons could be seen as a model for Copernicus' concept of the solar system: the planets (including the earth) moving around the sun. By 1690, people having no mathematic training could see for themselves that Aristotle's wrong. The astronomy he tried to popularize was Copernican!

In 1610, Galileo published his discoveries in a thin book, entitled in "Sidereus nuncius", (The starry Messenger). Within months, Galileo published his second edition. At age of 45, Galileo became well-known in Europe. At that time, Aristotelian tradition valued observations, its concern was primarily qualitative. Galileo's interest was more quantitative more than qualitative, with accurate measurements. As a pioneer in new science, Galileo showed how much ingenuity and precautions were required to obtain adequate results. At that time, many old-fashioned Aristotelians including Cremonini opposed and stood against Galileo at Padua. When Galileo in five years later reported his telescope observation with solid results, Cremonini even declined to look at the sky with Galileo's telescope.

2) 1610-1616: Returning to Florence, *"Dialogue" published*:

The year of l610 was a stormy year for Galileo. In June, he resigned his life appointment with Padue. Leaving Venice, he returned to Florence where he became "Philosopher and Mathematician" to the Grand Duke. With that position, Galileo gained his recognition, being free from academic teaching. He was able to continue his experiments, and consequently he was able to produce two books, i.e. "An Immense Design, being full of astronomy, geometry and philosophy. Then, he endeavored to establish the Copernican system on the basis of his new discoveries in astronomy and physics.

While in Florence, Galileo encountered so much resistance from traditional and diehard Aristotelians who even declined to peer through his optical instrument, or accused Galileo's flaw in the lens in the lens or optical illusions. Galileo could sense the resentment and hardening attitude of these colleagues from Pisa, Padua and Bologna. In April, Galileo traveled to Rome, with his telescope. He met with scholars such as Father Clavius and other Jesuit scholars, and demonstrated it what he had reported. At the same time, he left the telescope with them so these colleagues could look at it at their leisure time. Seeing the phenomena by themselves, these scholars became convinced of Galileo's new discoveries and enthusiastically honored Galileo.

The traditional and old Father Clavius, though unwillingly yielded but gracefully accepted what he had seen. Even so, when Father Clavius reported to a church commission which was chaired by Cardinal Robert Bellarmine, he did not

unequivocally supported the Copernican theory.While in Rome, Galileo was permitted to see Pope Paul V, who was favorably impressed by Galileo's report. At the same time, he visited then Cardinal Maffeo Barberini, a mathematician, and a member of a rich family in Florence, who later became Pope Urban VIII. Another honor conferred on Galileo was his election to the Lincean Academy, a scientific society which had been found by Prince Federico Cesi. With all these meaningful events, Galileo returned home, with full confidence that Copernican theory would be eventually and openly accepted. Those disgruntle faculty at Pisa secretly formed a movement, with a name of "Liga" fighting against this new theory. They adopted a new strategy, carrying this scientific inquiry into a religious and theological issue. They argued against Copernican theory was incompatible with the Holy Scripture. In 1613, when a formal dinner was given by Grand Duke Cosimo II (Galileo's employer), somehow Galileo did not go. In an informal debate, Cosimo Bostaglia declared that "any motion of the earth was impossible since it would contract Holy Scripture. After the dinner party, Grand Duchess Christina questioned Castelli (Galileo's student) on this issue. Afterward, Castelli wrote a full account of the discussion and sent it to Galileo. Consequently, Galileo decided that the time had come to meet the challenge head-on.

In a letter to Castelli, Galileo meticulously spelt out his position as a Scientist and a Catholic who wholeheartedly accept the Scripture. He fully affirmed his commitment to the truth and authority of the Bible, then he raised the question on its proper interpretation of scriptural verses. His pronouncement, later on became a famous dictum, as

"God has given us two Books, one of nature, the other Scripture. Both the Holy Scripture and Nature proceed from the Divine Word, the former as the saying of the Holy Spirit, and the latter as the most observable executrix of God's orders."

He further affirmed that

"the two can never contradict each other, even though they expressed in different languages for different disciplines: i.e. religion and ethics in Scripture; Physics in nature. Why then should be Bible be used to support the opinion of fallible philosophers against the others, to the jeopardy of its authority?"

Copies of that letter were circulated freely, and battle lines were drawn with both theologians and courtiers taking their sides.   Galileo intended to silence the illogical objections to Copernican, yet his enemies turned their arguments into an occasion of innuendo. So, in 1614, Galileo as a scientific and faithful Roman

Catholic was accused of undermining the Scripture and meddling in church theology.

Another unfortunate event came. On Dec. 20, 1614, Father Tommaso Caccini, an Aristotelian professor and Dominican friar, preached in the principal church in Florence. In his sermon, he made "Joshua's miracle of making the sun standing still, condemned the idea of moving earth as being very close to a heresy. He branded all "mathematicians as agents of the devil who ought to be banned from Christendom." In fact, Caccini almost charged mathematicians were identical with astrologers. Of course, Galileo was very much concerned to have been the subject on a Sunday sermon. Though in a later time, Caccini wrote a formal apology, it did not placate him. Somehow, the sermon on Sunday very much strengthened the opposition against Galileo. Not long after that, Niccolo Lorini, a priest sent a letter to one of the Inquisitors-General in Rome of the Holy Office, with a copy of the letter, accused Galileo and his followers as "orderly men and all good Christians, but a little wise and cocky in their opinion." The whole argument was one thing for scientists to speculate about nature, it was quite another thing for laymen to write thesis interpreting Scripture to fit their speculations.

When Galileo had heard of this bad news, he immediately submitted "Letter to the Grand Duchess Christina" to his friend Archbishop Piero Dini in Rome, asking him to show it to Cardinal Bellarmine. Unfortunately, in 1616, Galileo Gelileo who advocated Copernican theory of heliocentric universe, was *condemned in house arrest*.

3) 1616-1643: Condemnation, house arrest to death in home.

Now, Galileo had to do largely with encounter with Cardinal Bellarmine, who knew more and better informed in the Curia. The Cardinal was prepared to distinguish between two important questions: a) Was Copernican system true, being supported by convincing evidence?   b) Was it compatible with the Holy Scripture?

Now, Galileo knew well that the new cosmology was a true physical description of the universe, not just a conventional mathematical device to fit the data. It was one thing to show that the sun-centered model was compatible with the Scripture; it was quite another thing to prove that the Book of Nature supported that model. Galileo realized that he did not prove the earth's motion. His method was mostly hypothetico-deductive. To Cardinal Ballarmine and the other theologians, Galileo's procedures were essentially inductive. Such contingent arguments were not sufficient to force the reinterpretation of the Scripture. Galileo realized that he had to present the case. In 1615, Galileo finally found the action of tides which was due to combined daily rotation of the earth and its annual revolution around the sun. He presented this explanation to various audiences in Rome as a conclusive physical demonstration. Yet that did not convince the opponents.

In March of 1616 Galileo was summoned before Cardinal Bellarmine, who admonished him against advocating Copernicanism as a cosmology. If he refused to accept this, then the scientist would be enjoined before witnesses to "abstain altogether from teaching to defending this opinion and the doctrine, and even from discussing it." If Galileo refused to accept this admonition, then three steps would be taken, if necessary, they are "admonition, injunction and prison". If Galileo accepted the first, then that would be the end of the matter. He would not have to have any formal declaration in the public.

Galileo thought it again. He thought that the best thing to do is to accept the warning. He fully realized that he had to refrain from any argument. Simply, he just obeyed the church and her instruction, at least for time being. Galileo hoped that in the future he could one way or another persuade the church authorities to modify or change it.

Right after he had done this, Galileo was given an audience by the Pope. The Holy Father assured him of no more plotting by his enemies, so he had nothing to fear. Somehow, Galileo overheard the rumor circulating in Rome that he had hardened his heart, refusing his teaching the Copernican doctrine. To make thing clear enough and to set the record straight, Galileo asked Bellarmine a formal note describing what had been taken place. The Cardinal granted his request, giving a formal note saying that "Galileo had not publicly renounced his convictions nor been forced to do penance; he had only been informed that Copernican doctrine was contrary to Holy Scripture, and therefore cannot defended or upheld. With this note, Galileo left Rome with the impression that he could still use the new cosmology as a hypothesis. Yet, his opponents watched him for any misstep. In August of 1623, Maffeo Barberini became Pope Urban VIII. When Prince Cesi visited the new Pope, Barberini, who was also Florentine, and a friend of Galileo. The Lincean Academy decided to dedicate the new book "The Assay" (Il saggiatore) written by Galileo to the Pope. The book itself was an immediate success, even the Pope had it read to him in mealtime. In 1624 Pope gave Galileo several audiences. While Galielo was seeing the Pope, he tactfully reported the subject of a moving earth. He also alluded to the malice of his enemies, hope that the decree of 1616 might be rescinded, being not to avail. The Pope encouraged him to publish his tide theory, if he could make it clear as a theory, not a reality. Though Galileo did not achieve his objective, he was grateful that he could openly discuss Copernican doctrine one more.

From 1624 to 1630 Galileo published his "Dialogo dei due massimi sustemi del mondo – Tolemaico e Copernicano" (**Dialogue on the Two Principal World Systems – Ptolemaic and Copernican**) covering a wide range of subjects. The book revealed so much what Galileo had in mind. Galileo tried to make it as persuasive as possible. He presented it in a show. In 1630 Galileo went to Rome to get his book licensed. Pope Urbano VIII endorsed the idea of an astronomical dialogue provided it was strictly hypothetical. In February of 1632 Galileo finally presented the first printed copy to the grand duke. Though the book was popular,

within months rumors of disapproval by the church began to circulate. In August, an order came from the Roman Inquisitor to stop all the sales. A Commission of experts examined the Dialogue to assess its Copernican character explicitly implied in the book. On Oct. 1, Galileo was officially summoned to Rome to report to the Holy See.

In 1633, the trial and the verdict came. Galileo's trial was not the simple conflict between science and religion as publicly perceived. It was a complex power struggle of both personal and professional pride, envy and ambition, affected by pressure of bureaucratic politics. In the beginning, both judges and defendant were confused by the contradictory document of 1616. Galielo presented the admonition from Cardinal Bellarmine challenged the very basis for his trial. When the question was shifted to "Dialogue", it was obvious where Galileo stood. The argument for Copernican system was cogent, the refutation weak; so when Galileo declared that he had not defended Copernican, the judges became indignant. It was evident that Galileo had tried to fool them. It took only 5 days for them to declare that Galileo had maintained and defended *the Copernican astronomy as a valid theory.* Cardinal Francesco Barberini, the Pope's nephew, one of the Judges, tried to give Galileo a lenient sentence. After long discussion, Galileo finally agreed to make a confession. On May 10, Galileo pleaded for mercy on account of his poor health and advanced age. On June 16, a verdict was recorded:

"Galileo is to abjure on vehement suspicion of heresy in a plenary assembly of the Congregation of the Holy Office, then is to be condemned to imprisonment. at the pleasure of the Holy Congregation, and ordered not to treat further, in whatever manner, either in words or in writing, the mobility of the Earth and the stability of the Sun: otherwise he will incur the penalties of relapse. The book "Dialogue" is to be prohibited." The verdict was implemented on June 21. Finally, after further questioning and answering, Galileo renounced the Copernican view, and signed the deposition. The next day, Galileo heard the sentence, which declared the errors in his book of "Dialogue", which was banned, and he was condemned to a "formal prison of the Holy Office." At that time, Galileo pleaded to leave out two points, i.e.1) he was not a good Catholic, and 2) he had intended to deceive any one, After winning these two points, Galileo knelt again, and read aloud the corrected version of his confession:

"I, Galileo......... at age 70 .... Has been pronounced by the Holy Office to be vehemently suspected of heresy of having held and believed that the Sun is the center of the world, immovable and that the earth is not the center and moves..... With sincere heart and unfeigned faith I abjur, curse and detest the afore-said errors and heresies."

On June 30, 1633 Galileo was released to the custody of a friend and former

pupil, Archibishop Ascaio Piccolomini in Siena. In Dec. of 1633 the Pope allowed Galileo to return to Florence, instead of going to prison, and stayed at Galileo's small farm near Arcetri. Galileo was happy to be home again. Pope Urbano promised that the old man should suffer as little as possible, and continued to receive the pension he had granted in happy days. Though under house arrest for the reminder of his life, Galileo was glad to be home and near his daughter Virginia (Sister Maria Celeste). His daughter now could attend his father's need. Her death in April 1634 was a grievous loss to the old gentleman and scientist. Despite his loneliness, Galileo resumed his scientific writing, mostly on motion and applied mechanics with mathematic reasoning. They would prepare the ground for discussing planetary motion again, if the verdict could be rescinded or forgotten. Galileo was able to write his greatest contribution to new science by writing "Discorsi e demostrazion matematiche intrine a due nuove sciencze" (Discourse and Mathematic Demonstrations Concerning Two New Sciences). The book was completed in 1634. The manuscript was smuggled out of Italy, and published in Leiden of Holland in 1637.

In 1637, Galileo suffered from a progressive disease which deprived him of the sight in his right eye. It finally made him blind as he was planning to conclude his career with two more books. Though the Roman Catholic Church had turned her back on him, he neither withdrew from his church nor showed any irreverence toward the Church. He never blamed the church, but only some "wrong-headed individuals" Galileo had his conscience clear, said "*only I and God in heaven thoroughly know*".

Galileo Galilea was a mathematician, physicist, experimenter, inventor, entrepreneur, musician, writer, debater and a polemicist. For thirty some years, Galileo waged a battle against Aristotelianism of the scientific establishment. Though his attack was not personal, his opponents took it hurt, thinking his attack on undermining their scientific system and professional reputation. *He was a crusader*. His books and letters reflected his personality, character and his scientific insight and farsighted. Over his long life, he formed lasting friendships with a large variety of intelligent colleagues and powerful men. As a polemicist, Galileo in a way was potential to a university, church and state. *His long crusade was not only for Copernicanism but also as a new unified science drawing together mathematics, mechanics and astronomy. He advocated the pursuit of science to explain natural events, free from control of any philosophy, whether old or new. Galileo tried to keep the church, for its own good, from the mistake of making an article of faith out of any disputed scientific questions. Also, he wanted science to be free from he control of theology and philosophy*. He suffered for freedom of scientific inquiry from both the university and ecclesiastic establishment of his days.

In Nov. of 1641, Galileo was confined to bed by kidney pains, heart palpitation and fever. His two pupils, Viviani and Torricelli stayed with him. Although he was weak, he enjoyed listening to their scientific discussion. On Jan.

8, 1642, only one month before Galileo 78th birthday, Viviani wrote the following: "With philosophy and Christian firmness he rendered up his soul to his Creator, sending it, as he liked to believe, to enjoy and to watch from a closer vantage point those eternal and immutable marvels which he, by means of a fragile device, had brought closer to our mortal eyes with such eagerness and impatience."

The three Christian scholars devoted themselves to the astronomical studies with experimental methods over these years under restricted conditions. Consequently, they formulated the "*Sun-centered universe*" to replace Aristotle's "earth-centered" theory. *It was a historical landmark*. At the end of the year of 1999, US Academy of Sciences together with America Association for the Advancement of Sciences publicly proclaimed *Galileo Galilei as the Father of Modern Exp. Sciences*.

Based on what they had discovered, then Isaac Newton took up the studies in physics. He contributed with his universal gravitation theory. Also, Newton wrote extensively on sciences in relation to Christianity.

D) Issac Newton, 1642-1727

In the year of 1642, the world of science witnessed both the death of Galileo Galilea in Italy and the birth of Isaac Newton in England. Four scores of years later, Isaac Newton of Britain contributed his work in physics and mathematics to the birth of modern sciences.

Newton's parents were country folks who lived in a small farm in Woolsthorpe north of London. His father died at the age of 36. On Christmas day, friends came to assist the young widow with the birth of Isaac. Two years later, Isaac's mother Hannah remarried to the Rev. Barnabas Smith. When his mother and stepfather moved away, Isaac stayed with his grandmother who cared for him. Isaac grew up without any siblings.

Isaac was an avid reader in school. Early in life, he developed his self-sufficiency and resourcefulness, which served him well in his life and career. He had developed very un-usual skill in building mechanical toys. At the age of 12, Newton entered the Old King's School in nearby Grantham, which was known for preparing students for either Cambridge or Oxford. Newton was interested in chemistry, mathematics and mechanics. In addition, he always stood at the top of his classes. In 1658, his stepfather died, Isaac moved back to Woolsthorpe being with his mother with the farm. At the same time, he spent most of his time in nature-observation. The country farm life was not good for the young man, his mother decided to send back to school, completing his course at King's and prepared for Cambridge Univ.

In June of 1661, Isaac Newton entered Trinity College of Univ. of Cambridge. In those days the traditional Aristotelian philosophy was dominant in education, Copernicus, Kepler and Galileo were ignored. In 1662, the Royal Society of

London was chartered and established by King Charles II. The objectives of the Society was to Improve Natural Knowledge, stimulating scientific exploration. The Society's motto was " Nultius in verba " (translated literally "We don't take anybody's word for it"), expressing its policy and approach to sciences. The counterpart in France was the Paris Academy of Sciences found by Louis XIV in 1666. In the first 3 years, Newton followed the prescribed course, studying mathematics (algebra, geometry ad trigonometry), Latin and Greek. In addition, he studied physics and optics under a well-known scholar, Prof. Isaac Barrow, who held the prestigious Lucasian Chair of Mathematics. Prof. Barrow immediately noticed Newton's genius, and also introduced him to telescopes and current theories of light. All these awoke Newton's latent intellect. He read everything he could get hold of. He mastered Kepler's Optics, hew grounded lenses and built ingenious apparatuses. His dexterous fingers and mathematic mind lent him to build apparatus and optical instruments. With all these Newton was able to observe stars and light. Consequently, he was able to develop theory of light and color. He discovered the binomial theorem, an accomplishment that alone could have established his prestige in the history of mathematics. Then, he pursued a new way of calculating the areas of curved shapes. With remarkable energy and ingenuity, he calculated the area of a hyperbola to "two-and-fifty figures by the same method the Greek mathematicians in the years past had tried and failed. Thus, Newton laid the foundation of his methods of "fluxions". That method later developed into differential and integral calculus, the cornerstone of modern mathematics and an indispensable tool for scientific research.

In 1665, Due to an infectious plague season, the school suspended classes, Newton returned home. During this un-expected vacation at home, Newton found the solution to age-old problem of motion in the heavens and on earth. Newton was puzzled by the motion of moon, what makes the moon moving so evenly around the earth in an orbit of 27 and $1/8^{th}$ days. Fifty years ago, Kepler had discovered that the inverse-square principle applied, and that there must be some kind of attraction between the sun and the planets. Newton analyzed the moon's motion in term of centrifugal force, an endeavor to recede from the earth balanced by gravity. He discovered that for circular motion, the centrifugal force is measured by v/r where v is the velocity of the orbiting body and r is the radius of rotation.

a) Newton and his scientific studies:

According to report circulated among people, during this time at home Newton was sitting under an apple tree not far from the house, pondering a number of questions. When an apple landed at his feet, he began to think about the motion of the moon. The attractive force that caused the apple to fall extended to the top of the tree; did it also extended as far as to the moon? If so, what would be the attraction amounting to such a long distance. Consequently, Newton discovered the inverse-square law for circular orbits in the 1660, and laid the foundation for his later work in mathematics, optics and celestial mechanics. By

that incidence, Newton discovered the law of universal gravitation. His achievements in this period of time were phenomenal.

In 1667, the plague subsided, Cambridge reopened it doors. He returned to his school he had loved. About half year later, Newton was elected as a Trinity Fellow with annual stipend of L-100. With that honor he went home for Christmas.

At Cambridge, Newton was immersed himself in the construction of reflecting microscope, optics and new reflecting telescope in his laboratory. In July, he received his Master of Arts degree, opening the road to academic advancement. He welcome more than anything else was to pursuit of new ideas. At the request of Prof. Barrow, Newton reported his mathematical research in a paper entitled "On Analysis of Equation with an Infinite Number of Terms". Prof. Barrow thought of his originality and scholarship. He sent Newton's paper to many well-known mathematicians. After reading Newton's paper, these mathematicians had high regards of Newton's unusual contribution.

On Oct. 29, 1669, Newton was appointed **Lucasian professor of mathematics at age of 27**, he occupied the most famous chair in mathematics. He stayed in that position for 20 some years till he was appointed as Warden of the Mint by the King of England. While he was Professor, he was asked to give lecture of one week in an academic year, plus conferences with students twice a week. All these left him ample time for research. At age of 30, Newton was elected to a **member of the Royal Society of London.** In next year, Newton read his new paper on "New Theory about Light and Colors." It was a masterful sample of well-planned and executed scientific work, though some of them were not experimentally confirmed. In the Royal Society, Robert Hooke, who was then an excellent microscope expert and a mechanic genius, being different from what Newton had reported. The two gentlemen had debate on certain subjects. By and large, they got along well in scholastic world.

In the next several years Newton devoted to other subjects such as chemistry, practical invention, and also theology. He also tackled a complicated mathematic puzzle of planetary orbits. Years ago, Kepler had shown that the ellipse fits the observations of planetary orbits. Would it be possible to calculate the exact curve on the basis of the inverse-square law: the attraction between two bodies varies inversely as the square of the distance between them? Newton consequently proved that an ellipse would satisfy the conditions. It was the first time that Newton computed with precision the shape and speed of both celestial and terrestrial trajectories. He also produced a 9-page treated on "De motu corprum in gyrum" (On the Motion of Bodies in an Orbit). Prof. Edmund Helley of Cambridge recognized the precise mathematic analysis of "On Motion" constituted a revolutionary advance in celestial mechanics. Immediately, he went to get Newton's permission for its presentation to the Royal Society and for publication. Also, it was time for Newton to make his law of universal gravitation known to the academic world. So, Newton completed a three-part work that was

officially presented to the Royal Society in April of 1686. A committee was immediately appointed to oversee its printing. So in July of 1687, the "Philosophiae Naturalis Principia Mathematica" (Mathematical Principles of Natural Philosophy) came out in three volumes. The first volume sets the three laws of motion which extended Galileo's work and broke with the ideas of Aristotle and the medieval philosophers. The law of universal gravitation provides the basis for the science of mechanics, a major division of physics. Dealing essentially with forces and their effects, that science is fundamental for modern technology. The 2nd and 3rd volumes were on "System of the World" is Newton's crowning achievement. With these, Newton explained the orbits of Jupiter's satellites discovered by Galileo, and how Kepler's three planetary laws were consequences of universal gravitation. They discussed the earth's daily rotation and the movement of its axis in space, and explained how the gravitation pulling of the sun and moon causes the tides. Finally, Newton calculated precisely the motion of the moon. Years ago, both Copernicus and Kepler began to undermind Aristotle's system on the celestial front with their work in astronomy. Galileo's work attack was more practically with mechanics. His telescopic discoveries supported the Copernican system. With the law of gravity, Newton finally invalidated Aristotle's concept that the laws governing motion in the perfect region of heavens were different from those on an imperfect earth. Newton's synthesis was unrivaled till Albert Einstein related matter and energy in an equally universal and elegant formula: $E = mc^2$.

Newton was a superb mathematician. His conviction was different from Copernicus, Kepler, even Galileo. Often, he said that the world is what it is, let us try to explain all that we could by exact mathematic laws, to him it was the language of science. Newton was also open to other approaches. Though mathematics played a central role in scientific inquiry, theories much be confirmed by experiments. Mathematical truths should not ride roughshod over physical facts, but updated as new data became available. Newton was based on his confidence in his inductive methods, which undergird the objectivity and cumulative character of sciences. Newton also used what we call today the retro-productive methods; i.e. a) formulate a hypothesis,, b) deduction of the consequences and c) testing these consequences by observation and experiments. He also distinguished "natural philosophy" (science so-called in those days) and "hypothesis" (assumption, speculation). To Newton, the mission of science was to discover mathematical laws of nature's behavior – laws clearly deducible from and verifiable by observation of phenomenon. He made his position clear enough in 2nd edition of "Principles". Newton described how the attraction between two bodies occurs but does not explain why.

Newton's "Principles" as a scientific book was un-excelled among scientific writings. With his logics, detailed mathematic analysis, text clarity and breadth of contents. The book generated a great deal of interest in Cambridge and also in UK. It went into 3 editions. Newton ran the whole gamut of physical science, and its application in 17th century universe. He demonstrated a radically new celestial

dynamics on novel concepts of mass and inertia, force, momentum, an entirely new quantitative thinking for the next two centuries. The Principles articulated the interaction of mathematical theory with observed data, which firmly established the new scientific approach to describe nature.

In France and in the continent, Descarte and his associates resisted Newtonian ideas for a number of years. But, a century later, great mathematicians such as Laplace and Lagrange devoted their lives to completing Newton's work and extending it.

b) Newton's Biblical/Scriptural studies:

To Newton, the world of science was not all for his life. He was deeply committed to his dynamic faith in his Creator, who reveals Himself to humanity through Scripture and the world of nature. His God was the God of the Bible. He recognized Christ as divine Mediator between God and humankind, but subordinate to the Father. Christ, owing to his sacrificial death on the cross, he earned the right to be adored and worshipped. His understanding and knowledge came from the Bible. Miracles and prophecy were prominent in his studies. *He was a dedicated Christian*, being affiliated with British Anglican Church. He attended church services regularly, and took part in activities such as distribution of Scripture in poor communities. During his life time, he spent much more time on theology than science. He wrote somewhere one million and three-hundred thousand words on biblical subjects. He even attempted to calculate the times of Old Testament books. He emphasized much *quest for simplicity and unity.* To him, Christianity was not mere appendage to his science. His writings and manuscripts were assembled in a special library at Cambridge, and also in US and in Israel.

His studies in Bible and theology influenced his scientific activities. Newton had a high view of general revelation through the world or nature. To him, the beautiful system of sun, moon and planets could proceed from the counsel and dominion of an Intelligent and Superb Being. This Divine and Superb Being governs all things, as Lord over all. On account of his dominion, He is called The Lord God.

Newton made distinction between religion and science as set forth by Bacon's classic statement about the Book of God's Word and the Book of God's Work. He vehemently refused to use the Bible as an authority on scientific matters. He strongly objected to "those who introduced divine revelations into philosophy (science in a strict sense in our days), nor philosophical opinion into religion. Yet, this distinction was not a divorce. Although the books were not to provide the content of each other's teachings, they were bound together in many ways. Newton did not consider one to be sacred and the other secular. They were equal work as their respective teaching about God supplemented each other..

In 1703 Newton was elected President of the Royal Society of London, and was re-elected for his life time. In 1705, Newton was knighted by Queen Anne.

He died on March 20, 1727 at age of 85. He was buried in Westminster Abby with full honor. Newton's own view of himself and his achievement was modest, as he wrote:

" I don't know what I may seem to the world. But, as to myself, I seem to have been only like a boy playing on the sea shore, and diverting myself in now and then finding a smoother pebble or prettier shell than ordinary, while the great ocean of truth lay all un-discovered before me."

The well-known French mathematician LaPlace declared the "Principles" to be the greatest product of a human mind. British astronomer Edmund Halley wrote: "Nearer the gods no mortal may approach." Alexander Pope exclaimed: "Nature and Nature's laws lay hidden in night: God said, let Newton be! And all was light."

Conclusion

In 16-17th centuries, modern experimental sciences were born. This scientific revolution was due to Christian scientists, Nicholas Copernicus, Johannes Kepler and Galileo Galilea and their painstaking work. These scientists were devout Christians, believing the Creator God, and His created universe. They believed that through rational research and experimental results their faith would be strengthened. Their sun-centered universe eventually replaced the earth-centered one. Unfortunately, the Roman Catholic Church made a greatest mistaken by condemning Galileo to house arrest, a historical aberration in Christian faith in relation to sciences. The debate should be in essence a debt between university scientists themselves in institutes of higher learning. The debate should not be a

debate between Christians church and sciences. It was true that the Roman Catholic Church misinterpreted the Scripture. That was indirectly related to the debate. Unfortunately, the Church became a scapegoat. Even in 21st century, so many materialistic evolutionists use this as their justification to accuse the Christians and their churches. If they wish to examine the historical record, they would find their mistakes.

The birth of modern experimental sciences was mainly due to the Christian doctrine of creation, and also Christian scholars with a strong conviction searched and researched to know God's deity, power and wisdom as shown in the created universe. As a result of their painstaking efforts, modern sciences were born. We could conclude that *Christianity is indeed the Mother of Modern Experimental Sciences.*

Prof. Owen Gingerich of Havard Univ, in his book entitled in "God's Universe", 2006, said

"The Judeo-Christian philosophical framework has proved to be a particular fertile ground for the rise of modern science."

(pp#6). How true that was!

Literature Cited

1. Bernard Russell,   1961

   History of Western Philosophy, Unwind Univ. Press

2.   Charles Hummel, 1986

   The Galileo Connection: Resolving Conflicts between Science and the Bible.

   IVF Press, Downers Grove Ill.

3.   Peter Bowler and Iwan Rhys Morus, 1998

   Making Modern Science: A Historical Survey.

   Univ. of Chicago Press,Ill.

4.   Newton Keyes   1967

   Religion of Isaac Newton

   Univ. of Cambridge Press, UK

5.   R. Hooykaas, 1987

   Religion and the Rise of Modern Science.

   William B. Eerdmanns Publishing, Mich.

6. David C. Lindberg and Ronald Number,   2003

   When Science and Christianity Meet

   Univ. of Chicago Press, Ill.

7.   J. L. Heilbron,   2010

   Galileo.

   Oxford University Press

Chapter 6
The Dichotomy or Duality of Christianity and Science

" I join nearly all people of good will in wishing to see the two old and

cherished Institutions, our two rocks of ages: science and religion – co-exist in

peace while Each works to make a distinctive patch for the integrated coat of

many colors that   will   celebrate   the distinctions of our lives, uet cloak

human nakedness in a seamless covering called wisdom."

The late Prof. Stephen Jay Gould

Introduction

In Chapter 5, I discussed that the birth of modern experimental sciences was due to the Christian doctrine of Creation, and four devote Christians' rational research work. Our conclusion was that Christianity is the Mother of modern experimental sciences. In 20th to 21st centuries, both Christianity and sciences pated their company. The two disciplines went on their ways. Eventually, that has led to the present regrettable state of dichotomy or duality. In this chapter, I shall describe the historical background and prevailing culture at that time that led to this condition.

1. The Sun-centered universe, and aberrant episode with Galileo:

In Chapters 3 and 5, I mentioned Aristotelianism which included the earth-centered universe. This was firmly ground in institutes of higher learning in the European continent. With observation and experimentation, in 16th – 17th centuries Cupernicus, Kepler and Galileo Galilea demonstrated the sun-centered universe to replace it. The historical aberrant episode was the condemnation of Galileo by the Roman Catholic Church (RCC). The episode led to the frustration and disappointment of many scientists in those days. Regrettably, RCC did not take appropriate action in time to harmonize the situation. So, RCC was labeled as anti-rational and anti-scientific research work. This un-fair labeling has lasted so many years, even to the present century. Many materialistic evolutionists take the advantage of magnifying the situation. Atheists use it as something they could

utilize to attack the church and Christians. In 1996, Pope John Paul II acknowledged that the evolution theory was more than a scientific theory. That indicated that RC had adopted evolution as the second stage of God's plan for evolvement. Yet, the materialistic naturalists turned a deaf ear to this public proclamation. This has been the main and principal reason.

Once RCC had learned a lesson, the Church in 1980 under the leadership of Pope John XXIII and also Pope John Paul II established a Pontifical Academy of Science. By invitation, The Pope selected eighty renowned scholars of various scientific endeavors as members. Once every two to three years, they met to deliberate on different current scientific subjects which are under debate. With their recommendation on these subjects, the Curia and the Pope would decide what stand on these subjects they would take. That is the reason why since then the RCC has a rather united stand. For example, as I discussed in Chapter 12, on Creation narratives, there are five schools of thought. The RCC accepts theistic evolution as their valid theory of the origin of life and evolvement. That is nowadays why biologists who are members of RCC invariably cast their lots, and uphold this theory.

2. The rise of different schools of philosophies in Europe and in America:

Well-known British philosopher, **Bertrand Russell** (known as being not friendly toward Christianity, a scientific positivism scholar) in his "*History of Western Philosophy*" advocates "The Dark Age" in the 5th-12th centuries in the western world. For seven centuries, the RCC enjoys a monopoly of ecclesiastic authority and power. With the literal interpretation of Scripture and teaching, the Church considers herself that holds the key of deciding who goes to heaven and who goes to hell. In those days and to the people, this is a very serious question. Kings, nobility, and civilian governments have no alternative but being submissive to the Church. Higher educational institutions of learning are no exceptions. The intellectual windows are thereby closed. No progress in education and in other human endeavors has been made for that long period of time.

Then, Protestant Reformation came in the 16th century. The movement was led by Martin Luther in Germany and John Calvin in Switzerland. Once again, Christianity was revived and became a predominant religion in western Europe. Lutheran Church and Presbyterian Church came into existence. In the Protestant Church, Christ Jesus was once again exalted as the Lord and the Savior, the only Mediator between God and man. The Bible was the Word of God. It was an open book. Under the guidance and illumination of the Holy Spirit, Christians and clergy alike could read it, to interpret it and apply it in daily living. There was no authorized interpretation. Personal freedom and freedom of conscience were so much emphasized and practiced. Altogether this was a new movement worldwide.

Coming along with the movement was the Renaissance Epoch. Of this there were two trends. One trend was in Italy, with emphasis on classics, paintings, music and poetry. The other trend was in Germany and England, emphasizing

pietism, individualism and public ethics and workplace ethics. The Renaissance revived the western civilization and culture in the following centuries.

Concurrently, many schools of philosophies arose in western world, such as:

- Skepticism,
- Liberalism
- Rationalism
- Socialism and Communism
- Logical positivism
- Materialism
- Scientific Naturalism
- Evolution Theory/ Evolutionism
- Atheism
- Scientism
- Modernism
- Existentialism
- Unitarianism
- Pragmatism and Humanism

and many others. All these schools of philosophy and thinking are in one way or another incompatible with/to Christianity or even hostile. Gradually, many of these schools of philosophy infiltrated into the Christian circle, influencing their thinking and even taking the place of prominence in higher education and to some extent theological training in theological seminaries.

3. Evolution theory and evolutionism:

In 1859, British naturalist **Charles Darwin** published his book of "**Origin of Species**", advocating evolution theory in natural science. No doubt, the bio-scientific theory presents a great challenge to Christians and Christian church. It exerts a great influence in education in England. This led to the public debate between Bishop Samuel Wilberforce and naturalist Thomas Huxley, as a nation's news in Great Britain. The general public somehow considered this public debate, not as a personal, but as a debate between conventional Christianity and rational searching endeavor. This misconception lasted so long. Even today, materialistic, even atheistic naturalists use it as their justification to accuse Christians and Christian church as anti-rational research, to the extent of paying no attention at all what Christian religion contributes to personal living-style, family-living and

impact on nation's life.

In 1871, Darwin published another book, *"The Descent of Man"*, with graphic presentation of tree of life. This book presented even greater challenge to the Christians and their teaching of Creation in which humanity was created in the image of God. This caused even much more schism between Christianity and science.

In the 1950-55, the two very popular magazines, Life and Times in USA hired a much- accomplished artist, Mr. Rudy Zallinger to illustrate the evolution of human from chimpanzee on the basis of what Darwin had proposed in his second book. *Mr. Zallinger skillfully was able to produce two graphic illustrations (Fig. 1 and Fig 2), implying the phylogeny of human as evolved from chimpanzee and monkey*. These two illustrations were published in the two American most popular magazines (Fig. 1 and Fig. 2). The printing was repeated more than hundred times. They became so popular. People nowadays take them as "facts" in evolution theory.

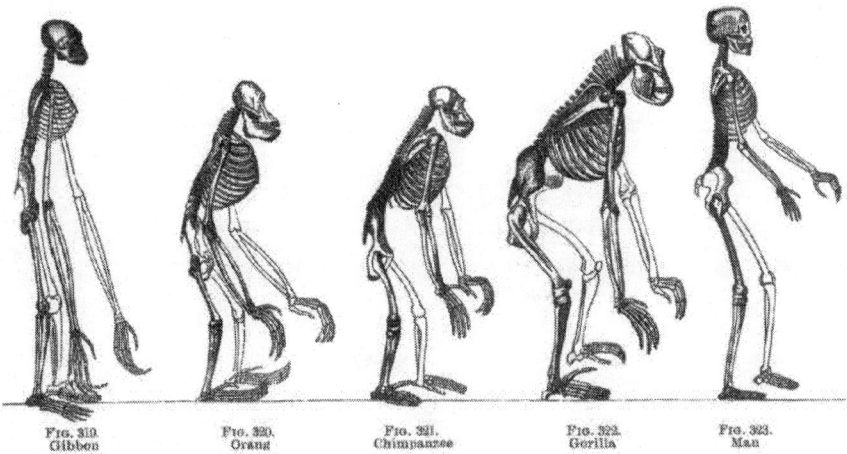

Fig. 1. Sketch of skeletons of gibbon, orangutan, chimpanzee, gorilla and human is arranged in series showing progression toward human form. (From: Thomas H. Huxley, Evidence as to Man's place in Nature, 1863;drawing by Mr. Rudy Zalinger, published in Life Time Magazine)

Fig. 2. Darwin's theory of human origin, an ape-like creature is shown involving through

a series of hypothetical intermediate forms into a modern human.

(the two drawings by Rudy Zallinger).

For years both *Life* and *Times* magazine enjoyed a wide circulation both nationally and internationally. In fact, the illustrations were printed again and again in popular magazines, even in textbooks. These two drawings were so popular to perpetuate the un-substantiated claim of human origin. Years later, people who knew nothing about the original intention were led to believe that this is the scientific truth. What a tragedy it has been not only to the public but also to the un-informed school children, not only in USA, but also elsewhere.

Evolution theory is in essence a biological science theory, formulated by Charles Darwin (1859). It was mostly based on *his observation, and then speculation and conclusion. There was no empirical experimental result of whatsoever for it*. It is speculation or theorizing more than anything else. The mechanism for variation, such as struggle for existence, survival for the fitted, gradual modification/horizontal variation through long years are mechanisms. The mechanism, in ordinary language, is something like "a way" or "a method". By this way or through this method, the organism attains its end. The origin of species is a theory, referring to its end. *The struggle for existence is a mechanism. The mechanism is a method or a way by which bio-organisms compete and survive it.* We should differentiate the mechanism from theory, or theory from mechanism. *Mechanism is mechanism. Theory is theory.* The two should not be crisscrossed. Evolution theory has two principal components. The two components are altogether different. One could accept the mechanism, yet could decline to take the theory. To accept the mechanism does not mean accepting the theory. One should separate the two components. Evolution theory as a theory, it should be taught as a biological or bio-scientific theory. Evolution theory should not taught as a bio-philosophy. Evolutionism is different from evolution theory. Evolutionism

is a doctrine, a religion, a philosophy, a worldview. Evolutionism is just like word similar to skepticism, or imperialism; it is a philosophical system. (cf. domains, on page #170, Fig (IV), (III), (II), (I)). Yet, most people in the public could not differentiate these two.

4. The separation of religion from state in USA:

In 1776 when United States of American was found, it was found on the constitutional principle of separation of church from the government. One of the reasons was the bitter experience the early founders of the Republic had learned while they were in England and European continent.   So they use this experience as guidance in formulating the constitution with separation of church from the state. Yet, not separation of the state of any religion. In the state or country, there are religions, more than one religion. The First Amendment prohibits the government making any law in favor of any one religion. This was a sound principle endorsed by all, irrespective of any religious faith.

Yet, the interpretation of this Amendment is up to the Supreme Court, which is composed of Justices (judges of the highest court). The Justices are human beings, though they have excellent training in law and jurisprudence, and rich experience in dealing with different cases. But, not body could deny the fact that human beings are human beings. Conviction, viewpoints and the way of interpretation does vary. This varies from Justice to Justice, and Court from Court. It is a matter of some or any governmental decision. It is whether or not in favor of one religion or another. It has been a subject of debate for years. Somehow the good and sincere intention of the early founding fathers end up sometimes not ideal and acceptable by majority of general populace in USA.

There are many such examples. In 1954 when I first came to USA, in commencement exercises on university campuses, there was a prayer offered at the very beginning of the event.   Protestant church clergy, or RC priest, or Jewish rabbi was asked to offer prayer. No one ever argued that the prayer was in favor or one religion or another. When I graduated with Ph. D. at Univ. of Minn., many of my fellow-graduates were very much touched by what church clergy uttered in his/her prayer. In those years, no one would consider that the prayer in public was a violation to the First Amendment. That was true in 50th to 70th. Beginning in 1980 it was considered as a violation. Public prayer was no longer allowed. This testifies the fact of different interpretations over time. When I applied for teaching position at the university, I filled-in my religious affiliation on the application form. That was a legal and logical requirement. Nowadays, it is illegal. USA is now a nation without a soul!

The current debate on equal time of teaching creation along the side of evolution theory is another case. Years ago, Christian creation was taught in public schools anywhere in the Union. Now, in late 20th century, only evolution theory is being taught exclusively in public schools. What a drastic change it took place in

USA!

The American Civic Liberty Union (ACLU) is an organization which makes use of every opportunity of changing US Christian heritage and legacy to a secular society. This is a great puzzle to the public. No body could predict what will happen in another half a century!

5. The War hypothesis or Conflict hypothesis:

In 1874, Prof. John William Draper published his book entitled in "The History of Conflict between religion and Science". In his book, using the case of a public debate between British Anglican Bishop Samuel Wilberforce and Prof. Thomas H. Huxley, he advocated a War hypothesis between rational research by science and irrational faith. Then, in 1896 Prof. Andrew Dickson White, who was then President of Cornell Univ. , wrote **another book entitled in "The A History of the Warfare of science with Theology in Christendom."** On the basis of his unhappy dealing with Christian fundamentalists while he was President on his university curriculum. He vehemently denied to hire faculty on religious preference to other criteria. His book intensified the debate and conflict. These two scholars expressed their viewpoints in such a very simplistic conclusion. But, the books made an important, and lasting impression on the mind of both intellectuals and common folks on the streets!

Fortunately, in recent years many academicians in history of sciences in both England and US advocated a **Complexity thesis.** They had done extensive research on the historical background, human factors and then prevalence social circumstances, they advocated a well-balanced viewpoint, and with a different thesis. It is our hope that this thesis would replace the damaging "War hypothesis." It is by no means easy! It takes an open-mind, seeking for the real truth.

As Prof. Ian S. Barbour said and well said:

"Conflicts were merely the product of misunderstanding on one side or the other."

This is indeed a fair and candid evaluation.

6. The Scopes' trial in Tenn., in 1925:

In USA, before 1920, Christian doctrine of creation was taught in public schools. This was more so in so-called Bible Belt, in the south. Citizens considered this as academic and sound in theory. In 1925, in Dayton, TN, Mr. John Scopes, a physics teacher as a substitute teacher in biology class, taught evolution theory the first time in biology class. This was considered as a breach by the School, and also the City Board of Education. As a consequence, Mr. Scopes' teaching was considered as his misdemeanor, with a fine of US$100.00. But, later on the Court reversed the decision by the Board. That unfortunate event initiated a

debate and conflict in school education between the two camps. It lasted for quite a good number of years. Nowadays, creation theory was excluded, and the evolution theory is being taught exclusively in school systems in USA. What a drastic change it has been in a matter of 50-80 years!

This unhappy but historical incidence was well known in the public, more so in the South. Literature is readily available. I am not going to take the time to repeat what had been transcribed.

7. The Equal Time Movement in USA:

Once the teaching creation hypothesis in public schools was excluded, the Christian public in the south was in a sad mood. Fundamentalists wished that some one else could stand-up and speak on their behalf. Then, the Equal Time Movement was born in time. This movement was led by an academician at Virginia Polytechnic Institute, Prof. Henry Morris, and then Dr. Duane Gish, a biochemist in Upjohn Co. in Kalamazoo of Michigan. Together with other like-minded individuals they launched a movement for Equal Time in Teaching in USA.

In USA, as a rule in a democratic society, the local School Board was an independent entity, deciding on their own textbooks used in classroom teachings. The Secretary of Dept. of Education exercises an overseeing role. It is the local School Board which will decide what biology textbook is to be used in that school system. So, this varies from the Board, and years from years. The school boards which are made of concerned local citizens chosen from different schools of thought and faiths. The composition varies from time to time, so does the decision as to the textbooks being adopted and being used. Therefore, the federal government does not have the authority to control whatsoever they choose. Basically, this is a principle of diversity in unity in democratic society. But, the election of Board members is influenced by different organizations, such as the American Civic Liberty Union, a radical and somewhat anti-religious entity. This organization tries to influence the outcome of election of school board. In addition, the faculty in natural sciences in American university/colleges were by and large taught by evolutionists more than any one else. Moreover, the judges at different levels nowadays are products of American universities, They are evolutionists more than anything else. They all consider Christianity as exclusively religious and supernatural whereas evolution theory as a valid, fact-proved theory. Therefore, Christianity or religion has nothing to contribute to school education. As a consequence, the equal time of teaching both theories in schools was denied nine times by the Courts.

In the 1970, a new school of thought on creation was revived, that was the Intelligent Design (ID). This group was led by Profs. William A. Dembski, Michael J. Behe, J.P. Moreland, James Kushiner, Phillip E. Johnson and Hugh Ross and many others. They revived what Rev. William Paley of Ireland had

proposed in 1802. They endeavored and proposed search and research with conventional practices, beginning with observation, hypothesis, and empirical experiments, results and then conclusion with an Intelligent Designer in creation. They argued that the cosmic system and, especially with the biological system having so much intrinsic, interlocking molecular mechanisms, have irreducible complexity. They can not be simply explained by what has been proposed in evolution theory. Altogether, this is a paradigm shift. Using this ID, they submitted it to the Board of Education for integration and in equal-time teaching. In nine times, they did it. In nine time, they were denied.

In August of 2011, Texas Governor Rick Perry was one of the Republic candidates for Republican Party for President. He was launching his campaign in New Hampshire, first-in-the-nation presidential primary state. Both hecklers and supporters confronted him with hard questions such as Social Security and Medicare, and also evolution theory. A young man, prompted by his mother, asked Mr. Perry whether he believes in evolution theory. He answered, "It is theory that it out there. It has got some gaps in it. In Texas, we teach both creationism and evolutionism in our public schools. It is because that we figure out that eventually you are smart enough to see what is proven and what is a speculation or extension. Then, you take what you believe the right one by yourself." Personally, I feel that this is the right attitude. As parents, we let the biology teachers present the evolution theory well enough to delineate what is known, and proven; and what is not proven but speculation without prove. Fact is fact, and theory is a theory. By all means, we should not close the students' intellectual windows. It is a terrible mistake to do so in the name of educaton.

8. Fundamentalism in USA and elsewhere:

In Christendom there are different schools of biblical interpretations. By and large, Christians and Christian Church have their fundamental doctrines, such as monotheism, special revelation and general revelation, the exegesis. To these basic and fundamentals they all subscribe. But, Christians do differ in interpretation and applications of biblical text. There is one group of Christians who subscribes more and often to the literal reading and interpretation. *They are so-called fundamentalists.* In addition, their attitude to social work as a consequence of faith, also to sciences is not positive or integrative. So, they do differ from others, esp. evangelicals.

The Christian fundamentalists by and large commit one mistake. They take literal reading of Scripture. Also, they take a *literal interpretation of Scripture.* For example, in the creation narratives (Gen. 1-3) the first day is a day of 24 hours, a solar day. No other interpretation is possible. They take certain scripture verses to prove something being scientific or philosophical or otherwise. They do not realize that the Scripture was written long before modern sciences came into existence. The language and contents are foremost theological, conveying one God who is the Creator of this universe, with humanity as living entity. The

Writers of the Holy Scripture write with the language of their days. The people in those days understand the message conveyed. The Scripture was historical, the writers used what they knew in that historical setting. The Scripture is also religious against the background of prevailing polytheistic religions of those nations in that time.

Fundamentalists sometimes point out a number of popular scientific bewildering theories or events to their views. Their stand against is so-called *literalism*. Due to the interpretation and its relation to sciences it has caused tension between Christianity and modern sciences.

9. Science and scientism:

In the last 50 years or more, science and technology have made great stride. No body could or would deny the wonderful progress being made, and knowledge has been exploded. Science and technology have contributed so much to the society, and have made life more enjoyable and comfortable. On account of it, scientists are inclined to think that science is the only way to knowledge. Without much thinking they uphold scientism. In college days they did not have a course *of "the philosophy of sciences". They failed to understand what science could accomplish, and what science and scientific methods could not accomplish.* Unknowingly, they adopted a thinking of scientism or materialistic naturalism. Their education is one-sided. It is not well-balanced. Knowing nothing of what religion could contribute to human welfare and society at large. What a pity it is! No wonder science and religion go their own ways.

10. Plurality/Pluralism in American society, and "de-Christianization in intelligentsia":

The USA was found by Christian puritans from England and European continent in 18th century. The early founding fathers were mainly Anglo-Saxon and western Europeans, with Christianity as the predominant religious groups. In 1930, Irish, Italian and Portuguese immigrants of Roman Catholic Church affiliation gradually came to this Continent. After that another wave of immigrants of Jewish nationality from East Europe and Russia came to this new Continent. They all were mixed and melted together in this great and new land. The society gradually and steadily became pluralized and diversified. In a way, Christianity and her impact on the society was gradually and proportionally reduced or diluted. No human conscientious efforts were made to achieve the natural end.

Of the many nationalities, the Jewish stands out as rather unique in culture and in practice. The Israelites emphasize so much in education and religious instruction in home and in synagogues. They are well-known in management and in finance. Gradually, they gained recognition and prominence in American society. The so-called *"WASP" (white Anglo-Saxon Protestant Society)* was gradually diminished her prominent role in society. This was very logical and

84

reasonable. Nowadays, in Wall Street of New York City, Jewish people enjoy a very prominent role in finance and in business. They work hard to gain their recognition. Nobody could deny them.

This was true in education as well. It was reported that in 1946, Yale college (now Yale Univ.) hired a first Jewish faculty, a philosopher by the name of Paul Weiss. Then, in a matter of years, there were eight Israeli professors on the faculty. In 1960, there were 260 Jewish faculty in the total faculty. In 1970, somewhere 22% of the total faculty members at Yale were Jewish. This growth was phenomenal. In 1969, the Carnegie Higher Ed. Foundation conducted a survey, with the result of showing 3% of total population of Jewish, yet 17% of them in higher education. Their distribution in specialty was: 36% in law, 34% in social sciences, 28% in finance, 26% in physics, 22% in humanity and history, and 20 % in philosophy. Well-known scholars such as Oliver Wendell Holmes in Supreme Court, Louis Brandeis, Felix Frankfuer, Jerome Frank Lerner, Robert K. Morton, Walter Lipmann, Albert Einstein and Robert Oppenheimer. Jewish scholars occupy 40% in total Nobel Prize winners.

Most of these Jewish folks are Reforming Jews, having very little Jewish religious inclination. They were very pragmatic, secular, smart and aggressive. Their worldview is by and large materialistic. Of course, there is a good percentage of them who are Orthodox Jews, even Hasidian in N.Y. and elsewhere. Together with other nationalities, they make up the plurality of American society. With that the impact by Christianity in society, in government and in schools are proportionally diluted and diminished. As some one else reported, there is a conscientious efforts made to diminish or dechristianize the American culture. As once written by Harvard Univ. Prof. David A. Hollinger, in his book entitled in " Science, Jews and Secular Culture", 1996.the multi-cultured or multi-civilized United States will not be the United States; it will be the "united nations" (pp# 306). The Jewish scholars have much to do with this. The clash between science and Christian religion in USA is a clash of worldviews and life-styles. The end of such a clash is a change of worldview and life-style. It is not that easy. Dechristianization (literally, get rid of Christianity) is what the materialistic naturalists try to do so that they could occupy the centre of the American arena.

11. Atheism in American and in the West:

Fifty years ago when I first came to US, atheism was not known, or looked down by people. In recent years, atheism has been in steady growth, and was somehow promoted by so-called academicians and politicians alike. Richard Dawkins, an ex-Professor of Popularization of Science at Univ. of Oxford is a self-acclaimed atheist. He has written a dozen books. Taking advantage of his university profession, he tried to downgrade Christians and Christian religion. His book of "God's Delusion" is an example. How much he knows Christianity? Did he look at Christianity scientifically if he claims himself as a scientist? His delution? Certainly, not mine. Or any Christian, so far as this matter is concerned.

Without studying it and experiencing it, how could he say that believe in God is delusion? Delusion to him? Or delusion to some one else? He can not make a conclusion of some one else's faith in God, on the basis of prejudice and personal misconception!

Many years ago, in USA Mrs. Marianne O'Hara tried to establish her atheistic organization, for propagation. Her personal life was in disarray. Her organization ended in bankrupt. His son denied her. In addition, he became a Christian. Mrs. O'Hara was kidnapped and murdered as reported by FBI. Her body was discovered in a river and recovered for burial with money contributed by the public. Her story was a subject of table talk for fun in bars and in slum district. Her atheism had very limited influence in American society.

With Richard Dawkins in UK; and Michael Ruse, Ronald Numbers, Christopher Hitches and Daniel Dannett in USA; atheism, as a "*disease of the mind*", seems prevalent in some sectors. In 2007 there were four books written by three American Atheists. I did not bother to read them. What is good about? It was reported that the International Union of Atheists grew to 5200 members in 2006. No body could figure out what could be the reason. Probably, the delution is with their atheistic life-style.   The question is this. ***Does atheism inspires them to do any good and sacrificial work***, as Mother Tereza had done in India?   ***Could atheism give them a sincere sense of forgiveness un-conditionally granted*** to a murderer by the Mannonite Christians in PA?   ***Did atheism inspire them to do missionary work among lepers in Africa***, in S. America?   Please read a book by Prof. Alister McGrath on "*Twilight of Atheism*", you will know something about atheism.

In this Chapter, I consider Richard Dawkins' conclusion as ridiculous. His conclusion is that any one who accepts evolution theory will eventually become an atheist. This is far from being true. People, even scientists could accept evolution theory, yet do not incline to accept materialistic worldview, he or she could not become an atheist. Some one else could take evolution theory as valid biological theory, yet does not accept scientism and materialism at the same time, he or she could not become an atheist. People such as Richard Dawkins who is a disciple of Darwinism, having a materialistic worldview, and also holding a scientism, ***all these three combined would lead him unquestionably to the road of atheism***. Of course, with these three altogether he becomes an atheist. Only through the combination of all these factors, he becomes his own atheist. To me, atheism is a matter of mind, not with soul or heart. It does not involve the totality of being human.

12. *The uprising and downfall of atheism in the world; and a challenge:*

Agnosticism and atheism are two entirely different worldviews.

a) Agnostics was a term first coined by Dr. Thomas Henry Huxley in 1869.

Very early in the Christian era, there were so-called "Gnostics", meaning

they know all the truth pertaining to life, even the existence of deity. On the contrary, there were those who did not claim all these. They professed that they did not know or did not intend to know it. So, these people were agnostics.

This term was coined in time when Darwinism had made known not long ago. Some of Darwin's disciples accepted Darwinism, yet they did not intend to know God and his existence, they were agnostics.

b) Atheism or atheists are altogether different. They proclaim no God, or they believe of no existence of deity. They deny God's existence. In some cases, they try to destroy it. Their mind is blind. When they see the beauty of the biological world and its complexity, they fail to derive a sense of awe. They could not come to any conclusion that all these are beyond what we human beings could do. It is so beautiful and so natural. Even Einstein perceived a higher intelligence somewhere in existence. You could use different terms to describe your religious feeling. Something is in existence.

In reading literature, we came to know that German philosopher and theologian F.D.D. Hagel and philosopher Schleiermacher were atheistic philosophers, teaching at Univ. of Berlin. Ludwig Fauerbach was one their favorite students. After attending their classes and received the instruction, Fauerbach in 1830 produced a book entitled in "Contribution to its critique of Hagel's philosophy of law" as a classic.

Let me share what I have read in literature, pertaining to atheism.

Three giants laid the intellectual foundation of atheism in German and Russia. They are *Ludwig Feuerbach (1804), Karl Marx (1818) and Sigmund Freud (1856-1939).*

Feuerbach was greatly influenced by two German philosophers-theologians, i. e. G.W.F. Hegel and F.D.E. Schleiermacher who taught at Prussian Univ. of Berlin, where Feuerbach was a student. With their teachings, Feuerbach, as a revolutionary thinker wrote his first book entitled in "Thoughts on Death and Immortality (1830). Authentic human existence is godless and limited to this life. His 2nd book on "Essence of Christianity (1841) as a manifesto of a revolutionary movement. To Feuerbach, Hegel and his philosophy opened up a new door that humanity invented the idea of God as a consolation and distraction from sorrow of this world. God was human creation, a product of a mind. It projects its longing for immortality and meaning onto an imagery transcendent situation, and gives its

name, "God" to his own creation. God far from being our master, should be our servant; man is God to himself", Feuerbach proclaimed/ claimed. Atheism was a response to the human desire for autonomy. He had robbed religion of any external existence. Feuerbach had his *"philosophical atheism"* and *"scientific atheism"*. By 1850, Feuerbach and his atheism were gradually waning. To British and Americans, Feuerbach's atheism was "freakish" and "exotic". Many philosophers at his time were lukewarm toward his ideas

Karl Marx envisaged revolution breaking out in the industrialized nations in Western Europe, though Marx himself was born into a reasonable comfortable middle-class Jewish family. He studied at Univ. of Bonn where young Marx was under the influence of Hegel. Unable to find a teaching position, Marx moved to Paris where he worked as a journalist. It was then Marx developed his ideas on social alienation of poor people under a capitalist economy. In fact, Marx was expelled from Paris because of his political activities. He and Friedrich Engels moved to Brussels where he devoted himself to a major study of a materialistic approach to history. In 1867 Marx wrote "Das Kapital". The notion of materialism was fundamental to Marx and his philosophy. He argued that every aspect of human life and existence was determined by social and economic factors. Material need determines the way the people live and think. Ideas and values were determined by the materialistic reality of life. This was significant for Marx and his understanding of religious life as well. His major ideas were shown in the "Communist Manifesto of 1848."

The idea of God was a human attempt to copy with the harshness of material life and the pain resulting from social and economic deprivation. To Marx, humans make religions; and religion does not make human. Religion is self-consciousnes and self-esteem of people who either have not found themselves or who have already lose themselves. Religion is the product of social and economic alienation. Change these conditions so that economic alienation is eliminated and religion will cease to exist. Marx's critique of religion was the most radical in 19th century, and even major influence on atheism in the 20th century. Yet, the historical and economic development in some socialist to communist countries in the last century or even the 21st century, has not vindicated Marx thesis in a realistic way.

Sigismund Schlomo Freud was born to a Jewish family on May 6th, 1856, in which Christianity was taken very seriously, in Czeck Republic. When he was 4-yrs old, the family moved to Vienna, he experienced the cultural golden age. In 1873 he entered the Univ. of Vienna, with a great deal of atheism at that time, studying medicine. Freud had a deep interest in philosophy and religion. Freud admired Feuerbach and his philosophy. He absorbed Auguste Comte's positivism ad Max's socialistic thinking. After all these, Freud thought that what he could do was to add some psychological foundation to the ideas of my great predecessors. Freud considered religion as an illusion and derived its strength form the fact that it fell in with our human instinctual desire. His strongest statement was found in

his "The Future of an Illusion" 1927, with a strongly reductionist approach to religion. To him, religious ideas are illusions.

Freud went on to develop a radical and original explanation of religion. This was grounded in his discipline of psychoanalysis. His original thinking lied not in society but in human un-consciousnes. In 1902 Freud was appointed to a professor chair in Vienna. He began to gather disciples at home and abroad, even in N. America. Out of this, the Vienna Psychoanalytical Society, 1908, and the International Psychoanalytic Association,1910 were found. Well-known figures such as Alfred Adler and Carl June were later on associated with.

Freud was a confirmed atheist long before he became a psychoanalyst. Basically, he believed that religion was dangerous, not least because it constitutes a threat to the advance of enlightenment and also the natural sciences. To him, religion arose through inner psychological pressure. At the logical level, Freud proceeded from his preconceived point to his predetermined conclusion. In his Autobiography, Freud portrayed a notion of expiating man's guilt through various rituals. To this, many of his supporters felt that such historical oversimplification was embarrassing and irritating.

Sir Richard Gregory (1864-1952) once made the laughing epitaph: "My grand-father preached the gospel of Christ; my father preached the gospel of socialism; and our generation preaches the gospel of scientism to atheism." This saying in a way described the *decay and deterioration of western civilization and Christian culture*. How regrettable and pitiful it is! We Christians in the East are sympathetic to their religious-philosophical situation. We should take precaution and prevention to this unfortunate tendency.

Some would ask me what do I think of this tendency and danger to/in our Chinese culture and society. My answer is definitely no, not likely. First of all, we Chinese are very much enlightened, and respectful to other religious faith. In our history, there is no religious warfare. Second, in Chinese society people of different religions faiths have lived harmoniously and peacefully. Thirdly, the Chinese religious heritage such as Buddhism with worship of ancestors is deeply rooted in people's thinking. Fourthly, western atheism and philosophy have not gained entrance into the thinking pattern among Chinese intelligentsia.

In our world today, especially in the academic circle, there are some well-know atheists. With their conviction, they have been writing articles and books about their believe and their life-style. Well-known people/scholars such as Richard Dawkins of England, and Ronald Number at Univ. of Wisconsin . I wish to challenge them with following questions. *Can atheism inspire people to do missionary work with love and compassion; or could forgive criminals, and do social beneficial work for the benefit of others?*

13. *"Anti-Evolution movement" so-called; and "anti-intellectualism" by*

evolutionists/Scientists:

In addition to atheists, there are many others who are devoted "disciples" of Charles Darwin.. *They accept evolution wholeheartedly and unquestionably as worldview or personal philosophy*. Anywhere they go, they proclaim "their gospel", that is evolutionism. In a way, they are akin to the atheists. There is a number of such professionals and university faculty members in USA and in England. *Prof. Richard Dawkins is well-known for his notorious writings*. He writes well and articulates well in public. Taking the advantage of being a professor for popularization of science (something of the past), he wrote more than a dozen of books, ridiculing Christians and Christianity. When you read his books, you get the impression that he pretends to know so much in sciences. In fact, he is a traditional zoologist, with Ph.D. thesis on young chickens in group-living. Nowadays, when he writes as a rule, *with a little bit of science, then he jumps into philosophy of science and worldview.* It is in the area of philosophy, he ridicules people and their faith. In his "Selfish Genes", he knows superficially molecular biology, and gene expression. *He treats "genes" as something like human, being selfish*. That is grossly simplifying the principles of molecular biology. Yet, *he spends a great deal of more time on bio-philosophy than bioscience*. Yet, people of little knowledge of molecular biology take what he describes as being very realistic and true. What a pity it is!

Richard Dawkins once wrote in his book "The Blind Watchmaker" that Darwin or Darwinism has made possible to be *an intellectually fulfilled atheist."* Darwin did not think himself as an atheist. Many times he said that "he is agnostic". At any rate, Charles *Darwin himself was not "an intellectually fulfilled atheist*. He never boasted about his un-belief; rather he approached it with remarkable caution. In his writing, he confessed that *he was "an agnostic"*. Shocking the mores of traditional believers may be Dawkin's pronouncement, but it certainly not Darwin's. To the end of his life, Darwin insisted that one could be *"an ardent theist and an evolutionist."*

In USA, Prof. Ronald Numbers of Univ. of Wisc., Daniel Dennett of Tufts Univ., Christopher Hitchins, Sam Harris and Michael Russ are well-known for their evolutionism. In 2009, while Univ. of Cambridge celebrated the 150th anniversary of Darwin's Origin of Species, these men were panel speakers. My wife and I deliberately went to both Cambridge and Oxford, listening to what they tried to say. At Oxford, Ronald Numbers fabricated and coined the term , the so-called *"anti-evolution movement"* in USA. In essence, "the equal time movement" was labeled as "anti-evolution movement". How well he could twist the venerable controversy to fit his personal bias and peculiar view!

In a review of Jerry A. Coyne's book of "Why Evolution Is True", 2009, Massimo Pigliucci wrote in Science, AAAS, Feb. 6, 2009, and labeled the "intelligent design' people engaged in *"anti-intellectualism"* in USA. What a polemic labeling it is! Both Ron Numbers and Pigliucci used such polemic terms to slash those who differ from their bio-philosophy or worldview. Are those who subscribe intelligent design or engage in equal time movement not intellectuals at

all? Their educational credentials are not very much alike to what both Ron Number or Pigliucci have? When we engage in debate or dialogue for mutual understanding, we should by all means avoid using inflammatory words! We should honor our enemies as much as we honor our colleagues.

Let me quote a book written by "Ms. Marilynne Robinson, a most admired novelist wrote a book entitled in "**Absence of Mind:** *The Dispelling of Inwardness from the Modern Myth of the Self*", Yale Univ. Press, 2010. Robinson derives from Dwight Harrington Terry's lectures on "Religion, in the light of science and philosophy". In the preface, Robinson aims to "examine one side of in the *venerable controversy called the conflict between science and religion*. In particular, she wants to question the kind of authority claimed by certain modern scientists, and raise questions about the quality of their thinking. In her first Chapter she focuses on what one might loosely call the socio-biologists, E.O.Wilson, Steven Pinker, *Richard Dawkins* and *Daniel Dennett*, who assert that our lives are ordered by overt or unconscious self-interest, that our minds are unreliable and constantly trick us, and that traditional religious belief is a primordial hold-over, certainly childish, sometimes deluded and generally embarrassing. Robinson vehemently argues that *such thinkers grossly simplify religious thought and testimony – and the ooze condescendingism.* "The characterization of religion by those who dismiss it tends to reduce it to a matter of bones and feathers and wishful thinking, a matter of rituals and social bonding and false etiologies and the fear of death, and this makes its persistence very annoying to them." Robinson notes that these same crusading debunkers consistently portray those who dare to disagree with them as "intellectually dishonest".

In particular, Robinson says, these "*para-scientists*" deliberately slight "the wealth of insight into human nature that might come from attending to the record humankind has left." She maintains that "we are not simply the instrument of selfish genes. Indeed, she suspects that the "modern malaise," our sense of emptiness and alienation, can be attributed not the "death of God" but rather to the widely promulgated, and reductionist   view of the self as wholly biological." (the end of quotation).

Can atheism inspire people for noble deeds and sacrificial social services?

To those atheists, I would like to pose a couple of questions. Can atheism inspire people for noble deeds in society and sacrificial services to people without means of repaying?

In Christian circle, there are well-known cases: Mother Teresa, a Roman nun who devoted herself to care poor-stricken people in India. Her services were not for one year, but for many years. Eventually, she was awarded with Nobel Prize for her work. There are more than thousands of Christian missionaries who are working around the world, with self-sacrificial services. Any Christian denomination could give you a list of such missionaries and their services. Not

only in developing countries, but also in under-developed countries in Africa, in Asia.

In Oct. of 2006, gunman Charles Carl Roberts I entered the West Nickel Mines School, a one-room Amish schoolhouse. He eventually shot ten girls of ages 6-10. He killed five of them before committing suicide in the schoolhouse. This became a national news in USA. The Amish people, especially those families whose daughters were slaughtered, publicly announced their forgiveness to this man. No human could do that easily, yet they did it willingly, without any malice. The Amish people and their community were widely admired. A large percentage of people admired this noble attitude. Their curiosity of the Amish faith and their life-style skyrocketed. Evangelical Christians by and large have a heightened interest in Amish spirituality. They hope with that insight they could deepen their own faith.

In Aug. of 2010, an International Assistance Mission, a Christian missionary organization did pioneering work in Afghanistan; six American workers were slained for no reason. Dr. Brian Carderelli, a Dentist from VA, and Dr. Tom Little, an Optometrist from N.Y. provided their Christian charity work, without any pay among poor Afghanistans. Mr. Dirk Frans, Exec. Dir. For the Mission said for these workers: "our faith motivates us, and inspires us. That is all we do. We do not proselytize people."

Atheists should ponder on these cases. Simply ask themselves of this question. Is atheism able to inspire people for noble deeds in society, sacrificial services in under-developed countries? Those who confess themselves as atheists should ask themselves, can I offer myself for this kind of service? If I suffer from any harm, can I offer forgiveness? Some atheists confess that their atheism in a way is "a religion". What kind of "religion" is that? All they do is to perpetuate their atheism for their own curiosity and intellectual satisfaction. Curiosity and intellectual satisfaction are non-productive at all.

14. In Christianity: traditionalism stagnant in science and in social issues:

If we Christians look at ourselves objectively and scientifically, we could not refrain from saying that many of our fellow believers, clergymen and officials try to maintain a status quo, and have a negative attitude toward sciences and social issues in our societies. What we need is something as

Dr. Bernard Ramm said in his book,

"Revelation/theology needs the perspectives of science, and science needs the light of theology. Both science and theology are human pursuits".

Prof. John Polkinghorne of Cambridge Univ. said in his book, "Science and theology are intellectual cousins. Scientific and theological inquiries are

parallel. "

We need to take time to reflect on their sayings! With these, we evangelical Christians should radically change our perspectives and change of attitude toward science, Science is not enemy. Science is neutral in value and in application. It all depends on how evangelical Christians consider/view sciences. This attitude would influence our attitude and our perceptions.

Is there a true dichotomy or a false dichotomy?

In 1986, American Association for the Advancement of Science (AAAS) with more than 300 societies and hundred thousand members of various disciplines), through the leadership of then Executive Director Dr. Alan Bromley suggested to Dr. Robert W. Hanson for a joint conference with scientists and theologians, for the sole purpose of dialogue. Quite a large number of scientists and theologians took part in such a meeting for several days. Their conclusion was that the dichotomy was a false dichotomy. It was due to principally the fault of two groups in such a dichotomy, i.e. scientific Creationism uses outdated scientific data in the Christian circle, and scientists who subscribe to materialistic scientism. On the other hand, there are so many scientists who are evolutionists occupy important positions in societies and organizations who are delighted to widen the scope of differences.

Let me conclude this chapter with quotations of both Galileo Galileo, Father of Modern Exp.Sciences, and Albert Einstein, the greatest scientist in 20th century, as follow:

Galileo Galilea, Father of Modern Experimental Science said in his famous dictum:

" God has given us Two Books, One Book is of Nature, the other Scripture. Both the Books of Holy Scripture and Nature proceed from the Divine Word. The former is the saying of the Holy Spirit, and the latter is the observed executrix of God's order. God is the Author of the Two Books. Therefore, the Two Books should not contradict each other. The Bible tells us how to go to heaven, not how the heavens go. "

Albert Einstein, the greatest Scientist in 29th century once wrote in his book,

"All religions, arts and sciences are branches of the same tree. All these inspirations are directed toward ennobling man's life, lifting from the sphere of mere physical existence and leading to the individual towards freedom."

Literature Cited

1. Bernard Ramm,   1945

History of Western Philosophy.

George Allen & Unwind Ltd., UK

2. David A. Hollinger,   1996

Science, Jews and Secular Culture: Studies in mid-20th Century American

Intellectual   History.,   Princeton Univ. Press, N. J.

3. Gary B. Ferngren, Ed., 2002

Science and Religion: A Historical Introduction. Johns Hopkins Univ. Press

4.   David C. Lindberg and   Ronald Number, Ed. ,   2003

When Science and Christianity Meet. Univ. of Chicago Press, Ill.

5. Ian G. Barbour, 1997

  Religion and Science: Historical and Contemporary Issues. Harper-Collins
  Press

6. John Polkinghorne, 1998

Belief in God in an Age of Science.

7. Russell Stannard, Ed.   2000

God for the 21st Century. Templeton Foundation Press, PA

8. Albert Einstein,   1956

  Out of My Later Years: Scientist, Philosopher and Man Portrayed through
  His Own Words.   Wings Books, N. Y.

9. Ruddy Zallinger,   1965

Early Man.   Life-Times Books, N. Y.

Chapter 7
Complexity Thesis: A New Insight in the Debate

"Only the men and women of intelligent and reasonable faith

have the desire, correct perspective and motivation

to harmonize the Scripture and science.

Men and women without faith cannot but clash the gears. "

Prof. Bernard Ramm

In 16th-17th centuries when Galileo Galilea advocated the sun-centered universe, it met with great resistance from both the academic circle as well as Roman Catholic Church. The reason was due to the fact that the earth-centered universe thesis was not only accepted as a valid thesis by the academic world at that time, but also as a doctrine of Roman Catholic Church (RCC). Unfortunately, Galileo, as a faithful member of RCC was condemned by the church. Eventually, the sun-centered universe theory was accepted as valid. The historical event was intertwined with personal interest of church high officials. That was regarded as aberrant event by those who look at the situation from both scientific and ecclesiastical perspectives. In 1996, Pope John Paul II, on behalf of the RCC, publicly acknowledged the misjudgment and mishandling. That did not satisfy some of those who were radical. Worse still is that many materialistic evolutionists/scientists who would be losing no time in attacking the Christians, and the Church for her wrong-doing, keep on their accusation and finger-pointing.

In Chapter 6, I cited the two historical events. One was the biological theory of evolution which appeared in 1895, challenging Christians and their faith. The second was the debate between Bishop Samuel Wilberforce and Prof. Thomas Huxley. Evolutionists & atheists waste no time in widening the gap between bioscience and Christian faith. The books written by both Prof. Andrew D. White and John W. Draper also contributed to intensify the debate, if not as a manifesto of war. The damage to intellectual and educational enterprise was indeed beyond calculation.

Fortunately, in the last 20 some years, a group of American and British historians of sciences undertook the task of re-examining the situation in 17th century. Their intent was to objectively examine not only the historical prevailing conditions in those days but also the inter-personal relationships which was combined to lead to this unfortunate event. Their endeavor was to probe at the root

of the debate so that they could render a fair judgment. The results of their extensive research led them altogether to a different conclusion. With their research results, they propose a complexity thesis which reveals the historical situation much more complex. Consequently, they have published their findings in two books, one of which is an encyclopedia of more than several hundred pages. The other treaty was shorter version for much easy reading. Their hope, as well as ours, is that the new thesis will logically and eventually replace the old one. With that we all will try to promote mutual understanding between life scientists and Christians in the coming years

Prof. Dr. William Whewell (1794-1866) was a well-known and greatly respected British historian, and mathematic physicist at Univ. of Cambridge. His many publications, specially the four books which described and clarified well the historical background for the birth of modern experimental sciences. The Christian doctrine of creation, and Christian scholars' rational research on this created world contributed so much to the birth. He said that "the RCC had acted against Galileo, that episode was an aberration". Especially, when we considered that in those days the teaching of Pope's authority in such a way that not only caused European countries leaving the church and but also Christian Reformation movement. All these made the Curia and officials so sensitive to any new philosophy, even new science emerged. Taken into consideration of many other prevailing factors, in 1911 both Profs. Whewell and John Hedley Brooks proposed the first time Complexity Thesis. Eventually, this new thesis replaced the old War Hypothesis.

In 2000. Prof. Gary B. Ferngren of Oregon State University took the led to edit a book entitled in *"The History of Science and Religion in the Western Tradition: An Encyclopedia". This significant piece of literature was a synthesis of 103 essays of more than sixty professional historians of sciences in both American and British universities*. The book has 10 divisions. The first division is "Science and Religion: Historical Background and their Relationship, with 14 subdivisions: the 1st, "Historical Introduction for Science and Religion. The 2nd, Conflict, the 3rd. divisions, 4th Knowledge, 5th Reasons, 6th worldviews, 7th God and Natural Science, 8th Predestination in Theology and its kind s, 9th Natural Theology, 10th Intelligent Design, 11th Miracles, 12th Theology, 13th Genesis and Science, 14th Critique in 19th century. The second division: individual scholars: their biography and views, The 3rd Div. Intellectual foundation and philosophical background. The 4th Division: Religion, its tradition and historical background, the 5th Div. Astronomy and Universe, 6th Div. Physics, 7th Div. Geology and Geography, 8th Div. Biological Sciences. 9th Div. Medical and Psychology, the 10th Div. folks' Sciences; to a total of 586 pages.

In this paragraph, I shall summarize what Prof. Colin A. Russell (British Free Univ.) writes in his essay on "The Conflict Between Science and Religion", pointing out the deficiencies of the War Hypothesis, as follows: 1. The War Hypothesis overlooks the other interactions between science and religion; 2. Fail to mention the collaboration between science and religions in the past years, 3:

the progress of sciences and its eventual victory, 4. The commonalities of sciences and religions, 5. partial or unnecessary factors; 6, the minor differences and slanted interpretations, All these were the attempts by those naturalistic scientists to move their marginal position to central role in British society.

In the Introduction, Prof. Ferngren, as Editor, shares his conviction and personal motive in launching this project. He treats the subjects with impartiality and candid attitude. There are sixty historians who contribute their essays, without preconceived personal bias or preference. They endeavor to be fair and honest maintaining a well-balanced attitude. They pay due attention to historical background and the prevailing scientific theories which led to this conclusion. They ask the question as to where conflict comes? Is there any possibility that science and Christian faith could work together? Could they be integrated?

In 2002, Prof. Ferngren, working with another 26 historians of science produced a shorter version on the same subject. It was entitled in "Science and Religion: A Historical Introduction" by Johns Hopkins Univ. Press. It was intended for much easier reading.

With two books, these 60 some historians of sciences endeavor to replace that slanted and erroneous view of war hypothesis or conflict hypothesis, with Complexity Hypothesis. They hope that those who are scientific and open-minded could join them in their endeavor.

In 2000, *Prof. Russell Stannard* wrote, in his essay as follow:

"A number of Neo-Darwinian biologists and philosophers who lose no opportunity to attack religious belief in God as infantile, and as incompatible with scientific knowledge. They advocate a war between science and religion. However, it is not biologists who establish these claims. It is rather a dogmatic materialism which interprets the biological evidence in a slanted way.

Prof. Alfred Norman Whitehead of both Cambridge and Oxford Universities, said as early as in 1926, as follows:

"Science over these years has made changes and progress much more that what theology has made. Christian theology has, on the two sides of the road to progress, discarded many hypotheses and theories in piles. Yet, on the two sides of the road to progress, science discarded much more hypotheses and theories as no longer valid. To those who have devoted their efforts in evaluating the progress of both theology and science, paying no attention to this fact will likely arrive at erroneous conclusion. Their slanted viewpoint in this

unnecessary debate is the eventual victory over theology is indeed an
oversimplified conclusion."

Those of us who are genuinely concerned in this debate should ponder on what Prof. Whitehead said.

Literature Cited

1. Gary B. Ferngren, Ed. 2000, 586 pages

The History of Science and Religion in the Western Tradition.

Garland Publishing   Co., NY

2. Gary B. Ferngren, Ed. 2002,   401 pages

Science and Religion: A Historical Introduction.

Johns Hopkins Univ. Press. MD

3. Peter J. Bowler and Iwan Rhys Morn.

Making Modern Science: A Historical Survey.

Univ. of Chicago Press, Il.

4. Russell Stannard, 2000

God for the 21st Century.

Templeton Foundation Press

5. Alfred North Whitehead,   1926

Science and the Modern World.

Univ. of Cambridge Press, UK.

Chapter 8
Philosophy of Sciences

"I am a passionate believer in the unity of knowledge. I believe that those who are truly seeking an understanding through and through, and who will not settle for a facile and premature conclusion to that search, are seeking God, whether they acknowledge that divine quest or not. Theism is concerned with making total sense of the world. The force of its claims depends upon the degree to which belief in God affords the best explanation of the varieties, not just of religious experience, but of all human experience."

Prof. John Polkinghorne

Before World War II, Universities in both European Continent and United States (in higher education) emphasized very much on research, with course work as secondary. The language requirements for advanced degrees were German and French, more important than English. These were referred to as *European* or *Continental System*. After the War, research center was shifted from Europe to American Continent. In early years, American universities adopted the European Continental System, with equal emphasis on research and course work. In degree programs, language requirement were German in science, French in literal arts and literature. In addition, a course on the philosophy of science was required. Generally, this was referred to as *American System*.

Years later, American universities found out that the language requirement was very heavy and challenging to American students. Somehow, many of the American students could not acquire the skill of learning foreign languages. As a result of this handicap, they took more than seven years to finish degree program. Considering this, many American universities, if not all of them, dropped the foreign language requirement.

One more factor may have something to do with this. In the 1960, Soviet Union launched her Spuntnik spaceship. American governments, The Congress and academic authorities realized the scienco-technological challenge, something needed to be done. Concerted efforts were launched in the nation. Consequently, President Dwight Eisenhower and his administration requested the Congress to modify the immigrant policy, opening USA for new immigrants. Following this policy, a large number of Europeans and scientists, and later on Asians came to the American shores, and took up their legal residence. At that time, literature in sciences were published less with German or French languages, but English as a

language adopted more and more. As a response to these two changes, most American universities dropped the foreign language requirements. At the same time, university authorities decided to increase the number of credits in course work and on term papers. Together with these, no more course on "The Philosophy of Sciences" was required in the curriculum. In those years I was near the end to complete my Ph.D. program at Univ. of Minn. I recalled that I had to pass two foreign languages, German and Spanish in my degree program. Fortunately, I passed these two, with ease. But, by no means they were easy.

After receiving my Ph.D., I was given a faculty position. In one of the social gatherings, Prof. Dr. Elvin C. Stakman (as one of the best known scientists in the world) spoke to me in a causal visit. With a mood of disappointment, he emphatically said that *"those who graduated from our university without taking a course of Philosophy of Sciences, knowing little what sciences could do and what sciences could not accomplish, are not scientists at all, but technicians!"* He and I agreed that this was true with graduates of other universities as well.

Nowadays, in our universities and professional societies as well, scientism is relatively common. Concerned scientists and university authorities often wonder why this is the case? This deficiency could have a lot to do with it.

In this chapter, I shall write and discuss the philosophy of sciences, as follows:

1. What is science? Its definition.

2. What are scientific methods?

3. Scientific hypothesis and theory.

    a. To falsify them

    b. To verify them

4. Scientific experiments and results, interpretations and implications.

5. Scientific principles and laws.

6. With scientific methods, what science and scientists could accomplish.

7. With scientific methods, what science and scientists could not accomplish.

8. The presuppositions scientists have while working on scientific projects.

9. Reports of scientific investigation and their acceptance by scientific communities.

10. The scientific view and the worldviews of materialistic/naturalistic scientists.

11. "Thought experiment".

12. The Christian view and the worldview of Christians-Scientists.

13. The types of sciences, the paradigm, and the domain of science.

14. The domain of philosophy and the domain of theology

15. The worldviews, and

16. Quotations by Nobel Laureates and well-known scientists

1. What is science? and its definitions..

German philosopher Emmanuel Kant once gave these definitions:

"Science, organized knowledge; religion, organized wisdom."

Prof. James Conant, Scientist and President of Yale Univ. defined

"Science is an inter-connected series of concepts and conceptual schemes that have developed as a result of observation, experimentation, and interpretation; and are fruitful for further empirical investigations."

Prof. Richard H. Bube of Stanford Univ., sad

"Science is both a way of knowing, and a body of knowledge derived from systematic research and interpretation of facts."

Prof. Salvador E. Luria, a Nobel Laureate in Biology said

"Science is nothing but educated common sense".

Prof. Owen Gingerich of Harvard Univ., in 2006, once said in his book that

" science is not simply a collection of facts; it is a grand tapestry, woven together from facts and hypotheses that unite these facts in an encompassing pattern of explanation." Also, " science works within a constrained framework in creating its brilliant picture of nature. But reality goes much deeper than this. Scientists work with physics, but (perhaps unwittingly) they also have broader system of beliefs, "metaphysics", a term that literally means "beyond physics". My lecture (at Harvard Univ.) presents a scientific tapestry of the physical world

(astronomy and astrophysics), but also wrestle with the metaphysical frame work within which the universe could be understood."

Prof. Richard Feyman (1918-1988) Nobel Laureate also said that

" Scientific knowledge is a body of statements of varying degrees of certainty. Some un-sure, some nearly sure, but none more absolutely certain."

Prof. Dr. Max Delbrueck, a Virologist at Calif. Tech. and Nobel Laureate also said pertaining to biology and biological phenomena:

" There are no "absolute phenomena" in biology. Life is so dynamic and lively. There are so much intrincacis of biological systems. Also there are so much extrincacies of their expressions. Science teaches us humility. How much we do not yet know."

Albert Einstein once defined and elaborated as

"Science searches for relations which they thought to exist, being independent of the searching individual. This includes the case where man is the subject… The scientific way of thinking has a further characteristic is "the concept which it uses to build up its coherent system are not expressing emotions. For the scientist, there is only "being", but no wishing, no value, no good or evil, no goal…. Scientific statements of the fact and relation, indeed, can not produce ethical directives.

I just quoted a number of definitions or characteristics of sciences as given above. The definition of science varies with individual scientist. Some of scientists do not have intention to define it. They do emphasize on the scientific methods used to obtain empirical data, and then systematize them. This is intended to stimulate further research by others. Definition could be revised if it does not explain adequately the phenomena and the fact, or fails to predict further probabilities.

2. What are scientific methods?

The methods used in empirical research by scientists vary, depending on the kind of science and what it researches for. Yet, the principles are the same.

For example, for those who are in life sciences, first, you have a field trip, looking carefully and systematically at what is involved, with naked eyes; also

with instruments of various kinds. Then, they survey the environmental condition under which this has occurred. Record them in details, and in book. Then, collect representative samples. Samples are being well-preserved. As investigator, you take them as quickly as possible to the laboratory. Based on your observation, you formulate your hypothesis on what has occurred. Then you design experiments, on the basis of what you know in your experience and what is reported in scientific literature. In planning, you choose the most appropriate experimental objects (living animals, plants or otherwise; or model system) for empirical research, with control as/for comparison. Remember, control is needed under all conditions. Then, judicially carry out the designed experiment. At regular intervals, you look at the experimental materials carefully, then well-recorded. If the experiment shows result of whatsoever, then record them. Regardless whether the results are what you expected or not expected, you have to repeat it at least one to two times so that the results obtained will be consistent and repeatable. Otherwise, the overall result is not considered as valid. As well-disciplined scientists, you carry out the experiments, firstly, to falsify your hypothesis. If you can not falsify it, then you try again to verify your hypothesis, one at a time (cf. Logician Karl Kopper) in a systematic and sequential way.

The instruments used in survey or in lab experiments vary with sciences. In life sciences, we use microscope, electron microscope, culture media to cultivate them, in incubators and greenhouse, eventually field work. In engineering sciences, you use machines and equipments in labs or factories. If you are in the social science, which is quite different from bio-sciences and mechanical or chemical engineering sciences. You first interview individuals, then a group of people (often time it is referred as coherst), collect adequate and appropriate results. Then, you analyze the results statistically for validity. All these tell us that depending on what kind of science you are professionally working with, you use your appropriate instruments. If the methods and instruments used are not adequate or appropriate, you could not obtain any valid results. You design appropriate and feasible experiments. First of all, you are to falsify your hypothesis. After that, you are to verify your hypothesis. All these are universal principles in science and scientific research work.

A)Thought experiment: There is one exception to this general principle. When Albert Einstein was formulating his relativity theory, together with some other related issues, he was in deep thinking and reasoning. Taking a couple pieces of paper, he wrote down what he was reasoning in principle. He was writing down, with formulas or equations. Eventually, he formulated his theory. He did not do any experiment at all. Nowadays, when you and I read the literature, especially his biography, people label that deep thinking and writing down, as *"thought experiment"*. Of course, in later time other physicists proved what he had thought of, and writing them down were experimentally valid. Einstein was a theoretician. With theoretic physics, he could do that. One formula of his could speak a lot of truth though no experimental work was done. This is one exception to the general principle outlined in this paragraph.

B)The Model or Model System":

In modern biological research, often bio-scientists adopt so-called *"model system"* for their research work. What is model system? It is *an intellectual framework in mind*, using a simpler material or "model" so that scientists could focus on one specific question at a time, and working in a sequential fashion in the complicated living system. For example, scientists intend to explore the biochemical mechanism of nerve system or digestive system. Both systems are completed and complex in human. So, through their intuition scientists could use simpler systems in small animals (for example, mice, nematodes, or insects). This gives them a strategy to tackle on point at a time. The models or model systems used often, as reported in scientific literature are *E. coli, yeast, nematode, fruitfly, and worm.*

Prof. James D. Watson, Nobel Laureate in DNA structure and function in 1953, said in his textbook of "Molecular Biology of the Genes" that "70-80% of the data in molecular biology in the early days were derived from working with a simple, enteric bacterium, i. e. *Escherichia coli*.

Prof. Dr. Max Born, Nobel Laureate once said,

"All great discoveries in experimental physics have been due to the intuition of men who made free use of "models" which for them not products or imagination, but representative of real things. "

In 2009, the Nobel prize was awarded to three American scientists, *Drs. Elizabeth H. Blackburn* of Univ. of Calif. at San Francisco, *Carol W. Greider* of Johns Hopkins Univ., and *Jack W. Szostak* of Harvard Univ. Med. School, for their work on "telomeres" which are replenished with an enzyme *telomerase*. Blackburn used an organism, *tetrahymena*, a single-celled organism found in pond water. Szostak extended Blackburn's work to *a yeast cell*. Both of them used simpler organisms as "model system". Their findings could be extended to aging process and other health problems in humans. That was the their rational on which they were doing their research work, and on which they were granted with the Nobel Prize.

3. Scientific hypothesis and theory:

Hypothesis and theory in science and scientific research are essential, valid and important. With hypothesis, scientists design empirical experiments first, and then carry them out. This is the first step in a research program. Let me use my specialty, i.e. microbiology as an example to illustrate it. For instance, somewhere in USA there is an occurrence of microbial infectious disease in cattle herd. Microbiologists go there and make observations, surveying what kind of cattle, seeing the environmental conditions and so on. Then, scientists collect samples,

e.g. infected areas. Then, with microbiological lab technique, they isolated aseptically the suspicious bacterial specimen, e.g. A, B, and C. (specimen should be more than two). They asked the question as to which one of the three specimens is indeed the causal pathogen? You will get the answer with empirical experiments.

With experiments carefully designed, with one suspicious factor under consideration, i.e. you subject specimen B for experimentation. Without empirical experiments and with results, you can not conclude that the B (in fact any one of them) is the pathogen. Your experiment should falsify B, that B is not the pathogen first; then to verify B, i.e. B is the pathogen. If you falsify B, then you try with A or C, having one pathogen under consideration at a time. These are the basic principles bio-scientists had to abide with, if they want to be bio-scientists indeed.

For your empirical experiment, you choose six healthy (or more) and young heads of cattle (being more susceptible to infectious disease), divided them into 2 groups. One group of four heads of cattle is aseptically inoculated with sample B, the two heads are not done anything with it, *serving as control.* All of them are kept for periodic observation in a room with optimal temperature, moisture, etc (being favorable for outbreak of the disease). In regular time intervals, you go to examine all six heads of cattle, seeing any one of them showing any sign or symptoms of disease (as you first ever observed in the field trip). You observe them for several weeks. If the four head of cattle being inoculated, show no sign or no symptom at all, you falsify your hypothesis of B as the probably causal pathogen. Or you verify B not the pathogen. You can not immediately suspect that C is the pathogen! Without empirical experiment, you can not say that. It is a guess work! So now, you go to specimen A. You do the exactly same experiment with A. If there is not sign or symptom with A, you could not even conclude that C is the causal agent. You may thought that C could be the suspected pathogen, but that is purely guest work. You have to run experiment with C, in exactly the same fashion. With C used in experiment, in 6-8 weeks, the four heads of cattle showed the symptoms, which are the same kind of symptoms of disease as you had first observed in your field trip. That is 100%. (if one of four is sick,   i.e. 25%, the percentage is not high enough to justify it). At the same time, the other 2 heads which are control show no sign/symptoms of whatsoever. So far, you have proved something. Then, you have to repeat this same experiment again, 2-3 times. In this way, your experiments have proved without any shadow of double that the C specimen is indeed the causal bacterial pathogen.

If necessary, you may have to conduct field experiment with a larger number of heads of cattle. You could prove C specimen that is indeed the causal bacterial pathogen, even in farming field. Science demands the experimental prove in a sequential fashion. Without empirical experiments, you could not arrive at any conclusion as valid. Even speculation or extension is not valid. Results obtained from empirical experiments verify/prove your hypothesis, after you first

falsify it, not vice versa.

With this, let me explain something else which is related to this. For example, in many years ago there occurred a serious outbreak of diseases in cattle. As what was reported in public literature, all these sick animals showed more or less the same kind of symptoms, as seemingly you have proved nowadays. So, on the basis of what you have proved today, you peculate that the disease was caused by bacterial pathogen C. You conclude that bacterial C would be likely the causal agent for that outbreak. Alas, this is an extension or speculation, or a theory. It is not valid at all! If somehow a group of people believe what is extended or speculated, they could believe it. Yet, you and others could reject it. It is a valid rejection. Those people who believed it, could not say that you are wrong. What they said could not stand up for an acid-test. In history of bio-sciences, there are indeed such misfortunes or wrong finger-pointing!

Or/ in the distant future, an outbreak of cattle's disease somewhere else, and also have more or less similar symptoms reported, you can't say that the outbreak is due to C-pathogen. To the past as well to the future, you could not extend your experimental results to verify your hypothesis or theory!

Science demands empirical experiments to verify or falsify your hypothesis or theory!

In conclusion, hypothesis could be falsified or verified with empirical experiments. Hypothesis is tentative, it is by no means final.. It can be revised, or replaced with another one, or discarded it completely. If it is verified by/with empirical experiment, then the hypothesis is valid as a hypothesis. It is true with this particular case. It could not be applied in other case. It is not true in overall realm or in the long run.

If the hypothesis is verified, then this hypothesis can be added to the existing principle. The scope of the existing principle is thereby enlarged. The principle is a total sum of all hypotheses with empirical validity that is systematized as a principle (cf. later section). Do not mix hypothesis with principle or theory. Theory is altogether different from hypothesis. Theory is again a total sum of principles assembled together and be systematized in a larger scope. Theory could not be proven one hundred percent. It is because what empirical experiment done with result is only true in that specific scope., not necessarily true all the time or in any case (cf. Karl Kopper). Theory is not law or postulate. I could not emphasize these principles enough so that we understand what is scientific hypothesis/theory.

4. Experimental results, interpretations and implications:

In the previous section, I explained that conclusion from empirical results obtained is tentative. It can be revised or rejected. It is because that fact that new data appears in the future, and shows it is different, and the old/former hypothesis should be revised. You may wonder why?

The reason is in a way simple, but with some scientific reason in it. Let me use the example given in previous section, and further elaborate it.

Some one else who works with the same bacterial pathogen C, with new method, and also in a different approach. With differential technique on culture medium, he has discovered that the C pathogen is indeed a mixed population of bacteria. This population has many different types of cells which differ from one another in their capacity in causing disease. In other word, bacterium C is composed of different sub-populations. The sub-population of cell/bacterium/organism is designated as C-12. It is the C-12 which is the causal agent (the real one which causes the disease; keep in mind that bacterium is single-celled organism. The sub-species is a lower category of classification). This scientist, with refined techniques, could separate C-12 from the others in the total population. So, he has C-12 as a single, homogeneous population. Consequently, this scientist could use C-12 for further studies, using the same kind of method in experiment. After inoculation with C-12, then in subsequent observation, this scientist discovered that the symptoms appeared on cattle inoculated are in much shorter time, i. e. in two days. Not only the time is shorter, but also the symptoms are quite different. The experiment is repeated a couple of times, with results consistent. With all these, the Scientist/Experimenter comes to a conclusion that the old conclusion should be revised accordingly, in view of the new result from his experiments.

This demonstrates well that empirical experimental results obtained, and even hypothesis derived from it/ behind it are tentative, not final. This principle applies to all scientific research, with no difference at all in other branches of bio-science.

When scientist reports his/her findings in a scientific paper, with interpretation, he/she can only explain it within the confine of what he has so far done. Above all, his/her interpretation should be confined to what the experimental results demonstrate, not going beyond its sphere or domain. This is very important. Often, researchers have such a tendency, as human beings, to interpret the result in such a way beyond what the result says. We all have the tendency to consider our work far more important than it is. As human beings we wish to proclaim that "It is final"! No, not at all. There is a temptation that scientist would like to interpret his/her result beyond what the experimental result tells.. For example, he/she interprets his/her result in term of its value in our society. It has become a theory of economics. When you and I examine scientific papers published in literature, such cases are relatively common. In other word, these scientists have made mistakes, going beyond what their result could tell /or going beyond their proper domain of science.

5. Scientific principles and laws:

Some other microbiologists will do very extensive work, collecting empirical

lab results with different bacterial pathogens in various hosts, as accumulated over these years. They collect them, classify them, and systematize them. Finally, they come to the conclusion that diseases caused by bacterial pathogens in farm cattle could be classified into three large categories, they are: a) diseases caused by pathogenic organisms: such as bacterial, fungal, parasitic and viral pathogens; b) inheritable or genetic diseases: no pathogens involved but due to genetic nature, it can pass on to succeeding generations, and c) nutritional or physiological or biochemical diseases: with no pathogen, but nutritional, and not inheritable..

On the basis of these categorizations, scientists could propose that farm animals could suffer from three kinds of diseases, as outlined above. This principle could be applied to cattle, sheep and hog. This conclusion seems simple, yet it comes as a result of systematization, and categorization of a large number of diseases with different causes. This becomes a scientific principle. This principle and its application are far greater, extending to plant diseases and human diseases. The scope is much greater.

Then, other scientists, on the basis of his knowledge and expertise, could extend this principle in an even greater scope. They conclude that disease is in principle *a deviation from normal, healthy life-pattern*. In other word, they use the normal and healthy condition as a criterion, and compare it with those abnormal conditions. This extension is even greater in principle and in scope. This becomes a scientific law or postulate.

In microbiology, there is a *Koch's postulate,* consisting of four steps. Nowadays, not only in microbiology, but also in public health, in cancer research and in genomic abnormality, scientists have to follow these four steps of Koch's postulate in order to prove the normal-abnormal situation in living organisms, and disease is a deviation. This postulates are the summation of knowledge accumulated over these years, and with many kinds of practical situation. Its validity and application are far greater. It is a postulate or a domain by itself.

6. With science and scientific method, what scientists could do and could accomplish:

In the last half a century, we all have witnessed the amazing progress made in sciences, with scientific methods. With their results and being applied in a practical way as technology, they have made our lives far more comfortable and enjoyable. A great deal of progress has been made. No one could deny this.

Sciences and knowledge have entered into many new frontiers, new technologies and new sciences. For example, jet travel has made our travel far easier and faster. Medicine and medical technology have saved many lives. Nowadays, scientists are contemplating genomic diseases and treatments; embryonic stem cells in transplantation and cloning technologies. All these indicate what scientists with their knowledge and skill could do and could

accomplish, making meaningful contributions to society and human living.

In this created universe, scientists with their innovative mind could find so many interesting projects for research. With appropriate methods they could achieve their objectives. In the last half a century, scientists and technologists have made great stride in many areas. Jet travel takes us to anywhere in hours or in days. With TV we could see what has happened in the other parts of the world. With computer, we could communicate to people on other continent in a matter of minutes. These are marvels! We could fall into the pit, that is, we can do all things and anything in this world. That is scientism! We scientists have to be aware of the followings so that we would not entertain the idea that science has become almighty tool, and we scientists have become almighty in work. There are many areas, we scientists, with our knowledge and technology could not do. Science is not almighty. It has its proper domain, and its limits as well. Let me share with the following paragraph.

7. *With science and scientific methods, what scientists could not do and could not accomplish:*

First of all, we have to realize the fact that *science of whatsoever kind carries no ethical value* in itself. By nature and in essence, science is neutral so far ethical value is concerned. For example, *atomic energy* is a type of physical energy. It could be used in medicine, agriculture and engineering with the practical and ultimate benefit for humanity and society. It is good use of the energy. On the other hand, we could construct atomic bombs which could be used to slaughter hundreds even thousands of innocent lives in war. This is bad use of atomic energy. The practical use of it is quite different from the inherent nature of the atom and atomic energy. We have to differentiate the two, one is the inherent nature of atom and atomic energy. The other is the use of this wonderful source of energy. The atom itself, and its activated energy for practical use, are two different things. For good use or for bad use is what we use it for. Atom and atomic energy do not carry any ethical value in themselves.This principle could be applied in other areas as well.

(a) Value or ethical value: They are abstract description of a life dedicated to noble principle, for example, Christian missionaries and their sacrificial services, statesmen and their public service. You could neither measure it with meter nor see its weight with a scale. Scientists could not do any experiment to determine its value. Value or ethical value does not fall into the category of science. With science and scientific methods of whatsoever kind, scientists could not do anything about it, and could not accomplish anything of it.

(b) Meaning of life: What you live for? Mere physical existence! Jesus said in public, in answering to the devil's temptation: "Man does not live on bread alone, but on the Word of God." Life has a higher objective, which can't be seen or be measured with meter. You do not see any value beyond what you eat

and you sleep, and work! When you die, that is the end of it! Others live for higher goal in life, with meaning, with daily sacrifice and meaningful contribution. Could any one measure it with a meter? Or weigh it on a scale? Do some experiments with it? No, it is not in the domain of science.

(c) Aethetics: Have you ever read a biography of Mr. Abraham Lincoln? Or Jesus of Nazareth? Or John F. Kennedy? JFK was assassinated while he was in his prime youth. To-day, we see Kennedy Airport in New York, and Kennedy Performing Arts Bldg. in Washington, D. C. Their lives and contribution to human society are very much envied by young people, today! Aethetics is not a subject for scientists! So many millions of people claim that Jesus is their Savior. He delivers them from evil and wrong-doings! Can we scientists measure the claim on scale or with meters? They are not in the domain of science. Science can do nothing with it. But, to some of us, the claim is so real and so precious.

(d) love or hatred: How much your dear mother loved you?   Twelve inches or two pounds? Can any renowned scientist perform an experiment to determine it its weight or its length? No, it is not something you could measure or weigh. Also, you could not submit it to scientific experimentation. Yet, motherly love is so real and so important. You can feel it. You describe your mother's love with your emotion and in words. Some one else stands by could sense what you are saying. He could not deny it that is something you consider it important and valuable.

Hatred is also in the same category. You could sense it, and experience it, and even describe it. Yet, you could be subject it to scientific experimentation.

(e) Genuine religious faith and doctrines: Whenever you see an artificial portray of Jesus Christ, invariably you are inspired. During Christmas season, you and I hear Christmas singing, "Oh, come and let us worship Him and let us adore Him". We Christians believe that he is God incarnated, and died a sacrificial death of the Cross in redeeming believers from their sins. God is some one else who is in heaven, also in our hearts. No body could deny the truth and the reality of genuine faith. Only those idiots-scientists try to prove the non-existence of God with their scientific methods. Religious faith is not in the domain of science. To those who experience God's love in daily living could describe it to you. To those who have genuine faith is so real. It is not delusion, as Prof. Richard Dawkins has labeled and explained it in his book. To him, it is delusion!

(f) Philosophy and philosophical views: In etymology, there are different domains of knowledge (please consult 13 in this Chapter). Scientific knowledge is one domain, and philosophy is another domain which is larger than the domain of sciences. In USA people receive Ph.D. (doctor of philosophy) as the higher degree or highest degree, after M. S. and B.S. That means you have passed the domain of science, and your knowledge has already entered the domain of philosophy. By and large, theology is an even larger domain, larger than philosophy. That is the why science of whatsoever kind could neither prove the non-existence of God nor

the existence of God. So, it is with philosophy, more so with theology.

(g) Why human (you and I) exists? or why we live?   The purpose of life or living is not a material thing. It is a question bigger than ourselves. Yet, in this society of ours, there are people who live for mere existence or bread alone. Beyond mere existence they do not have any idea of why they live for. Noble idea for living, for example, the living of Mother Teresa and the reason why she lived such a noble life is not a subject of science. It is in her genuine faith in God, or her viable religion which inspired her to live in such a meaningful life.

(h) Why the universe exists? Again, this is a question of bigger than yourself. You could neither   design a scientific experiment to prove it not to disprove it. For those who have genuine religious faith, they believe that the universe exists for a purpose to glorify God, the Maker of the universe. To those atheists, there is no purpose, not any meaning at all.

(i) Questions in metaphysics and theology: The ultimate question is theistic or atheistic, or pantheistic. It is in the domain of theology, pertaining to the existence of God.

(j) The worldview: What are mentioned or described in 6) to 10) could be collectively described as worldview. Every body has a worldview. The worldview will either influence or determine how we as humans look at the world. Again, it is either theistic or atheistic, or pantheistic.

(k)   "125 Questions: What Don't we Know?"   In 2005 when *American Association for the Advancement of Science (AAAS)* celebrated *her 125th Anniversary,* listed *125 questions that we do not yet know scientifically. Cf. Anniversary Issue, July 1st, 2005*

The Senior Science Editorial Board of AAAS suggested q't convey the questions that point to critical knowledge gaps. At first, they thought of 25 questions. Quickly, they realized that 25 questions wouldn't convey the grand sweep of cutting-edge research, finally ended up with 125 questions. Then, they listed 25 highlighted questions in no special order as one group, and the other 100 questions grouped under scientific disciplines.   For those who are interested in knowing them in detail, please consult Science Vol. 309, July 1st, 2005. Due to the constraint of space in this book, I choose some of these questions as follows:

For example: What is the universe made of? What is the biological basis of consciousness? How and where did life on earth arise?   What determines species diversity? Can we selectively shut off immune responses? How hot will the greenhouse world be?   Will Malthus continue to be wrong?. Scientists could ask hard questions. With their endeavor, in another 25 to 50 years, they may be able to have partial answers to these questions, no answer at all.   To you and to me, these questions would make us humble enough to answer these questions as how little we know, or how far we have to go.

All these eighteen areas (a to k, under different disciplines) are not subjects for sciences to prove or disprove; or up to the present time, we know very little. Even in another decade or more, with scientific advancements at a faster speed could not enter into these areas for scientific inquiry. If any one attempts to do, ultimately, he or she could be disillusioned. It is because the fact that these questions are not scientific questions. They are in the domain of philosophy, or domain of theology or the domain of worldviews.

Prof. Owen Gingerich of Harvard Univ. in 2006, also mentioned seven questions having no answer (as related to the "efficient cause of "Aristotle's how"):

How <u>Homo sapiens</u> came into being (other than being created by God), 2) How our DNA is related to all forms of life, 3) How atom emerged? 4) More uranium than god on earth crest", 5) what the universe is made of? 6) are we alone in this universe, and 7) what genetic changes have made us unique. These questions are for philosophers, if not for theologians.

Prof. Arthur Peacocke of Oxford Univ., also said,

"What sciences tell us is true about nature. It can not falsify what is true about human relationship to God. ......Indeed, because the world is created by God, knowledge through science must enhance and clarify our understanding of God and his relation to the creation, including humanity,"

Let me cite one example. In 1993, the 40th anniversary of the publication of the double helical structure of DNA and its functions, we molecular biologists assembled on the campus of Univ. of Chicago for a celebration of three-days' International Congress. It was a huge gathering of more than 400 scientists, with 12 Nobel Prize winners presented. The molecular biologists, especially the geneticists tried to evaluate the progress made in the last 40 years. At the same time, they contemplated on what to do in the coming 10 years, with even greater contribution to science. Three Nobel Prize winners, **Francis Crick** (molecular biologist, Univ. of Cambridge), **Gerard Edelman** (molecular immunologist at N.Y Univ) and **S. Tonagawa** (mol. immunologist, at MIT) announced in the Congress that they give up their current research projects, and would enter into neurobiology, a relatively new discipline. With their knowledge and experience they intended to find out the "God-spot" in the human brain as to why those people believe God and worship one un-seen deity. Also, why people have a sense of conscience, "soul-spirit" so called. Once they find the "*God-spot*" in human brain, then they will study how this "God-spot" functions, giving religious people a sense of worship, and also the conscience. Quite a good number of participants applauded and admired their ambition. At the same time, they looked forward to having their new findings.

After 10-years' painstaking and consistent research endeavor, the 3 eminent molecular biologists wrote their books with their research results. In his book, " The Astonishing Hypothesis: *The Scientific Search for the Soul*" of 300 some pages, in 1994, Prof. Crick concluded, with his experimental results, that "*your joys and your sorrow, your memories and ambitions, your sense of personal identity and free will, are in fact no more than the behavior of a vast assembly of nerve cells and their associated molecules.*" Prof. Edelman also published his research result in a book entitled in "The Phenomenal Gift of Consciousness" Yale Univ. Press, as "*The nerve cells, their responses and their reactions, just as electronic pulses in an electronic wire.*"

Their scientific and painstaking research work of 10 years have given them any concrete and specific answer? So many of the participants were greatly disappointed! Why? Because "soul-spirit" and "a sense of deity and worship" are not material. These are not physical matters. They are not subjected to empirical scientific research work. Every body knows by intuition that people somehow have a sense of existence of deity, and an urge to worship, or an urge to live noble and honest living, yet they could not prove it with scientific methods.

Dr. Erwin Schroedinger once said:

" *although life may the result of an accident, I do not think that of consciousness. Consciousness can not be accounted for in physical terms. For consciousness is absolutely fundamental. It can not be account for in term of anything else.*"

Another eminent British neurobiologist, a Nobel Prize winner as well, *Prof. Dr. John Ecclid*,who was a Christian and a scholar commented on their empirical results as follows.

"*Though these three eminent molecular biologists acknowledge "God-spot",or even they could find such a "God-spot" in human brain,they still could not explain how the "God-spot" functions in molecular terms. It was because the question was not in the domain of science.*"

8. *The presuppositions scientists have while working on scientific projects:*

Many scientists tend to acknowledge that while they engage in scientific research work, they are very objective. They harbor no subjective viewpoint. Is this true? The answer is "not necessarily true."

Whether you are a scientist or not a scientist, we all enjoy looking at the vast universe, this world of ours. When you travel by air, look-up at the blue sky, you feel it is so vast. You look down, you see terrains after terrains. When you travel

by ocean-liner, you see this beautiful huge body of water, seemingly no-end horizon. You feel that you are so small in this vast universe. You derive a sense of awe! Likely, you will ask yourself a question, where this beautiful universe came from? Who is holding it in this vast space? For what purpose it exists?

You have an answer or you do not have any answer. If you are agnostic, you would say I do not know, or it is so natural. If you are an atheist, you would say that it is a material world with no meaning of whatsoever. If you are man or woman of faith, you will say that there is an intelligence behind it. If you are a deist. For example: *Dr. Albert Einstein* once said that he was a deist of Apinoza's type. *His problem was that he could not pray to a personal God, and get an answer*. If you are a Christian or Roman Catholic, you will say: yes, there is an almighty God, who answers our prayers and directs my ways. You are/I am one of these 3 or 4 types of person. If   it is so, you have your preconceived supposition.

Biologists study the living things and/ or naturalists study this world. They have their viewpoints. No one could deny this. It is pre-conceived   or "in-born" in your mind. This is our worldview. You and I may use different terminology describing it. If you accept/believe evolution theory wholeheartedly, you are an evolutionist, naturalist, or agnostic or atheist. This worldview in one way or another would influence our thinking even at the   end of our scientific research. Let me give you an example.

In 2002, US National Academy of Sciences, AAAS and others sponsored a dialogue on Harvard University, with more than 300 scholars, on "Science and Faith" for two days (I was one of the participants). In the morning there are plenary sessions, and small group discussion in the afternoon. Interesting enough is the fact that eminent scientists acknowledged that in one way or another our worldview would influence our research and career.

Prof. D. William Phillips (Nobel Laureate, 1997 in quantum physics) of Univ. of Maryland was one of the Speakers. He is well-known for Christian faith and activities in the community. In one of the dialogue sessions, Dr. Phillips was the target, being asked of his Christian faith in his research career. This is how he answered.

"When I design an experiment, I design it as a trained physicist. I design it with my training in   scientific principles and methods. There is no such a thing as Christian experiment. My Christian faith does not enter into my design.   Even when I and my colleagues carry on the experiment designed, my Christian worldview does not enter into it, even to the conclusion of my empirical experiments. Because all these are in the domain of science and scientific methods. Yet, when or after I have

analyzed the results and the phenomena shown in my empirical experiments, I have found that the quantum phenomena are so different from classic physics experiments. The phenomena are different that would lead me to admire the intrinsic nature of quantum physics which is so different. At this time, I have a sense of wonder which I myself could not explain them with words. A sense of awe, metaphysics comes to my thinking and my mind. At this time of the whole process of empirical research, I have my Christian worldview. With this Christian worldview, I admire the One who creates and holds the mystery of this vast universe.

Then, Prof. Phillips turned his comment on something else. He said, "years ago, I had the opportunity of participating in the so-called "Manhattan Project". The Project was designed to make our ammunitions better and better, for wars. I declined to take part in such a project. *It is because my Christian worldview, and my personal ethics would allow not me in so doing., and would not give me a free conscience working on such a project.*"

No one else in the whole conference would like/was able to argue with Prof. Phillips!

9. Reports of scientific investigation and their acceptance by scientific communities: Scientists should abide with another scientific to philosophical principle, i. e. uniformity of scientific research and principle. In this world of ours, you see the macrocosm or the microcosm with regularities, orderliness and uniformity. What we see or we do to-day could be seen in years to come. What we scientists have demonstrated in one locality could be demonstrated in the other locality. The mechanisms are the same, but the principles we arrive at may vary. Laws are universal. What you have demonstrated and achieved could be demonstrated/achieved elsewhere. As scientists we all accept these principles. What we have reported as valid results could be repeated by some one else in other place. Scientists have to be honest enough to earn others' trust. If you "artificially fabricated your results", you betray your profession and betray the trust by other scientists. You will loss your reputation as a scientist. No more respect would be bestowed upon you any more. This is un-written consensus in the scientific community. This is our acceptable standard. Otherwise, there would no be such a profession, and no more scientist and no more scientific research.

Prof. Dr. Bruce Albert, Editor of Science, weekly scientific journal by AAAS, in an editorial article in Sept.5th of 2008 wrote:

"Scientists have an absolute obligation to honesty. They must accurately report how they arrived at their discoveries, as well as the discoveries themselves. Thus,

our journals must insist on detailed description of all the methods used, so as to allow other scientists to reproduce the results in a straightforward manner. The appropriate place for most of this information is in the easily expandable Supplementary Materials that accompany each article. Authors, reviewers, and editors of scientific manuscripts should therefore constantly ask themselves whether results are valid and genuine."

Prof. Dr. Michael Bishop, molecular virologist at Univ. of Southern California, a Nobel Laureate once wrote:

" Scientists depend upon the truthfulness of their colleagues: Each of us builds our discoveries on the work of others: If that work is false, our constructions fall like a house of cards and we must start all over again. The great success of science in our time is based on honesty."

10. The scientific views and the worldview of materialistic/naturalistic scientists:

In the 16th to 19th centuries, the worldview of naturalists/scientists was "vitalism". It describes that all living things manifests living phenomena summed up as "vitalism". This was a generic and philosophical description. In 1944, Austrian scientist **Dr. Edwin Schrodinger**, a physico-biochemist, published his book entitled in *"What Is Life?"*. He defined "life" simplistically in physico-biochemical term, as composed of bio-macro-molecules such as polymers and proteins. His definition of life had a profound influence on the thinking of scientists in the succeeding years, turning their attention to fundamental composition of cells and tissues.

In 1950 and onward, proteins with their enormous kinds, as fundamental building materials in various structures and catalytic functions in all living entities were the focal point of research and teaching at colleges. Proteins were considered the fundamental bio-material of cells. So much attention was given to them. In 1953, the structure and function of DNA were made known to the scientific world. By then, DNA and RNA as proven the genetic materials with capacity of self-duplication, are far more significant than proteins. So, attention was shifted to DNA and RNA. Naturalists and Scientists took them as the criteria of "Life". Life science entered a new era of molecular biology. Once you find DNA or RNA in the test tubes, Scientists/naturalists/materialists considered the "Origin of Life". Evolution theory was revised and entered into biochemical and molecular evolution, as the current theory. *This was the worldview of "life" in the 19th to 20th centuries.*

Scientists as well as laymen know well that you could not equate "Life" as we see in ourselves and daily activities as simply as physico-biochemical substances in test tubes. The laymen know well that you and I, as a living being, could think, love and hate. Certainly, the proteins even the DNA/RNA in test tubes could not manifest all these functions. So, the worldview of life is simplistic, and reductionism at the extreme! Yet, evolutionists and/or materialistic philosophers consider it as "the milestone" in science!

In 1970, French molecular biologist, **Dr. Jacques Monod**, a Nobel Laureate, in his book of "*Chance and Necessity*", a well-known book in scientific literature. Using DNA as a criterion for life, he cited two basic requisites in "Life". One is the replication of DNA necessitates the pairing of nucleotides in function (Necessity), and mistakes in mutation as a function of "chance". In scientific principle, they are true and correct. But, extending them to the domain of philosophy of science is something questionable. At any rate, again this was considered as another "milestone" in bio-science in 20th century.

All these could be summed up as naturalistic/materialistic worldview, denying any supernatural. This universe was not pregnant with life, no meaning and no value. Man and woman live in the world alone. He/she is made of bio-materials after all. There is no divine endowment, no value and no meaning. Once you die, that is the end of it! There is no hope of any kind!

11. The scientific view and worldview of evangelical Christians; the paradigms:

Evangelical Christian/Scientists have altogether a different worldview. Galileo Galilea, the Father of modern experimental sciences used the metaphor of two books, i.e. The Book of Scripture and The Book of Nature. The former is the Special Revelation of God, and the latter is the Work of God. God is the Author of these Two Books, therefore they should not and world not have contradicted against each other. In 19th century, Christian scholars such as W. Dawson, John Pyre Smith, Hugh Miller, Asa Gray, James Orr' in 20th century such as John Ecclide, Charles Townes, John Phillips, Kenneth Miller, Robert John Russell, and British scholars such as John Polkinghorne, William Bragg, Arthur Peacocke, Keith Ward and Alister McGrath, all these scholars upheld this classic worldview. They have seen no conflict between Scripture and science. For years these scholars have been building bridge between the two disciplines. They integrate well these two disciplines in their worldview as Christian worldview. This worldview is altogether different from the worldview of materialistic/atheistic worldview.

In this respect, I do suggest this to our Christian theological seminaries and colleges by addition one course to their current curriculum, i.e. one course on "The Philosophy of Science." Now, we live in a scientific era. As world citizens and world Christian ministers, we should know something about this

fundamentally important subject so that our ministry will be more effective and more productive.

Paradigm as defined by Logician **Thomas Kuhn** as, *"paradigms are fruitful ways of looking at the world.* They are the ways to determine the categories to be employed in understanding the phenomena; the relations that hold between the entities thought to exist, the problems that need to be addressed, the research methods to be used, and the kinds of outcome expressed from their applications. Paradigms such as: Newtonian dynamic, Cupernician astronomy, Maxwell's mathematization of electromagnetic, Einstein's relativity, Darwinian evolutionary biology, DNA hereditary materials, and Linnean classification. When paradigms change, the worldview with themselves change with them.

12. The types of sciences and domain of sciences:

In accordance to **Dr. Karl Popper** (1902-1994), well-known Logician, science could be divided into the following categories: *theoretical, conceptual, structural, functional, exact and descriptive sciences*, etc. Biologic science is not an exacting science, such as physics and engineering. Biologic science is a descriptive, interpretative science, or experimental science.

As Nobel Laureate, *Prof. Francis Crick of Univ. of Cambridge once said,*

"in biological science, one observable phenomenon could be described

from different angles.

The description could be multiple and varied, more than one description possible." Therefore, bio-science is different from structural science or theoretical science such as mathematics or physics. The theorems are conceptual. No body has seen "universal gravity theory". But, we all know that the ripen apple could fall to the ground, as Isaac Newton had first observed and formulated. You have not seen the gravity itself, but the action of gravity as a phenomenon. Science and its explanation should remain in the confine/domain of science. *It should not go beyond. If it goes beyond, then, this is in the domain of philosophy or worldview.*

13. The domain of philosophy and the domain of theology:

I shall illustrate the domains of science, philosophy and theology in different domains,and gradually enlarging domains, and finally worldview, as follows:

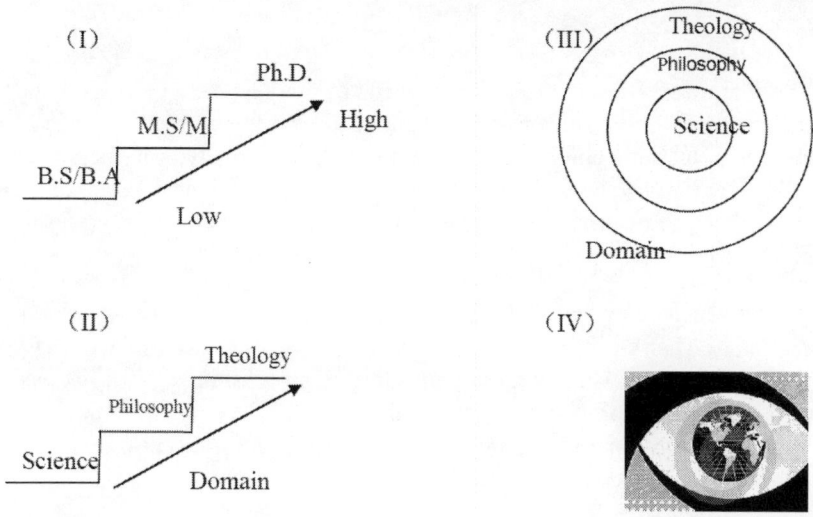

(I)

(III)

(II)

(IV)

*Worldview*s

Figure #1 illustrates the academic degrees granted by US colleges and university, i.e. the bachelor degree to master and then Ph.D.;

Fig. #2, science as the smallest domain, then philosophy to theology as the largest domain;

Fig. #3, science is the lowest domain, then philosophy to theology as the largest domain in knowledge, and

Fig. #4, with our eyes we see our academic learning in worldview.

Additional comments: Pertaining to names of colleges/schools and degrees granted at UK and USA.

In UK, the European or Continental System, Schools of Engineering, agricultural and medicine were called "Faculty, for example, Faculty of Engineering, Faculty of Agric., and Faculty of Medicine; whereas schools of laws, humanity and literature were called College of Laws, College of Humanity and Literature. When degrees were granted, to the former, would be Doctor of Engineering, Agric. and Medicine; whereas to the latter Doctor of Philosophy of Law and Ph. D. of Humanity and Literature. Why is there such a difference? The difference and distinction were based on the degree of sophistication of the disciplines. In the former, it is limited in scope and in depth of learning, in the latter it is more depth and more in scope. As shown in Fig. #3, science is the smallest domain, then philosophy is larger than science, and theology is larger that

philosophy in scope and in depth.

14. Worldviews:

What are worldviews? Only the scientists or scholars have their worldviews? Or the common folks/citizens also have their worldviews? Yes, every one irrespective of learning and or degrees conferred by university or no degree at all, we all have our worldviews. You and I may use different terms in describing our worldviews, but in essence they are the same when we look at the bigger scheme and bigger than ourselves.

Worldview is the way in which each one of us looks at the world, we ask the question as to what meaning is there? Why the universe exists? for what? We all live in this world, for what? with any meaning or no meaning at all? Irrespective of having religious faith or no religious faith, you and I invariably come to have our worldviews. It is the total sum of our knowledge and perception of what we see this world and also we who live in this world.

The worldview is something like a sun-light glass you use. With that, you and I see the world, receiving different perceptions of it, and then giving a different reaction to it. The worldview is something like a coin you hold it closely before your eye (with one eye closed). If you hold the coin close to your eye, you see nothing else but the coin itself. That is all you see. If you hold the coin far away from your eye, then you will see the coin as small as it could be, with surrounding things else, that is a bigger picture. This would illustrate the key point, that is, your worldview will determine how small a picture you could perceive when you look at the world with a coin covering your eye. Also, you will see how big the picture you could perceive when you hold the coin away from your eye.

In other word, our worldview would determine what kind of perception we derive when we look at the world of ours. If you are a materialistic/atheistic in worldview, you perceive its coldness, with no meaning of whatsoever. Life has no meaning and no value. It is not worthy of living. Death is the end of everything! If you are a man/woman of genuine religious/Christian faith, you will see that this world of ours is created by God with a purpose, and ultimate objective for goodness/blessings of humanity, and his enjoyment, with value, with meaning. What a vast difference it makes!

Logician Thomas Kuhn defines worldviews as

> **"They provide a large framework for describing what reality is**
>
> **and how it operates. They tell how reality ought to be.**
>
> **They convey meaning and purpose."**

Let me illustrate with our daily experience in eating or in having a banquet.

120

You go to good restaurant, you and your friends enjoy a good meal. If you have your friends eating at home, with your dear Mom cooking her meal for you. You and your friends could enjoy the meal just as good as you eat it in a restaurant. Since the dishes are prepared carefully judicially by your dear Mom, you eat with a sense of love and appreciation, you enjoy the meal far more and far better. It is because you realize the fact that the meal is prepared by Mom with love and tender care. You derive a sense of deep love and appreciation when you enjoy the meal at home. What is great difference it is!

Worldview is how we as human beings look at this world of ours, and perceive it with a sense of appreciation of its value and purpose, or no value or no purpose at all. *Dr. James W. Sire* (1997) once defined as

"A worldview is a set of presuppositions (assumptions that may be true, partially true or entirely false) which we hold (consciously or subconsciously, consistently or inconsistently) about the basic makeup of our world."

In his 4th Ed. Sire revised as

"A worldview is a commitment, a fundamental orientation of the heart that Can be expressed as a story or in a set of presuppositions about the basic constitution of reality, and that provides the foundation on which we live, move and have our being."

15) Quotations by renowned scholars and theologians:

"All religions arts and sciences are branches of the same tree. All these aspirations are directed toward ennobling man's life, lifting it from the sphere of mere physical existence and leading the individual towards freedom." by *Dr. Albert Einstein*, the Greatest Scientist of the 20th century. He also said, " *Science can only ascertain what is, not what it should be. Religion, on the other hand deals with value and purpose.*"

By Johannes Kepler, the Father of modern astronomy.

"Science has become a valuable tool, but dangerous, that needs ethical guidance for constructive use. It is essential and vitally important that we appreciate and understand the value and the limitations of science so that we would enhance science and Christianity as partners in enhancing humanity welfare and blessings."

By Prof. Dr. John Polkinghorne, former President of Queen's College, Univ.

of Cambridge and Cannon Theologian of Liverpool.

"Science and Christian theology are "intellectual cousins". They both are concerned with interpreted experience, and with quest for truth about reality. Scientific and theological inquiries are parallel."

Conclusion

In the early years of 20th century, those who pursued a higher degrees at academic institutions and universities in USA were required in their overall curriculum to take a course of "The Philosophy of Science". With this course, the future leaders of sciences and literature would know how much sciences could accomplish, and at the same time know how much sciences could not do or could not accomplish. With this course, they will have an appropriate/adequate appreciation of sciences. In addition, they will know, in a progressive fashion, the domains of science, philosophy and the worldview.

Literature Cited

1. Del Ratzsch, 2nd Ed.,2000

   Science and it Limits: The Natural Science in Christian Perspectives

   IVF Press, Wisconsin.

2. Bernard Ramm, 1954

   Christian View of Science and Scripture.

   Moody Press, Chicago, Ill.

3. Thomas Kuhn, 1962

   The structure of Scientific Revolution.

   University of Chicago Press, Ill.

4. Keith B. Miller, Ed. 2002.

   Perspectives on an Evolving Creation.

   Wm Eerdmans Publishing House, Mich.

5. Stanley L. Jaki, 2000

   History of Science and Religion in Western Tradition: A Symposium.

   Garland Publishing Co. N.Y.

6. Joshua Lederberg, Eric Kandel et al, 2002

   Unity of Knowledge: The Convergence of Natural and Human
        Science.

   N.Y. Academy of Sciences, N.Y.

7. Bertrand Russell, 1961

   A History of Western Philosophy.

   Aldens & Mowbray Ltd, Oxford, England

8. Karl Popper, 1959

   The Logic of Scientific Discovery

   Hutchinson Press, England

9. Steven Shapin, 1996

The Scientific Revolution

University of Chicago Press, Ill.

10. Alfred North Whitehead, 1926

Science and The Modern World

Cambridge Univ. Press, England

11.Albert Einstein, 1956

Out of My Later Years.

Wings Book, N.Y.

12. James W. Sire, 1974,4[th] Ed. 2004 (revised)

The Universe Next Door: Basic Worldview. Inter-Varsity Press, Ill.

Chapter 9
Christian Philosophy of Life Sciences

"Science, especially natural sciences, investigate the created things in the universe with empirical methods .In essence and by nature, scientists do not attempt to investigate the Creator who is beyond the domain of science. Religion, especially Christianity tries to understand and know the Creator with philosophic-theological contemplations. By necessity and in essence, Christians appreciate the divine design, purpose and the value of human beings as created by Him."

Prof. Kenneth A. Koestler

In 16th and 17th centuries, modern experimental sciences were born as a result of Copernicus, Kepler and Galileo in their rational and empirical research. They advocated the sun-centered universe, with results of astronomy, physics and mathematics. Then, Isaac Newton discovered the universal gravitation in physics. These four pioneers were dedicated Christians. There were many other Christian scholars such as Antonie-Laurent Lavoisier, Robert Boyle, Carl Von Linne, Louis Pasteur and Francis Bacon, they made their contributions in their specific areas. This is something Christians who are in the scientific fields should know, with a sense of pride and gratitude.

In 1802, Irish scholar William Paley, who was involved in Natural Theology at that time, advocated in his book, *"The Watchmaker"*, a divine, intelligent designer (in a metaphor of a watch, with a watchmaker) of the universe, who is the Lord Jehoval, the Maker of the Universe. This became the philosophy of science in general, and bio-science in particular.

In the 20th century, Christian scholars felt that Rev. William Paley as shown in his philosophy of science was much influenced by Isaac Newton's physics. They thought that the watchmaker could be too mechanistic. It did not imply the dynamic, fluidal and ever-changing conditions of living things. They suggested that the "Watchmaker" metaphor should be enriched. Others did agree to this argument. But, the principle of an intelligent designer of the universe was valid metaphor.

In 1859, Charles Darwin advocated evolution theory with his publication of

125

"The Origin of Species". The mechanisms proposed were adaptation, sexual reproduction, competition and survival for the fitted, eventually with new species evolved. No doubt, Darwin's evolution theory presented a tremendous challenge to Christian faith.

In 19th-20th centuries, there were many schools of philosophies arose in Europe and consequently in USA. Gradually, these philosophies infiltrated into institutes of higher learning and eventually Christian theological seminaries. So many of these scholars could be due to the fact they were not happy with their life-styles. At the same time, they could not find answers to their problems in daily living. Some of them became agnostic even atheistic. They pitched up against institutional churches and teachings. The schism of Christianity and science became a reality in learned societies. This became very acute situation in USA. Fortunately, there are many scholars who devote their energy and time to build "bridge" between these two major cultural forces in western world.

What we Christians need is a scientifically viable and sound philosophy of life science. With this, we evangelical Christian scholars could look at the living world with our conviction and our worldview. In this chapter, I shall endeavor to present such a philosophy of life science, with reference and quotation of three American scholars.

A. Four eminent American scholars and their publications:

1. Bernard Ramm, 1954

Christian View of Science and Scripture.

William B. Eerdman Publishing Co., Mich.

2. Bruce H. Reichenbach and V. Elvin Anderson, 1995

On Behalf of God: A Christian Ethic for Biology.

Wm. B. Eerdmen Publishing Co., Mich.

3. Keith B. Miller, Ed., 2003, 527 pages

Perspectives on An Evolving Creation Wm. Eerdmen Publishing Co., Mich.

This 3rd book is compendium of article written by 20 some Christian professionals in areas of astronomy, physics, and biology, together with the staff members of the Center for Theology and Natural Sciences at Univ. of Calif. on Berkeley Campus, such as Robert John Russell, Director, and Prof. Mark A. Noll of Wheaton College. These scholars accept the Theistic Revolution Theory.

For a well-balanced view, I choose Christian scholars in different schools of thought of Creation hypothesis.

Personally and professionally, I always maintain a fair and balance treatment

of any subject under discussion so that we Christians have a broad view and unity in our philosophy of bio-sciences.

1. Bernard Ramm, 1954

Christian View of Science and Scripture.

Wm. Eedermann Publishing Co., MI

In this book, Prof. Ramm (Bethel College and Theological Seminary, St. Paul-Mpls., MN) advocated the Progressive Creation theory. At the same time, he endeavored to develop a Christian philosophy of life science. His objective was to harmonize Christianity with Science, with four major themes, pp#22.

a). The doctrine of Creation is fundamental to Christian and Biblical theology,

b) Science needs the light of revelation,

c) Revelation needs the perspective of science, and

d) Both science and theology are fundamental human pursuits, p## 33-37.

These four major points are indeed dicta , and universally valid and important.

Then, *Prof. Dr. Ramm* also points out:

a) Mistakes peculiar to the theologians: He has been un-sympathetic with science, or suspicious of it, or fails to understand science.

(1) To identify a given worldview with its science, with the Bible

(2) To derive too many empirical or specific data from the general assertions of Genesis 1, for example, the conflict between Aristotelianism and science, not Christianity with science. Try to prove minute points of geology, biology, botany or anthropology from it is impossible, and should not attempted.

b) Mistakes common to both theologians and scientists:

(1) Theologians and scientists may pronounce some scientific theory as final, and this can cause conflict. Theory is not final, hypothesis is not a fact. Premature judgment by either scientist or theologian may cause unnecessary conflict.

(2) They fail to be keenly aware of the imperfections of human knowledge in both science and theology. Scientific theory is somewhat fluid under our feet. The same is true with exegesis.

(3) The misinterpretation of Bible by scientist or theologian. For example, the creation of the universe is at 4004 B.C. If the scientist insists that the Bible teaches that the earth is flat, or heavens solid, or that there are pillars supporting the sky, or that the entire solar system came to a rest at Joshua's command, or universal flood. Both scientists and theologians must exercise unusual care in their interpretations of the Bible.

c) *Mistakes peculiar to scientists:*

(1) They have an anti-religious attitude. No knowledge of whatsoever can be learned without some sympathy or kindly feeling toward the system. Dogmatists are in sciences as well as in theology.

(2) Opposition to Christianity at the level of science is in many instances simply localized or vocalized opposition to Christianity in general. Therefore, anti-Christian man takes pleasure in making the gap between science and Christianity as wide as he can make it. In this instance, the gap between science and Christianity is in reality the gap between faith and un-believe.

(3) Scientists tend to be emphasizing scientism, i.e. exalting scientific method and scientific knowledge with reference to philosophical construction.

(4) Those who hold a scientism philosophy tend oversimplify both scientific methods and reliable knowledge. Reductionism is the effort made by scientists to explain the complex by the simple, and the higher by the lower. What is left un-mentioned is as vital to the scientific methods and knowledge as what is mentioned

(5) They pay no attention to teleological thinking such as validity of purpose, meaning, intelligence, wisdom and guidance as possible categories of the real.

(6) They have a prejudice against the supernatural. If theologians and scientists have been careful to stick to their respective duties, and carefully learn the other side when they spoke of it, there would have been no disharmony between them.

Prof. Ramm summarized the Christian worldview, as follows:

1) Theistic

2) humanity not to worship nature and/or created things

3) God creates the world with spiritual purpose

4) Personal intelligence

5) He sustains the world by His providence

6) Regularity of nature manifests the consistency of God

7) The laws of nature are the laws of God

8) Uniformity of nature is a biblical notion, and

9) we do not deny natural law. When we so speak, we are speaking religiously, theologically, metaphysically and teleologically.

Prof. Ramm and his conviction and philosophy of science, as contained in this book have great influence among evangelical Christians and scholars. Many of them subscribe to his viewpoints and conviction. In 1960, he relocated in California, teaching at Baptist Seminaries. He continued his scholarly writings. Then he published: 1) Protestant Biblical Interpretation, in 1970, and 2) Offence to Reason, 1985.

Evangelicalism in USA:

Prof. Ramm, Dr. Carl Henry, (the first Editor of *Christianity Today*)   and Evangelist *Dr. Billy Graham,*   together with Francis Shaeffer, Arthur Gasser, Kenneth Kantzer, Joseph Bayly, Vernon Grounds, Stan Guthrie, Edward   John Carnell, James Kennedy and many others began an *evangelical movement in USA.* Books written by some of these evangelicals were "*Evangelism and Social Responsibility*", and "*Evangelicals for Social Actions*". The magazine "*Christianity Today*" became the bastion of voice.   As evangelicals, they believe and uphold biblical, and fundamental teachings and doctrines. In addition and above that, they emphasize 1) maintain a positive attitude toward sciences,   2) encourage Christians to take part in social justice and work in the society, as the Lord Jesus had taught them "not out of the world, but sent into the world.", and 3) maintain an open-mind and ecumenical in attitude to fellow Christians and others, and willingness to cooperate with them. It is true that many Chinese churches

worldwide are fundamentalists, with some evangelical. It is due to the teaching and influence of former missionaries. That could be the reason why Chinese churches in Taiwan, USA and elsewhere are liable to split, even due to tiny differences in practices, not very much in doctrines. In a way, evangelicalists and fundamentalist are not easy to delineate. They are mixed together., being evangelical in one time, and fundamental in another time. The American Christian churches in USA elsewhere are by and large more evangelical in theology and in practices than churches. No one is able to pinpoint it any time. It is true also with Chinese churches.

Before I wrap up this section, let me cite what Prof. Ramm and his commentary on Creation as mentioned in Genesis narrative, as follow:

"Genesis, Chapters 1ˢᵗ-3ʳᵈ give us a "divinely inspired reconstruction" and "theology by narration". It is Hebrew reflection on creation and on the nature and origin of sin expressed by telling a story.. Adam is both "generic figure" and "the person who in Jewish history" is the head of both the Jewish people and human race. The Bible and Science, therefore, are both correct when viewed within the proper perspective of each. I opt neither for the rejection of geological findings that point to a great age of human kind nor for a purely mythological interpretation of the Biblical narrative. Geology and Scripture share historical character of the Genesis narrative."

"God was the Author of both creation and redemption, being built from the assumed agreement between true science and the Bible."

2. Bruce R. Reichenbach and V. Elving Anderson, 1995

"On Behalf of God: A Christian Ethic for Biology

Wm. B. Eerdemans Publishing Co., Mich.

Dr. Reichenbach was Prof. of Philosophy at Augsburg College, MN, and Dr. Anderson was a well-known Prof. of Genetics at Univ. of MN. Both of them were well-known evangelical Christian scholars. They have written many books on philosophy and ethics. As the sub-title shows, this is a book on Christian ethic for biology. This is what I have intended to introduce to the Christian public.

They wrote that "in Genesis Chapters 1 and 2, God the Creator of the universe gave three commandments to Christians as stewards, i.e. *1) Be fruitful and increase the population to fill the land, 2) to rule the land as the representatives of the Ultimate Ruler, and 3) to work with and to care for the*

property of the Owner. Stewards have these "tending functions." To conclude, "nature is so important that God seeks to renew and re-create it, partly through His stewards".

By and large, what these two scholars have written could be summarized in four categories:

> *1). The Lord's commands to Christian stewards:*
>
> *a) be fruitful and increase in number,*
>
> *b) to rule over the universe, and*
>
> *c) to care for the universe.*
>
> *In both qualitatively and quantitatively.*

2) Christian stewards and stewardship,

3) Moral and social responsibility, and

4) To utilize man's intellectual faculty

 a) in subjectivity

 b) in imaginative creativity, objectivity, and

 c) for human health and environmental protection.

To elaborate them as follows:

1.The Lord and his commandments to Christian stewards:

When God, the Creator and Sustainer creates both male and female in his image, then He gives us three commandments. As stewards, we have to utilize/exercise our God-given faculty, wisdom and intelligence to fulfill these functions, both qualitatively and quantitatively. Modern methods are readily available. We utilize them to fulfill our obligation, but also for the benefit of humanity for the present generation as well for the coming generations. We have to exercise them with moral responsibilities to God and to our society at large. This is an holy and solemn responsibility.

In the "garden", the snake as metaphorically conveyed to us was a very cunning creature. It is the agent for temptation for evil and downfall. God has created us with a free will, choosing between good and evil, to obey or to disobey. Therefore, humanity has to know and to realize what is God's will, and to what extend we have to carry this command, not violating moral and social responsibility.

The Lord God first created male and female in his image. On the basis of this first creation as a pattern, we conclude that a) Christian family is the union of one male and one female. 2) The union is both inclusive and exclusive; the most

131

intimately and physically, emotionally and spiritually. 3) Procreation is their responsibility between husband and wife. 4) to care and to nurture is far more important, Pregnancy is a matter of 10 months or more, the nurture is life-long, both qualitatively and quantitatively. 5) how many children is up to the parent's decision, in consideration of their ability, resources and planning. 6) caring and nurturing include both physically, intellectually and morally.

Thomas Melthus advocates population control in view of the resource available in this planet. So better people is more important than more people. Prof. Baron Commoner of Washington Univ. in St. Louis, MO also advocates the limited resource in this "planet" as "a spaceship" in this huge universe. Conservation and preservation are not optional.

In 2012, when Christine Legarde, the International Monetary Fund Managing Director was in Washington, D.C. for a meeting., she asked not only European policy-makers, but leaders worldwide, to take decisive steps to meet the *world crisis*. She said that, "We are facing triple crisis: *1) economic crisis, 2) environmental crisis and 3) increasingly, a social crisis.* "The planet is getting warmer and warmer, with un-known and possible dire consequences down the line. The global economy is still rocked by turmoil, with uncertain prospects for growth and jobs. Across so many societies, the gap between the have's and have not is getting wider, and strains are getting fiercer. As these threats feed off each other, we all need to pursue joint solutions by restoring financial stability, accurately pricing energy including renewable sources and promoting inclusive growth. The world leaders will gather to reduce poverty, advance social equity and ensure environmental protection. Sustainable development must spring from macro-economic and financial stability, adequate supply of energy, and renewable sources and promoting inclusive growth. What Ms. Christine Legarde said in public is very much what we evangelical Christians have been proposing for both governments and private citizens.

Food scarcity, security and policy:

By 2050, it is estimated that there will be additional two billion people on this planet. With parts of the globe have been facing resource shortage, especially food scarcity and security, we should consider now what it will take to feed the 9 billions' people.

To address the future food supply, we should address a series of complex, inter-connected and inter-woven , often conflicting issues. Logically, we have to produce more with limited farmable land on this planet. We must do so in a way that promoting water and soil conservation, and improve the livelihoods of farm workers and agricultural communities.

The demand of a collaborative effort, the likes of which we have not yet attempted on such a large scale. We must reach out broadly and engage the entire food and agricultural supply chains: from organic and mainstream farmers and

ranchers to nutritionists, development experts, processors, retailers and consumers.

We are grateful to the growing interest in our societies in food production from an increasingly diverse set of stock-holders, we are at a tipping point in food and agricultural policy, and have a unique opportunity to make changes today, and will impact future generations. From consumers who are concerned about health, and supporting their local economies to the military, which is worried that over a quarter of 17- to 24-year-olds are too over-weight to serve their country. People are finding that food and agriculture policy must be a national priority.

Prof. Martin Rees, former Chairman of the Royal Society of London, in the 150th years' celebration of the Evolution theory by Charles Darwin, on the campus of Cambridge University pronounced/discussed his viewpoint and conviction of *"Our Final Century"* of humanity. He warned us that man-made change in world environment, and the advancement of technology if not under control, would lead us to the last century of this universe of ours! (cf. the last chapter in this book).

We can't influence change from within our current silos, and without asking: what is inspiring? What is working? And what isn't? Perhaps, most important is what is missing: what we need is a new and systematic approach. Otherwise, when problem is tackled in one place, like squeezing a balloon, it will simply bulge out elsewhere. Four of the ten leading causes of death in our USA are related to diet and obesity. At the same time, in 2012, more than 16 millions of children lived in food insecure households, where they do not have consistent access to adequate healthy food. As a latest study estimates that in an egregious squandering of precious resources, more than 600 pounds of food are wasted per person per year in USA. This is very alarming!

If it were easy to reduce food insecurity or improve nutrition, we all would be healthier. But so much goes into our dietary decisions: culture, social influences, media and forces of supply and a demand, As a collective, all of us must work to address questions such as: What steps must been taken to encourage people to eat smartly? How should the roles of the public sector, agricultural producers, food manufacturers, distributors, retailers and advertisers be re-defined so there is a larger supply and demand for healthy foods. Many good ideas are percolating to address this problem: from controlling portion size in restaurants to doubling federal food stamps to mandating more physical education in schools.

The medical community, health and school officials, the foreign assistance and development community, food marketers, agricultural producers and civil society, including private foundations, must come together to answer these questions, and take action, collectively.

At its core, the future of any food system depends on the viability and vitality of its farm business and workers. More must be done to help them thrive. Because of the high cost and low incomes, in farming enterprises, many workers small and

medium-sized farms depend on off-farm income and a need of second or third job to sustain their livelihood. Because farms differ by size. Use of hired workers, types of commodities raised, and production practices, they each have unique sets of workforces issues.

Clearly, we need a systematic approach to agriculture and farming practices in 21st century. The first step in driving positive change is to develop a broad framework for actions. You and I should eat every day, we should care about ensuring access to nutrition and affordable food for ourselves, our families, our communities and future generations.

2) to rule over the universe: This includes a) to watch for, b) to protect c) to guard and 4) to manage. Humanity as steward has to make use of whatsoever atmospheric and environmental sciences have learned and proposed. We utilize the principles and the methods to fulfill our responsibilities. We are not "playing God" but as instruments in his hands for his work.

In modern society of ours, there are many problems and practices which were not known in ancient society. For example, abortion, in vitro fertilization, biological insecticides, genome project, embryonic cells and cloning, extinction of bio-species are current subjects. The Scripture gives us only general principles. So, it is up to Christian stewards to exercise their faculty, learning and ability to discharge their stewardship.

3) As stewards, Christians are required to be faithful and devotional (1 Cor. 4:2), and administered with gainful and profitable responsibilities (Matt. 25:14-30). This is profitable for this generation, and also for generations to come.

3. Keith B. Miller, Ed. 2003

Perspectives on an Evolving Creation

Wm. B. Eerdman Publishing Co., MI

This book is a compendium with articles contributed by more than 21 scholars, 528 pages. They all belong to the school of *Theistic Evolution*, now known as God's Fully-Gifted Creation. They profess to be called as *Bible-believing, evangelical Christians*. They believe/accept God's creation as the first stage of God's overall creation, then with "the *inborn seed*" as proposed by Augustine, as the second stage of God's over-all plan of creation. Their specific name is "Theistic Evolution".

In the preface, Dr. Miller, as Editor said, "I am convinced that science is not only a profession but also a Christian vocation. Part of that vocation is using scientific knowledge to ascertain God' creation……. *The objective of this book is thus to provide a wide-ranging and authoritative evaluation of evolutionary theory from those with to deepen our understanding of God and of our calling as Creation's stewards as an orthodox Christian perspective* …. Our scientific

and technological society is in desperate need of a theological foundation which can give its purpose and moral value. While we are orthodox Christians with a high view of Scripture ….. We all represent well-informed and thoughtful integration of science and faith.   pp # xi to xiii.

1). *Prof. Howard Van Till* of Calvin College, MI, wrote in Chapter #14, as follows: *" Let's us be candid. We Christians disagree about a lot of things….. Christians have not been able to agree on their evaluation of scientific concept of evolution. Some see this concept as one that is clearly and forcefully forbidden by scripture teaching. Others see it as something on which is silent, an idea that will have to be evaluated on its scientific merit alone.   Some see the evolutionary paradigm as an un-welcome threat to cherished Christian doctrines, while others welcome it as a stimulus to re-articulate historical Christitan theology in light of what the science has learned about creation."*

2). *Prof. Robert John Russell,* the Director of Center for Theology and Science, at Univ. of Calif. on Berkeley campus, wrote in Chapter 15th: "Special Providence and Genetic Mutation: A New Defense of Theistic" as follows. *"For over a century, Christians have found ways to accommodate or to integrate the Darwinism theology of biological evolution into systematic and philosophical theology.   God's action plays a key role in biological evolution". Pp#356.   God is the Creator of the universe per se; without God there would be no universe, nor would the universe exist moment by moment. Granted that God maintains the efficacy of nature, whose regularities, which we call the Law of nature, manifest God's faithfulness and rational intelligibility as Creator. ' pp#345.*

3). *Prof. Mark A.* Noll of Wheaton College, wrote in Chapter 4, " Rev. Charles Hodge and B.B. Warfield of Princeton Theological Seminary, *refused to countenance any permanent antagonism between the two realms of human knowledge: what humans, by God's grace, could discover about the natural world (which owed its origin to God), and*

135

what they could learn, again by grace, about the character and act of

God from special revelation in the Bible. Pp#62-63.

For brevity and economy of space in this book, I quote only three scholars and their conviction and viewpoints. Readers could consult the book for more and for more detail. This book is a wealth of biblical knowledge as well as scientific knowledge. You will be rewarded with dividend if you read it.

I wish to take this opportunity to say a few words to my Chinese fundamental Christian clergymen and Christians about the school of Theistic Evolution, and those who believe/uphold this Christian doctrine of creation in relation to evolution theory. My experience over these years tells me that these colleagues and fundamental fellow-believers feel un-easy about it or hear it. Their face will become "flushed red" once they hear the name of this school of creation hypothesis. So many of them consider them as "compromisers", and "on the other side of the aisle", to a point of short of calling them "heretics". What a shame it is. They close their intellectual window! Those who accept theistic evolution theory are evangelical Christians, and have a high regard of the Scripture (as Dr. Miller said in his Introduction). They accepted creation as the first stage of God's creation, and evolution or evolving as the second stage of God's overall creation. As I said before, evolution theory should not be interpreted exclusively as anti-Christian. Above all, this is a group of evangelical scholars who accept both creation and evolution. We should consider them as fellow-saints of the same body, God's Church.

In Aug. of 2009, when both Christine and I attended the 150th anniversary festivity of publication of the Origin of Species, we had the privilege of meeting both Prof. Brian Heap and Prof. Denis Alexander, Director of Faraday Institute for Science and Religion at Univ. Cambridge. We enjoyed the Christian fellowship with two fellow saints/ scholars. Prof. Brian Heap, who was former Foreign Secretary, and then Vice President of Royal Society of London, and was a church elder at Cambridge. We also met Prof. Denis Alexander. In fact, I bought one of his book, being entitled in "Creation or Evolution: Do We Have to Choose?" 2008, by Monach Books, I read it, trying to find the answer to the question Prof. Alexander posted on the cover page. The answer was that you could accept both creation and evolution at the same time, without any compromise.

In US, Prof. Francis S. Collins, who was, years ago Prof. and Dept. Chairman of Human Genetics, University of Michigan. Now, he is the General Director of National Institute of Health (NIH). In his book entitled in "*The Language of God: A Scientist Presents Evidence for Belief*", by Simon & Schuster. Inc., 2006. In reading his book, you will find that he also accepts both creation and evolution.

In addition, there are hundreds of such evangelical Christians who subscribe this school of scholarly thought. We should respect them. We should embrace them as our brethren in Christ.

Conclusion

In this chapter, I take the liberty of using three books, written by Christian scholars, showing their philosophy of bio-science. In a way, their philosophy of bioscience is mine too. If it is not so, I would not quote what they presented in their books and scholarly writings.

Thomas Aquinas once said, "If you want to know God's mind, first you have to exercise your own mind." In other word, to know God's revelation, human intelligence as being endowed by God should be fully exercised.

Prof. Stanley Jaki of UK, in his book entitled in "The Road of Science and the Ways to Good, 1978, Univ. of Chicago Press, once wrote,

"Science has an ethical dimension. If the road of science is leading to the ways of God, this has to be also true of the connection of science with ethics. The scientific discoveries are the fruit of the painstaking self-exertion of genius."

pp# 247 & 307.

To sum up, I shall say that the Lord of universe and Creator who created us in his own images, with value and dignity, and also with endowed intelligence. With our intelligence and learned disciplines, we exercise our innate capacity to find out in what ways He created us for his glory. Therefore, we evangelical Christians should have an unified philosophy of science and nature. This is what the two chapters I present them to the Christian public.

Literature Cited

1. Bernard Ramm, 1954, 368 pages

   Christian View of Science and Scripture.

   Wm. B. Eerdman, Publishing Co., Mich.

2. Stanley L. Jaki, 1978   120 pages

   The Road of Science and The Way to God

   Benner Publishing, UK

3. Bruce R. Reichenbach and V. Elvin Anderson 1995, P353

   On Behalf of God: A Christian Ethic for Biology

   Wm. B. Eerdman, Publishing Co., Mich.

4. Arthur Peacocke, 2001

   Paths from Science toward God

   Onward, Oxford, UK

5. Keith B. Miller, Ed, 2003

   Perspectives on An Evolving Creation.

   Wm. B. Eerdman, Publishing Co., Mich.

6. Francis S. Collins,   2006

   The Language of God: A Scientist Presents Evidence for Belief.

   Simon & Schuster Co., N.Y.

7. Denis Alexander,   2008

   Creation or Evolution: Do We Have to Choose?

   Monach Books, UK

Chapter 10
The Ways to Knowledge and Truth

"Christianity and science are different responses to nature.

They nevertheless share some vital components,

i.e . both are faith community activities.

We should consider them allies rather than enemies.

Dr. Charles Hummel

In Chapters 8 and 9, I have presented rational approach to philosophy of science in general and bio-science in particular. In this chapter, I shall present some other ways by which we could arrive at knowledge and truth.

In his public ministry, the Lord Jesus said that "man shall not live on bread alone, but on every word that proceeds out of the mouth of God." (Matt. 4:4). What the Lord Jesus teaches his disciples in those days and to us in this time is this. There are two kinds of living philosophy. One kind   is to live on bread alone. Everything is material, the life-style is materialistic.   The other way is to live on both bread and the Word of God. In other word, one is material whereas the other is non-material. He does not belittle the bread, but we live on more than bread. What things other than the bread? To me, mental to intellectual to spiritual realms or life. Man is made of body (material, physical), soul (emotion, mind and intellect) and spirit. All these three areas of the "total human being" have to be satisfied. Therefore, in our human society, there are libraries, museums, theaters, music concert halls for us to avail of. All these will provide the ways we could arrive at knowledge and truth. In Christian church, we do teach the human beings worship God by the spirit. "For God is spirit, those who worship Him must worship in spirit and in truth. (John 4:24).

A. The different ways in acquiring knowledge:

1. Creation of knowledge: Based on what we know, launch into unknown territory or new frontiers.

2. Discovery of new knowledge: a)   discovery of new things, & b) acquiring new knowledge of   existing thing, etc.

3. Systematization of knowledge: a) categorizing & b)systematizing.

4. Integration of knowledge: a) merging & b) unifying.

5. Transmission of knowledge: a) teaching & b) printing for transmitting

6. Dissemination of knowledge: a) publicizing   & b) multi-media

7. Archivization of knowledge: a) storining & b) upkeeping

8. Application of knowledge: a) translating & b) using.

B. The different ways of knowledge:

1. Inspiration: music, poems, painting, and religious inspiration.

2. Instinct:

3. Rational search and research:

4. Meditation

5. Revelation

6. Contemplation

7. Perception.

Briefly elaboration as follows:

1. Inspiration: George Handel (1685-1759) was inspired by the Holy Spirit, with the scripture verses he had memorized, with his music talent he composed the symphony "Messiah". In Christmas season, when we sing this Messiah either in a concert or in church service, we all are inspired/moved/touched by the Spirit. Automatically and unconscientiously we echo with quiet singing or deep meditation/ in our mind and spirit. Beethoven, Bach, Malher and Tchaikovsky; Felix Mendelssoln (1809-1847),Frederic Chopin (1810-1849), Wolfgang Amadeus Mozart (1756-1791), and many other renowned musicians left a legacy behind with their work. Every time we hear them in concert hall, we all are inspired and echoing with our mind and spirit.

The Italian painter, Mr. Michaelangelo painted so many wonderful and exquisite paintings. When both my wife and I had the privilege of visiting St. Peter's Cathedral and Sistin Chapel, we saw his painting on the ceiling and on the wall, you and I are spontaneously   inspired, and admired his great work.

When we go to the Smithsonian Art Galleries in Washington, D.C., where we could see so many   exquisite   paintings by various artists. We are inspired, often with a sense of awe. When go to cathedral, we feel the difference while songs/hymns were offered by those who have genuine Christian faith. They will singing with feeling and spiritual conviction. Do you feel differently when some one else in reading the Bible? Those who have genuine faith in God and his redemption in Christ, will read them with spirit and feeling, as compared with those who just read the black words on white paper, with no feeling. All these will make people feeling differently!

Scientists or non-scientists couldn't deny the fact that inspiration is a way we

could attain wisdom and spiritual knowledge.

2. Intuition: Every body, man or woman has instinct. Probably, female has more. When you see something which is either provocative or inductive, immediately you have intuition. For example, when you see a painting or photograph which provokes to lust, or to hate, which is quite different from inspiration. You know the difference. Sometimes, instinct will lead to destructive conduct or emotional action. You know that you have to exercise restrain or discipline.

3. Rational search and research: Scientific research work is in essence a rational activity. Based on what you know or which has been report, you, using your mind and training, try to extend what you know with rational methods, using logical reasoning. It differs from what you compose a music or doing a painting. Often, you succeed in what you do. Keeping in mind, this is the only way we could attain knowledge. There are many other ways as well.

4. Meditation: Meditation is a spiritual and intellectual exercise. This is often practiced by those who have genuine religious faith, such as Christianity or Buddhism. Those who exercise this often, share their experience by reaching a "non-self" situation. They could go on without foods for a couple of days. Christians also do exercise this either before or after church service. When they come to a church service, they take the time on meditating some scriptural verses or a hymn or a sermon with inspiring contents. They could attain what the Psalmist saying "He leads me to lay down in green pastures, He leads me beside quiet waters."

5. Revelation: Those who believe omnipotent and omniscient God will often feel they have received revelation when they read Holy Scripture. They not only read the words, or hearing a hymn, and through meditation and contemplation, they receive revelation from God by the Holy Spirit. Christian ministers receive divine revelation when they prepare messages by meditation on the Scripture they read, and through prayers. Likely, their messages will contain something which is above their own reasoning or meditation.

6. Contemplation: Contemplation is something that falls between rational searching and spiritual meditation. Philosophers, artists and those who have genuine religious faith often practice this. Through it they will reach either a rational or spiritual condition, and receive something that is above ordinary thinking. Contemplation could lead noble activities and products.

7. Perception: Perception is a reaction or feeling when see something which is so inspiring. It will eventually lead to give you a permanent feeling of beauty and nobility. This is one kind of intellectual and mental exercise.

These are seven ways people could attain knowledge or wisdom, depending on prevailing condition and also one's intellect and mental state. In one way or

another, every one experiences it from time to time. Those who specialized in psychology or psycho-analysis suggest that these probably have much to do with one's education, profession and religious faith. It varies from case to case. Genuine religious feeling is not superstition. It is something that their faith is so dynamic and so practical. Education and experience have something to do with it. But it is not confined to it. In other word, those who have had a good education could experience some of them, and also those who have very little formal education could do the same. They are not conditioned by education or professions.

Chapter 11
Believe and Christian Faith system

"The Bible reveals the mind of God, the state of man, the way of salvation,

the doom   of inner, and the happiness of believers.

The doctrines are holy, its percepts are binding,

its histories are true, and its decisions are immutable.

It is the traveler's map, the pilgrim's staff,

the pilot's compass, the soldier's sword and the Christian's charter.

It contains light to direct you, food to support you, and comfort to cheer you.

It is a mine of wealth, a paradise of glory and a river of pleasure.

Read it to be wise, believe it to be safe and practice it to be holy.

Read it slowly, frequently and prayerfully.

It should fill the memory, rule the heart and guide the feet.

Owned, it is riches; studied, it is wisdom; trusted, it is salvation; loved, it is

character; obey it, it is power."

Author unknown

Introduction

As Christians, whenever we are meeting on university campus, or in our church, we share our faith with our friends/colleagues. With sincere desire and friendship, we do this. Once awhile, at the end of our conversation we would invite them to accept our Christian faith. Not too infrequently, our colleagues would reply, "if you could show me the person Jesus Christ,   I see him. Then, I would accept your Christian faith". Or "demonstrate what the Bible teaches is practically true.". "If I practice what is being a good man, don't you think that is good enough?" There are so many and many answers to our invitation.

To many of our friends who do not have any genuine religious faith, Christianity is superstition or lack of rationality. If this is the case, it would take quite a bit of conversation to come to the point. To the others who have in one way or another come into contact with Christians or Christianity, it will be less challenging. Let me analyze their answers, with much objectivity as possible.

143

In essence, *what is faith, intelligent and reasonable faith?* Do you have to see it in order to believe? Not seeing it makes it impossible to believe? Why you have to accept the Christian Bible, Or Christianity only? Can you scientifically prove your Christian faith, or substantiate it with circumstantial evidence? What difference it would make if I take any other religion? How much Christianity influence the society, family and personal life-style? I shall endeavor to answer these questions in the following paragraphs.

1. What is believing/faith? Its consequences?

In principle, faith is based on partial evidence or fact you either can see it now, or take it as reasonably trustworthy. It is true that there is *a part of it which is not seen. It is based on what you see* or you could accept, you reason the part which is not seen now whether it is true or reasonably reliable. *If you could see everything now, why you and I have to believe it*? It is because something which is not present and not seen now, but you and I believe it reasonably reliable in the past, or even in the future. This is what we refer to   belief. Seeing everything necessitates no belief. If we could see everything present as fact, why have we to believe? Is this true or logical?

For example, you and I believe that years ago there was a well-known scientist, Dr. Albert Einstein. Why? And why you believe it? It is because fact that at the present time, even though, he is not here, Dr. Einstein once lived, and made great contribution in science, you and I believed. There is a relativity theory he had formulated. There are many photos available, through he is not here.

Again, you and I believe that in China there was a great man, the founding Father of the Republic of China, Dr. Sun Yet-Sen. The reason why we all believed it is because at the present time, there is partial evidence of his life and his contributions. Based on the partial (incomplete) evidence seen, then we extend it to the part of the evidence which is not here. If they can be seen and touched upon, then you and I do not have to believe. In theory and in practice, to see is to believe is illogical.

The genuine faith we Christians talk about and we take it wholeheartedly is not something just talking about. It is not a lip service. *Genuine faith as we Christians practice is that which will affect/effect the whole human being, including your mind and your intelligence, eventually it will lead to action.*

In Christian church doctrine, there are two aspects of the dynamic faith and resultant action.

In Christian church history, there are many such examples. In the early era, when Roman Emperor Nero falsely accused the Christians for the burning of part of the Rome city. Consequently, he condemned them to death, and had them fed to lions in the Collosium. It was so cruel and inhuman. Yet, those early Christians accepted the false accusation, and the death penalty. After the gates of

the Collosium opened, those dear saints were led out.   The Christians knelt down before the crowd and the Emperor, and accepted the verdict, they prayed earnestly and sincerely. They accepted their fate without a word of   protest. They all died! How could they do so?   *It was their genuine faith in God, and in his eternal judgment!*

In China, while in the Qin Dynasty many western missionaries were falsely accused by the Qin Government, they were condemned and be beheaded. Before the execution, these dear saints sang Christian hymns, with praising to God, before they were put to death. *What made them so differently and so courageously*? It was their genuine faith in God and in his eternal judgment! *Faith affects the whole person*!

Years ago there was a dear Chinese Christian old lady, Mrs. Xu who lived in Hong Kong. Her son was a multi-millionaire. Mrs. Xu saved every single penny of what her son had given to her. Then, she gave it to missionary work. She donated her site of burial to a Chinese minister, as a sincere sacrifice. It was because of her sincere faith in the Lord Jesus, and the resultant work/action to others.

Rev. W. H. Griffith-Thomas, 1861-1924, once defined faith and Christian faith as:

"Faith affects the whole of man's nature. It commences with the conviction of the mind based on adequate evidence; it continues in the confidence of the heart or emotion based on conviction. It is crowned in the consent of the will, by means of which the conviction and confidence are expressed in conduct"

Prof. John Polkinghorne, former President of Queen's Colllege, Univ. of Cambridge   once said:

"Christian faith is not blind. It has its rational. It begins with the existence of omnipotent God as supreme Intelligence, which is partly seen in the created world as evidence, and partly unseen so we have to take it by faith. To those who believe, the genuine faith has profound impact on their daily practical living".

"The book of Hebrew 11:1   in the New Testament of the Bible says:
"Faith is being sure of what we hope for, and certain of what we do not see. Jesus the Savior while in public ministry, said that "Believe in me, also in the Father."

Faith is an important ingredient in our daily living. It is essential and important for us. Without it, we could not live a day at all. When you are sick, you go to a medical doctor for assistance. You have to exercise faith in your medical doctor, and what he is to prescribe for you is what you actually needed. If you do not have such a faith, you do not know what is to do. When you keep your saving in a bank, you have to believe that the bank is fully credited, and your money is 100% guaranteed. When you go to have a meal in restaurant, you believe that the chefe is not crazy, adding poison to your meal. When you drive a car, you believe that every body will observe the signals. Otherwise, you will be nervous. No faith, then the whole society will be in chaos. Faith is a very important and necessary ingredient in our lives and daily living. To those who have grown up in the west, faith matters. Personally, you can not be human until you are religious. Or put in the other way, you can not be religious until you are human. *Faith is a part of your being*. History tells us that many wars were waged because of misguided faith, or no faith of any kind.

2. Who is Jesus, and why we believe in Him?

How could you get to know a stranger, or some one else you meet in social gathering? By and large, there are three ways. The first and most common way is *his own introduction by/with words*. The second way is *the introduction by your friend or colleague* whom you know well. The third way is the fact that *some one else writes a letter of introduction*. The other possible way is in time past you read news about him/her in a journal/newspaper, with his/her picture on. So you have some knowledge of him/her. This is a possible way.

First of all, *Jesus of Nazareth was a historical. He claimed that he is the Son of God* (John 10:36, 30). *Extraordinary claim demands extraordinary evidence.* In various time in his life, indeed, Jesus proved/exemplified his claim. Then, John, the Baptist seeing him, he proclaimed that "*behold the Lamb of God*" (John 1:29, 34 & 36).

Jesus Christ himself substantiates/exemplifies his claim with the following facts:

a) Jesus performed a miracle of transforming water to wine at the wedding in Canaan (John 2:1-11). This was the first one of many miracles He performed to substantiate his own claim. Consequently, the people and also the public dully acknowledged it.

b) Not long after that, Nicodemus, a Jewish man, an official and well-schooled in the Old Testament, acknowledged Jesus "a rabbi comes from God, for no one can do these signs that you do unless God is with

him". Nicodemus' acknowledges Jesus was based on what he had known the Jewish claim of being God Himself.

c) In the four Gospels which are the authentic historical record of his life, his teaching, miracles performed and his final death on the cross:

   1)Jesus healed a man's son who was on the verge of death, with his words (John 4:46-54), the second miracle.

   2)He fed five thousand people with two fishes and five barley loaves. With this miracle, Jesus claimed that he came from the heavenly Father, giving them "true bread of God from heaven,….gives life to the world. Consequently, the crowd acknowledged Him as "truly the Son of God'. (Matt. 14:33).

   3)He restored man's sight from blindness;, and later on He restored another two blind men's eye sight. and

   4)He could rebuke a great storm on the sea, and brought a great calm. The people who were with Him marveled, saying " what sort of Man is this"

The four Gospels recorded many other miracles, and how the people of his day publicly acknowledged Him as the Son of God.

Saul of Tarsus who was a rabbis and well educated under Gamaliel, very well-known scholars in those days, persecuted the Christians with every bit of his energy. Then, he was genuinely converted while he met Jesus in a vision while he was traveling on the road. His conversion was genuine and thoroughly, he was blind for a few days. Consequently, *he was transformed, becoming the great apostle with a mission to reach the Gentiles.* No one could transform a man so thoroughly and so amazingly. In a later day when he was persecuted for his work among the Greek-speaking Jews, He testified that he had seen Jesus in a vision, and accepted Jesus as his Savior. In his life time, he traveled extensively, bringing the good news to people in the Roman Empire. No greater apostle than Paul of Tarsus was known in his time, also in later years.

The history of Christianity and his church of more than two thousand years are full of examples! Any one has doubt could examine the record.

Jesus of Nazareth is a wonderful Man, a Model, a Healer, a miracle Performer; above all He is a Savior, and God-Man (God incarnated)!

Some one else who wrote a historical document as follow:

"While Jesus was in the world, he did not have a spot to lay down his Head. Now, there are homes by millions, welcoming Him to come, occupying the seat of preeminence. He did not write any music or compose any song, yet today in the world of ours there are thousands and thousands of hymns and songs which praise Him as Savior and Lord. He did not write a single volume of book, yet in the world there are countless books which are written of Him and about Him, his teachings and his example. He never led a group of soldiers, yet today there are millions and by millions who would like to claim to be his soldiers, following Him. While he lived, he never conquered any nation, yet in the world to-day, there are many kings and Queens of nations who acknowledge Him as Lord of Lords, King of Kings. Who is He?

Jesus. He is God, the only God and Savior!"

3. Why believe the Bible, not any other holy writ?

The Bible is a compendium of sixty six books, with thirty nine in the Old Testament and twenty seven in the New Testament. There were more than forty individuals, including kings, statesmen, scholars, philosophers, poets, physicians, fishermen, farmers and common citizens who contributed their writings. These contributors lived in different eras/ years, and in various places. They did not meet for a conference on a common theme or what they were going to write about, and the division of labor. The whole writing itself lasted more than one thousand and six hundred years. If all these were the cases, likely, their writings would be varied, and probably contradictory in many ways. If this were the case, no body would be surprised at all.

Yet, the whole Bible is in such a unity and in harmony, having only one theme, with one message. The message is how God, the Creator of the universe has been dealing with people in different ages. The central message is the coming of his only begotten Son, Jesus of Nazareth to dwell among the people, redeeming them from their sins with His substitutional death on the cross, then rising from dead and ascending to sit on the right hand of the Almighty on high. It is something like a great symphony with so many pieces of instruments, yet in such a harmony and unity. All these testify that the Bible is unique, and is the Book for centuries and centuries. It is being translated into many and many languages, including tribal. It is read by millions and millions of people all over the world. It is the most popular book, being sold in astronomical number. It is because that the Bible deals with the essential and most important issues in humanity, and also gives the ultimate answer to human quest.

In both the Old Testament and New Testament as well, there are prophecies,

foretelling something in the future. All these have been either fulfilled or authenticated with discoveries by modern science research work. One outstanding example is the prophecy pertaining to the Israelites and their recovery and re-establishing it as a nation. Archaeology and paleontology are full of recorded cases for any one who is willing to examine them with searching mind.

Let me be more specific:

1) In Old Testament, there are many so-called *types (of shadows)*, and in the New Testament there are ***anti-types***. For example, the Israelites celebrated their Passover with slaughtered lamb and blood. In the New Testament, there is so-called antitype, i..e. Jesus of Nazareth offered himself as a lamb of God, being sacrificed for the sins of the people of the world. You and I have to read them along these lines in order to appreciate the spiritual meaning of them.

2) The Jewish Talmud is a compendium of books of wisdom. Even today, the learned Jewish folks read them every Sabbath day celebration. The Holy Bible is much more than what the Talmud could offer, being more than any Greek sages and their philosophies.

3) Any one of us read the Psalms, the Proverbs and the Ecclesiastes, will be impressed with the wisdom and aspiration, in addition to the beauty of the pose and the language.

4) The four Gospels written by Jesus' disciples and followers are written in simple and straightforward language. Learned scholars and people with very little education could understand it and appreciate it. They could absorb the messages conveyed and applied in their daily living.

5) The Bible does not necessarily prove the existence of God with evidences in the world. The Bible affirms the existence of God, and his manifestation of wisdom and power in the world.

6) In the world population, a very high percentage is Christians with different ethnical differences and languages. They sincerely consider the Bible as their "Book".

7) Modern sciences could assist Christians and scholars to search, to know and to prove the existence of God, his love and his care of the people of the world.

4. Why should I believe Christ Jesus, and Christianity?

Religion exists in every civilization of the world. This is shown by/in anthropological evidence. Some religions are primitive whereas others are highly sophisticated. In essence, it is the spontaneous outgrowth of inner aspiration to divine. To such a divine, man responds with a sense of reverence, and in worship. On the human side, there are some individuals who are somehow endowed with supernatural wisdom and intellect who will be able to perceive the inspiration and reception codified or a code of belief and a system of theology.

Christianity is altogether different. The only God Jehovah moves people to write down what is revealed to him through inspiration. The Spirit of God will move such man to write down what God reveals to him. The Spirit will move him and guide him, utilizing his training, knowledge and wisdom, to write down what is inspired. The Holy Script is totally inspired by God, using human language or word to reveal God's wisdom, will and percepts.

The Founder of Christianity is a God-Man by the name of Jesus, born of virgin Mary. He grew up in Jewish civilization and religious culture.   While he was 30,Jesus of Nazareth first launched "*a movement*" known "Nazareans" which was composed mainly with Jewish people, and Greek-speaking Jews, much later with so-called "Gentiles" (people other than Jews). He called them out of the world, becoming his disciples, with a genuine sense of self-denial, sacrifice and service with love. The Movement was considered by the Roman Empire at that time as illegal, underground and rebellious. That was the reasons why they met in homes and underground meeting places. He also called them out to form a new humanity, known as "the Church", a community of individuals of renewed mind and hearts. Above all, these disciples were/are willing to bear their crosses, rendering meaningful services to the world. The message delivered by Jesus, and even his disciples was/is a message of salvation, and renewed community living and personal sacrificial services. Nowadays, these groups become the organized church in existence all over the world. It is because that while He was living and ministering, he proclaimed that He was to build-up his church on the rock of genuine faith and sacrificial services.

In later time, his Jewish disciples such as Peter, James and Matthews went around in Judea, proclaiming Jesus as the Messiah they had looked forward for his coming. Then, Paul of Tarsus, a learned rabbis, together with his co-laborers went to region beyond and in the Roman Empire, declaring Jesus as the Savior of the world. Also, they wrote different letters (epistles known), expounding the truth of believing and living both individually and collectively as a Church. For quite awhile, the infant church abode with the so-called apostles' teaching. As years

went by, these early disciples passed away. Then, local elders and shepherds were raised up, carrying the torch forward. The teaching of these early disciples became gradually varied and diluted. To maintain its authenticity and trustworthiness, the early Christians and church-office bearers (elders and overseers, or bishops) called for conferences. In addition, they collected the writings and edited them to one book what we now have, The Bible, and evangelical church teachings.

The early Christian Church in the apostolic era or/to post-apostolic era, as described in the Book of Acts, which in essence is a book of early church history and her practices both locally and universally.

The early Christian Church was one of those social entities under the Roman Empire and her rule. Then, the Roman Emperor, Constantine once in a vision saw Jesus and his cross, was converted to Christianity. He became a firm believer and disciple. Out of his love and devotion, he proclaimed Christianity as the state religion, and all the citizens became Christians. That was *why there was a Roman Catholic Church (Catholic means universal)*, which was in existence with the early apostolic Christian Church side by side for quite awhile. Even today, there are both Churches in existence, with minor differences.

By and large, the evangelical Christian, Protestant so-called, Church was/has been more in zeal and in missionary services. Beginning in early years, they sent missionaries to various nations of the world, a movement seen today. Owing to the different nations as sending entities, with both man power and financial resources, they adopted different names, for example: Lutheran Church, Episcopalian Church, Presbyterian Church, Methodist Church, Mennonite Church and the Church of the Brethren, and so on. They exist not only in those western countries but also in eastern countries such as China, Korea and India and so on. In the early years of the movement, the eastern churches, due to infancy and limited resources, relied very much on the western churches. That was quite true for several centuries. Then, the 20th century arrived, it was an era known as an independence movement worldwide. Not only the civilian governments became independent and self-supporting, but also the churches as well. This was/is a historical characteristics. So nowadays, you see this independence and self-reliance almost everywhere and anywhere.

Though the Christian church is, by nature and in term of administration, independent. Yet the essential/inherent nature of *Christianity or the Church is international in scope and in practice*. In Christ, or in Christianity, as the New Testament declares that there is neither Jew nor Greek. All is one in Christ. So, Christianity is universal in nature and in practice. As Christian, you or I could go to any church in any locality, you or I will be cordially received into mutually profitable and enjoyable fellowship. In Christ, *Christians are brethren. There is one family in worldwide scheme*.

Please do examine all these. You will find Christianity unique. It is because the Founder, Jesus of Nazareus is unique. His personality is unique. His teaching

is unique.

In summary, Christianity is characterized by/with:

1).Her uniqueness, though she has some features in term of ethics common with other faiths.

2).One God, monotheistic.

3).He is the Creator of the cosmic universe, and He upholds it even today

4).This universe demonstrates his deity, wisdom and power.

5).Jesus of Nazareus is the One died in substitution for sins of others. On the third day He rose from the dead. Now, He is seating on the right hand of the almighty.

6).He is coming again to this world, though the time is not announced specifically.

7).The Holy Bible is a holy book, being inspired and profitable in teachings and living.

8).The Christian church is universal in nature and in practice, with high standard of morality in daily living.

9).The faith is rational, though could not proven with rational, scientific research.

10).Christ Himself, with his teaching could change drastically man's life. This change is so radical and so completely. Christians refer it as "new birth".

5. *Is Christianity or Christian faith scientifically sound? Can it be authenticated by scientific methods?*

In essence and in principle. Christianity and her teaching are in the domain of theology, a domain far greater than the domains of both philosophy and science. Therefore, *it is beyond what science and scientific methods could prove or authenticate*. The Bible had been written long and long before modern experimental sciences came into existence. Therefore, the language of the Bible is pre-scientific. It is true that in the Bible, especially in the Old Testament, description of nature and natural phenomena were included. So, the description is not scientific, yet non-scientific. It is religious. It is philosophy. It is theology.

Additional information:

Mr. Lee Strobel, a journalist, and with law degree from Yale Law School, and formal legal affairs Editor of Chicago Tribune was an atheist. His journey from atheism to Christian faith was documented in Gold Medalion, with several books entitled in "The Case for Christ", "The Case for Faith", "The Case for a Creator" and "The Case for Real Jesus" (Zondervan, 1998-2002).

In these books, he investigated the evidence for Jesus Christ, the Bible, The Creator and many other historical incidences recorded in the Bible. With a searching attitude and spirit, he gathered evidences from his journalist's search for truth, even scientific studies on them, With questions in mind, he interviewed Christian scholars such as Craig Blomberg, Bruce Metzger, John McRay, Edwin Yamauchi and many others. Consequently, he had "eyewitness, documentary evidence, corroborating evidence and scientific evidence of the Savior, the Bible and the historical incidences". Invariably, he proved all these are true and as fact, and published them in books. There are too many for me to mention them in this chapter. Readers who are interested in knowing these or in reading these books, I give one book in literature cited at the end of this chapter.

In later years, Mr. Lee Strobel became a Minister of the Gospel. He served as teaching Minister at Willow Creek Community Church in Chicago, and Saddleback Village Community Church in Orange County, Calif.

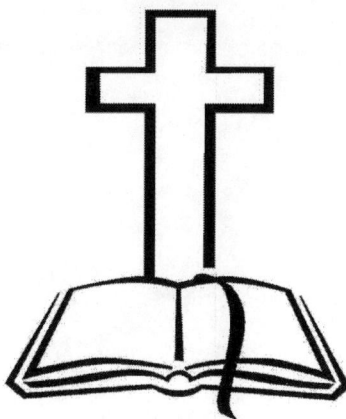

Conclusion

Christianity is in essence is rational religion. It was found by the God-man Jesus of Nazareus of Israel more than two thousand years ago. While on earth, Jesus proclaimed that He is the Son of God, being confirmed by his miracle, teaching and work. The Bible is inspired by God, as the most reliable document. Christians are his disciples. They believe Him as the Son of God, and accepted Him as the Head of the Church. With means at their disposal, they endeavor to proclaim Him as the Savior of the World.

Literature Cited

1. The Holy Bible.

2. Lewis S. Chafer, 1947

    Systematic Theology,   Vols. 1-8

        Dallas Theological Seminary Press, TX

3. Alfred Edersheim,   1883

    The Life and Time of Jesus: The Messiah.

        MacDonald Publishing Co., McLean, VA

4. Millard J. Erickson, 1983

    Christian Theology

        Baker Book House, Grand Rapids, MI

5. Fred. F. Bruce,   1969

    New Testament History

        Doubleday Co., N.Y.

6. Stanley L. Jaki, 1975

    The Road of Science and the Ways to God.

        Univ. of Chicago Press, IL.

7. Lee Strobel, 1999

    The Case for Christ, a Journalist's personal investigation of the Evidence

    for Jesus. Zondervan Publishers, Grand Rapids, MI.

Chapter 12
The Doctrine of Creation: Five Schools of Thought

" There is little real conflict between science and religion properly understood. God is the author of both modes of knowledge, so there can be no fundamental disagreement. Scientists and theologians should tend their own distinct sphere of knowledge and not intrude upon the other's intellectual territory."

Rev. John Henry Newman

"The origin of the universe and the living things can be talked about not only in scientific terms, but also in poetic and spiritual language, an approach that is complementary to the scientific one. Indeed, the Judeo-Christian tradition describes the beginning of the world in a way that is surprisingly similar to the scientific model."

Prof. Victor Weisskopf, Physicist at MIT

The doctrine of Creation is an important Christian and theological doctrine. In principle, it is derived from the book of Genesis, Chapters 1 to 2, the creation narratives. The book of Genesis is a book of beginning, i. e. the beginning of the cosmic universe; of humanity and also of the living things on earth, and their subsequent horizontal development. The Creator, the Lord God Jehovah is the only and true God that both Israelites and Christians worship. The Bible is God's Word, his revelation to humanity. The Bible is consisted of the Old Testament and the New Testament. It is the Christians' Holy Book. The Old Testament (OT) is written in Hebrews language, an ancient language. The first book of OT is Genesis. It is the creation narratives. It is written in Hebrew language, an ancient language. The creation narrative is derived from the book of Genesis. This is what this chapter is all about.

The Hebrew Bible uses the ancient words, rich in implications. For example: the word of creation has different words for it, implying different cannotations. For example: God creates out of nothing, the Hebrew word *bara (creation ex nihilo,* creation out of nothing) is being used, and used   three times, as follows:

155

1) Genesis 1:1, the creation of the cosmic universe,

2) Genesis 1:21, the creation of conscious living things, and

3) Genesis 1:27, the creation of Adam in His image.

In Hebrew language, there is another two words, *asah* and *yasta*, which are very closely related to "being created", with different implications. In the creation narrative, these words are translated into English, as "brought forth", "yielding", "bearing fruits", "be fruitful and multiply", "swarm with" ," bring forth" and "made", indicating innate capacity of growing or further development. In Gen. 1:27, both bara and asah are used, when Adam and Eve were created.

The different Hebrew words used and their sequence in appearance, used in expression do convey different meanings. *These are the subjects of rational studies*, and scholars over these years do pay attention to them in their research. *Scholars also pay due attention to what modern sciences and their result* could afford any assistance in their searching for meanings. On account of these emphases, *scholars do differ in their conclusions*.

The Hebrews and Christians do believe one God (i.e. monotheistic) who is the true God, the Creator of this cosmic universe, humanity and the living things. *He is unique and omnipotent and omniscient*. He is the true God whom they worship and proclaim. The other gods made by hands or with crafts are no god at all, being not worthy to be worshipped. *The book of Genesis presumes the existence of God the Creator*. God forbids the worship of false gods in any form by his chosen people.

It is true that in the creation narratives, *there are descriptions of natural phenomena*, such as light and darkness, seasons and vapor. These are necessarily scientific descriptions. *They were written long before the birth of modern experimental sciences. Though the narratives are not scientific in essence, being non-scientific, yet they are not un-scientific (cf. Prof. William Phillips,Nobel Laureate, 1997)*.

Sciences such as biology, geology, physics and astrophysics with their findings do aid Christian scholars in their searching for meaning. With this, scholars do arrive at different conclusions.

Therefore, all these have made Christianity unique and different from other religions of the world. With all these research, scholars do arrive at five schools of thought on creation. This is what this chapter will discuss and their relationships.

Why five schools of thought on Creation narratives/theory:

In the following paragraphs, I shall share with readers (of evangelical and fundamental Christians) of what I have studied in the Holy Scripture and Christian

literature, and also current literature by others the five schools of creation narratives. In dealing with such a subject, it could easily cause misunderstanding. In order to avoid this, I endeavor to explain in this paragraph.

I myself am an evangelical Christian in both doctrines and practices. I accept the Holy Scripture as God's revealed Word, for our instruction. So, what I share with you is an *evangelical Christian conviction and viewpoint*. But, I know that other Christians reading/looking at the Scripture from a different position may have different conclusions. It is logical and scientific.

Therefore, they may have a different purview and conviction. We should not be surprised. What we Christians should avoid it is this. Do not label some one else with a different conviction as wrong or heretic.

Five Schools of Thought of Creation:

On the basis of their report and development, there are five schools as follows:

A. Theistic ~~*Creation,*~~ Evolution *renamed as Fully Gifted Creation,*

B. Progressive Creation,.

C. Fiat Creation, renamed as Scientific Creation in 1999, and

   Biblical Creation   in 2002,

D. Intelligent Design, and

E. Theistic Evolution.

A. The summaries/primaries of Five Schools:

a. Theistic Creation or Fully- gifted Creation:

There are two major points;

1.God, the Creator of the cosmic universe. He is the source or the first cause. He first creates. He creates with "Seed" with it. With the seed, it has the innate capacity of further development or growth in accordance with God's overall creation plan. This was what Augustine of Hippo first proposed. This embraces natural sciences and their principle/methods as the second phase of God's creation.

2.Of all the God's creation, man created is the last and the most important one. Every created is for the humanity as ultimate. Accordingly, God could create the first humanity (Adam and Eve) directly, or use the other choice. God could take some creature who was so akin to humans, as hominoid.   To such hominoid , God breathes into, such a hominoid will become a living soul (This method mode

of creation is generally referred to as "derived creation").

3.What the Lord your God created at the beginning is not what we see them in this universe nowadays. He might have created several kinds. Then, in a horizontal fashion what is created could develop and vary in appearance. This could take much longer time than what we human beings could observe them in one generation or two. In essence, those who believe and uphold this school of thought take both bara and also asah or yasta in sequence. They take science and scientific principles in the second phase of God's overall creation, i.e. development. As the English name implies, Theistic (God) evolution (evolvement).

4.Those who believe and uphold this school of thought consider themselves as evangelical Christians, having a high view of the Holy Scripture.

b. Progressive Creation or Development Creation:

There are two important parts:

1.God the Creator creates, i.e. creatio ex nihilo, supernatural creation out of nothing. It is a miracle.

2. After that, the Lord God creates succeeding generations in progressive fashions with increasing complexities, creation de novo, over time. This is the innate creation potential, development in horizontal fashion. The second phase of creation could be accomplished in six days, not necessarily in chronological sequence, as evidenced by modern sciences. This is referred to as creation actual.

3.The Lord God upholds the cosmic universe today with his wisdom and power, with care and dull attention. The Lord God gives humanity whom he had created the wisdom and knowledge so that humanity could take proper care in order to fulfill God's overall creation under the leading and guidance of the Holy Spirit. Those who believe and uphold this school of thought fully accept God's creation as described in the Holy Scripture and also the scientific principles and methods in the second phase of God's creation.

For the sake of future and further explanation of other schools of thought, I shall mention some additional and secondary variations/differences between these two schools of thought.

1)Day as described in the creation narrative is solar day, what humans could see it by themselves.

2)The "gap" between verses 1st and 2nd in Chapter one in Genesis could be accepted, if they choose so doing, as a time of renovation or waiting for new creation.

3)Both Theistic Evolution and Progressive Creation accept science in

creation actualization, as the second phase of God's overall creation.

4)They decline to take completely the evolution theory. It fails to give an accurate account of life's beginning. Also, it fails to explain why humans are unique and different from other higher animals.

5)Scholars of these two schools are Trinitarians.

6)They accept the full authority of the Bible, including the creation narratives.

7)They acknowledge that humanity as created does have a sense of morality and value before God, and accept fully his commandments.

c. Fiat Creation or Scientific Creation or Biblical Creation:

The important components of this school are as follows:

1)Scholars and theologians believe and uphold that what God commands/says: "let there be", then there will be what he says. He is the Authority, therefore He commands. This is what Fial means.

2)The cosmic universe is a young earth, less than 10,000 years.

3)God creates in six solar days, the day of 24 hours of Gregorian calendar.

4)Hebrew word "bara" is used in Gen. 1:1, 21 and 27; asa and yasta are used in the other verses. In other words, there are creation ex nihilo and creation.

5)God creates humanity in his own image, a human being as we know him today.

6)Noah flood was universal, the original creation was destroyed.

7)Not accepts Day-age hypothesis, no gap between Gen. 1:1 and Gen. 1:2.

8)Accept micro-evolution, no macro-evolution.

9)Literal reading and interpretation of the Creation narratives.

10)They profess that they are fundamentalists, errenoucy of the Scripture; the Bible is beyond the science domain, therefore scientific methods could not prove or disprove what the Bible says.

d. Intelligent Design:

This school is altogether different from the other four schools in principle:

1)It does not begin with God and his creation. Instead, it begins with

scientific rational research, using empirical methods.

2) With observation and formulating hypothesis, then they design experiments to falsify or verify the hypothesis. With experimental results obtained, they look at both macrocosm and microcosm. With macrocosm, you see regularity and beauty in this world. With microcosm, for example, a cell with interlocking and interwoven molecular mechanisms, an irreducible complexity. All these could not achieved or arrived at with evolution theory and its mechanisms

3) At the end, they conclude with/by inference that there is an intelligent design and an Intelligent Designer, God the Creator.

e. Theistic ~~Creation~~ Creation

This was first proposed by two British scientists/naturalists in 1996. Then, in 2002 it emerges again in literature. The main points of this school is very much approximated to Theistic Evolution. God creates the universe, humanity and living things. The Creation narrative does not tell us how God creates. Humanity as being created is different from other higher animals in quality. With God's breathing, man becomes a living soul.

I. The secondary differences and importance:

These five schools of thought also differ from one another in some minor areas. I shall briefly describe them as follows:

A. The question of "day":

The Hebrew word for day is "yom". In the Old Testament, this word appears more than one thousand times, being use in different circumstances. Once awhile it referred to an epoch. In other times, it denoted a long period of time or a season. It is true that the word was used to refer to a solar day more than any other use. On account of these various uses, scholars could not agree to have one conclusion.

B. Scholars of the five schools agree that the Creation narratives in Genesis was theological, i.e. monotheistic, being testimonial against the background of polytheism in the surrounding nations in ancient time.

C. In addition to being theological, there is additional attribute:

1. Chronological and sequential in nature: Fiat Creation,

2. Poetic: Theistic Evolution,

3. Picturesque   and poetic: Progressive Creation.

D. The question of "gap" between verses 1 and 2 of Genesis Chapter 1:

1. Yes, it has: Theistic Evolution,

2.No: Progressive Creation and Fiat Creation.

E. The age of earth:

1.Old earth: Theistic Evolution, Progressive Creation,

2.Young earth: Fiat Creation.

F. The age of humanity:

1. Less than 6,000-10,000 years: Fiat Creation,

2.More tha 10,000 years: Theistic Evolution, Progressive Creation.

G. Relation to natural sciences:

In general, all scholars accept development with variation in horizontal fashion after creation, especially the mechanism for variation. It is a matter of how far you go.

The relationships among Five Schools:

A. Common denominators and important differences:

1.They all hold a high view of the Holy Scripture. They are creationists, being either fundamentalists or evangelicals.

2.They all realize the different Hebrew words denoting creation ex nihilo (bara) and creation and then development (yasta or asah)

3.In the secondary phase, they do differ, i.e. to what extent they accept what natural science and report could offer to their exegesis.

4.To Evolution theory, they differ in acceptance in degree, not in mechanisms for variation.

B. Scholars do differ in some minor points, such as "gap", "Noah's flood" and "age of earth and humanity".

We all know, these schools have come to existence more than one thousand years. So many scholars over time took part in formulation and conclusion. Even in one school of thought there were many scholars taking part. In minor points they differ also. No one has absolute assurance of what is the right answer. It is a matter of approximation.

II. Historical development of these five schools:

A. Theistic Evolution/Fully Gifted Creation:

This is the oldest school. Saint Augustine of Hippo first proposed/advocated this hypothesis. First, the Lord God creates, He creates it with "Seed" in it. So, then or in later time seed germinates, grows and develops. Thomas Aquinas further affirmed it, elaborated it. The Roman Catholic Church accepts this school of thought. In Protest circle, the Christian Reformed Faith, i.e. the Presbyterian Church accepts it. (cf. Howard Van Till, 1999).

B. Progressive Creation:

In the 1950, Prof. Dr. Benard Ramm at Bethel College and Theological Seminary in St. Paul, MN published his book entitled in "Christian View of Scripture and Science". In this book, Prof. Ramm, as an evangelical scholar, not only formulated philosophy of science and bio-science, but also advocated "Progressive Creation". With his training in biology and then theological education, he was well qualified to do so. He writes such a book, with breadth and depth. The book won Moody Year Book Award. What he proposed has an immense impact on the thinking of Christian scholars in his time.

In late 1950, I came to pursue my graduate studies at University of Minn,majoringin microbial physiology of parasitism, and virology. On the university campus, I purchased some leisure reading books, Dr. Ramm's book was one of them. I undertook a personal intensive study, I found it very evangelical and thought-provoking. I wholeheartedly accepted his Progressive Creation as the leading theory. I had the privilege of attending some of his lectures at the Seminary. I found them very profitable. In my Christian ministry in later years, I referred to his book and used the progressive creation in presentation.

In 1960, Prof. Ramm relocated in Calif., teaching at Western Baptist Theological Seminary, with further writing on Christian exegesis and apologetics. Several books entitled in "The God who Makes a Difference: A Christian Appeal to Reason", 1972; "Biblical Authority: Is Scripture Alone?", 1977 and "Offense to Reason" 1985.

Together with Evangelist Billy Graham, Dr. Carl Henry (first Editor-in-Chief of Christianity Today) , Prof. Ramm, and some other scholars, thcy were considered as leaders of American Evangelical Movement. What they advocated was the positive attitude toward science (instead of negative attitude by majority of Christians and clergymen), and active participation by Christians in social services to the society.

C. Fiat Creation/Scientific/Biblical Creation:

United States of America was found by those pilgrims migrated from western Europe and England to the New World in 16th century. These pilgrims were devout Christians, suffering from religious restriction on their faith. While they migrated to this new continent of North America, they intended to establish a Republic on sound Christian principles, honoring God in government and in public life style. At the same time, they remembered so well that in the old countries Christianity as a religion was under state control. The Christian Church and her clergy were so much depended on the State and her treasury for supporting and supplying. There was no freedom of conscience. The Christian Church became an attachment to secular authorities. What the pilgrims wanted most was the separation of the state from religion/ separation from religion from the state.

Once this republic of United States of American was firmly established, the Constitution did stipulate the separation of the state from religion. The Bible was highly esteemed as the Holy Book by both the people and government officials. Down in the south, in the so-called Bible belt, this was even more so. So, Creation, probably Fiat Creation at that time, was one of the core doctrines of Christian Church. It was taught exclusively in public school systems.

In 1925, in the city of Dayton of Tennessee, a substitute teacher by the name of John Scopes, taught evolution theory in biology class. This was considered by the City School, as a breach of the teaching code. So Scopes was penalized with a fine of $100.00. This caused a great deal of dissatisfaction by a percentage of citizens. They protested against this decision, filing a suit against the School Board in court. The Civil Liberty Union (CLU) which was a secular and liberal organization in USA. With a team of lawyers and resource, with a secular bent, joined in this protest. Eventually, those who upheld creation were defeated. The general mode in the south was in lowest elbow. The Christians and fundamentalists wished that some body else could come and rescue them from terrible disgrace!

In due time, Prof. Henry Morris of Virginia Polytechnic University with Fiat Creation arrived on the scene. Under his leadership he and his group were greatly welcome. As a result of this, *the Fiat Creation hypothesis was most popular among the Christian fundamentalists*. Then, Dr. Morris created the "Creation Research Institute and Society" with thousand and thousand members. Financial support and donations came to endorse his endeavor. He wrote a paperback book entitled in "*Scientific Creationism*". The periodicals from the Institute amounted to millions in circulation, not only in USA but also worldwide. Consequently, Scientific Creation has become the most popular school of thought among the Christian fundamentalists in USA, probably elsewhere as well.

One of the cornerstones of US democracy was the fact that textbooks of biology and other subjects were chosen by city/local Education Board. The Board

members were elected, varying in composition from years to years. Beginning in 1950, the State Boards of Education in USA were citizens being slanted to evolution theory. As a result of this trend over the years, evolution theory has been taught to the exclusion of Christian creation.

Prof. Morris, with his associate Dr. Duane Gish, a biochemist, and many others launched an "Equal Time Movement" in USA. They went to the School Boards and presented their argument for equal time of teaching both evolution and creation. Eight times the School Boards declined.

Above all the District Court ruled that "creation in invoking God is not in the context of naturalistic biological science, as ground rule." The scholars of Intelligent Design jointed them, the 9th time the Court upheld its position.

During the time of campaign, then in Christian Church at large in the 70th was debating another issue of Biblical Inerrancy. The adherents embraced this as one of their components. Somehow, moral degradation was also incorporated. Then, radical extremists somehow began hair-splitting, name-calling and finger-pointing at others who did not subscribe to their view. It generated so much non-charitable feeling, even hostile attitude. This trend regrettably spread elsewhere. Christian testimony to the world has suffered greatly and unnecessarily. World Christian leaders wish that this could be somehow stopped before going to be worse.

Personally, I also encountered unpleasant incidences when I was invited to conduct seminars on science and faith, especially in California where Creation Research Institute with earnest advocates was located. As evangelical Christians we should differentiate our primary from secondary. Our first fidelity is to the Scripture. Our secondary is to which school of thought we accept. They are two different things. We could maintain our high degree of fidelity to the Scripture, yet we could accept different school of thought of creation. Do not take the second as the first, and vice versa. Above all, our Christian fidelity is to the Scripture. One school of thought about explaining the Scripture is not the Scripture itself.

D. Intelligent Design (ID):

As early as 1802 Irish Theologian, ***Rev William Paley published his "Natural Theology: The Watchmaker"***. He used the watch as a metaphor, illustrating the designer of a watch, i.e. there is a Watchmaker in this cosmic universe. When you see a watch, naturally you will think of a watch-designer or maker. Though he is not standing in front of you, you do speculate of such an individual, by inference. The individual parts of a watch can not incidentally jump together by themselves to form a well-designed and functional watch. In science, we do accept inference as one of the valid method of making conclusion.

The hypothesis was by and large acceptable to the academic world at that time. This was thirty some years before "The Origin of Species" by Charles

Darwin (1839). In fact, Darwin referred to Paley's hypothesis in his writing.

Logically, Christians in general have accepted this as a valid view in seeing both the macrocosm and microcosm. In 1980 or thereabout, a number of North American scholars such as Drs. William A. Dembski (mathematician-theologian), Michael Behe (biochemist), J.P. Moreland (philosopher) and Hugh Ross (astronomer-physicist), with their semi-scientific writings not only endorsed this watchmaker hypothesis but reinforced it. The hypothesis became more popularized. A large number of Christian scholars joined them in their efforts.

Then, these scholars joined those who were trying to propose equal time movement. Once again, in 2005 the Kansas State School Board voted again their attempt. This was the 9th time of denial.

1. Some other issues:

Theologians, Bible scholars and scientists keenly realize the challenging task of biblical exegesis and interpretation of the creation narratives, as follows:

(a)The Old Testament has different Hebrew texts. So are the Greek texts. By and large, these texts vary very little. In interpretation, attention should be given to this.

(b)The Hebrew language is an ancient language, having her advantages and disadvantages.

(c)The creation narratives have threefold objective: as a theological document, historical record, and testimonial against the heathen nations (with idol worship in the surrounding nations). They were written many thousand years ago.

(d) The Hebrew language is a rich language. There are many synonyms and antonyms. Yet, the paradox is that the description of time, the gender, feeling and emotion are not exact as compared with what we do nowadays. This will be further elaborated in the following paragraphs.

(e)The Lord God creates living things and human beings, without giving us the details as to which methods or ways He used to create. It is to this area, modern sciences, especially biology to molecular biology, physics and chemistry could contribute. Due to the inherit nature of sciences, the methods could differ, and vary from time to time.

(f)Creation by definition is a miracle, which can't be repeated. It was done without witnesses. Therefore, at present time what we could speculate is to approximate at the best.

(g)Scholars of different schools endeavor to use modern sciences as supplementary. The difference is a matter of degree, or to what extent they go.

(h)The conclusions they arrive at are varied.

A. The unique characteristics of Hebrew language:

There is no gender (male or female) in usage, somewhat being similar to old Chinese. The descriptive terms for day and night are "the light" (day, the sun, the bigger light) and "the darkness" (night, the moon, the smaller light). The Hebrews deliberately use lunar calendar. The moon (full moon or half moon) is an indicator of farming seasons and time of seed-sowing and harvesting time. A day is counted from the sun-set of one day to the sun-set of the next day, with darkness and light as alternating periods. The emotional seat are liver and the other visceral organs. Their counting is comprehensive, being not specific enough by our standard. This is true in describing the kinds of marine life in both water and ocean, etc. The Writer records/writes what he could see and observe, without asking the questions as to the mechanisms, why or when, or how long or short, and what?. He knows God and he knows God creates. The narratives are in essence theological more than anything else. Using the language we use to-day, we may say their lack of specificity. Because of all these, we could not use science or scientific language to read the narratives. In essence, it is not scientific recording, yet not non-scientific (i.e. the narrative does describe natural phenomena and facts which are in the domain of science of to-day).

For years, the Jewish people used their language on daily basis. They knew the ways they describe phenomena and living animals or plants. So, therefore, we can not say deficiency, but uniqueness.

B. The age of heavens/cosmic universe:

The English translation is correct (Chinese version uses singular number, heaven). In the beginning God creates the heavens and the earth. The Hebrew word "bara" is used here, meaning creation out of nothing (creation ex nihilo). No date, no time, no method is given.

As Christians you accept the record by faith. Yet, living in the 21st century, people who are not in the Christian circle would not be satisfied with such a simple answer. They could ask for or demand specific information or data. This is what Albert Einstein once said "the incomprehensible is made comprehensible". For this very reason, there are scholars of Christian faith or otherwise have endeavored to answer this question with specific data. So, in this section, I shall quote what scientists/scholars have so far proposed to explain this issue. This is given for your information. Keep in mind, what they have done is approximated to the real situation, at the best.

Heavens and earth are different in nature, so the scientific methods scholars/scientists have used varied. For search and research on the age of heavens, the methods used are astronomical, such as telescope for observation, asteroids

and other bodies coming down from the sun, then analysis of them, calculations and deduction. For earth, methods such as geological, fossils and radioactive dating techniques, etc.

a). The age of heavens:

Jewish scholar, Dr. Gerald L. Schroeder who had received his Ph.D. degree at MIT, with a major in physics and astrophysics is currently teaching at Weismann Univ. in Israel. So far he has written a dozen books on science in relation to faith. As a Jewish scholar and of faith, he knows the Hebrew language. He accepts the Hebrew Bible. He is a disciple of Jewish scholar, Moses Maimonides, and wholeheartedly accepts his commentary on the Old Testament. In 1997, he published his book entitled in "The Science of God: The Convergence of Scientific and Biblical Wisdom". In Chapter 3, With mathematic formulae and calculations, he concluded that the cosmic universe is both 6-days and 150 million years' old, using C-14 dating system; by cosmic rays smashing into nitrogen (N) atoms near the top of earth's atmosphere; isotope separation mass spectrometers; and radioactive decay series of uranium-thorium; with the universe in expansion.

He concluded with two figures: one is six days, the other is somewhere within the 100-200 million years, taking the average as 150 million years. Why two figures? He advocates two ways to look at the universe. One is from God's perspective, that is 6-days. The other is from man's perspective on this earth, 150 million years. They are not in conflict.

b). Dr. Hugh Ross, the founding scholar of "The Reason to Believe" in Calif.:

Hugh Ross received his Ph.D. degree in astrophysics at Univ. of Toronto, with Post- doc experience at Calif. Institute of Technology. Among his many writings, one book entitled in "Creation and Time: A Biblical and Scientific Perspective of the Creation-Date Controversy" is very much pertinent to this quest. In Chapt. 9, he gives his view on the age of heavens, with the following table:

Measuring methods	Age of the heavens: 10 billions' years
Relaxation time of star cluster	>4
Erosion of Mercury, Mars	>4

Star stream interaction in galaxies	>8
Expansion of the universe	1.55 +_ 4.0
Color-luminosity fittings	18.00 +_ 2.4
Deuterium abundance & mass density	19.00 +_ 5.0
Anthropic principles	17.00 +_ 7.0

The age of universe 17.0 + _7.0 billion- years

c). Prof. Dr. John Gribbin, of Sussex Univ., England, Prof. of Astronomy:

In his book entitled in "The Birth of Time: How Astronomers Measure the Age of Universe", he traced scholars in past centuries such as Lightfoot, Ussher, Lyell, Buffon, Hutton, Lord Kelvin, Helmholtz, Edwin Hubble, Allan Sandage, Gustav Tamman; and George Ellis who had worked on this subject, and concluded differently. Prof. Gribbin considers himself as an Insider, assaying the age of universe.

Prof. Gribbin together with John Ellis, using Hubble telescope in Arizona state and radiometric decay isotopes U- 238 (lifetime 4.51 billion years) U-235 (1/2 time 713 million years) , and other materials, came to the conclusion of 130-150 billion years.

d). American Association for the Advancement of Science : AAAS is the largest Scientific professional society, with more 100,0000 members (naturalists, atheists, agnostics and Christians), publishing the weekly magazine "Science". Their estimate is somewhere in the neighborhood of 140-160 billion years.

2. The age of the "earth":

a). Dr. Richard Bube, Prof. of Electric Engineering at Stanford Univ., an evangelical Christian with Progressive Creationism, has written "Human Quest", with his estimate, using the following materials:

Earth crest cool from molten to its present state

Salinity of oceans/oceanic water

Recession of moon from earth

Transformation of igneous to sedimentary rocks

Radioactive decay of K-40 and Uranium 235

Isotope ratio

Radioactive decay products

Radioactivity of age of meteorites

Rocks and dust from Apollo 11.

Prof. Bube takes the means value: 45-47 billion years.

b). Dr. Jeffrey K. Greenberg, theistic evolution scholar of Wheaton College, IL., using rocks and geo-chemical compositions, with geophysical methods, arrived at the age of the earth, 20 billion years.

c). Dr. Henry Morris, well-known scholar of Scientific Creationism advocates young earth theory, with less than 10,000 years.

d). Dr. Bernard Ramm, of Progressive Creationism, advocates the age of earth, at least 40 billion years.

3. The age of humanity:

This was debated among scholars of both Fiat Creationism and Theistic Evolutionism. For this reason, I shall limit my brief review in following section.

*Scholars of Fiat Creationism/Scientific Creationism/Biblical Creationism:

They calculate the age of humanity on the basis of two genealogies as given in Matt. 1:1-17 and Luke 2:23-28. The two genealogies have so much in common, yet they differ in minor points.

Matthews describes Jesus as the Messiah to the Jews, beginning with Abraham to Joseph, the husband of Mary. From Abraham to David, 14 generations; then from David to Babylonian captivity another 14 generations; then from Babylonian captivity to the birth of Christ Jesus, another 14 generations. Altogether, there are three of 14 generations. The message was mainly to the Jews,

i.e. Jesus as the Messiah, the descendants of Abraham. Luke records from Joseph to Adams, Jesus is the Son of God, i.e. the descendants of Adams; mainly a message to man, the Greeks.

Bible scholars, in their research, discovered that in Matt. 1:1-8, as compared with the record in I Chronicle 2:10-12, several names were missing. Matt. Omits Ahaziah (2 Kings 8:25), Joash (2 Kings 12:1) and Amaziah (2 Kings 14:1). With these names omitted, the Matt. geneology could come have 3 times of 14 generations as parallels. Matthews' geneology includes four women. With these women included in the geneology, Matthews' record is not exclusively from Adams to Joseph. To the Jews, Jesus is the Messiah, a descendant of Abraham, as a royal descendant very important and significant. Knowing all these, scholars conclude that probably when Matthews or Luke collected the geneology data and then have it being modified . After all, the geneology is not given primarily for this very purpose.

In 1642, Dr. John Lightfood, Vice President at Univ. of Cambridge endeavored to calculate the years when humanity was first created, on the basis of what is given in Genesis, Exodus, 1 and 2 Kings and 1 and 2 Chronicles of the Old Testament. With such calculation, he came to the conclusion of 3828 years. This was the first time scholars endeavored to estimate when humanity had been created. Then, in 1950 Irish Episcopal Bishop, Rev. James Usser tried to do the same the second time. He came to a conclusion of 4004 years. This figure first appeared in King James' authorized version, generally referred to as Scoffield Reference Bible. In the early 1950 to 60, the Scoffield Reference Bible was very popular in English-speaking world. Then, the young earth creationism (less than 10,000 years) came into existence as its consequence, and it was popularized.

Many Christian scholars did not endorse it. They thought that 6,000 to 10,000 years were not long enough for the formation of the earth. Based on what they had studied, they counter-proposed the old earth hypothesis. The scholars on these two camps debated and argued. Christian testimony of unity suffered un-necessary. World citizens wish that this would come to an end soon.

In 1999, scholars of three schools met for a dialogue, and in a format of debate and answer. With Christiana virtue of forbearance, representatives of each school presented their basic tenets and in turn, and then debated and reached a consensus. Eventually, they jointly published   a book entitled in "*Three Views on Creation and Evolution*" (cf. Literature cited). We hope that this kind of dialogue for mutual respect could be expanded and extended to other areas on subjects of general concern.

Before we close this section, let me share with you again on the proper use of genealogies. Christian scholars agree that the genealogies as given in both Matt. and Luke to show us both the royal and common lineages of our Lord Savior Jesus. To the Jews, the Lord Jesus was/is the Messiah, descendant of Abraham (the father of faith) and David, being entitled to the royal line, as given in Matt. To

the Greek and the Gentile world, the Lord Jesus is the Savior, the Servant, descendant of Adam, as given in Luke. These are the primary purposes. As Christians we do not have the liberty of using genealogies for the calculation of age of humanity. With names missing further indicates the inappropriate use of them. Beginning in the 1950-60 or thereabout, the Scoffield Reference Bible was no longer attached to the KJV. But, the post-effect even to this day could not be neglected.

*Theistic Evolution/Fully Gifted Creation:

In 2003, a book entitled in "Perspectives on An Evolving Creation" under the editorship of Keith Miller, gave their view. They considered Adam and Eve had lived at least 40,000 years ago.

4. The question/debate on "the day":

In Genesis 1:3-5, "God said, "let there be light, and there was light. God saw that the light was good, and he separated the light from the darkness. God called the light "day", and the darkness he called "night". And there was evening, and there was morning" --- the first day. Gen. 2:1, 2, "Thus the heavens and the earth were completed in all their vast array. "By the seventh day" God had finished the work he had been doing; so on the seventh day he rested from all his work."

The Hebrew word of day is "yom". It appeared more than thousand times in the Old Testament. Often, "yom" refers to a day. But, it also refers to an epoch, a long period of time and geological span of time. The Hebrew count their day from the sunset of a day to the sunset of the next day;, with evening (darkness) and day (light) as alternating , of 24 hours. Also, Gen. 1:16, God made two great lights – the greater light to govern the day and the lesser light to govern the night. This was on the 4th days after vegetation, seed-bearing plant created on the 3rd days. This appears to contradict to what we know plant photosynthesis under sun light. So, Christian scholars have debated on these issues. Was the day a solar day of 24 hours? Was the total creation done in a chronological sequence? How could plants thrive without light? Let me show what and how scholars explain them.

British Old Testament scholar, Prof. Frederic F. Bruce of Sheffield University, in his Dictionary of Old Testament says: There are eleven definitions of days as given by scholars of the past. One of them is in metaphoric and figurative, "a period of natural light, figuratively, one period of alternative light and darkness". Therefore, a day will have a period of darkness (evening) and light (morning and day time). This seems to coincide with the way the Hebrews count their one day from sunset (darkness) to the sun-sunset of the next day. From the 7th day on, God and his creation is still going on.

Jewish scholar, Dr. Gerald Schroeder knows the language well (cf. the age of heavens). He considers the six days are solar days of 24 hours. "Erev" in Hebrew refers to disorder, chaos and mixture; "boker" is the root of "orderliness". In other

word, from disorder to orderliness is what modern sciences have proven the case. So, he believes that the day in Genesis is a solar day of 24 hours, and the creation narratives are chronological. The age of the universe is somewhere in 150 millions' years. In other word, there are two ways to look at it: one is from God's perspective, the other from humanity's perspective.

American astrophysicist, Dr. Hugh Ross and his book "Creation and Time" explains Hebrew words "yom", "ereb" and "boqur" and their differences. There are 3 possibilities: (1) from sunrise to sunset, (2) from sunset to sunset, and (3) one period of time. Yet, he considers   (2) is likely the case.

William Wilson, another scholar considers "yom" a period of time. In English, we often say "the day of my suffering", and "the day I endure the hardship." Ereb" referes to sunset or the end of the day; while "boqer" for sunrise, the beginning of a day. On the 7th day, "no evening and no morning" implies that the Lord has been continually working in new creation. In John's gospel, Jesus once said, "my father works, so do I".

Dr. Bernard Ramm, in his book "Christian View of Science and Scripture", says that "day" is metaphorical, and poetic. The Lord God creates in six times, six solar days of 24 hours, yet not in chronological sequence such as 1st, 2nd and 3rd, etc. It is pictorial-revelatory day (pp#222-224). The Genesis narrative is not a matter of time, but a revelation of an almighty Creator.

In my reading, so far I have not found any adequate answer to the question of photosynthesis by plant (3rd day) without the sun light (4th day). This lends a solid support to poetic or picturesque description of the creation narrative.

5. The "gap" between Gen. 1: 1 and Gen. 1:2:

Some Bible scholars considers a "gap" between verses 1 and 2. They based their reasoning on Isaiah 14: 12, "How you have fallen from heaven, O morning star, son of the   dawn! You have been cast down to the earth, you who once laid low the nations."

Luke 10:18 and Rev. 9:1 refer to archangel Lucifer was casted down as a devil while he boasted and intended to be equal with God. Because of this, the earth was onced ruined, and this was a curse. God had to re-create the world again. This was first suggested by Irish Scholar, Thomas Chadwick, without indicating the length of time of such a "gap".   To this hypothesis, scholars of Fiat creation vote "no". Yet, some Christians of this school accept it so that they could use it as additional condition to meet with the challenge of evolution theory in term of the time. So far, Fully gifted creation and intelligent design hold their silence. Progressive creation considers   it as a time of re-creation, if there is such a gap.

6. The debate on Noah's flood:

In Genesis, Chapt. 6-9 record the floor in Noak's time. Biblical scholars sought to answer the question whether this flood is universal or local. It is true the text, "….the waters increased they lifted the ark high above the earth, and all the high mountains under the entire heavens were covered……every living things on the face of the earth….." so scholars such as Drs. Henry Morris and John Whitcome (in their book of "Genesis Flood), and others of Fiat creation advocate universal flood. This has become a foundation stone of this group.

Prof. Bernard Ramm advocates "local flood" in Asia Minor only. These are what he says, or questions he asks. "The Writer records only what he could observe". "Where comes this huge amount of water if it were universal? The Hemalayan mountain range, and its peak spread more than 2,400 miles. Is volume of water large enough to cover them? Where the water goes and how it is discharged?"

"To take the 2 samples each of all the living things to the ark takes so much time". In addition, geological record indicates local flooding. Many countries do have record of flood quite huge in scale. But, nations such as Japan, Egypt and some in Africa have no record of huge flood". All these questions are hard to give adequate answers.

For scholars of Theistic evolution, with evolution as the second stage of creation, they have no problem with either one of the two theories. As indicated in literature, a high percentage of scholars accept local flood as likely the case.

7. "Each after their kind":

In classification, there are different categories, i.e. species, genus, family, order and class, in an ascending sequence of scope and number. How do we consider/identify to which category "each after their kind"?

Biblical scholars, especially those who have certain degree of training in life sciences consider species, even genus is too narrow in scope. It does not allow any leeway to include the horizontal evolvement of living things. So, many of them do propose "order" or even "class" as what the creation narratives refer to "each after their kind."

8. Creation versus evolution, the debate and the difference:

In my presentation. so far as I could write are as follows: Scholars of five schools of thought accept evolvement or "evolution" in horizontal way. Again, we as scientists have to differentiate mechanisms from principles. Mechanism is one thing, concluding principle is another thing. Mechanisms such as adaptation, modification, struggle for existence, and survival of living things are well-known. They are mechanisms. The question is how far and how much. It is a matter of degree. Those who are in the creation camp do accept these mechanisms as valid. The difference is the final result of evolving or evolution, as a principle. In nature,

we know well that evolving or evolution eventually leads to degeneration/decay. Extinction in large scale is well known, and firmly established in biological sciences. It is in the final conclusion we differ. We, evangelical Christians do accept the horizontal evolution/evolving. In other words, we accept the mechanisms of evolution, they are: adaptation, struggle for existence. What we differ is the final theory. Evolutionists, with randomized mutation and in concert, they advocate evolving for better species, is where we differ.

9. Biblical exegesis:

In this section, I shall devote exclusively to biblical exegesis in relation to science and its principles. Please refer to Chapter 19 for details.

We evangelical Christians in scientific disciplines should pay due attention as to how we interpret the Scripture, especially the Genesis. As I quoted Dr. William Phillip's conviction and the way what Genesis is in its content. It is in essence not scientific writing (non-scientific)   yet not un-scientific. So, in our interpretation, we have to exercise an extra degree of carefulness. It is more so if we interpret it in a literal way (that is literal reading and literal interpretation).   Literal reading or/and literal interpretation has its proper place and usefulness. For example, if we read and interpret "the day" as solar day of 24 hours, and 6 days in a sequence, we may have difficulty in harmonizing with scientific way of reading and interpretation. It is in this area we have difficulty or conflict. As given in this chapter, there is "poetic way" or "picturesque way" or "picture-revelatorial way". We may have to think twice before we announce the way we interpret them. It seems that it is in this specific area we come to the conflict, not only among ourselves with theistic evolutionists (cf. Sections A and B of this chapter), to a greater degree with evolutionists.

10. Prof. Bernard Ramm and his comments:

Let me conclude this chapter with a quotation by Prof. Bernard Ramm, His conviction and viewpoint are what I myself consider most appropriate, acceptable and inclusive.

"Genesis 1 -3 give us a

"divinely inspired reconstruction" and "theology by narration". It is Hebrew reflection on creation and on the nature and origin of sin expressed by telling a story. Adam is both "generic figure and the person who in Jewish history is the head of both the Jewish people and human race". The Bible and science, therefore, are both correct when viewed within the proper perspective of each. I opt neither for the rejection of geological findings that point to a great age of

human kind nor for a purely mythological interpretation of the biblical narrative. Geology and Scripture share historical character of the Genesis narrative."

God was the Author of both creation and redemption, both built from the assumed agreement between true science and the Bible."

Conclusion

Bible scholars, theologians and scientists acknowledge the fact that the study and exegesis of the creation narrative are by no means an easy task. The narrative is written in an ancient language, Hebrew. It is a very rich language with so much in synonyms and antonyms. In essence, it testifies that the Lord God as the Creator. He has an exclusive power of creating either ex nihilo or creating. Humanity is created after his own image. The narrative is both theological and historical. By definition, creation is a miracle which can not be repeated with any modern scientific endeavor. It was written long before the birth of modern experimental sciences. Therefore, it is not scientific, yet not un-scientific.

In this chapter, I endeavor to present the five schools of thought in historical perspective and their inter-relationship. With these we evangelical Christians will appreciate their common denominators. Under the overall creation, there are differences in secondary, even in tertiary points. With these we shall have a mutual respect and understanding.

Some Christian scholars accept evolution theory as the second phase of God's overall plan of creation whereas other decline to have any correlation. In Chapter 13-A, under organismal creation I present an integrated scheme of both creation and evolution, for your information.

Literature Cited

1. William A. Dembski, 1999
    Intelligent Design: The bridge Between Science and Theology.
    IVF Press, Il.
2. _____, 1998
    Mere Creation: Science, Faith and Intelligent Design.
    IVF Press, Il.
3. Gerald L. Schroeder, 1997
    The Science of God: The Convergence of Scientific and Biblical Faith.
    Broadway Books, N. Y.
4. Hugh Ross, 1994
    Creation and Time.
    NAP Press, Col.
5. Richard H.Bube, 1971
    The Human Quest
    Word Books, TX
6. I. D. Morehead, Ed., 1994
    The Creation Hypothesis: Scientific Evidence for an Intelligent Designer.
    IVF Press, IL.
7. Henry M. Morris, 1991
    Scientific Creation.
    Master Books, Calif.
8. Henry M. Morris, 2000
    Biblical Creation
    Master Books, Calif.
9. J.P. Morehead and John Mark Reynolds, 1999
    Three Views on Creation and Evolution.
    Zondervan Publishing, Mich.
10. Malcolm A. Jeeves and R. J. Berry, 1998
    Science, Life and Christian Belief
    Baker Books, Michigan
11. Bernard Ramm, 1954
    The Christian View of Science and Scripture
    William B. Eerdman Publishing Co., Mich.
12. Keith B. Miller, Ed., 2003
    Perespectives in an Evolving Creation
    Wm. B. Eerdman Publishing Co., Mich.
13. John Henry Newman, 1996
    The Idea of a University.
    Yale University Press, New Haven, Conn.

Chapter 13
Evolution Theory: (1) Organismal Evolution

"People of good will wish to see science and religion at peace, working together to enrich our practical and ethical lives…I propose that we encapsulate this central principle of respectful non-interference, accompanied by intense dialogue between thetwo distinct subjects, each covering a central facet of human existence.

Late Prof. Stephen Jay Gould

In 1859 Charles Darwin, a British naturalist published his epochal writing, *"The Origin Species"*. The book itself and description are based on his expedition in Central America, specifically the island of Galapagos. He observed the diversity of birds and finches, and also their morphological similarities. With data collected, upon returning to England, he analyzed them in a systematic way. Then, he theorized the formation of new species under the natural island conditions through 1) adaptation, 2) multiplication through sexual reproduction, 3) acquisition of new morphological characteristics and variabilities, 4) *struggle for existence*, 5) survival of the fitted, and 6) "natural selection", and then 7) "the origin of new species". This was a new theory in natural science.

In 19th century, some naturalists accepted this theory whereas others maintained a reserved attitude. Those who accepted Darwin's theory looked at the biological world of diversity through these mechanisms. Also, they predicted that in the future generations, likely by the same mechanisms. Therefore, they considered Darwin's theory as a unifying theory.

Charles Michener in his Introduction of Great Books proclaimed it as "the greatest intellectual revolution since the advent of Christianity". Mr. Walter Cronkite considered it as "road map of civilization". Yet, scientists and scholars do differ from one another in viewpoints.

In 1871, Darwin published his second book entitled in "The Descent of Man". In this book, Darwin speculated that mammals, on the basis sexual selection, mental-intellectual faculty, were evolved from lower categories. He even extended this to human beings. Finally, he asserted that monkeys, chimpanzees and human were evolved from a common ancestor. In other word, he denied that humanity was created by divine creation. This definitely came into conflict with Christianity,

and what the Christian Church believed and taught.

It was Prof. Thomas Huxley, a contemporary of Darwin, who had suggested "struggle for existence", being added to Darwin's theory. Based on what Thomas Melthus had proposed the shortage of food supplies due to increasing population. For survival, people had to struggle. Herbert Spencer popularized the theory through his writing. The evolution theory became popular in British society. It stirred up a great deal of debate. The Anglican Church felt the challenge, and arranged a debate between Prof. Huxley and Bishop Wilberforce. Somehow, the citizens did not consider this as a personal debate. They considered it as a conflict between Christianity and evolution theory. Even today, some irrational evolutionists use this as an indication of anti-rational research by Christian church.

In 1925, in Dayton, TN, a substitute teacher by the name of John Scopies taught evolution theory in biology course of city school. In those days, Christian doctrine of creation was taught exclusively in the southern USA. Therefore, Mr. Scopies' teaching was considered a breach of the regulations of school systems. He was fined for one hundred dollars. To this, Evolutionists protested against it. This led to the debate between William Jennings Bryan and Clarence Darrow in the Court. This event became a national news. Also, it created the impression that Christianity through her teaching and evolution theory were in diametrically opposing camps. Somehow, the pendulum swung to the other extreme, i.e. evolution is being taught exclusively in secular school systems. In recent years, fundamental Christians of Scientific Creation have tried to restore the status of creation on equal basis of teaching. They began launching an Equal Time Movement. They have tried tirelessly over these years. Up to this day, they were denied nine times in Courts. Prof. Thomas Huxley once claimed that "those who accept evolution theory can't be sincere Christians." Personally, I deny this claim.

Over these years, the evolution theory has been evolved from one single theory to many theories. In fact, to radical evolutionists, this becomes not only a bio-philosophy, but also a worldview. It is in the domains of bio-philosophy and worldview, evolutionists and creationists have fundamental conflict.

In this chapter I shall discuss the evolution theory at three biological levels, they are:

A) organismal evolution,   1859-

B) biochemical to molecular evolution, 1953-   , and

C) from bio-macromolecules to cells, tissues and organs,   1957/58 to   .

At the end of organismal evolution, I shall share with *my integrated scheme of both creation and evolution*.

A. Organismal Evoultion (at the level of individual organism)

In 1859, Darwin in his book discussed basically at organismal level, emphasizing population more than individuals. Scientifically, it is valid today, with its scope being enlarged.

In 2001, **Prof. Ernest Mayr of Harvard Univ.**, published his book of "**What Is Evolution**?". In Chapter 5, under Variational Evolution, he presented Darwin's five major theories of evolution, as the way he understands them, pp#86 as follows:

1) The non-constancy of species, the basic theory of evolution,

2) The descendant of all organisms from common ancesters, branching evolution,

3) The gradualness of evolution, no saltation, no discontinuities,

4) The multiplication of species, the origin of diversity, and

5) Natural selection.

In order to understand Darwin's evolution theory as current, as presented by Prof. Mayr, I shall use more or less his format for my discussion and evaluations.

1) *The non-constancy of species, the basis theory of evolution*:

(a) The species, as originally used by Darwin in his days, and in his book, was "a population of individuals, with constancy of species". With advancement in biology, especially in microbiology and molecular genetics, we know now that "within a species, there are individuals which are genetically different". This is something Darwin did not know in his time. His biology under discussion was population biology. Carl Linne, as the founding father of classification, long before Darwin, defined "species as constant, with limit". Now, all those who are versed with modern biology, know that within a population the individuals, (especially with bacteria and other lower organisms), are genetically different. Therefore, Prof. Mayr incorporates this new concept into Darwinism, as non-constancy of species. This is a change in concept and in definition.

With constancy of species, there is no room for sub-species, even new species with minor morphological difference. Therefore, Prof. Mayr took the liberty of changing it to "non-constancy of species". Not only changing it to non-species, he even defines it as the basic theory of evolution. This was not the basic theory of Darwin's theory of evolution, as originally defined/given in his book! This is a new version by Prof. Mayr!

What Prof. Mayr presents in "What Is Evolution?" is modification of Darwin's original (in fact, it was defined by Prof. Carl Lenne, long before Darwin).

It is "What is Evolution theory in 20th century! It was not so in 1895! That was 150 years ago!

In this connection, I wish to point out the fact that evolution theory over the years has been modified in concept. It is because the old definition could not accommodate new facts. Therefore, evolutionists such as Prof. Mayr has to modify it. To modify it so that sub-species or new species with minor morphological differences could be accommodated or introduced. You and I should know that the intermediates between species is one of the cornerstones of modern evolution theory. One important scientific fact is the new, sub-species or/even new species produced with genetic mutation. By and large, genetic mutation will lead to the formation of members within the species with minor difference in morphology or in physiological functions, basically genetic differences as manifested. Therefore in Prof. Mayr's presentation, #3,"no saltation" (large differences) and "no discontinuities" (genetic mutation is continuous, one step at a time). We all know that with/by genetic mutations, there are minor changes and graduate changes (no discontinuities).

Because of these new principles, Prof. Mayr, in Chapt.5, wrote about "Evolutionary Developmental Biology". Chapter 5 is an extensive treatment. Basically, Prof. Mayr is dealing with so-called "neo-Darwinism". It will take a great deal of background in modern biology, especially molecular genetics. On account of space, I have to omit them in my evaluation. Those who are interested in more and in details should read Mayr's book.

2)*The descendant of all organisms from common ancestors – branching evolution*:

Darwin first observed on Galapagos Islands that there were three morphological varieties of mocking birds. They were mocking birds with minor morphological differences. Based on observation, then Darwin speculated that these three varieties could be, years ago and also through many years of evolvement, evolved from one species of mocking bird. Due to the isolation by islands, these birds were unable to interbreed among themselves. Then, he speculated, even theorized that they were the products of "branching evolvement" (branching evolution).This was exclusively a speculation and a pure theory. It was without any empirical, rational research, let alone extensive and systematic research.

It was true that Darwin in his "Origin of Species" once said, "*There is such a grandeur in this view of life, with its several powers, having been originally breathed into a few forms or into one; and that from so simple a beginning, endless forms most beautiful and most wonderful have been, and are being involved*". Reading this exclamation, we would say that by implication, Darwin did consider such a branching evolvement of mocking birds.

It is true that Darwin in his second book, "The Descent of Man", did speculate humankind was somehow evolved from chimpanzees and monkeys. But, he did not say clearly in his first book. Based on this exclamation and speculation by Darwin, Prof. Mayr modified it to become "branching evolution, the descendants of all organisms from common ancestors". In fact, Mayr concludes that this was Darwin's major contribution to evolution theory. He says, "*this chain of inferences led Darwin to the ultimate conclusion that all organisms on earth had common ancestors that probably all life of earth had started with a simple origin of life*." (pp#21) One of Darwin's major contributions was to have proposed the first consistent theory of branching evolution." #19.In order to support this *inference*, Mayr went on one step further by mentioning 1) morphological similarities, with Linne's classification scheme, 2) embryological evidence   (Ernest Haeckel's contribution) and 3)   vestigial organs, 4) ecologico-geographical distribution, and 5) genes and similar nucleotides sequences.

Once again, I would like to mention that all these are based on circumstantial evidences. They are not empirical data from laboratory studies, or ecological or genetic experiments in those days. They are not yet empirically proven.

In this conjunction, let me evaluate the classification in relation to evolution theory   with the following figures and description, for clarity.

In 1758 (long before Darwin)", Swedish scholar Carl Van Linne invented/established the classification of living things. Since then the schemes have been used by biologists universally. Linne's nomenclature of living species with his "binominal system" (with two words either in Latin or latinized English/German), (cf. following 4 figures).

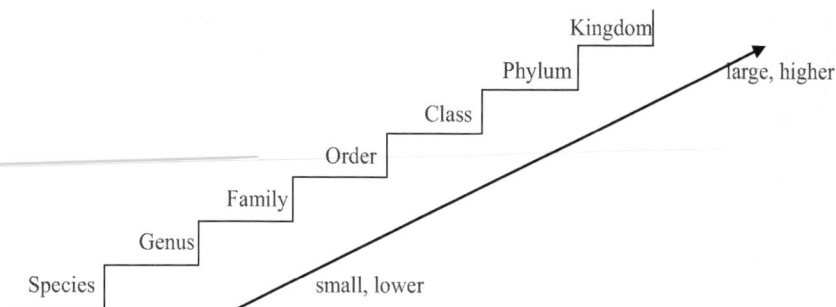

Figure 1.   Classification scheme, in large categories

(macro-evolutional).

By Stephen C. Liu

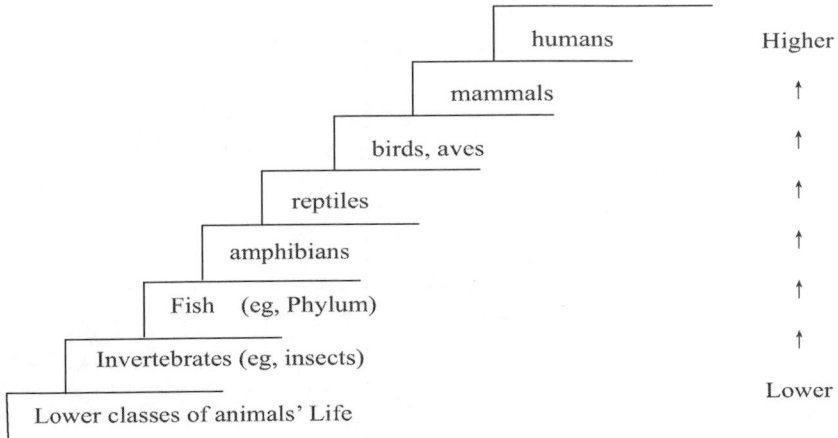

Figure 2. Classification of animals (in common names)

By Stephen C. Liu

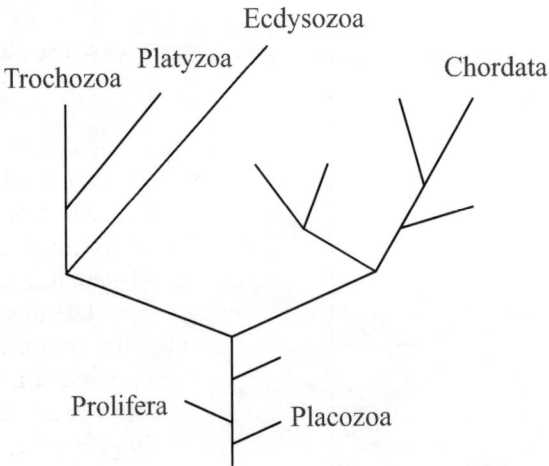

Figure 3 Branching evolution in higher animals (taken from Mayr, #52)

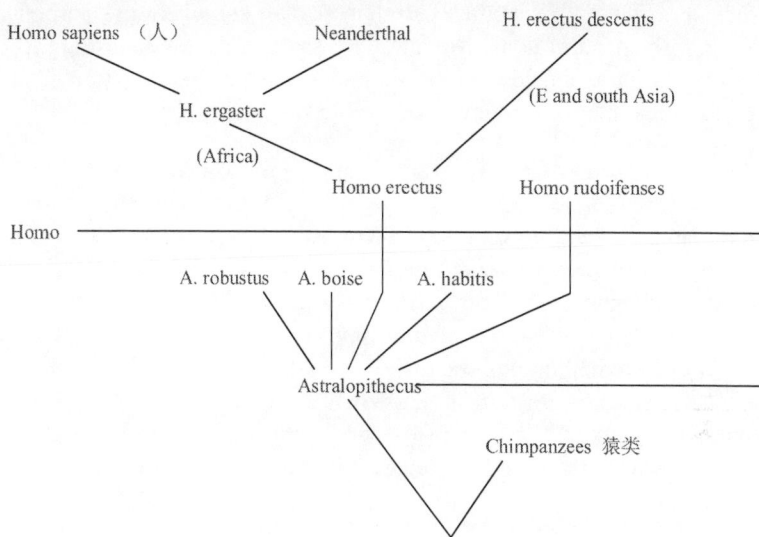

Figure 4.   Branching evolving of human and chimpanzee

(adopted from Mayr, figure #11-2, p#224)

Classification does tell us something. Among the members of one species/even one genus, or between species/genus are phylogenetically related. Not only their morphological characteristics are close enough, even their physiological functions, to some extent genetic variabilities. This is what we professors teach in both undergraduate and graduate courses, in/as scientific subjects. It is based on their phylogenetic relatedness, we conduct lab tests of new drugs or anything new in animal models. With valid results obtained, then and eventually we go to human, even in clinical work. All we scientists could say is that they are phylogenetically related, that is all we could tell. Whether there is an evolvement (evolution) for better or for worse, we can only speculate them, or infer them. There is no way to perform empirical experiment to demonstrate one way or another. It is true that we do have intermediates between one species. With genetic mutation (natural or induced) we could have variants with either morphological or physiological variations. These variants would give us another kind of evidence that they are phylogenetically related. Once again, that does not means that they are evolved. If we do say so, then that is conjunction or inference.

Biologists, whether they are Christians (having religious faith) or scientists having no faith, do agree that there is a horizontal dimension (versus perpendicular) of evolving/evolution/variations or variability. Over the long years of horizontal variation, especially those grown in isolated environs will lead/end to morphological or even physiological variations. This is well known or demonstrated. So, we have keep the two kinds of variations, i.e. horizontal and

perpendicular variation in mind. Through sexual conjugations, perpendicular variation (in the sense from one generation to next generation, in a straight way or perpendicular fashion) does lead to variations too. But, this variation is gradual, and over many and many years, even generations.

One more point I wish to mention. Prof. Linne, so far as I could tell was a Christian scholar. In 2000, I was in Upsala of Sweden. I had the privilege of visiting his lab at Upsala university. I saw one plaque hanging on the wall, with the inscription of " **Deus Creavit, Linneaus disposuit**". The literal translation is "God creates, Linne systematizes". His Christian faith is clearly shown in the display. Of course, whether his Christian faith had anything to do with what his scientific work is something no one knows. Also, whether the systematic had any implication in his Christian faith is unknown, at least to me. Again, this is just circumstantial evidence. I just want to share with you of my visit and personal experience. As scientists, we should separate the two as separate disciplines.

Coming back to the subject of branching evolution, let me conclude with two more points. When more plants or animals are discovered/known and classified, the number will be increased. Minute differences will be discovered among these new varieties. Eventually, we shall have branches and branching in grouping them or classificational schemes. This is logical. Then, the second point is the question of phylogeny. At the bottom of the issue is whether all these varieties come from the same ancestry or different ancestry. Again, it is a matter of inference and speculation. In biology, pertaining to phylogeny, there are two schools of thought. One is mono-phylogeny; another one is poly-phylogeny, i.e. the former is one origin or one ancestor, the latter is many origins or many ancestors. Up to this date, we biologists have not solved this basic question of phylogeny. This question has so much to do with what Prof. Mayr writes branching evolution, and what I elaborate in these paragraphs.

3)*The gradualness of evolution (no saltation, no discontinuities):*

What Prof. Mayr refers to "gradualness of evolution" is one step at a time (gradualness) in a progressive fashion of characteristics (continuity) in genetic mutation (evolution). Mutation is always one step at a time. This will lead to having mutants, with minute differences in characteristics. In either spontaneous mutation or induced mutation, mutants will be isolated with lab methods, manipulation in the field. Then, they will be characterized. Mutation is always gradual, i.e. in sequential fashion. With mutation (with microbes, insects or plants or animals, as model systems in lab experiments) will yield/lead to the formation of mutants. The mutants differ from the parental organism in minute characteristics. Mutants themselves will differ from one another in minute characteristics (micro- evolution). Therefore, mutation is gradual in modification of characteristics. There are no large discontinuities or gaps. Saltation in Greek means large jump. That refers to no big changes by/in mutation (macro-mutation).

(1)With the advent of molecular biology in 1950-60, molecular biologists know that mutation is due to alteration (deletion or addition; transition or inversion),of sequence of nucleotides in nucleic acids (DNA or RNA) in chromosomes. Through transcription and then translation, proteins (or polypeptides) will be formed/produced.

In principle, there are three types of mutations, especially with induced mutations: They are:

(1)Harmful mutation, or detrimental mutation,

(2)Neutral mutation or point mutation, and

(3)Beneficial mutation.

Mutation in nature is by and large harmful mutation, i.e. with deletion of nucleotides. Neutral mutation is due to point mutation, with no effect on the end products.

Beneficial mutation is conferring acquired characteristics to an organism. It is true that with laboratory manipulation we could transfer genes to an organism. Nowadays, with cloning technology we could transfer genes to another organism. Years ago, we knew acquisition of plasmid by transfer, could confer drug resistance to the recipient. With these two mechanisms, mutation, in a way is beneficial. But, keep in mind, the first one is by lab manipulation only. The second one could happen both in nature by chance, and in lab by manipulation.

In evolution, especially in neo-revolution, genetic mutation is an important mechanism. As mentioned in previous section, mutation could either add or delete genes. Therefore, it is matter of by choice, not by necessity. With harmful mutation, the organism would not be able to advance, or to gain any acquired characteristics. Evolutionists know well that this is roadblock to evolution.

Mayr, in his book, chooses to mention beneficial mutation only in order to advance his theory. To us scientists and to the public as well, this is bias more than fair treatment of the subject.

What we could conclude in this section is this. Genetic mutation is by/with minus variations. Therefore, it is micro-evolution. There is neither discontinuity nor saltation,   i. e, no macro-evolution. Let us keep all these principles in mind.

(2)Gradualness could be due to another mechanism:

Plants, especially of lower categories, grown in isolated environmental conditions (ecological) over years will also gradually change (variation) through adaptation. Eventually, this will probably lead to formation of sub-species (horizontal variation).Prof. Mayr was a specialist in this sub-discipline. Beginning in 1940, he advocated an "evolutionary synthesis", with bio-eco being

incorporated as something new. It was not generally accepted until 2000. In his writing Mayr proposed a number of names for such varieties or subspecies, such as: allopatric, peripatric, dichopatric, sympatric, instaneous, parapatric speciation etc. Such scientific (Greek) naming are strang to the public. Even to professionals. Even so, all these are minor changes, being in the category of micro-evolution. That means "gradualness" of evolution, no saltation or discontinuities.

The most important point for all of us to know is this. Micro-evolution is in one category whereas macro-evolution in another category. The prefixes micro and macro mean small and large variations/changes. They are different in categories. Also, they have arrived at these categories through different mechanisms.

For micro-evolution, we all know well, i.e. through genetic mutation or geological-ecological induction to variation. As scientists we know well that we can use one to substitute for the other. In other word, micro-evolution has its mechanisms whereas macro-evolution has its mechanisms. If we keep these clearly in our mind, then we do not have any difficulty in understanding them.

But, difficulty comes when some irrational evolutionists insist on using the mechanisms in micro-evolution for macro-evolution. Not only they insist on using them in such a way, they even insist on the mechanisms for micro-evolution could work for macro-evolution. This is so-called "coupled". This creates the un-necessary debate.

Profs. Drs. G. L. Stabbins and Francisco J. Ayala, two well-known geneticists, said, in their article in Science, AAAS, Vo. 214:967-971, 1981, wrote:

"The decision as to which among alternatives (macro- evolutionary) is correct can not be reached by recourse to micro-evolutionary principles. Thus, macro-evolution is an autonomous field of evolutionary field of evolutionary study and in very important sense, epistemologically, macro evolution should be de-coupled from micro-evolution."

Prof. Mayr wrote, in his "Toward a New Philosophy of Biolgy" 1998, #pp 103,"Stebbins and Ayala are quite correct in stating that macro-evolution is an autonomous field of study. It should develop its own mechanisms to support it. Theories are not inter-transferrable and reducible."

Evidently, Prof. Mayr contradicts himself in principles in two different books of his own.

Before I conclude this section, let me say one more important point. When we accept *micro-evolution* and its mechanism does not mean that we also accept *macro-evolution. The two are altogether different*. When we decline to accept

macro-evolution, it does not means we also decline to accept micro-evolution. We non-evolutionists could accept one, and at the same time refuse to accept the other. In theory and in practice, we should make clear this distinction.

By and large, the debate is due to the fact that people fail to differentiate mechanisms from principles or vice versa. *Mechanism and principle are two different things. You and I could accept the mechanisms as valid and acceptable, yet decline to accept the final principles*. They are different. They are not coupled, or linked together. Fail to differentiate these two will lead un-necessary debate, even fight.

4) *The multiplication of species, the origin of diversity:*

Prof. Mayr, a specialist of ornithology (birds) knows very well multiplication of species through sexual conjugation. Eventually, this will lead to the diversity, but within that of species. The question is whether different species could engage in sexual conjugation or intercourse.

Carl Linneaus originally defined what constitutes a species? The definition given was that "sexual incompatibility between species. Within a species regardless how much they differ one from another in morphology, even in other characteristics, they could inter-breed through sexual conjugation or sexual intercourse. If they could not do so, then they should be considered as different species." This definition stands well, even today.

A good example is among human beings (***Homo sapiens***). In this world of ours, there are different races (sub-races will be more appropriate in systematic). They differ with/in skin color, i. e. yellow, while, black (even different shades) and even somewhat red. To some extent their hairs and hair types are different. Yet, one important fact is that they could inter-marry, producing offspring. Often, their "hybrid" will be different from their parents. When/if they continue to inter-marry, the differences will be further and more pronounced. Yet, they remain as human beings. All in all, they all belong to *Homo sapiens*, one species with varieties or sub-species. Under all circumstances, they are human beings. Today, in our modern society, these are very common. We all know these well.

Evolutionists consider the evolvement of humans from chimpanzee and monkey, as a theory. *If this is the case, then they human and chimpanzee should be able to engage in sexual intercourse in the past, or in the present time*. So far, we have not seen any such thing ever happened nowadays. It happened in the past? If this was the case, they should be some kind of vestiges or proof. Up to this day, we have not heard from any one, or have presented any fossil sample or anything else.

Prof. Mayr defines this as biological speciation. In addition to this, he adds topological speciation. As given in the previous sections, Mayr was considered as a specialist in geo-eco field (cf. page 127, under (2) gradualness). Charles Darwin

observed three kinds of mocking birds on Galapagos Island. He theorized that they were evolved from one species, from common ancestry. He took another big step. He even theorized that all living things were evolved from one common ancestor (cf. #123, (B), *Common ancestor, branch evolution*).

5) *Natural selection:*

Mayr considered "Struggle for Existence" (Chapt. 5), "adaptation" (Chapt.6) and "natural selection" (Chapt. 7) as cornerstones of modern interpretation of evolution theory. In fact, it was Alfred Russell Wallace, in 1858, who had suggested to Charles Darwin that" natural selection" being added to his theory.

Wallace had five major points:

1. Any species, if it is not restricted by environmental factors, the number will be doubled in every generation,

2. In general, the size of that population is relatively constant,

3. The resources available is limited,

4. There is a struggle for existence among the individuals in a population, and

5. Inheritable characteristics are heritable in succeeding generations.

" Survival for the fitted", as suggested by Herbert Spencer to Charles Darwin, was "a passive response/mechanism" rather than a "active force" for selection. "survival for the fitted", or "fitted for survival" is a circular statement. Mayr denied this circularity. He emphasizes that due to the acquisition of certain morphological or physiological characteristics, the species would be in a better position to compete for survival. Even so, it is a passive mechanism. In nature, if plants are not selected, eventually they will degenerate. To a large extent, and eventually they will face extinction. The reasons why they are better survived, are due to selection of better varieties by plant breeders. In 2007, the World Conservation Union published "A Red-list" with 16,306 endangered biological species, as compared with 200 in 2006.

For years, Evolutionists have been debating among themselves, pertaining to the level of struggle for existence. Is it the individual member in a species? or the genus? or the whole population? or the gene? or the environment? *No final agreement has been reached*.

In recent years, British Biologist or a specialist in chicken behavior, Richard Dawkins advocates that it is the gene (cf. The Selfish Gene) that determines the outcome. Evidently, he is a naturalist, or a biologist at organismal level. *I take it*

that Dawkins knows very little of how genes are activated, and what induces or inhibits the activation. In addition, there are activation site and suppressor site for gene activation in the immediate cellular environment. These will determine activation or suppression of gene expression by molecular inducers or repressors. In all cases, gene or genes do not have that kind of autonomy, as advocated by Dawkins. These are well established principles in molecular biology, though complicated and interwoven principles. Yet, I just mention it as a level in mechanism of evolution in biology, and for public information.

Most evolutionists do consider environment which exerts the selection. Let me cite two well-known cases as reported in scientific literature of recent years.

One was the peppermoth (*Biston belularia*) in Manchester, an industrial city in England. There were two populations of moths, one white, the other gray (protective colors against the grayish color of the trunk due to smug).With the adaptive/protective color, the peppermoths could avoid the devouring by birds. If there is a new species formed, which is the driving/evolving force? The birds? the environment? or something else? To answer this question, Prof. Michael Majerus of Univ. of Cambridge took up this study. He reported his 20-years' studies, in Science, Vol. 304:1894-1895, July 25, 2004. His discovery/conclusion was the environment, not the birds. The peppermoths hid themselves in small holes on the trunk ("niches" in ecological term). His conclusion was that *the peppermoths remained as the same species, no great change at all*.

The other study was on the spiders on Hawaii islands, by Dr. Rosemary Gillespie. She undertook the study to determine which was the driving/evolving force, and under what ecological conditions do spiders respond and changes (induced). She reported under "The Ecology and Evolution of Hawaiian Spiders". Her conclusion was the spiders found their "niche", thereby they adapted to the conditions in the "niche". Once again, she confirmed the general principle in which the environmental conditions (in "niche), determining the changes in the spiders' response.   (American Scientists, March-April issue, 2005).

These two recent studies confirmed environmental condition, exerting selective pressure on the organisms for change or variations. But, the change was minor change, i.e. "sub-species". Therefore, they were in micro-evolution.

These five theories were considered by Prof. Dr. Mayr as the five major theories of evolution in   "What Evolution Theory is?" published in 2001. To my knowledge, these are only a fraction of what evolution theory is in 21st century, mostly at organismal level.

In the context of evolution theory at organismal level, let me review once again the principles, models and methods in genetics in general, and molecular genetics with microbes (such as fungi, bacteria and viruses as model systems) in particular.

In 2010, Jerry Foder and Massimo Piatelli-Palmarini, two forthright atheists as they professed to be, published their book entitled in "What Darwin Got Wrong", 286 pages, ISBN 9780374288792, by Farrar, Straus and Giroux, N.Y. These two authors accepted the historical and entirely material reality of evolution. But, like many earlier critics, they cannot accept natural selection as the only mechanism of adaptive evolution. (cf. Science, Books, #692,May 7, 2010.

In fact, much earlier time, both Profs. Ed. O.Wilson (2002) and Owen Gingerich (2006) said the same thing. Both Wilson and Gingrich were professors at Harvard University. In other word, the mechanism for evolution as proposed by Darwin,, and also Mayr was not yet a settled principle.

B. Microbial and molecular genetics: mutation, frequency of mutation and mutants:

Genetics and genetic mutation are cornerstones of neo-evolution at organismal level. One level down will be molecular genetics (cf Chapt. 13- B). In his book of "*Molecular Biology of the Gene*" (1st Ed.), *Prof. James D. Watson, the co-discoverer of DNA helical structure in 1953*, once said, "the knowledge of molecular biology and genetics is derived mostly from working with Eschericia coli." In conceptual scheme, one level lower than organismal is molecular. So, molecular biology and molecular genetics are closely linked together, in molecular evolution (cf. Chapt. 13-B) In molecular genetics, in addition to E. coli and many other bacteria used as models, such as phages, animal viruses and plant viruses. In this section, I shall briefly review microbial and molecular genetics, especially in mutation, mutation frequency and mutants.

a)There are several ways in studying mutation with microbes:

1)Spontaneous mutation: in nature or in lab.

2)Induced mutation: with UV, and chemical mutagens, in lab.& in field.

b) Three types of mutations: cf. pp#127

1)Frequency of mutation:

(a) in spontaneous/natural conditions:

with E. coli, *one gene: one in one million per gene;*

two genes, tenfold less, one in ten millions;

three genes, another tenfold less, one in hundred millions.

(b)induced mutation with mutagens:

The frequency is higher than natural/spontaneous mutation. Even so, the mutation rate is still low. Working with two genes, the mutation rate is lower than with one gene. The rate of mutation is progressively lower and lower. The kind of

mutagens also has something to do with it. The stronger the mutagen, the higher the frequency. No general estimate can be given.

So, in general principle, to obtain mutants for any molecular/genetic studies is a very challenging undertaking. In addition, the isolation of mutants (with minute differences in characteristics) is a formidable task. The late Prof. Joshua Lederberg invented "the replica method" in isolating auxotrophic mutants of _E. coli_. That made the job much easier. So, in microbial to molecular genetics, to have mutants is a formidable. At any rate, with painstaking work, scientists could obtain mutants with desirable traits. In the last forty years, molecular biologists have made great stride in elucidating the intricacies of molecular interwoven mechanisms of living systems. They were using mutants in comparative studies and genetic studies. Prof. Horace Justus described all these in his book, "The Eighth Day (8th) of Creation: The Makers and Making of Molecular Biology". Read this book, for your intellectual enjoyment.

Charles Darwin observed variations among birds and turtles. He did not know what mechanisms which would induce variations. It was Gregor Mendel working with pea plant, thereby discovered "genes" and their inheritance. Since then molecular geneticists/biologists have made great stride in elucidating gene structure, functions and products. Eventually, all these led to molecular biotechnology as we stand to-day. By the side, this new discipline has something to do with evolution theory. That is the reason why I briefly review then so as to offer something essential to understand the next section, Evolution Theory B, Biochemical and Molecular Evolution.

Prof. Owen Gingerich, one of Mayr's colleagues at Harvard Univ., once said in his book, " Evolution in a Darwinian world has no goal or purpose. The exclusive driving force is random mutations sorted out by natural selection from one generation to the next. .... ". I am happy to concede that ample evidence demonstrates that natural selection is a major force at work, though I would be hesitant to say that this is the exclusive driving force." (pp#97-98). In addition, he said, "*whether an atheist or theist, a thoughtful person can only stand in the awe of the way this universe seems designed as a home for mankind.... We can hope that our increased scientific understanding will eventually reveal more to us about God the Creator and Sustainer of this cosmos.*"

C. My conviction and stand in evolution theory:

Likely, some of my readers wonder as to my conviction and stand in term of evolution theory. In this section let me share with you. In principle, as an evangelical Christian and molecular biologist, I wholeheartedly accept creation theory. When we come to the interpretation of the creation narratives, I may differ from others in secondary and minor points. In essence, I accept creation as the first stage of God's overall plan. After creation, the God Creator has been continuing working and creating, even to-day. This is seen in horizontal variations

in biological world. This is muh more than perpendicular dimension. So, the second stage of God's overall plan is evolving, which would lead to diversification of kinds in the biological world. This applies to both animals and plants, even to human beings within a limit. By and large, this progressive evolving is gradually going down the hill. This would lead to degeneration (from generation to generation), eventually to extinction. This would continue if there is no intervention by biologists or agricultural specialists (plant geneticists and breeders). The overall balance is dependent so much on these two factors, and their inter-reaction. The end-results would vary from time to time, and will continue on going over a long period of time.

Let me illustrate all these with diagramming/figures as follow.

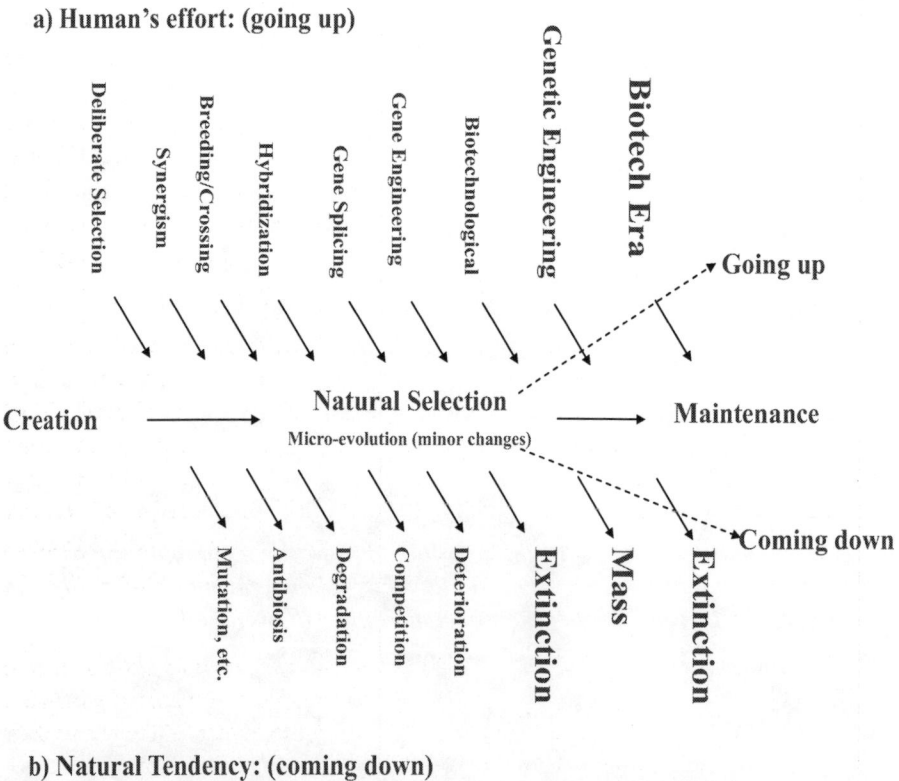

a) Human's effort: (going up)

b) Natural Tendency: (coming down)

Fig. 5   An integrated scheme of both creation and evolution theories.

By Stephen C. Y. Liu

D. "Anti-evolution movement" in USA?

In July of 2009 while Univ. of Cambridge (Darwin's Alma Mater) celebrated 150th anniversary of publication of "The Origin of Species", with one-week's Conference, I went to join 400 some participants. The theme was "*The Impact of Darwinism in the world*". By invitation, speakers presented their findings, and then opened for dialogue. By and large, speakers spoke on mechanisms more than principles of Darwinism at different levels. Then, Univ. of Oxford followed it with another five-days' conference on "*The Religious Responses to Darwinism*", with 80 some participants. To my surprise, Prof. Ronald Numbers of Univ. of WI slanted his talk on so-called "Anti-evolution Movement" in USA! This was the first time we ever heard of such a polemic phrase used in public speaking by a devoted evolutionist. He and a handful of speakers used "equal-time movement" in USA, as subject to be attacked as anti-evolution movement! In order to support and justify their accusation, they used both "Scientific creation" and "Intelligent design" as "the agents" of such a movement. Deliberately or intentionally, they did not include "Theistic evolution" or "Progressive creation". To scholars in these two schools, evolution theory could be accepted as a bio-science theory and in the second stage of overall theory of "creation". Of course, they reject the theory as a bio-philosophy or worldview. Prof. Numbers twisted it to organize his talk. To me, as well to other evangelical Christians in the conference, this is something deliberately slanted in order to justify their "false accusation." It is certainly no fair to use the time for such a un-justified accusation. Of course, no body was scheduled to give a reasonable response to this false accusation.

Personally, I did not have any regret of going to the conference on Cambridge campus. In fact, I learned something. But, to the conference on Oxford campus, I had regret of going. But, after all, I learned "something" new! Why? Over the last 10-15 years, open-minded scientists, irrespective to their conviction or viewpoint, did participate in conferences elsewhere, most in USA. In such conferences, we were eager to go where "*we could built bridge of mutual understanding and respect*" with open mind. The conference on Oxford campus was in reality a denial to such genuine efforts, betraying the original idea of dialogue by scientists and theologians

Let me emphatically say this. *There is no such movement in USA*. It is true that in USA there are scholars who deny evolution theory in wholesale fashion. Even so, no body could label them in "anti-evolution movement". They have their rational. As scientists they have their right. They do have doubt about the totality of evolution theory. They may accept mechanisms, but decline to take some principles of evolution theory as valid. Also, they deny evolution as a bio-philosophy or worldview. There are other scholars who are "theistic evolutionists". They consider evolution as second stage of God's overall plan of creation. I, as a microbiologist/molecular biologist, have my own integrated scheme, as given in previous section.

All in all, Prof. Ronald Numbers was too simplistic on one hand, and too much dogmatic and authoritative on the other. Above all, he is too judgmental. Taking the advantage of being a speaker, he accuses those who differ from his viewpoint as "anti-evolution movement" This is not fair at all. He certainly abused his privilege as a speaker in the conference!

E. Teaching "Evolution theory" as a scientific theory in high school curriculum, in USA:

Teaching evolution theory is not an issue in Europe, even in Canada. USA is the only country exceptional. Seventy five percent of population in Uk accepts evolution, yet only 47% in USA. This is a difference, being interesting to the public. Why? This is something every concerned citizen of the country wants to know.

In 2003, a book entitled in " Darwinism, Design and Public Education" edited by John A. Campbell and Stephen C. Meyer, and was published by Mich. State Univ. Press, 634 pages. The book is divided into 4 parts. The first part is dealing with Darwinism; the 2nd, scientific critique of biology textbooks; 3rd, the theory of intelligent design; 4th, critical responses. Then, there are Appendices A, B, C, D, and E.

In this section, I shall take the *Appendix A., US Commission on Civil Rights Hearing: on Curriculum Controversies in Biology, 21 Aug. 1998*; and Appendix B., Helping Schools to Teach evolution by Donald Kennedy. I shall present a summary of Appendix A, on teaching evolution in schools in USA.

Appendix A. pp#559-586, *Civil Rights Hearing, on 21 Aug. 1998*, chaired by Berry, Commissioners Anderson, Horner, and George; and panelists, Drs. Stephen Meyer and Eugenie Scott.

Chairperson Berry stated the objective of the hearing: It is a Civil Issue entailing rights of the teachers, and also the First Amendment of the students for knowledge. Students should not be deprived of their right to knowledge and Creation-evolution controversy in USA . Then, Horner and George added some other specific subjects such as: 1) teaching on Life Origin, 2) diversity of the living world, and 3) theories and alternative theories, 4) scientific theories have religious implications. Should they be excluded in public school teaching? Religious implication of evolution theory. Then, Panelists expressed their convictions and stands on these issues, and then open for question-and-answer.

Scott: 1) evolution theory is state-of-the-art, 2) evolution is not inherently atheistic. It is methodological neutral, 3) evolution is not inherently philosophical system, 4) alterative theory could be taught. 4) It should be secular, and not religiously based, 5) we can't tailor to suit all people, and 6) difference in teaching religion and advocating religion. 7) of course, as Director of Nat. Center for

Science Ed., I opposes the inclusion of creation sciences and intelligent design, in public school teaching.

Meyer: 1) It is a demarcation issue. For example, science and/or explanation, if it is extended to the domain of philosophy, then to worldview, it is no longer science, or scientific theory. So much in explanations in evolution is not empirical, remaining to be verified. Yet, it is extended to philosophy. It is philosophical more than scientific. For example, variations through common descent, this is an extension to philosophy. This is the boundary. *No one could verify the mono-phylogeny or polyp-phylogeny*. There are many other areas that need verification with empirical scientific methods. 2) *No body would oppose teaching evolution theory as a biological scientific theory. It should be in scientific, as a theory*. This is the limit and the boundary, the demarcation. Once it is in *philosophical explanation, it is no longer a scientific, let alone the worldview*. 3) the origin of life has not experimentally be verified. Biochemical evolution is a probability statement. It is a reconstruction with biochemistry and principles. It is scientific, and scientific theory, not scientifically verified, 3) *Darwin's evolution theory is a theory, with some mechanisms scientifically sound and acceptable*. Mechanism is different from the theory. 4) *Darwinism is much more than science*. Then, you have demarcation issue. If evolution theory is science, then, so is design theory, 5) any discussion in class, as alternative to evolution or other than evolution is intimidated by lawsuit. Students have no or little exposure to discussion/debate on scientific problems with Darwinian viewpoints. That is viewpoint discrimination, and above all, the violation of human rights, 6) intellectual window of students and of future generations of students should not be closed, allowing other possible or theories in the coming centuries, 6) evolution theory could be interpreted in broader theistic framework. *In Christendom, there is a theory of theistic evolution, and creative evolution*, 7) USA is pluralistic society. Cultural differences of citizens should be taken into consideration in school education.

Mr. Sybrandy, as a participant gave the following statement: in "Edward vs. Aquillard", 1987 96 LED, at #525,#526; "We do not imply that a legislature could never require that scientific critique of prevailing scientific theories be taught. In a similar way, teaching a variety of scientific theories about the origin of mankind to school children might be validly done with a clear secular intent of enhancing the effectiveness of science instruction... You can present religious material as a part of secular program of education. It does not violate the Constitution.

Evolution theory is a scientific theory in crisis, and theories are in a state of flux. Students have the right to an un-biased instruction. When we deprive students of certain scientific fact and certain scientific theories merely on the basis that it happens to support a certain religious viewpoint, that should not be excluded from teaching the children."

Appendix B is an advice by Dr. Donald Kennedy, as helping schools to

teach evolution. No one would question academic qualification of Dr. Kennedy. But, this appendix is an advice by him, with his expertise on the subject. "We cannot answer the central questions about life – Why do so many species exist", he said these in the first paragraph. Yet, he thinks that all these questions could be answer with principles in biochemistry. Yes, this is science, not philosophy. We all should have these in demarcation of domains in our thinking.

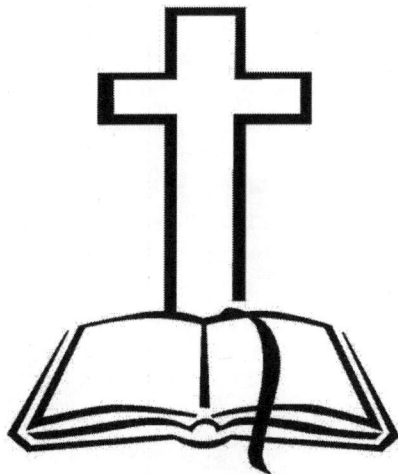

Conclusion

In 1895, Charles Darwin, in his book of "The Origin of Species", advocated evolution theory, with several mechanisms. In 150 years, the theory has been evolved to become scores of theories. In this chapter, I took Prof. Ernst Mayr's five major theories as given in his book entitled in "What Evolution Is?", as the basis in my presentation. I hope that I present it as positive as possible. It is true that I evaluated Mayr's five theories in the light of what we know in modern biology. I hope that I did not give readers an impression of tearing the evolution theory to pieces. In order to present it positive, sometimes I have present the negative sides so that we could appreciate the positive side of the story.

Evolution theory does present an intellectual challenge to evangelical Christians. In fact, as evangelicals we do accept evolution as a bio-scientific theory. Darwinism assists us to see the world, being no longer static, but in dynamic process. Adaptation and natural selection are valid mechanisms in bio-world. But, there are other mechanisms as well. Nature is a very complex of inter-reacting forces. To present evolution theory as fact or bio-philosophy or worldview, we have our right to decline it. In this chapter I have tried to present it as a valid scientific theory as possible.

The important question which often asked by scientists, Christians alike, and also the public, is this. Was Charles Darwin himself an atheist, or otherwise? In any of his publication, what did he publicly or privately acknowledged his

conviction? What he said about his own personal religious faith. It is true today that *many evolutionists claimed that Darwin was an atheist*.

So far as I have read or searched in literature. This is what I found it out, as follows:

" *Charles Darwin, in 1879* while working on his biography, *confessed his personal religious faith as follow*:

"My personal judgment on Christianity or religious faith fluctuates so much and so often. Even in my most fluctuations I have never been an atheist in the sense of denying God. I think that generally (more and more as I grew older) but not always, that an agnostic would be more corrected description of my state mind."

My only regret is this. I copied down these words from somewhere, I did not write down where this was published, so I could not give a citation of literature. But, I am honest to say that this is not my fabrication.

Prof. Alister McGrath of Oxford once wrote that
"The religious implications of a Darwinian view of life are contested. It can be interpreted in a Christian, agnostic or atheistic view of life. all depends on your worldview when you consider Darwinism."

Literature Cited

1. Ernst Mayr, 2001

    What Evolution Is?

    Basic Books, N.Y.

2. Douglas Futuyama, 1998

    Evolution Biology

    Sinauer Associates, Boston, MA

3. Charles Darwin,   1859, 1993

    The Origin of Species

    Ramdom House,   N. Y.

4. Benjamin Lewin,   1998

    Genetics VI

    Oxford Univ. Press, N. Y.

5. John A. Campbell and Stephen C. Meyer, Ed.,   2003

    Darwinism, Design and Public Education

    Mich. State Univ. Press, E. Lansing, MI

Chapter 14
Evolution Theory: (2) Biochemical to Molecular Evolution

" Religion and science are not mutually exclusive, but complementary.

At a time when faith and science seem for a clash.

Is it possible for theologians and scientists to share a common belief or at least

to develop a kind of truce to allow a meeting of mind?"

Fr. Hans Kung

Introduction and Historical perspectives:

Aristotle, the Greek philosopher-naturalist, in centuries ago, advocated a theory of *"abiogenesis"* or *"spontaneous generation"*. The basic tenet of his theory was that inorganic elements could be evolved (through a series of biochemical reactions) to become bio-organic living entities. This was known as either naturalism or Aristotetlianism. At the same time, there was another theory. That was the *"biogenesis", i.e. living things produced living things*. This theory was taught by Christian church at large. The Church believed that the God Creator created living things in various kinds or categories. Then, through sexual conjugations, these large categories of living things could evolve to become diversified biological entities in this universe. These two classic schools of thought existed side by side over the centuries. Institutes of higher learning, depending on the faculty members and also their affiliations, taught either one of the two theories or two theories side by side. Yet, Aristotelianism was a dominant philosophy in the west for many centuries. Therefore, this was the predominant philosophy which was firmed implanted in the mind of scholars. No one could challenge it till the 16th -17th centuries.

In 1680, Dutch naturalist *Antonio Van Leeuwenhoek* (1632-1723), with his "microscope" (a magnifying glass mounted on a rod, with adjustable screws) observed very small "wee animalias" (moving things) under his microscope. He made sketch and drawings, then reported his findings at Royal Society of London, a well-known scholarly society at that time. Then, they debated on how "these little "wee animalias" (in fact, they were bacteria) were originated. After that, Lazzaro Spallanzani, an Italian doubted the spontaneous generation of these "wee animalias". He designed a relatively simple experiment in which water and weeds were mixed in a glassware. Thcy were heated to a boiling point, sealed, preventing any dust falling into the glassware. He observed this simple experimental set up

daily over a period of time. He did not find any "*wee animalias*" ever developed inside the glassware. But, once outside air was allowed to go into the glassware, then "wee animalias" were seen. He concluded that without introducing "dust" (they carried the "wee- animalias" on the surface), once they were killed by boiling water, they would not any wee-animalias be ever developed. Nowadays, with advanced technics we came to know what **Antonio Van Leeuwenhoek** had discovered were indeed "bacteria" under his microscope. So, he was honored as the founding **Father of Bacteriology** (later time, microbiology). As a result of this discovery, spontaneous generation met with challenge, if not being defeated.

In 17th and 18th centuries, chemistry was emerging as a new discipline. British scholars Joseph Priestley, Henry Cavendish and Antonio Lavoisier proved that oxygen was essential for living things to be originated and developed. Then, those who had upheld spontaneous generation argued in reply to Spallanzani's work. When water in the glassware (after boiling) was cooled down, you expelled the air, creating a vacuo. Without air, nothing could be ever developed. This was correct and justified.

In 1860, well-known French Scientist, Louis Pasteur (Nobelist), with a specialty in fermentation designed one epoch-making experiment. He designed an Erlenmyer flask with a side-tube bent a couple of times to a small opening at the end. He more or less repeated Spallanzani's work with water and weeds in the glassware, then brought to a boiling. Then, it was cooled down. Through that little opening at the end of bent side-arm, oxygen could freely enter. But, the bent extension arm would prevent dust particles being carried upward by the air current. In other word, dust particles were unable to enter and dropped the microbes carried on the surface, to the boiled water-weed mixture. In those days, it was an outstanding and genius design for experimentation. Pasteur observed for days, even for weeks. There were no bacteria ever developed, or "life" originated. He proved without any doubt that oxygen was needed. But, dust particles could not enter the heated liquid. So, consequently, no new crop of microbes were ever originated or developed. Pasteur's conclusion was "omni viva e vivum", by interpretation "only living thing will produce living thing". Once the side-arm was broken or the flask was cracked, fresh air with dust particles carried to the liquid was brought in, then new crop of bacteria would be developed in the liquid.

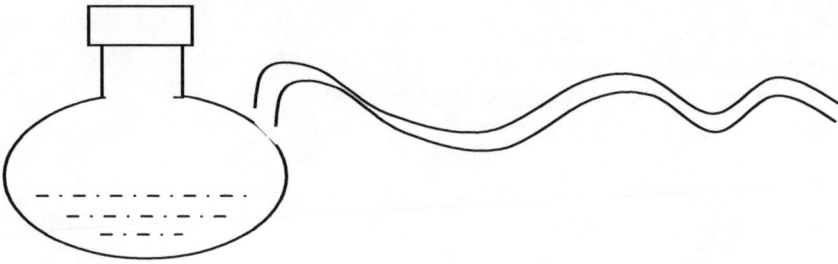

Fig. 1   Louis Pasteur's bent glass side-arm and experiment. By Stephen C. Liu

In fact, the biochemical to molecular evolution of 21st century is indeed the revival   of spontaneous generation of the old days.

A. *The definition of "life" or "living entities"*:

Virology, the studies of viruses of plants, animals or human was my major in under-graduate and graduate studies in college. In a way I know it better than any other disciplines. In late 19th century, it was emerging as a new discipline. It was probably due to the fact they were so minute in size. Without electron microscope, you could not observe them. Only with living cells or tissues as culture, they could be grown in vivo. Virions (virus particles) are made of proteins (on the outside as coat) with either DNA or RNA (in the core). *They replicate themselves only in the living cells or tissues* (known as replication). Viruses are model systems used in research, having a great deal to do with molecular evolution in biology.

In 1882, Russian virologist, D. J. Iwanowski studied tobacco mosaic virus (TMV) in plants. He ground diseased tissue and obtained the expressed juice after filtration (generally bacteria or fungi would be excluded). With such filtered juice, he was able to reproduce the disease in plants. To define such a characteristic, he coined a phrase, "fluidum vivum contagium", by interpretation, "living contagious fluid".   In1898, two German virologists, Fred Loeffler and Henrick Froelich discovered the foot-and-mouth viral disease (FMVD) of cattle. In 1900, American scientist, Dr. Walter Reed discovered smallpox viral disease. In 1915-57, British Frederick Twort and French D'Herelle simultaneously discovered bacteriophages (abbreviated as phages). All these viruses had an inherent ability to self-replication *in vivo* (in living cells or systems). On the basis of all these, scientists in general and virologists in particular recognized "*self-replication*" as the first sign/prerequisite of living thing. This criterion was also adopted as a first prerequisite of living entities in molecular evolution. Once something having the

ability of self-replication, this is taken as "living" by molecular evolutionists.

In the 50th to 60th of 20th century, biochemistry became a new discipline. Proteins (made of amino acids) were essential ingredients of all living cells, amounting to 50-80%. They were found in cytoplasm, cell membrane, and surface receptors, etc. They were conjugated with nucleic acids in chromosomes. Because of their ubiquitousness, scientists at that time took them as the inheritable materials. Biochemical evolutionists took them even one more step. Once they have found amino acids anywhere, they consider that is the beginning of "living" entities.

At that time, they did not recognize "*self-replication*" as a prerequisite for living entities. Even so, *this is a wholesale simplification to the extreme*.

In 1953, when double helical structure of DNA was elucidated and made known to the scientific community, DNA or RNA replaced proteins as the genetic materials. Biological sciences entered into molecular era. On account of this, biologists shifted their attention from proteins to nucleic acids, i.e. DNA or RNA. With that recognition/acknowledgment, scholars who wholehearted accepted evolution theory following the trend, entered into molecular evolution. Once again, these molecular evolutionists consider that once you have something which is made of either DNA or RNA, with self-replication ability, then these entities could be considered as "*living entities*". Again, this is a simplification to over-simplification. But, this is science. To them, science is built exclusively (to molecular evolutionists) on materialistic premises.

In 1954, Austrian Biophysicist Erwin Schroddinger wrote/published a book entitled in "*What is Life?*" In his book, he advocated/proposed/defined (as explained in previous sections) "life" exclusively on biophysico-biochemical basis. Such "life" has two characteristics: 1) it derives its energy from sun radiation, being from disorderly to orderly, and 2) it possesses a "specific blue-print" for inheritance. Of course, these two prerequisites had been long before recognized in general biology. It was a matter of transferring them to evolution. Dr. Stuart Kaufman, in Calif. proposed that 'living entities" should possess "interlocking and interwoven self-organization".

All these prerequisites have been fully accepted in general biology.

In 1959, British Biochemist of Univ. of Cambridge, Prof. Dr. Malcohm Dixon (specialized in enzyme biochemistry) also published his "*What is Life*". He fully recognized physico-biochemical basis of living entities. But, he recognized something else above the merely physico-biochemical basis, that is dynamic living phenomenon as we always see in human daily living state. Prof. Dixon advocates three types of "life" as follows. 1) "material life", that is life of a cell or cells/tissues/organs. It involves food-intake, energy-generated and absorbed, cells formed. All these are very complicated and interwoven metabolic processes, with various enzymes and pathways implied. So complex and so complicated, they are

subjects of our intensive empirical research. We understand them as where we stand to-day. 2)" body life". As a living being, we speak, express our emotion in love, and in hope. This is far more complex and complicated. All these fall into the category beyond science domain. We could not perform any empirical experiments to ascertain them in details. 3)" Life eternal", this is in the philosophic-religio-theological domain, being far greater than science domain. All these three kinds of life, people irrespective of religious faith of one kind of another, not only recognize them, but experience them daily and personally. Who could deny them?

Prof. Dr. William Bragg of Univ. of Cambridge, a Nobelist, universally acclaimed scientist, once said:

" Life is so wonderful and so dynamic.

Such an integrated system could ever be originated spontaneously?

No, not at all "

B. Biochemical evolution:

In 1953, Mr. Stanley Miller, a graduate student at Univ. of Chicago, undertook a Ph.D. thesis research work, under advisorship of Prof. Dr. Harold Urey, a Nobelist, on biochemical origin of life. He used so-called "primitive air" (supposed to exist in early universe's upper sphere) which was composed of: NH_4 , CH_4, H_2O and H_2, in a specially designed apparatus (Fig. 2).Then, with reducing agent in it, he applied electric spark through the content in the glassware, with heating source underneath. Let it go for several days. After the operation, liquid was found in the glass. He isolated glycine, the simplest amino acid (of twenty kinds), and two more amino acids from the liquid. Then, with paper chromatography he was able to identify them.. With this result, he submitted his paper to Science, AAAS for publication. At first, it was denied by AAAS. Then, through manipulation, he eventually got his result published in Science, on July 10th issue of l953. In his interpretation of such simple experimental result, Miller and Urey did not believe that they had created "*life*". They felt that they had made a significant start in the laboratory to unravel the problem of origin of "life". The premise behind his interpretation was glycine, as one of the simplest amino acids, could be assembled to form polypeptides, eventually protein. Since protein is present in living cell, so they had the first step toward "life".

Interesting enough, this was publicized in secular literature and newspapers, as valid. That was science, exclusively being built on materialistic philosophy and worldview. Even, in scientific literature, it was quoted from time to time as valid hypothesis. To no body's surprise, in the l990, Mr. Stanley became Prof. Stanley in Calif.   He died in 2000.

In 2007, other scientists tried to repeat Stanley's experiment. This could not be repeated, unless some reducing agents should be added to the mixture.

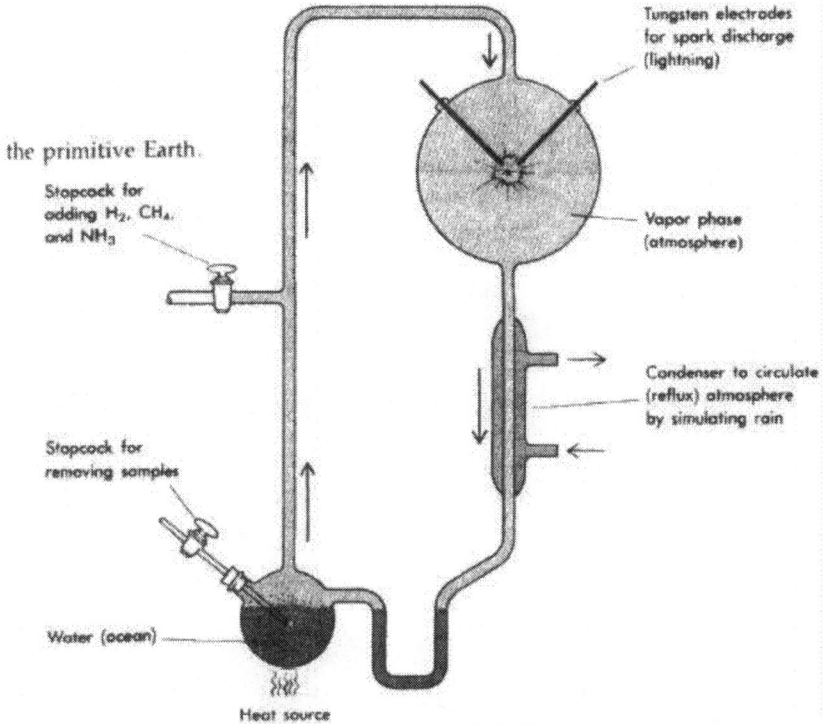

Fig. 2 Stanley Miller's experiment (taken from a letter of Dr. Antonio Lazcano to Stephen Liu)

Illustration of both biochemical evolution and molecular evolution, as follow"

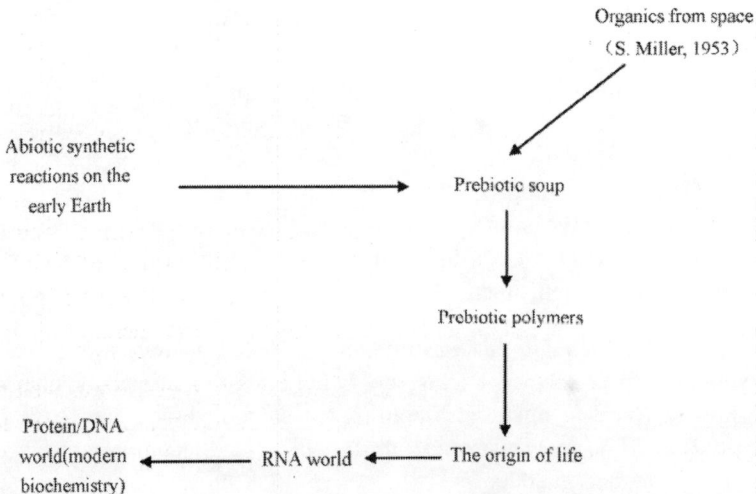

Fig. 3: Biochemical & Molecular Evolution, by Stephen C.Y. Liu
（cf. Jeffrey L. Bada and Antonio Lazcano, 2003, Science, AAAS）

C. Molecular Evolution:

In 1924, Russian scientist A. L. Oparin published his book entitled in "Origin of Life on Earth". Based on his scientific materialistic/Communistic philosophy, he first proposed the inorganic origin of life. He coined the so-called *"primordial soup"*. In this "soup" there was a series of inorganic chemical reactions, leading to formation of bioorganic molecules, then evolvement to *"life"* . His theory had an impact on the thinking of evolutionists in the West. Biochemical to molecular evolution had its root in Oparin's philosophy and worldview. As I mentioned in previous section, in 1956 biochemical evolution began in USA. Then, the double helical structure and functions of DNA were made known with Crick and Watson's report in 1953. DNA/RNA replaced proteins as the genetic materials. That ushered-in the molecular biology era. In 1960, Profs. Salvador E. Luria, Max Delbrueck and Alfred Hershey, Nobelists elucidated the intra-molecular mechanisms of hybridization of DNA in genes. French molecular biologists, Francois Jacob and J. Monod demonstrated the functions of *operons*. Evolutionists incorporated all these new discoveries in their theory. Molecular evolution was born in the 1960.

Prof. Arthur Kornberg, a Nobelist biochemist at Stanford Univ., in 1961, used bacteriophage T-4 as a model system in his experimental work. With a short T-4 DNA template in test tube, together with A,T,C,G (4 types of nucleotides) and their synthetic enzymes, he and his collaborators were able to extent/increase the length of T-4 template. Since we knew DNA as genetic materials with self-replication capacity *in vitro/in vivo*, you have the first sign of "living". With such experimental results, they advocated the origin of life at molecular level. This was well accepted by academic circle in both USA and elsewhere.

In 1987, Nobel Laureate James D. Watson published his "Molecular Biology of the Gene". His book became a standard textbook used in gradual schools in USA. In Chapter 28, the title was "The Origin of Life", pp# 1098-1163, explaining the molecular origin of life, from both scientific and materialistic worldview. It was done by a well-known scientist. Who could deny it. The book was reprinted in several subsequent editions.

In 1988, Prof. Geoffrey Zubay of Columbia Univ. published his "Biochemistry", 1266 pages. Chapt. 33 entitled in "Origin of Life" by Profs. James Ferris and David A. Usher. This thick and well-written textbook was adopted by many graduate schools in USA, probably elsewhere.

In other word or in summary, the molecular origin of life was well publicized, and accepted by scientific community all over the world. Let me say this again. All these have been written on premise of materialistic philosophy and worldview. It is because it is science.

D. Evaluation of both biochemical and molecular origin of life in Evolution Theory:

1). By two eminent Evolutionists:

a)**Prof. Antonio Lazcano**, univ. de Mexico,   Science, AAAS and also in a letter written to me:

"Since we never know in full detail the origin of life, it is no surprising that it is becoming a target for intelligent design creationists. The geological and chemical evolution evidence required to understand life's beginning remain insufficient and difficult to be understood.

It is true that there is a huge gap in the current description of the evolutionary transition between the pre-biotic synthesis of living beings. Even the un-anticipated discovery in 1982 – the research teams directed by Thomas Cech and Sidney Altman – of catalytic RNA molecules (ribosymes) which can be loosely described as nucleic acids that simultaneously have characteristics of DNA and enzymes has not closed the gap. Instead, that and related discoveries have led to a more precise definition of what should be understood as the origin of life. The origin of protein synthesis is still not understood, our understanding of the origin and early stages of biological evolution still has major un-solved problems, but they are recognized by the scientific community as intellectual challenge, and not as required metaphysical explanations, as proponents of creationists would love it. Creationism is a danger to science education that should be addressed by a constructive dialogue and collective action by imaginative researchers and educators on both sides of the bordor."

(the end of quotation)

b)**Prof. James D. Watson**, in "The Molecular Biology of Gene", Vol. II, 1997, pp#1161-

"Questions of molecular evolution are far trickier because it is harder and sometimes even impossible to do the right experiments.......Questions of molecular evolution becomes even more daunting when we try to speculate about the very earliest life forms. We have seen that even the best fossils preserve, only the durable parts of an organism; the macro-molecules that most

interest to us are lost. As a result, we must attempt to reconstruct ancient organisms by examining living organisms (molecular fossils) and by designing model experiments that mimic that condition thought to prevail on the primitive earth. Unfortunately, it is impossible to obtain direct proof of any particular theory of the origin of life. The sobering truth is that even if every expert in the field of molecular evolution were to agree on how life originated, the theory would still be a best guess rather than fact."

In this chapter, we have presented one possible scenario for the origin of the first "living molecule", that would replicate and evolve. Our purpose has been to show how the recent discovery of enzymatically active RNA species has it possible to speculate usefully about the molecular origin of life. Aside from the intellectual challenge of trying to imagine how life began, such speculation inevitably inspires specific experiments that sharpen and modify the speculations themselves…….

Although the scenario we presented is most likely to be true in detail, it surely contains important elements of the truth. Showing up how life could have begun is a first step toward how life actually began."

These paragraphs were written by Prof. James D. Watson. The foremost known molecular biologist in the 20th century. We all should take them as valid statement, and future predictions as well.

2). By Stephen C. Y. Liu, microbiologist and molecular biologist, the Author of this book:

As a microbiologist and molecular biologist, I write this section, expressing my appreciation and evaluation. I am in no way to criticize them. Personally and professionally, I accept them as science and scientific theories. In fact, I taught them in both undergraduate and graduate classes.

As a scientist and an evangelical Christian, I personally see things a wee higher than the materialistic worldview. This worldview of mine is built above the scientific and materialistic one. I see something "un-seen", yet real to me. But, this is neither science nor scientific view. As I wrote and described in Chapter 8, this falls into the domain of worldview. The worldview is larger and higher than philosophy and science (cf. pp#119 , with illustration, Fig.III and IV).

Professionally, I do not deny the biochemico-physical basis of life. Life is made of essential biochemical macromolecules in a huge conglomerate, which we call "human life". I see another dimension of human life. That is, we humans could think, talk, hate and love. Life is so dynamic and wonderful. No body could

deny all these! This is what and how I consider "life". Altogether, it is another dimension! We scientists, irrespective of our religious faith could not deny this. So, it is how and why we choose to see life. To me, to see life at biochemical and molecular basis is a simplification and oversimplification at the extreme!

Pertaining to the debate between evolutionists and creationists in USA, I personally feel that

There are *four areas* we all have to pay more attention, also as my *conclusion of this chapter*.

(1) *Mechanisms and principles are two different things*. Adaptation and genetic mutation are mechanisms. Common ancestry and mono-phylogeny are principles. If we take mechanisms as principles, likely we will end in dispute. The same is true when we take principles as mechanisms. This mistake is relatively common, even among scientists.

(2) We often have crisscrossed our territories. *If we stay in our area of our specialty, not tramping to the other side, there would not be any conflict*. Evolutionists try to interpret their result in term of bio-philosophy or worldview (not in scientific way). Creationists want to interpret their religious conviction in scientific way. We deliberately crisscross these two territories/domains. Therefore, we have unavoidable conflict.

(3) Another thing is that we fail to see the *difference between science and worldview*. Science and worldviews (or religious conviction or faith, believing God or not believing God is faith; theistic or atheistic worldview is worldview) are in two different domains. Science has its limit (cf. Chapt. 8, the philosophy of Science). Anything we could not perform empirical experiments is not empirical science, and

(4) *In creation theory there are five schools of thought* (cf. Chapt. 12). Scientific/biblical/fiat creation (young earth, universal flood and literal reading/interpretation of Scripture) is one of them. Intelligent design is another school. In the debate, evolutionists often quote these two schools as representatives of creationism. This is not true. There are another three schools. Scholars in Theistic evolution take evolution as the second stage of God's overall plan of creation. Those who uphold progressive creation consider evolution as a valid scientific theory. Once again, evolution theory could not give adequate explanation of origin of life.

(5) I personally have creation and evolution integrated in an overall scheme, with creation in the first stage and evolution in the second stage (Chapt. 13-A, Fig. 5, pp#192) . What my view differs from the other two schools is in later time of the two major stages. After creation, both plants and animals will eventually deteriorate unless we humans do something to improve the quality of both plants and animals. In evolution theory, with randomized mutation (no aim or no

objective), plants and animals will eventually be degenerating to extinction. The reason why they do not go down over the year is because agronomists/ plant breeders/biologists try to select better varieties and hybridize them.

Literature Cited

1. Stanley Miller and L. E. Orgel, 1974

    The Origin of Life on Earth

    Prentice-Hall Co, N. J

2. James D. Watson et al, 1997, 4th Ed.

    Molecular Biology of the Gene

    Cold Spring Quantative Biol. Press, N.Y.

3. Malcohm Dixon, 1959

    What is Life?

    IVF Press, IL.

4. Erwin Schroddinger, 1954

    What is Life?

    Cambridge Univ. Press, N.Y.

5. Geoffrey Zubay, Ed. 1998

    Biochemistry

    Addison-Wesley Press, MA

6. Antonio Lazcano, 2005

    Teaching Evolution in Mexico: Preaching to the Choir

    Science, AAAS Vol. 310:787-789

7. Roger Y. Stanier, et al, 1965

    Microbial World, 3rd Ed.

    Prentice-Hall Press, N.J.

Chapter 15
Evolution Theory: (3) Macro-Molecules to Cells, Tissues, Organs & Human

"At the core of the problem between science and religion is the deductive character of theology and the inductive characteristics of science. The two processes are fundamentally different. It is when a person switches the methods from one arena to the other that the difficulty, confusion, and conflict commence."

Cardinal John Henry Newman

In this chapter, as a continuation of Evolution Theory, I shall present what beyond macro-molecules; i.e. cells, tissues, organs to human being (in a very comprehensive way), as the last step. Generally, textbooks or scholars seldom take up this subject as a part of evolution theory. Lately, there are two books appears in literature, dealing with this particular phase of evolution theory. Using these two books, I shall present it as a part of modern evolution theory.

1. Christian de Duve,   2002,   341 pages

> *Life Evolving: Molecules, Mind and Meaning*
>
> *Oxford Univ. Press, N. Y.*

2. James D. Watson, Nancy H. Hopkins, J.W. Roberts, Joan A. Steitz
> *and Al. M. Weiner,*

> *Molecular Biology of the Gene, 1161 pages, 4th Ed., 1997.*

> *Benjamin Cumming Publishers, Calif.*

Both de Duve and James D. Watson are Nobel Prize winners. The two books, 1500 pages altogether, with illustrations and tables, are well-written for advanced courses in biology. To the general public and for your information, what I could do is to summarize them.

A. From inorganic elements to bio-macromolecules to higher organisms to man.

A schematic presentation:

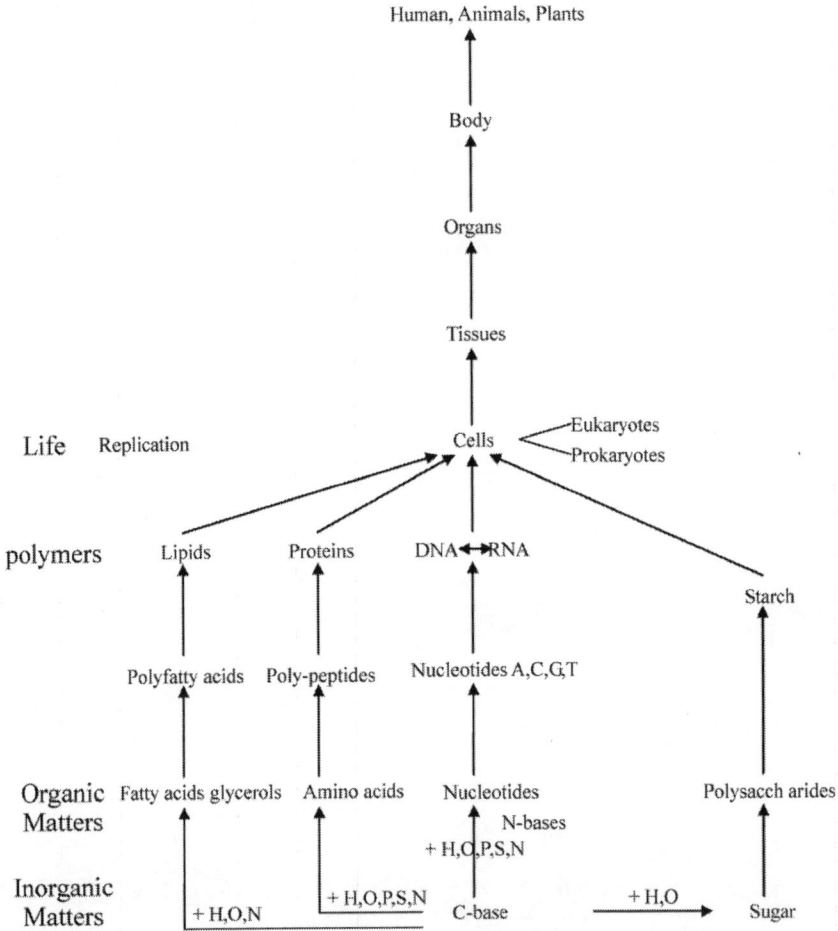

Fig. 1. Four kinds of polymers to cell, tissues, organs, to higher organisms

(overall biosynthetic work goes upward), by Stephen Liu

Fig. 1. in general principle, beginning with inorganic elements (with C as the skeleton), with addition of N (nitrogen), S and P, four kinds of polymers (starch, lipids, proteins and nucleic acids) are formed. So far and to this point, all these steps could be done in the laboratories. Beyond this point, everything is a matter of speculation and extension. Then, they are brought together to form cells, then tissues, organs and eventually plants, animals and humans. This is an oversimplification scheme. Yet, this is on materialistic ways what bioscience is

nowadays. This is what in colleges we teach in undergraduate classes and graduate courses. In general principle, scientists should not introduce anything that supernatural. If we do that, that is no longer in the scientific context (as what is said in school boards in their decision on textbooks).

In research universities in USA, some laboratories have been working on the tissue production. So far, scientists are able to produce synthesized skin for grafting on burnt patients. So far we have not succeeded in synthesizing one single animal cell in laboratory, let alone tissues, organs. Keep in mind, these are general principles. In theory, they are acceptable. Yet, we can not substantiate them in vitro up to this point.

B. Biochemical evolution to molecular evolution, then to species: (Fig. 2)

Biochemical to Molecular Evolution to higher categories of living beings

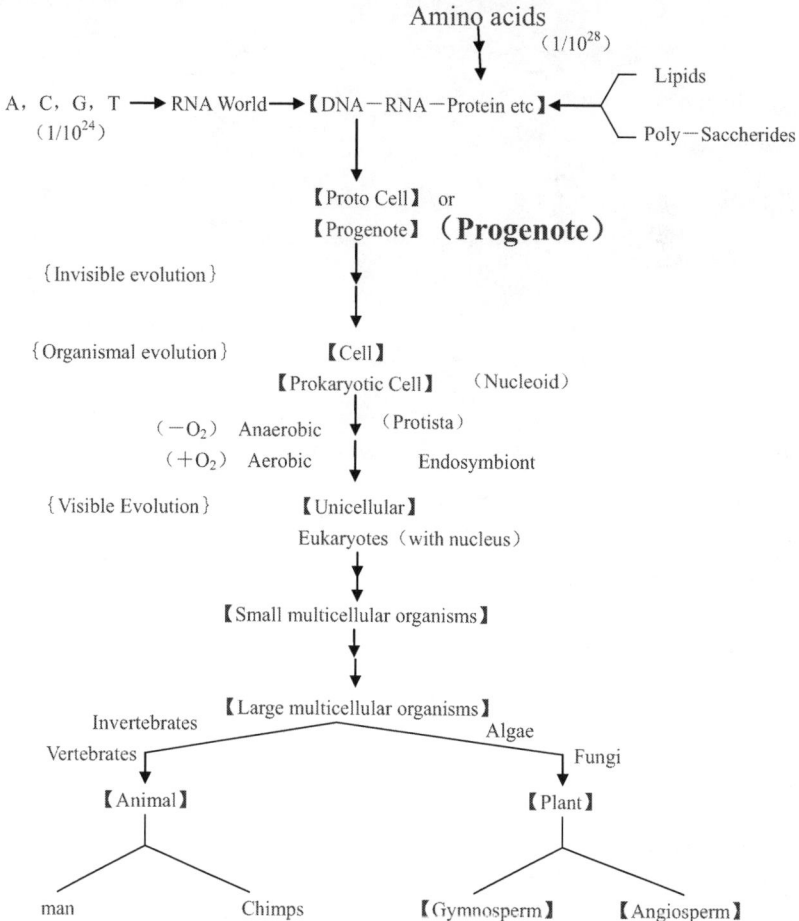

Amino acids

$(1/10^{28})$

Lipids

A，C，G，T ⟶ RNA World ⟶ 【DNA−RNA−Protein etc】 ⟵

$(1/10^{24})$

Poly−Saccharides

【Proto Cell】 or
【Progenote】 **（Progenote）**

{Invisible evolution}

{Organismal evolution}　　　【Cell】
　　　　　　　　　　　【Prokaryotic Cell】　　（Nucleoid）

$(-O_2)$　Anaerobic　　（Protista）
$(+O_2)$　Aerobic　　　Endosymbiont

{Visible Evolution}　　　【Unicellular】
　　　　　　　　　Eukaryotes（with nucleus）

【Small multicellular organisms】

【Large multicellular organisms】

Invertebrates　　　　　　　　　Algae
Vertebrates　　　　　　　　　　　　Fungi

【Animal】　　　　　　　　【Plant】

man　　　Chimps　　【Gymnosperm】　　【Angiosperm】

Fig. 3. Biochemical to molecular evolution to higher categories of living beings. Scheme/illustration downward, by Stephen C. Y. Liu

The biosynthetic reactions (in the first stage) to progenote (primitive cell) as given above, then it begins the evolutionary processes to higher categories of living beings. In scientific principles, they are scientifically valid in phylogeny and in classification (systematic). They are taught in schools, universities and graduate schools. So far and in reality, they are hypothetic and scientific theory only, without any experimental proval.

Progenote, primitive cell was coined by Prof. James D. Watson. It is generally accepted in the scientific community.

C. The evolution of progenote:

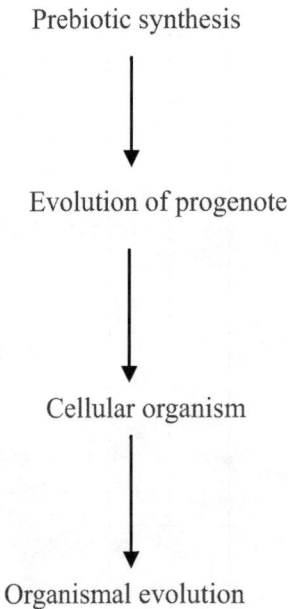

Prebiotic synthesis

↓

Evolution of progenote

↓

Cellular organism

↓

Organismal evolution

Fig. 4. Biosynthesis to progenote then to cellular organisms (progressive downward)

(taken from: James D. Watson et al 1995, Molecular Biology of the Gene. PP #1155)

Figure #3 illustrates biosynthesis in prebiotic soup, then to hypothetic progenote. Once progenote is formed, it has the ability of "self-replication" as living entity, to cells. From here on, cells will multiply to million cells, then to an organism. It would be more advisable for readers to look at the Figs. 1, 2 and 3

together, getting an overall view of biosynthesis, though overlapping.

Evaluation and Conclusion

Dr. Christian de Duve was a Belgian and naturalized US citizen. He shared Nobel prize with another two cell biologists, in1974. In his book, he acknowledged that in teens he was a Roman Catholic. While studying in college, he was influenced by European philosophies and social upheaval. He gave up his faith, and became an agnostic. In Chapt.13, pp#205-207, he listed the uniqueness of human, being quite extensive, such as a) being rational, b) having analytic abilities, c) abstract thinking & expression, d) ascetics, e) moral, e) responsibility and loyalty. This list contains much more than what evolutionists in general would like to admit. To some extent, his Catholic background had somehow an impact on his thinking.

In Chapt. 13th, "Becoming Human" (#189-207) he elaborated more on "the origin of human consciousness". Based on studies conducted with lab animals in group living, he advocated that moral consciousness origins from lower animals. In constant association with others, such lab animals would gradually develop animal nature and behavior, such as sex drive and emotion outburst. Such phenomena and behavior were due to physiological response, making an imprint on the nervous system. This was how animal or human consciousness developed and originated. This is the way most evolutionists would consider how human consciousness originated, exclusively on evolutionists' premises. In essence, Duve denied the human consciouseness, moral laws were endowed by the Creator. As a renowned cell biologist, he takes evolution as his personal philosophy, being entirely secular.

In the last several chapters, Dr. Duve dealt with the question as to "How About God in all That?" He openly confesses that he does not need God or religious faith in relation to science. In conviction and worldview he is an agnostic (pp#302-303). He mentioned that some other scientists/colleagues are atheists, such as British chemist Peter Atkins and naturalist Richard Dawkins, Hungarian immunologist George Klein, and American Steven Weinberg. Of course, they openly deny deity as evidence of God in nature. Duve said that in some way, *"atheism is in some way a religion"*.

In this chapter as a whole, I presented what the two eminent biologists considered the evolution of macromolecules to cells, tissues, organs and then the whole organism. With this chapter, we come to the end of "the evolution theory" at three levels. As scientific principles taught in our schools, they are scientifically valid and acceptable. It is in the domain of worldview scientists do differ.

Literature Cited as given in the Text

Chapter 16
Some Other Theories on Origin of Life

"Exclusion of creation/religion in science teaching was naïve and un-lightened."

Fr. Hans Kung

In Chapters 12 and 13, the two major theories of origin of life, i.e. *Biogenesis* (Chapt. 12) and *Abiogenesis* (Chapters 13, 14 and 15, evolution theories at three levels) are discussed. In reality and in substance, biochemical to molecular evolution are the revival of the old and traditional *abiogenesis hypothesis*.

In this chapter, I shall present some other theories which are diametrically at the opposite end to evolution theory. It is because that in last 30-40 years we scientists entered into the search of life with/in extraterrestrial studies, and also geological excavations for oil. By and large, these theories have been proposed by agnostics to atheists.

A. The *Panspermia*, i.e. life comes from other planets:

As early as 1821, French scientist Sale-Gyon de Montivault first proposed that life had come from other planets. Then, German scholar, H. E. Richter suggested that the meteorities carrying microbial life from other planets. Pursuit to this theory, in 1903 Swedish Svant Arrhenisus, a Nobel Laureate extended this to say that bacterial endospore carried by meteorites to this planet while the temperature drastically lowered down, with abundant moisture available, these endospore germinated and developed into life. Then, he coined the term pamspermia.

B. Microbial life in the depth of earth:

In recent decades, in search for the source of oil, international petroleum companies devoted a great deal of efforts in search, specifically the depth of earth, 500 meters to 2.8 miles down to the earth. Many university research labs. joined them in this effort. What they found sulfur bacteria in some rocks, and also some filamentous fungi. With these, some geologists interpreted the early evidence of life on this planet (cf. Scientific American, 1988)

C. Life transported from Mars:

Australian astrophysicist, Dr. Paul Davis, in 1999 published his book entitled in *"The Fifth Miracle: The Search for the Origin and Meaning of life"*, Simon & Schuster, N.Y. Based on the finding of trace of some microbes on meteorite ALH84001 in 1984 in Antarctica, and also the report by Mr. Daniel Golding, Dr. Davis advocated that " in 30 billion years ago, there was sign of microbial life on Mars." All these indicated the existence of primitive life on Mars. Then, this could be transported to earth in unknown time. "Did Life Come from Another World?" Scientific American, Nov. 2005, both David Warmflash and Benjamin Weiss theorized several pamspermia carried by asteroids or comet. Paul Davies in Science, Vol. 328, April 23, 2010 once again argued (in an interview) viral DNA dispatched by a far-away civilization may have since become incorporated into the DNA of organisms on our planet. Once again, all these are speculations more than anything realistic.

D. Life came from other planets:

Two British scholars, **Prof. Francis Crick and Leslie Orgel** advocated that in years ago spaceship carried first primitive life from other planets. All these are scientifico-philosophic speculation as to the origin of primitive life coming from other planets.

In recent years, the "Space Exploration Research" conducted by NASA in USA is a seemingly hot topic. United States acknowledged that this was a new dimension/territory of scientific exploration, with both scientific and military significance. The government appropriated a large sum of money for this program. Russian and even China followed the lead. In 2007, China launched spaceship " Shen-Zhou" with two astronauts. It was considered a feat with success. The European Union, Canada, Japan, Israel, India, Brasil and South Korea followed the suit, appropriating more than 100 billion dollars for such programs.

This presents a great scientific and intellectual challenge to the scientific communities, with job available. Up to this date, scientists have tried to find out whether is there any water on the moon and Mars. Once water is found on these planets, then they would consider the possibility of "life". Moon and Mars are large planets. In one of these days, scientists could trace out any sign of water channel, likely they would suggest the existence of life. Of course, this is scientific exploration. Once you have circumstantial evidence, no one could deny the logical extension of such an evidence. Years ago, scientists speculated any tract of nitrogen on the moon. As we all know that nitrogen and carbon are the two chemical skeletons of organic matters. Once you have found the trace of these two skeleton elements, the logical extension would be the existence of life. All these are based on the premise that life is nothing but lifeless organic matters. As scientists we all know that this is an oversimplification of "Life" to the extreme.

Conclusion

In this chapter, I present some other theories of origin of life. As I said in

The Introduction, the theories given in this chapter are diametrically opposing to the biochemical and molecular evolution (or origin) of life. They are speculations or theories more than anything else. They lack the empirical data to support them. So, we take them on the face value. Let me quote once again *Prof. James Watson's* saying. though he was talking about the molecular evolution. The principle is the same.   He said

"questions (of molecular evolution) become even more daunting when we try t speculate about the very earliest life forms. We have seen that even the best fossils preserve only the durable parts of an organism;(the macromolecules that most interest us are lost.) .. It is impossible to obtain direct proof for any particular theory of the origin of life.   The sobering truth is that even if every expert were to agree......... on how life originated, the theory would still be a best guess rather than a fact."

This is the conclusion given by a well-known bioscientist and professor of molecular biology.

Literature Cited

1. Paul Davis,   1999, 304 pages

    The Fifth Miracle: the Searching for the Origin and Meaning of Life

    Simon & Schuster, N. Y.

2. Christopher McKay, et al, 1996

    Search for Past Life on Mars: Possible Relic Biogenic Activity in Artisan

    Meteorite ALH84001, Science, AAAS 273

3. Svent Arrhenius, 1908

    Worlds in the Making. Harper, London, UK

4. Francis Crick,   1981

    Life Itself: Its Nature and Its Origin. Simon & Schuster, N.Y.

5. Christian de Duve, 1995

    Vital Dust: Life as a Cosmic Inperative, Basic Books, N. Y.

6. James B. Miller, Ed. 2001

    Cosmic Questions, N.Y. Academy of Sciences, Vol. 950

7. David Warmflash and Benjamin, 2005

    Did Life Come from Another World?

Chapter 17
Paleontology and Evolution Theory

" I am personally persuaded that a superintelligent Creator

exists beyond   And within the cosmo......

The Judeo-Christian philosophical framework has proved to be a particularly

fertile ground for the rise of modern science."

Prof. Owen Gingerich, Harvard Univ.

In Chapter 14th and 15th, I dealt with evolution theory at three levels. In general, either through genetic mutation in a stepwise manner, or geographic isolation for many years, minor modification to new sub-species of varieties could be produced. This is what biologists and evolutionists refer to as micro-evolution or minor changes. The mechanisms for such minor changes have been accepted by those evolutionists and non-evolutionists. The focal debate is so-called macroevolution, i.e. large changes or saltation. The mechanisms for such major changes, as most evolutionists agree, should be decoupled (separated) from what is known in micro-evolution. Such major changes could not be visually observed in life-time of scientists. No empirical experiments could be performed. Therefore, it is a matter of speculation and extension on the basis of what we could observe. This is the debate.

Another debate is whether living things were originated from one ancestor (monophylogeny) or more than one ancestor (***polyphylogeny***). As a scientific theory, this is not yet settled or agreed upon by both evolutionists and non-evolutionists. As proposed by Charles Darwin, and also by evolutionists, human and living things were evolved from a common descent. That is ***monophylogeny***. Yet, in USA, more than 40% of citizens believe that the human species was created by God, rather than evolved from a common ancestor. In western countries, Christians occupy a high percentage in population. They do not accept evolution of man. They believe that God created different "kinds", i.e. major categories of living things. Then, in a horizontal fashion, these major groups could evolve to lead to minor changes (polyphylogeny). So are Roman Catholic, Jewish and even Moslems

One additional point should be mentioned. As I elaborated in Chapter 12, in creation there are five schools of thought, including both young earth and old earth. In Christendom, some Christian scholars refuse to accept evolution theory in a wholesale fashion. Others accept evolution as the second stage of God's overall creation. Theistic Evolution is one of them. It has been known in both academic circle and in general public. Roman Catholic Church upholds theistic

evolution. That was why Pope John Paul II in 1996 affirmed that evolution theory was more than a theory, implying no conflict between evolution theory and Roman Catholic's faith. By and large, the evolutionists fail to understand all these. In argument, they mention only the "biblical creation" or "scientific creation" (young earth group, the literal reading and interpretation), as if there were only one school alone. They erroneously create such a barrier for mutual understanding, and reciprocal acceptance among evolutionists and non-evolutionists.

A. *Macro-evolution or major changes:*

Geologic Era	Fossils (+ +) , (+) , (−)	mys,(start to present	Major events , (Animal Fossils)	Major events (Plant Fossils)

When coming to macro-evolution, most evolutionists argue, not on the basis of direct observation and rational empirical experimentation; but on testing hypotheses against the predictions they make. They argue that nothing in science is ever absolutely proved. "Facts" are hypotheses in which they could have high confidence, because of massive evidence in their favor . All these are no longer in science, but in the domain of philosophy, even worldview.

Evolutionists often say that the fossil record will give good support to their theory. In other word, paleontology would provide the evidence for macro-evolution. If there is evidence, how much is there? How much validity or invalidity is there of the evidence? Are they scientifically sound and acceptable? This is the subject of this chapter.

B. *Geologic era, million years, and fossils (animals & plants):*

in Table 1 Geologic Era

Cenozoic	+ +	0.011	Human's	Herbaceous
Pleistocene	+ +	1.8	Giant mammals perished, Social life of humans	Mostly extincted
Pleitocene	+ +	6.0	Chimpanzees, monkeys, donkeys, etc	Trees extincted monocotyledons
Miocene	+	25.0	Mammals,hominides	

		+			
	Oligocene	+ ±	38.0	insects , early mammals	forests , dicotyledons
	Eocene	± +	54.0	Hoofed animals , carnivorous	
	Paleocene	± +	65.0	Lower mammals	
2	Mesozoic(reptiles)				
	Cretaceous	+ ±	135.0	Dinosaurs extinct , birds , lower mammals	monocotyledons , dicotyledons, gymnosperms
	Jurassic	+	181.0	birds , huge Dinosaurs	dicotyledons , evergreens
	Triassic	+	230.0	Dinosaurs , amphibians	Gymnospers,
	Appalachian				
3	Paleozoic（primitive）				
	Permian	±	260.0	repetiles , insects	Mosses,
	Pcnnsylvanian	±	320.0	reptiles , insects. amphibians	mosses , gymnospers
	Mississippian	±	345.0	sharks	
	Devonian	±	405.0	Sharks, amphibians	forests , gymnosperms
	Silurian	±	425.0	Wingless insecs , fishes	algae , trees
	Ordovician	±	500.0	Fishes appear , corrales	Sea weeds
	Cambrian	+ + +	500.0-600. 0	Modern animals, trilobs	Sea weeds

| 4 | Proterozoic | ± | 1600.0 | Oceanic primitive | Primitive aquatic algae |
| 5 | Archeozoic | ± | 3600.0 | | |

Table 1. Geological Era and stages with appearance of living things

C. *The classification (systematic) of living things (using common names):*

In biological sciences, there are classification systems. In classic literature, we use Latin, Green, or Latinized word so that biologists worldwide understand them. This is very true in paleontology. In this chapter, I am trying to use common names as much as possible for the general public.

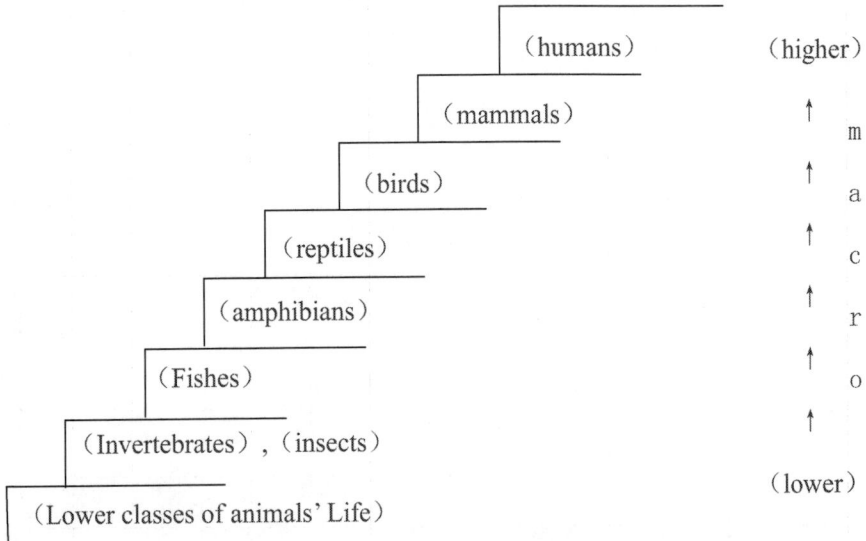

（humans）   （higher）

（mammals）   ↑   m

（birds）   ↑   a

（reptiles）   ↑   c

（amphibians）   ↑   r

（Fishes）   ↑   o

（Invertebrates），（insects）   ↑

（Lower classes of animals' Life）   （lower）

Fig. 1   A simplified classification scheme of animals (using common names)

(Compare with Fig 1 pp#181 & Fig 2#182)

By Stephen Liu

In general, fossils are found in cold region or in hot and dry regions. Under such conditions, their remains could be preserved as fossils. Learning from experience in excavation, the lower animals to amphibians, due to their soft tissues and organs, living in aquatic conditions, their bodies hardly preserved. No fossil could be found. If they were found, often the fossils were incomplete. By and large, paleontologists work with those in higher categories. Even so, their fossils are scarce. Therefore, fossil samples were collected from different

regions, then assembled in one central location. Even so, In order to substantiate evolution theory, attention should be focused on finding intermediate forms between major categories (cf. Fig. 1). For example, from invertebrates to fish, having teeth or different kind of teeth is critical. From amphibians to reptiles, appendages or feet and their lengths should be closely examined. From reptiles have teeth, and birds could fly with wings, but having no teeth. Coming to monkeys, chimpanzee, to human, pay attention to whether they could stand straight, having thigh bone, thumb and small finger's size and their degree of angle so that they could grasp more firmly articles. Attention should be paid to whether there is intermediate form. If there is, this should be found in fossil remains.

In general principles, the characteristics used in identifying phylogenetic relationships and differentiations are:

a)Morphology:

Skull size and capacity, pedals and dexterity: in early era

b)Physiological and functional differences, and

c)Genes and hybridization, etc: in recent years

D. Primates including monkey, chimpanzees and humans, and their time's frame:

Order Primates	(Order Primates)			
Sub-orders	Prosimii	Anthropoidea		
	Lemuroidae			
	Lorisidae			
	Tarsiidae			
	Anthropoidea	Catarrhini		
		Cercopithecidae		
			Lemuridae	Old & new world monkeys & apes
			Lorisidae	
			Tarsiidae	
			Anthropoidea	

		Cebidae	Cercopithec da	
		New world monkey	Old world monkey	
			Hominoidea	
			Pongidae	
			Pan:Chimpanzee	
			Gorilla:Gorilla	
			Pongo:Orangutan	
			Homiminidae	
			Homo:man	

Table 2. Order Primates, and sub-orders

Prof. Carl Linne's classification, mammals have 32 orders. Primate is only one of the Orders, including Lemurs, Lorises, Tarsiers, new world monkey and old world monkey; Then gibbors, siamangs, orangutan, gorilla, chimpanzee and humans. Evolutionists believe that sometime in the past there existed a population of apes-like creatures that split into sub-populations, one of which gave rise to the gorilla and the other of which split once again to give rise to the chimpanzee and man. The ancestor of apes and man is in much dispute. Very little is known about it. So much of it is hypothetical.

E. Suggested phylogenetic scheme for hominioids:

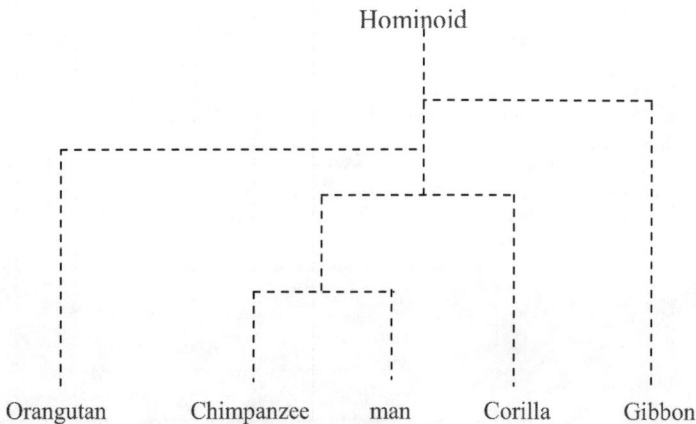

Fig. 2. A hypothetic phylogenetic scheme for the hominoids

As given in this chapter, the fossil samples collected at various places, and then assembled together for analysis by palenontologists. With such a samples collected from diversified regions, scientists have found them difficult to classify them under reasonable categories. As compared with what we know in nature, the samples, though numerous in a way, are relatively small. The best speculation they could reach will be likely a approximation at the best. Therefore, the reliability of such report is questionable. Conclusions reached are even more questionable and debatable. They could be used only as indirect evidences.

F. The conclusions reached by Evolutionary Paleontologists:

Paleontologists and anthropologists acknowledge the fact that fossils (fossum in Latin) collected were collected in fragments of skeletons, skulls, teeth and bones of relatively hard organs of higher organisms. They were buried in deep layers of the earth in relatively dry region or very cold region. Though seemingly a large number is assembled together, they represent only a small fraction of animals or/and plants of higher categories. Lower categories, due to the soft cartilages or remains, the lower categories are not preserved. The chromosomes and their DNA are what molecular biologists interested most are lost. What these scientists could do are to assemble them as much as possible, and study them carefully as possible. So, scientists and non-scientists fully realize the validity of such a study, though systematically and analytically as possible. They report their findings. Then, based on what they know, they suggest hypothesis. Then, with what they have already known, they propose their speculations or conjunctions.

Late report by two American scientists, Johnson and White, 2007.

Figure 5, both D. Johanson and T. D. White, in Science, AAAS:1104, 2007proposed,on the basis of more critical analyses of the fossils which were collected from various regions for a comparative studies. Even so, there was no conclusive evidence.

Hominoid

Orangutan   Chimpanzee   man   Corrilla   Gibbon

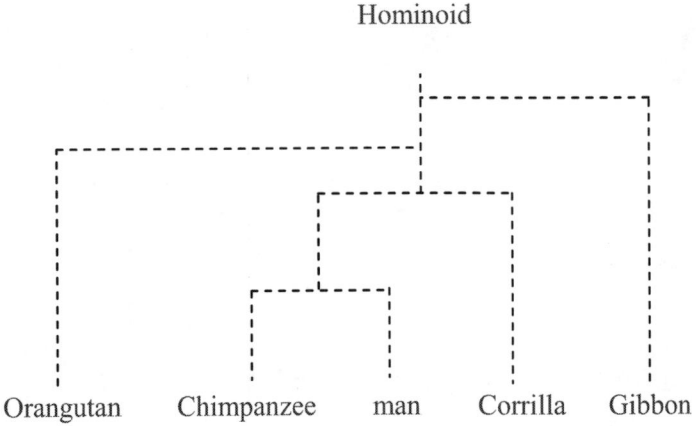

Fig. 3. Family tree of man and A.africanus, by Johnson and White, 2007

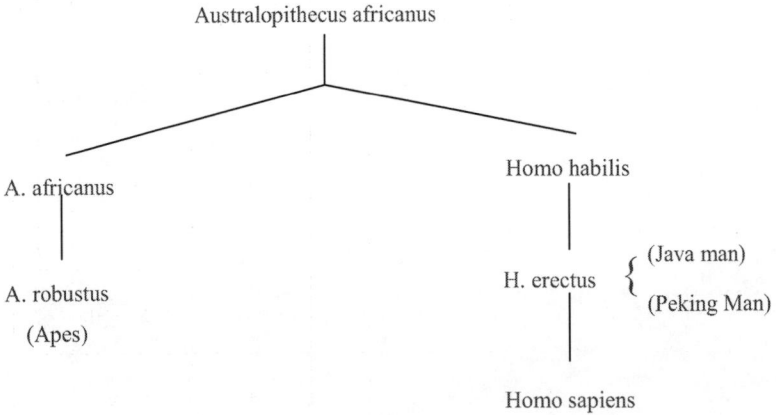

Australopithecus africanus

A. africanus

A. robustus

(Apes)

Homo habilis

H. erectus { (Java man)
                (Peking Man)

Homo sapiens

Fig 4. Fossils of man and their times of appearance:

G. The fossils of men and the time frame they appeared:

0	Modern Man (Homo sapiens)	
1	Cro-Magnon	50,000 yrs
2	Neanderthal	80,000 yrs
3	Swanscombe	300,000 yrs
4	Heidelberg	500,000 yrs
5	Java	400,000 yrs
6	Peking	400,000 yrs
7	Australopithecus	1,000,000 yrs
8	Zingjanthropus	1,750,000 yrs
9	Late samples in northern China	?
10	Primitive ape-man of S. Africa	800,000 – 2 billion yrs

Table 4. Fossils of Man and their appearance

Paleontologists and anthropologists have been debating on these data and their validity. They have not yet come to their conclusion.

H. Conclusions given by eminent evolutionists in recent years:

Evolutionists and paleontonologists who have devoted to the study of this subjects in recent years have come to the conclusions, as quoted here, regarding with fossils and their findings.

Fossils (fosilium in Latin) refer to those skeletons (skulls, bones, teeth, etc) are remains of those living things once existed on this planets, and then they were

preserved in hot-dry region of cold climate area. As compared with the enormous number of animals and plants on this planet, millions to billions the fossils and their number are relatively small. In addition, only those of high categories with relatively hard remains could be fossilized. Lower categories due to their soft to fragile constitutions, these of lower categories were not fossilized. What scientists could study today is only a fraction of the total number if they are fossilized. By and large, fossilized remains are fragments, seldom as a whole entities. They were collected at various times and in different localities with varying conditions, and studied. Scientists realize all these. They acknowledge the fact that they could only study what is available, and come to conclusions, as approximation as possible. So, they interpret their conclusion with consideration and reservation. Readers of to-day should keep all these in their mind when they read their reports and books.

Prof. Douglas Futuyma, of N.Y State University is one of well-known paleontologist and evolutionist of our time. His book enitled in"Evoultionary Biology" is a standard college textbook, and should be read and consulted by those who are interested in this subject. In fact, the geological time scale table given in this book, is taken from his book. In Chapter 6, "Evolving Lineages in the Fossil Record" begins with such a paragraph, as quoted:

"Although some of the history of evolution can be inferred from living organisms, it is only in the fossil record that we can hope to find reasonable direct evidence of their history. The fossil record tells us of the existence of innumerable createures that have left no living descendants, of great episodes of extinction and diversification, of the movements of continenets and organisms that explain their present distributions. Only from this record can we obtain an absolute time scale for evolutionary events, as well as evidence of the environmental conditions in which they transpired. The fossil record, moreover, provides an independent check – although a very in-exact one – on some inferences of living organisms."

It seems to me that there are some controversial and contradictory statements if we read them slowly and carefully. If fossils are so fragmentary and scanty, how they represent the total picture of living entities? If so, how could they give us a total picture? How could we compare them with what are living on this planet? Which one, the fossil record or the living things today could give us the direct evidence? How could we compare them?

Prof. Ernst Mayr in "What is Evolution", said in pp#14-19, Chapt. 13, his discussion on fossils as follows: Why does the fossil record fails to reflect the gradual change one could expect from evolution? Only an incredible small

230

fraction of organisms that had once lived are preserved as fossils!"

Well-known molecular biologist of Harvard Univ., Prof. James D. Watson, in his *"Molecular Biology of the Genes"*, *in Chapt.28,* *"The earliest examples of anatomically modern human fossils have been found in Africa, suggesting that a band of the earliest humans left Africa and that their descendants migrated throughout Europe, Asia, and finally America. Although the theory that modern human (Homo sapiens) first emerged in Africa is widely believed, the fossil evidence is unlikely to be complete, and there is nothing to exclude the possibility that modern humans evolved on another continent, and then migrated to Africa."* In fact, in recent years, there is such evidence and theory.

"Can we address the question of what Homo sapiens originated by examining the molecular fossil record that is written in the DNA sequences of present day humans? ....Cytochrome c, mitochondrial /DNA seems to be ideal"

In the chapter's conclusion, Prof. J. D. Watson said

"Questions of molecular evolution become even more daunting when we try t speculate about the very earliest life forms. We have seen that even the best fossils preserve only the durable parts of an organism; the macromolecules that most interest us are lost. .. It is impossible to obtain direct proof for any particular theory of the origin of life.   The sobering truth is that even if every expert in the field of molecular evolution were to agree on how life originated, the theory would still be a best guess rather than a fact."

These words come from a Nobel Laureate. If this is the case, the so-called "molecular clock" be considered as one of the ways to ascertain the relationship of living things, scientifically reliable? The answer would be "not likely".

Conclusion

Lately, there are several articles related to the subject of fossils and paleontological evidences, they are summarized and quoted here as a summary.

a)There remains some gaps in the fossil records.

b)Very few fossil remains of chimpanzees or gorilla have been un-earthed. The closet relatives of humans. One such gap has been the near-total absence of ape-like fossils from 12 and 7 million years ago, a period during which monkey-like apes (or apes-like moneys) must have diverged to give rise to the ancestors of to-day's remnant trident of chimpanzes, gorilla and human.

c)It is not proper to call Proconsul an apes, a monkey, or even a monkey-like ape or an ape-like monkey, proconsul is what it is...... "The ape in the tree" is a fine account of new ways to puzzle out the behaviors of fossilize animals from odd scarpes of bones. Reading it, I got the sense that maybe we should fuss a little bit over geneology, and pay more attention to ancient landscape, environment, climate, diets, and behaviors. We really need to find a lot more fossils.

d)In 1947, Pan-African Congress of Prehistory suggested that Africa could be the origin of human. This conclusion was based on the studies of three partial skulls, of 154,000 – 160,000 years. Scholars named them as Homo sapiens idaltus. Idaltus is an African word for earlier.

e)About one third of the fossils, scholars have so far examined were dug and un-earthed .

f)In May, 7th, 2010, Science by AAAS reported: "The Neanderthal project, which took four years, and involved 57 scientists, is the latest and most astonishing example of the recovery of scientifically useful information from ancient DNA.

The new data answer a few of the many questions about modern human beings' relationship with their last big hominin competitors, who died out about 30,000 years ago. The data also hint at what <u>Homo sapiens</u> and – but <u>Homo neanderthalensis</u> did not – that may have made the difference between survival and extinction.

The findings show that modern humans and Neanderthals interbred, probably in the Middle East, between about 100,000 and 80,000 years ago, soon after modern humans migrated out of Africa and before they diversified, through chance and natural selection, into the ethnic groups that exist to-day.

g) Proto-humans and chimpanzees diverged from each other about 6.5 million years ago. Modern humans and Neanderthals diverged about 300,000 years ago. One a genetic level, Neanderthals and modern humans are almost as closely related as to-day's ethnic groups are to each other.

h) The fossil records are often used by evolutionists to support their theories of origin of life. With such a small number of unearthed samples, conclusions drawn should be carefully evaluated. The intermediates are the keys to bridge-up the gaps. As Nobel Laureate James Watson said, *pertaining to molecular evolution with so much missing, The sobering truth is that even if every expert in the field of molecular evolution were to agree on how life originated, the theory would still be a best guess rather than a fact.*

Literature cited

1. Duan T. Gish,   1995

    Evolution: The Fossils still say "No"!

    Institute for Creation Research., Calif.

2.   Douglas Futuyma, 4th Ed.

    Evolutionary Biology

    Sinauer Associates, Boston, MA

3.   James D. Watson, et al,   1997

    Molecular Biology of the Gene

    Benjamin Cummings, Boston, MA

4.   Jonathan Wellls,   2000

    i-cons of Evolution: Science or Myth?

    Regency Publishing Co.,

5.   Science, AAAS,   May   2010.

Chapter 18
Are Big Bang theory and Creation narratives
Compatible and Mutually Explainable?

"Big Bang and subsequent physical and biological evolution
are firmly established beliefs in the mind of nearly all scientists.
When set side by side with the story of creation in Genesis,
they appear to give a more convincing account of material creation.
But, the two accounts have different purposes.
The scientific one makes no mention of God and creation.
On the other hand, Genesis is primarily concerned with.
The divine truth of God and creation and God's relation to humankind.

Prof. Ted Burger

"The most un-intelligible thing about the universe is made   intelligible."

Albert Einstein

"The origin of the universe can be talked about not only in scientific terms,
but also in poetic and spiritual language. The biblical statement, as an approach
that is complementary to the scientific one. Indeed, the Judeo-Christian
tradition describes the beginning of the world in a way
that is surprisingly similar to the scientific model."

Prof. Victor Weisskopt,
Eminent Physicist, MIT

235

Introduction

On April 24th, 1992, scientific societies and establishments all over the world announced "The Big Bang" theory, a beginning of time, as the greatest discovery in astronomy and astrophysics in the century! Newspapers, periodicals and science magazines all over the world carried this headline!

As a reaction to this announcement, Roman Catholic Church acknowledges that the Big Bang theory is compatible to Creation narratives in the book of Genesis. They are being able to mutually explain the two theories. The Christian Church worldwide has no official representative organ. No official announcement was issued. It is more so with the Chinese evangelical church at large. Therefore, it is a matter of professional judgment, and personal choice.

This chapter will present briefly the principles of Big Bang theory and related subjects, as follows:

A. The Big Bang theory, historical perspectives and principles,

B. The Anthropic principle,

C. The Creation narratives in Genesis,

D. Scholars and their views, and

E. Is Big Bang Theory compatible to Creation narratives and mutually explainable?

A. Big Bang Theory: Historical perspectives and principles:

1)The beginning of this universe had been discussed long before the Christian era. The Jewish, Christian and Muslim tradition, the universe started at a finite time in the past. It was necessary to have "The First Cause" to explain the existence of this universe.

2)Greek philosopher, Aristotle, in 340 B.C., in his book "On the Heavens", put forward two arguments: the earth was the center of the universe, being stationary. The other was that Sun, moon, the planets of Mercury, Venus, Mars, Jupiter and Saturn moved in circular orbits about the earth. Then, Polish priest, Nicholas Copernicus proposed sun-centered universe. (cf. Chapt. 5, the Birth of Modern Exp. Sci.)

3)Issac Newton, in his "Philosophiae Naturalis Principia Mathematica,, postulated a law of universal gravitation. The gravity causes the earth and the planets to follow elliptical paths around the sun, and there were an infinite number of stars.

4)*In 1924-29, American Astronomer and Astrophysicist Dr. Edwin Hubble,* using the Cosmic Background Explorer Satellite (COBE) observed the cosmic

space. He reported that ***there was a time, called the Big Bang*** when the universe was infinitesimally small and infinite dense; and the uniform expansion of the universe.

5)***In 1965, Arne Penzias and Robert Wilson at Bell Lab.***, using sensitive microwave detector on the background response, discovered that the universe was/is expending, (based on a suggestion made by George Gamow that the universe was very dry and hot, glowing white hot) therefore there is a beginning. In 1978, the two men were awarded with Nobel Prize. All these are the greatest intellectual revolution in the 20th century (Stephen Hawkings, "A Brief History of Time: From the Big Bang to Black Holes, 1999).

6)In 1970, Roger Penrose, a British mathematician and physicist, working together with Stephen Hawking with mathematical formulae and their calculations, came to the conclusion that there must have been a Big Bang singularity provided only the general relativity is correct and the universe contains as much matter as we have observed.

As a result of these Scientists' keen observation, studies and calculation, the Big Bang theory has been established. There was a great deal of endorsement by Maxists and materialists who believe in scientific determinism, and also a lot of opposition from Christian church's Radicals who feel that the theory would smack of divine intervention.

B. The early and later events in the Big Bang:

The picture of a universe that started off very hot, and cooled as it expanded is the basic principle known. It is in agreement with all the observational evidence that scientists have reported. For steps in details with accuracy, let me quote what Prof. Stephen Hawkings wrote in his book.

At the Big Bang itself, the universe is thought to have had zero size, and so to have been infinitely hot. As the universe expanded, the temperature of the radiation decreased.

One second after the Big Bang, it would have fallen to about ten thousand million degrees. This is about a thousand times the temperature at the center of the sun. At this time the universe would have contained mostly photons, electrons and neutrinos (extremely light particles that are affected only by the weak force and gravity) and their antiparticles, together with some protons and neutrons. As the universe continues to expand and the temperature to drop, the rate at which electron/anti-electrons pairs were being produced in collision world have fallen below the rate at which they were being destroyed by annihilation. So most of the electrons and anti-electrons would have annihilated with each other to produce more photons, leaving only a few electrons left over. The neutrinos and anti-neutrinos, however, would not have annihilated with each other, because these particles interact with themselves and with other particles only very weakly.

About one hundred seconds after the Big Bang, the temperature would have fallen to one thousand million degrees, the temperature inside the hottest stars. At this temperature protons and neutrons would no longer have sufficient energy to escape the attraction of the strong nuclear force, and would have started to combine together to produce the nuclei of atoms of deuterium (heavy hydrogen), which contain one proton and one neutron. The deuterium nuclei then would have combined with more protons and neutrons to make helium nuclei, which contain two protons and two neutrons, and also   small amounts a couple of heavier elements, lithium and beryllium." (pp# 117-118)

This picture of a hot early stage of the universe was first put forward by Dr. George Gamor in 1948. In his paper, he made a remarkable prediction that radiation (in the form of photons) from the very hot early stages of the universe should still be around to-day, but with its temperature reduced to only a few degrees above absolute zero (-273 F)

Within only a few hours of the Big Bang, the production of helium and other elements would have stopped. And after that, for the next million years or so, the universe would have just continued expanding, without anything much happening. Eventually, once the temperature had dropped to a few thousand degrees, and electrons and nuclei no longer had enough to overcome the electromagnetic attraction between them, they would have started combining to form atoms. The universe as a whole would have continued expanding and cooling, but in regions that were slightly denser than average, the expansion would have been slowed down by the extra gravitational attraction. This would eventually stop expansion in some region and cause them to start to re-collapse.

As time went on, the hydrogen and helium gas in the galaxies would break up into smaller clouds that would collapse under their own gravity. ....The earth was initially very hot and without an atmosphere. In the course of time it cooled and acquired an atmosphere from the emission of gases from the rocks. This early atmosphere was not the one in which we could have survived. It contained no oxygen, but a lot of other gases that are poisonous to us. However, there are other primitive forms of life that can flourish under such conditions. They would thus have reproduced themselves and multiplied in oceans.

The first primitive forms of life consumed various materials, including hydrogen sulfide, and released oxygen. This gradually changed the atmosphere to the composition that it has today, and allowed the development of higher forms of life such as fish, reptiles, mammals, and ultimately the human race.

This picture of a universe that very hot and cooled at it expanded is in agreement with all the observational evidence that we have today.   (Stephen Hawkings, #3pp- 117-123).

C. The Anthropic Principle:

Literally, this means "We see the universe the way it is because we exist".

The whole history of science has been the gradual realization that events do not happen in an arbitrary way, but that reflects a certain underlying principles and orders, which to us Christians be divinely inspired. At first sight, this universe is the region where we live seems in such a smooth region. It is in this region where galaxies and stars formed and are conditions right for the development of complicated self-replicating organisms like ourselves who are able of asking the question, why it this so? This is exactly what the anthropic principle is. For intelligent life being possible, the law of sciences include: the fundamental numbers, like the size of electric charge of the electron and the ratio of masses of the proton and the electron are here and met. The remarkable fact is that these values of these numbers seem to have been finely adjusted to make it possible the development of life. If they were slightly different, stars either would have been unable to burn hydrogen and helium, or else they would not have exploded. We can take all these as evidences of a divine purpose in creation, and the choice of laws of science as support for the anthropic principle.

There are two versions of the anthropic principle, the weak one and strong one. The **weak anthropic principle** states that in a universe that is large or infinite in space and/or in time, the conditions necessary for the development of intelligent life will be met in certain regions that are limited in space and time. The intelligent beings in these regions should therefore not be surprised if they observe that their locality in the universe satisfies the conditions, both physical and chemical, that are necessary for their existence. *If it had been different, we would not be here!*

The strong version of anthropic principle says that there are *either many different universes or many different regions of a single universe, each with its own initial configuration and with its own set of law of science*. Of these universities, only in a few universes that are like ours would intelligent being develop.

D. Comments made by renowned scholars:

Prof. Stephen Hawking, "it is the discovery of the century!" and " Science seems to have uncovered a set of laws, that within the limits set up by the uncertainty principle, tell us how the universe will develop within time, if we know its state at any one time. These laws may originally decreed by God, but it appears that he has since left the universe to evolve according to the laws. .... The whole history of science has been the gradual realization that events do not happen in an arbitrary manner, but they reflect a certain underlying order, which may or may not be divinely inspired." (## 122).

In 2010, Prof. Hawking published his second book "Perfect Design" on this subject. His conviction remains pretty much the same way.

Prof. Owen Gingrich of Harvard University, an evangelical Christian Amish scholar, wrote in his book, "God's Universe", as

"for several decades, theists and atheists have been wrangling over the meaning of the anthropic principle. For theists, the anthropic principle may not be a proof of God and his existence, but it is surely a pointer to a creative Super-Intelligence at work."…. "I am personally persuaded that a Super-Intelligent Creator exists beyond and within cosmos, and that the rich context of congeniality shown by our universe, permitting and encouraging the existence of self-conscious life, is a part of the Creator's design and purpose. We can hope that our increased scientific understanding will eventually reveal more to us about God, the Creator and Sustainer of the cosmos." (Pp#39-40)

Prof. Victor Weisskopt, eminent physicist at MIT said,

"The origin of the universe can be talked about not only in scientific terms, but also in poetic and spiritual language. The biblical statement, as an approach that is complementary to the scientific one. Indeed, the Judeo-Christian tradition describes the beginning of the world in a way that is surprisingly similar to the scientific model."

Prof. Michael Polanyi philosopher, in his book of "Personal Knowledge", said:

"The Book of Genesis and its great pictorial illustrations, like the frescoes of Michelangelo, remains a far more intelligent account of nature and the origin of the universe from a Christian perspective than the representation of the world as a chance collection of atoms, as grossly simplistic in science. For the biblical cosmology continues to express the significance of all the fact that the world exists, and that man has emerged from it, while the scientific picture denies, as

atheists contemplate to do, any meaning to the world, and indeed ignores all of

our most vital experience of the world."

Prof. Michael Turner of Univ. of Chicago:

" Un-believably important, the significance of this can not be overstated."

Sir Prof. Fred Hoyle of Oxford University

" a super-intelligence was at work!"

Dr. George Smoot of NASA Goddard Space Flight Center, Greenbe, TX, Nobel

Laureate of 2006 said,

"what we have found is evidence for the birth of the universe.

It is looking at God and his work."

Dr. Smoot shared the Nobel Prize with Dr. John C. Mather, for their work using COBE Satellite at Lawrence Nat. Lab., Calif. Drs. John Barrow and Frank J. Tipler of Oxford Univ.,*" for any form of life to exist, it has to meet the astrophysical number and physics"*.

Stephen Liu's comment:. In recent years those who are totally evolutionists/atheists to advocate biochemical and molecular evolution with simplistic view of life, should know the anthropic principle. For any life to intelligent life to be originated/developed on this planet has to meet the stringent requirements in physics and astrophysics. In recent, under NASA programs, they have tried to find so-called "extra-terrestrial life" (for example, Prof. Paul Davies of Australia). Years ago, they endeavored to find any nitrogen present (essential element of nitrogenous compounds such as proteins and nucleic acid) on Mars. Lately, they tried to see any trace of water which is essential for life. Once Dr. Davies suggested bacterial endospore transported from other planets could be the first sign of life on Mars. All these are their theories or imaginations or assumptions. So far, no scientific proof is available. We hope that their labor is not in vain.

E. The Creation narratives in Genesis:

Genesis Chapt. 1, verses 1-2,

" In the beginning God created the heavens and the earth. Now the earth

formless and empty, darkness was over the surface of the deep,

and the spirit of God was hovering over the waters" (NIV version).

We evangelical Christians consider these being theological and pictorial, and poetic. They are not scientific (non-scientific), yet not un-scientific (describing

241

supernatural and natural phenomena). We should say that these are more theological, declaring the almighty God the Creator and his almighty and wisdom. They are non-scientific, why. It is because that the narratives were given before the birth of modern experimental science.

I have consulted five sets of Bible Commentary written in English language. The New Bible Commentary which was written a great number of British theologians and scholars, and published by Inter-Varsity Fellowship Press. It has a very high scholarly standard. It has been consulted by those who have a genuine desire to study the Bible. The Commentary has this paragraph,

> *"Creation account does not claim to be scientific…….. If it had been written in accordance with scientific ideas of the present day, it would be mostly outdated and inaccurate in a century's time…… Yet, it is a scientific in substance. ……… The biblical record of creation is rather to be regarded as piscturesque narrative, affording a graphic representation. . The opening chapter must be regarded as divine revelation …… The account of creation is given with a spiritual and religious aim."*

Pertaining to the Big Bang theory, there are following quotations by scholars.

1)*Dr. Ted Burge, Prof. Emeritus of Physics of Univ. in London wrote,*

"The Big Bang and subsequent physical and biological evolution are firmly established beliefs in the minds of nearly of many and many scientists, if not nearly all. When set side by side with the story of creation in Genesis, they appear to give a more convincing account of material creation. But, the two accounts have different purposes. The scientific one, of course, makes no mention of God. Genesis, on the other hand, is primarily concerned with the divine truth of God and creation, and God's relation to human kind."

2)American astronomer/physicist, Dr. Hugh Ross the Founder of "The Reason to Believe" says,

"If the universe arose out of a big bang, it must have had a beginning. If it has a beginning, it must have a Beginner."

3)Prof. Howard Van Till , American astrophysicist of Calvin College, Michigan, says:

"We have spoken of the Big Bang as the opening episode of cosmic history – the beginning". As Christians, we naturally associate the concept of beginning. As Christians, we naturally associate the beginning with the opening line of Genesis 1 – the majestic announcement with which the first creation narrative opens. It is tempting, therefore, to equate these two "beginnings", and thus to view the Big Bang theory as a scientific version of creatio ex nihilo. We believe these two concepts differ in substantial ways, and should be treated as distinctly different ideas, owing to a) Big Bang is totally other than God, and b) its causality and c) continuity."

4)Prof. Stephen Hawking said:

" If the density of the universe one second after the Big Bang has been greater by one part of a thousand billion, the universe could have collapsed after ten years. On the other hand, it the density of the universe at the time had been less by the same amount, the universe would have been essentially empty since it was about ten years' old."

Conclusion

The Big Bang theory was well formulated and promulgated by astrophysicists and astronomers all over the world in 1992. It was based on observation with cosmic telescope, and then calculated with mathematics to their best abilities, and compared with what scientists have known. Astrophysicists and astronomers came to the conclusion of it, as a scientific theory. Big Bang is the beginning of time. It was 5 t0 14/16 billion years ago, such an event had happened.

In 1965, Drs. Arno Penzie and Robert Wilson of Bell Lab. were awarded with Nobel Prize for their painstaking work. Then, in 2006, Dr.George Smoot and John Mather of NASA were also awarded with Nobel prize. Certainly, all these carrying weight and confirmed the scientific trustworthy to the theory.

The anthropic principle as being a sequential to Big Bang theory is also well established and accepted by most scientists, if not all.

All these in principles show that the Creation narratives as given in Genesis is Christian theological description. They are complementary and supplementary. One gives the physical science of creation whereas the other gives a theological one. They are theoretically complementary. They are mutually explainable, at least to th Auther of this book.

In 2002, while Prof. Dr. John Polkinghorne, former President of Queen's College of University of Cambridge, particle mathematic physicist, and Cannon Theologian of Liverpool, accepted the Templeton Award/Prize, he said,

"The Big Bang and the evolution are compatible with belief   in God as Creator".

Nobel Prize winner, Dr. Robert Jastrow, in his book of "God and the Astronomers" by W.W. Norton Book Co., in 1996, said:

" the Big Bang theory appears to support the biblical doctrine of Creation.

Literature Cited

1.Hugh Rose, 1945

The Creator and the Cosmo: How the Greatest Scientific Discoveries of the Century. NAV Press, Colorado.

2.Stephen Hawking, 1988

A Brief History of Time: From the Big Bang to Black Holes.

Bantam Books, N.Y.

3. Howard Van Till, Robert Snow, J.H. Stek and D.H. Young, 1990

Portraits of Creation: Biblical and Scientific Perspectives on the World's Formation.

Wm B. Eerdmans Publishing Co, MI

4.Russell Stannard Ed., et al, 2000

God for the 21th Century. Templeton Foundation Press, Penn.

5.Bernard Ramm, 1954

Christian View of Science and Scripture.

Moody Press, Chicago, IL.

6. Francis Davidson, A.M. Stibbs and E.F.Keven, 2003

New Bible Commentary. Wm. B. Eerdmans Publishing, MI

7.Robert Jastrow, 1996

God and The Astronomers. W.W. Norton Co., N.Y.

8. Owen Gingerich, 2006

God's Universe.   Harvard Univ. Press, MA

Chapter 19
Stem Cells and Cloning Research Regenerative Medicine: with cells and organs

"My view is that the third millennium of Christian existence will bring a new integration of scientific and religious thought the development of a more global spirituality, and a retrieval of some of the deepest spiritual insights of the Christian faith, which have often been underemphasized or overlooked."

Prof. Keith Ward

In 1999 when the Annual Conference of American Association for the Advancement of Sciences (AAAS) was convened, with more than 3,000 scientists of different specialties in a huge assembly hall, the Chairperson announced that " *Stem Cells Show Their Potentials: Challenge for a New Century*". This was an important and meaningful announcement, calling for attention and also scientific work in the coming years.

I. Historical:

The second half of 20th century was considered as "Molecular Biology Era". In biological research, molecular biologists have made great discoveries and great stride in accomplishments.. In 1935, the molecular structure and functions of DNA was announced. That ushered the molecular era! Since then, molecular biologists have been working on genes, their structure and activation and termination, then genomics, and now stem cells and clonings. No body knows what will be next?

In the early dates, molecular biologists were using "*model systems*", such as E. coli, yeast, mouse (pl. mice) in their empirical work. Prof. J. D. Watson said once in his textbook that more than 50% of the information in molecular biology up to that point was derived from working with *Escherichia coli* in vitro. These model systems are either cells or small animals, due to the simple fact that they are smaller in size. As a rule they multiply fast. In cloning research mouse was the choice. The first mouse cloned from differentiated cells were reported in 1998 by Prof. Wakayama and his colleagues at the University of Hawaii. Many laboratories around the world had experience in early mouse embryology, and achievement seemed certain to herald a rapid expansion of the research effort on cloning with embryonic cells. However, in practice, it proved difficult for other

laboratories to replicate these results. So far only six laboratories have reported successive cloning of mice. The Roslin Institute at Edinbough, Scotland was the first research institute   which cloned farm animals, such as goat, pig and cattle.

In the last twenty years the embryonic stem cell, somatic stem cell and cloning research led to regenerative medicine. This has been a fast-growing field of research endeavor in USA and elsewhere. In a matter of years, so many scientific papers have been published. In 2000, 49 articles were published. By 2011, the number increased to 654. USA was by and large the leader in this area, and China as the second.   In May of 2012, American Association for the Advancement of Science published a supplement of 72 pages entirely on "Regenerative Medicine in China", with 71 articles. All these show that this field of research with clinical application has been increasing by leap and bound.

In this regard, allow me do a wee bit of reminiscence in my teaching-research endeavor in the People's Republic of China. I remember so well that in the year 1980 the diplomatic relations between USA and China was normalized. Consequently, China opened up to the outside world the first time. So many westerners and outsiders took the initiatives of visiting and lecturing in China. I was one of those fellows in the international crowd. With the invitation by Chinese Government's Ministry of Education and Ministry of Forestry and Agriculture, I went to China, the land of birth, and the land I had never seen since 1950. With a sabbatical leave of six months granted the Universities in Michigan, I taught "Molecular Biology of Animal Viruses" at the Chinese Academy of Agricultural Sciences in Beijing, with 128 senior faculty members coming all over the land. To my surprise, they knew nothing about Molecular Biology. They took "chemical microbiology" as molecular biology!   DNA, RNA and gene and gene expression were practically unknown to them. It was due to the simple fact of isolation and deliberate separation by Chinese Communist Government. University faculty members were in despair and in need of modernization of their learning and university curriculum. Then, another three months were spent at Fudan University, teaching "Molecular Virology" in a nationwide lecture with 120 some Chinese scholars. While I was at Fudan University, Prof. Ming-Chi Wang who was a plant virologist, a graduate from University of Minnesota. He was many years senior to me. In fact, he was instrumental to get me going to China in 1980. Prof. Wang was asked to give a television lecture on modern virology and molecular biology. He requested my assistance in providing the lecture materials. So, I took Prof. David Baltimore, a well-known molecular biology/virology at MIT, his seven molecular classifications of viruses. This molecular classification on the basis of viral genomes of either DNA or RNA, was to replace the traditional classification. Prof. Wang did not know anything pertaining to this molecular classification devised by Prof. David Baltimore. This shows how much Chinese scientists were behind the time. This provides a stark contrast between we knew in the West, and how far behind the Chinese scientists were in scientific disciplines.   In the 1950 to 80, molecular biology and its research were in booming in USA and in the western world. So, the course of molecular biology of

animal viruses was most welcome. The courses I taught opened their mind and to a new vista. In the following fifteen years, by official invitations, I returned to China. I taught similar courses elsewhere. With these, the Chinese animal industry and research were modernized. Progress was made so rapidly and amazingly.

This particular separate issue on "Regenerative Medicine in China" could testify this fact.

II. What are "embryonic stem cells", "somatic stem cells" and "induced pluripotent stem Cells ?

Historically in science literature, and up to this point of time, There are three types of stem cells, as follows: (cf. Fig. 1. An embryo with embryonic stem cells (eight in number).

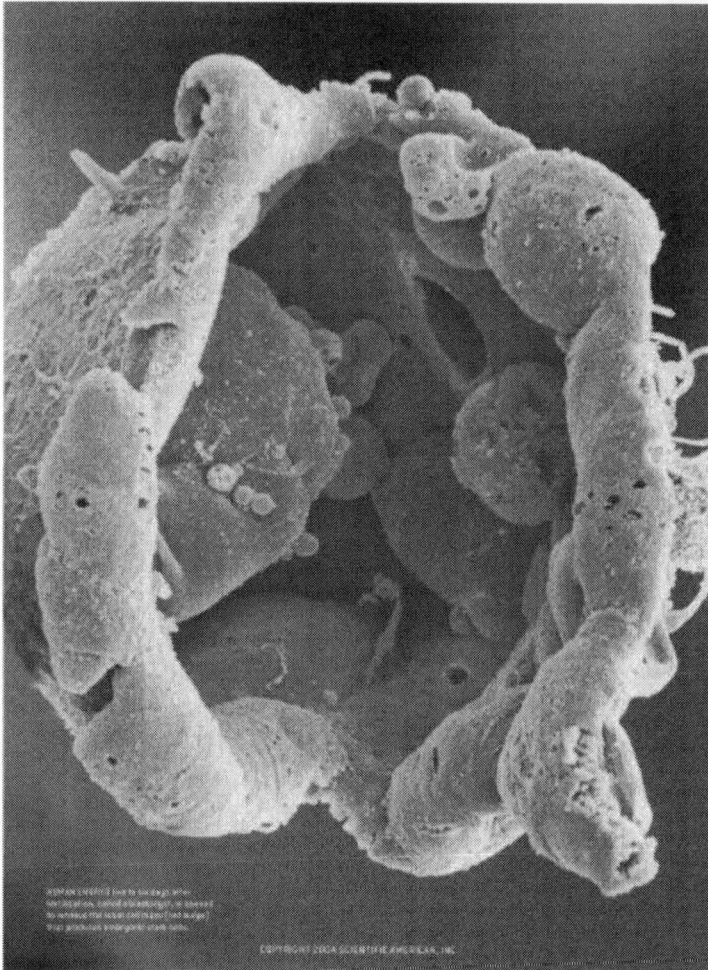

Fig. 1 An embryo with/and embryonic stem cells (taken from Roslin Scientific Pub.)

An fertilized egg in the female (by sperm from the male) will be eventually developed into *an embryo,* which at the very initial stage has *embryonic cell, one*. Then, one cell will divided into two cells , two to four and eventually in *eight cells in an embryo. So, they are referred as embryonic stem cell, 8 in numbers.*

A) *embryonic stem cells,*

B) *somatic stem cells, and*

C) *induced pluripotent stem cells (iPS)*

In this section, I shall discuss the general biology and principles of stem cells, and cloning technology, as I have studied and learned from the colleagues at Roslin Institute at Edinburgh of Scotland. In 2002 when I was on my lecture tour in Europe and England-Scotland, I had the privilege of visiting the Roslin Institute. On that particular day, Dr. Ian Walmut, the Leader of a team of researchers who had cloned the goat, was on business trip elsewhere, so he was not available. Dr. John King, Dr. Walmut's close colleague, was kind enough to conduct the tour, showing us the labs and equipment, the operation room and the animal house. In addition, he explained the principle and the technique in detail to us. Also, he provided us with some literature and reports for our use. So, what I am writing here in these pages are taken from The Roslin Institute's publication, and my notes taken on that particular visit. Due to the constraint on pages, I shall limit my discussion in principles and with some lab techniques.

A) Embryonic Stem cells (ESC):

What are the stem cells? Why they are called stem cells? Using the metaphor of a plant, you have the stem and the branches. Human has 220 types of cells (they are referred to as "branches"). These"branches" are coming from one type of cell, that specific type of cell is referred to as "stem cell". This type of cell is taken from the embryo (in human). So, you have "embryonic stem cells". This type of cell, have the endowed capacity of self-replicating (self-regenerating) capacity. Due to this capacity, they could be led to differentiating to form different tissues and organs, if being properly induced. Here, you see the potentiality and usefulness in repairing and regenerating. Because ES originate in this primordial stage, they retain the "pluripotent" (many-potent) ability to form any cell type in the body.

Less than 7 days after the human egg is fertilized, the developing embryo contains 100 or more cells that have yet to differentiate. The embryo is a hollow ball, consisting of an outer cell mass (later become the placenta) and an inner mass which would become the fetus, inside the womb. These cells continue multiplying, beginning to specialize by third week. The embryo at this stage would contain three distinctive germ layers (endoderm, mesoderm and ectoderm, cf. Fig 2) whose descendant would ultimately form hundreds of different types of

human body.

In summary, embryonic stem (ES) cells are derived from the portion of a very early stage embryo that would eventually give rise to an entire body. Because embryonic cells originate in the primordial stage, they retain the "pluripotent" ability to form any cell type in the body (see the following paragraphs).

1). How to isolate the stem cells from the fertilized embryo?

To create embryonic stem cell lines, scientists in the lab remove the inner cell mass from a blastocyte created in the lab, usually left over from an attempt at fertilization in vitro. The inner cell mass is placed on a plate containing "feeder cells" (cells will supply nutrients and growth factors to the new cells) to which it soon attached. In a few days, new cells grow out of the inner cell mass and form colonies. These cells are called embryonic stem cells only if they meet two criteria: they display "surface markers" which would characterize the embryonic stem cells. They undergo several generations of cell division, or "passages", demonstrating that they constitute a stable, or immortal (not dying) cell line.

These embryonic stem cells could be isolated either individually or in groups. Then, they could be cultivated in Petri dishes, then Erlenmyer flasks. Once they are in this stage, they are no longer in embryo, they are on artificial culture medium. Of course, scientists working with their lab technicians will supply all kinds of nutrients for these cells to grow. Growing such cells in vitro takes a great deal of knowledge in human nutrition, physiology and biochemistry. It is by no means easy. What scientists could do is to create conditions which are approximated as possible to the natural. In addition, they have to be stimulated with growth factors so that they would grow and multiply. In nature, such stimulators are available from the human endocrine system. There is such a complicated and interlock molecular mechanisms involved. This is what molecular biologists specialized in cloning have to do. Up to this date, they have made some breakthroughs at cellular to organismal levels2.from the embryonic stem cells, three layers of tissues will be formed:

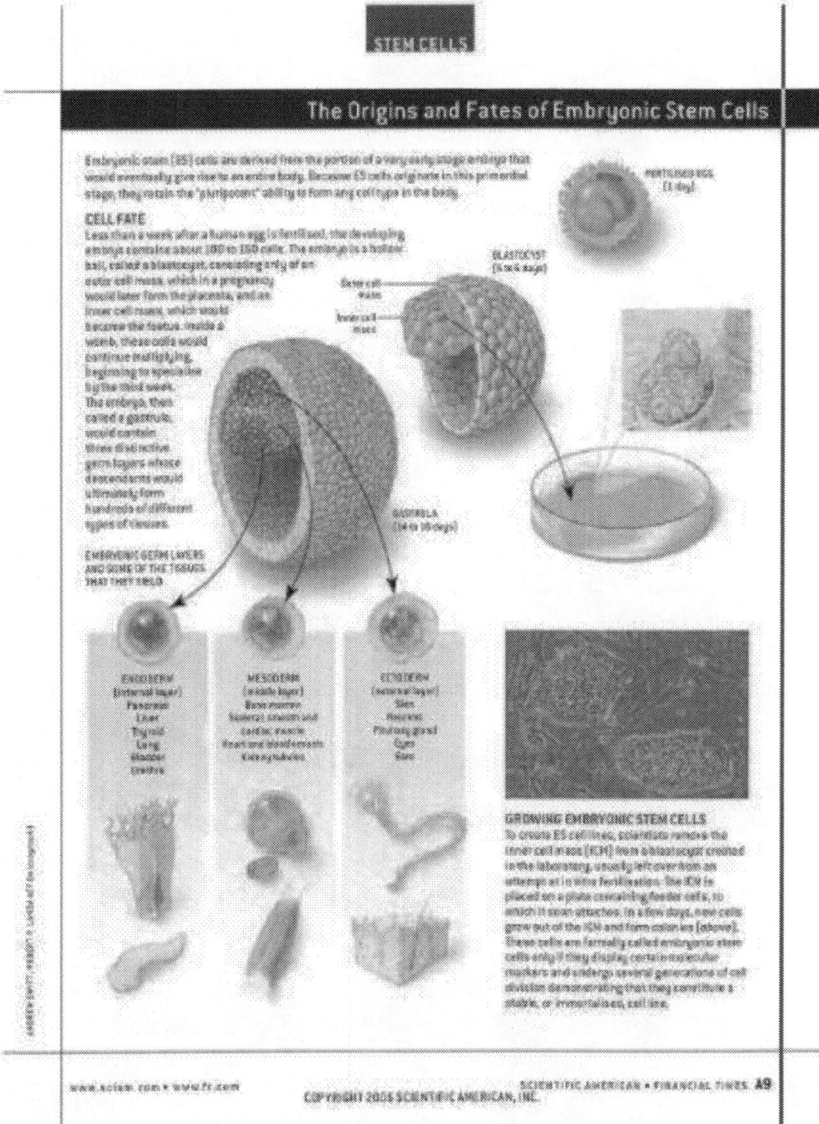

Fig. 2. Origin and fate of embryonic cells, (from Roslin Sci. Pub.)

showing that from the eight embryonic stem cells, and the subsequent three layers, i.e. endoderm, mesoderm and ectoderm of tissues are developed, then tissues are produced from these three layers,

2). Somatic stem cells or mature stem cells:

In human umbilical cord, bone marrow, blood, skin and some other organs, q number of scientists isolated another type of stem cells, they are *somatic*

(bodily) stem cells or mature stem cells. These cells have the innate capacity of multiplication and renewal, but only to a limited degree. They are being able to multiply, yet to the tissues or organs from which they are originally isolated, no other.

Because they are very close to embryonic stem cells, so these cells once isolated, could be use as *"model system"*, elaborating growing and multiplying mechanisms *in vivo* and also *in vitro*. The results obtained from such cells could be used to apply to/project for embryonic stem cells. With this type of cells readily available, scientists have so far succeeded in making skins for burnt patients and some others tissues. At the same time, bio-scientists have been working on other organs in regenerative medicine (cf. Regenerative Medicine in China,   2012).

B. Induced pluropotent stem cells   (iPS cells):

In 2009, Japanese molecular biologist, Dr. Shinya Yamanaka succeeded in producing an induced pluripotent stem cell (iPS) in the lab.   That was an outstanding breakthrough in cell technology, being able to turn the "clock" backward. This offered a great deal of hope in clone and in cloning, and also in regenerative medicine. Dr. Yamanaka was awarded with Lasker Award for his work. The iPS offered a great incentive to the clone and cloning studies.

In July of 2009, Chinese scientists in Mainland China had bred mice from cells that might offer an alternative to human embryonic stem cells. This technique could help sidestep many of the explosive ethical issues. One team of scientists led by Dr. Qi Zhou of Chinese Academy of Sciences created 37 iPS cell lines. Of these lines, 3 of them produced 27 live offerings, the first one they named Tiny. One of the offsring, a 7-week-old male went to impregnate a female and produce young of its own. Altogether, these researchers bred at least 100 first-generation mice and hundreds of 2nd generation mice that genetically to the mice from which the iPS cells were derived. This experimental results gave hope for future therapeutic interventions using patients' own programmed cells.

The second group led by Dr. Shao-Rong Gao of National Institute of Biol-Science in Bejing. They created five iPS cell lines. One of which was able to produce embryos that survived until birth. The work was a proof that iPS cells were functionally equivalent to embryonic stem cells.

These two teams published their results on line. The findings were welcome by supporters   of human embryonic stem cell researchers and some institutions. They thought this as a long-sought vital step in proving that the cells could be useful as embryonic cells for studying and curing human diseases. Dr. Konrad Hochedinger of Harvard Univ. said that "this clearly says for the first time that iPS cells pass the most stringent test." Richard M. Doerflinger of the US Conference of   Roman Catholic Bishops said that " No body   has been able to find anything that embryonic stem cells can do that these cell can't do."

The Chinese scientists said that ," continued research on embryonic stem cells remains crucial to validate iPS cells. It remains unclear which cells will turn out to be most useful for different purposes," Again, There are people who harbor the fear in their thinking that rogue scientists might misuse the technique to attempt to clone humans. Dr. Jonathan D. Moreno of Univ. of Penn., as a bio-ethicist said *"This is a paradigm case that shows the old debates are rapidly being transformed into something even more complicated."* Others dismissed such concern, saying many scientific, ethical and regulatory hurdles remain. They said that just because the process works in mice does not necessarily mean it would work in humans. In USA, human cloning is outlawed. Federal regulators could step in to prevent it when it is needed.

C.Clones and cloning technology, with embryonic cell's nuclear materials:

By definition, clones are replicates of organisms by asexual replications. So, such clones are asexual replicates, *they are cousins*, sharing genetic make-up, and therefore their patterns of growth. They are not in father-and-son relationship. This method has been in use by plant biologists for a long time. These replicates have been used/ practiced in farm vegetables, such as potatoes and strawberries. Using this technique for replication in farm animals, even small animals is much more complicated, requiring much more knowledge and techniques. Therefore, cloning animals should be given due consideration of their scientific complexities.

In biological research, we have been using small lab mouse (plural mice). Being small in size, and multiplying both asexually and sexually fast, they have been created with asexual technologies (cloning). With such small lab animals, great stride has been made, mostly in genetic crossing , even with gene-transfer techniques.

Keep this basic and important principle in mind when you engage in cloing research. *Sexual reproduction* is altogether different. They are through sexual conjugation/intercourse, entailing male and female as partners. Cloning small animals, and even farm animals is technologically possible, but it scientifically takes a great deal of advanced knowledge and lab manipulation. If any one attempts to do it with big animals, even human, he/she should ponder on the problem and the difficulties before they attempt to do anything about it (cf. letter to Scientists by Ian Wilmut et al 2004). In addition, they are other issues involved (viz. at the end of this Chapter). In cloning human being is altogether different business, with so much ramifications (cf. later sections) and should not be attempted without due consideration and under all circumstances.

1).*Cloning technologies for small and farm animals*: so far, there are two technologies.

a)Nuclear transfer, and

b)Nuclear replacement.

a)**Nuclear transfer** is to transfer a part of the nucleus from one animal to another. First, with lab technique, scientists have to remove/deplete a part of the nuclear material of the total one, from the recipient so that there will be space for receiving the transferring nuclear material from the donor. With the space provided for the transfer, then scientists would transfer the donor's nuclear material to the recipient. This is a very delicate operation. By and large, scientists succeed in only a part of it. Therefore, it is by and large a gross technology, with low percentage of success, with birth deformities common or early death of the whole animal.

Fig. 3   Domestic and farm animals so far cloned successful
(From Science, vol. 316, 15 of May, 2007).

255

In 2001, Dr. Ian Wilmut and his co-workers cloned sheep Maggie and Doly with this technology. It made a big splash of news worldwide! Dr. Wilmut reported later that one out of 175 times was "successful". If miscarriage, prenatal death and others were taken into consideration, it would be one of thousandth. The animals survived with deformities, diseases and earlier death.

In 2002 while I was on lecture tour in England and Scotland, both my wife and I had the privilege of visiting Roslin Institute.On that particular day,   Dr. Walmut was on speaking tour elsewhere. His colleague, Dr. John King cordially received us, and showed us the lab, the operation room, and the farm, and then both Maggie, Doly, and some others. These poor animals suffered from deformities and arthritis. In 2003, they died earlier, with much shorter life-span than the normal death.

b)*Nuclear replacement* entails to transfer the whole nucleus of the donor to the recipient.   Once again, this was crude technology. The rate of success was also very low, animals survived with deformities, disease and early death.

Though the two cloning techniques were imperfect, scientists did use them to clone farm animals. Up to this date, more than 20 lab and farm animals have been cloned, They are: wolf, muflon, African wild cat, dog, sheep, mule, domestic cat, buffalo, mouse, goat, rabbit, horse, gaur, cow, pig, rat and ferret (cf. map, Science/AAAS, May 18, 2007, pp#991). We have seen some cloned animals that are phenotypically normal. Nonetheless, a large proportion of cloned fetuses die in utero, and some are also born with malformations. But, for most species cloned so far, a subset of clones show normal physiological parameters and are currently aging normal. Although the percentage of normal animals born from embryos is extremely small, it underscores the fact that this man-made procedure can sometimes, albeit randomly work.

2).*Cloning with somatic cell nuclear material.*

Since 2006, attempts were made to use somatic stem cells in cloning.   No success has been reported. But, this is a new area of endeavor.

D. Some difficulties and concern with cloning technology:

There are quite a few questions which should be seriously considered

1)   Technological methods:

As Dr. Walmut and co-workers reported, the two technologies so far used in transferring nuclear materials were not perfected. Success rate was very low. Cloned animals were born with birth defects,   and ended with early death. To use those two technologies for cloning higher animals should be given due serious consideration. It is even more serious business if any one else contemplates in

cloning human. A combination of human nuclear material with that of animals should under all circumstance be discouraged, if not prohibited. The cloning technology remains to be further researched for improvement, perfection if it is possible. For this reason, the US government would not permit any such attempt, especially with federal government funding. Somatic cells, though less potent, as model system could be used for further research. The oocytes and limited source of supplies remain as a technological issue. The feeder cells used were able to induce tumors. All these issues remain to be resolved.

In 2003 Drs. Walmut, R. Prather and Prof. Schatten jointly wrote a paper which was published in Science/ AAAS, Jan. 17, warming the scientific community that no one else should attempt to use these two technologies for any cloning on humans!

The two technologies so far developed were imperfect, with high percentage of early death! Yet, there were a few radicals who turned deaf ears to such warning. They got nowhere!

2) *Legal ramification, ethical issues and social /moral/religious implications:*

Do donors of fertilized embryos have the legal right to the derived cell lines? Who has the final saying in cloning? If cloning does not work with the animals,the meat of defect animals could be used for food. But, working with any species higher than farm animals would require serious consideration. Animal rights certainly would protest against such attempts.

To sacrifice/kill living embryo is a philosophical, ethical and religious issue. Christians in general and Roman Catholic Church consider that life begins with fertilization/conception. To kill fertilized embryos is considered a crime. It is very serious ethical issue. The defective humans being born of cloning will be a serious burden to families, to society and to the nation. The US Bioethic Advisory Council and UNESCO considers this matter seriously, and sets up guidelines that should not be violated. US Presidents, with administrative authority allow only federal funding research with existing cell lines, and somatic cell lines. Lately, President Barack Obama authorized, through NIH, more federal fundings for such research, and at the same time increased the number of cell lines for use in research work.

Molecular biologists contemplate on using these technologies for curing curable and incurable diseases in humans, They have been using both embryonic stem cells, somatic stem cells and tissues generated for repair.. With certain degree of success, scientists intend to go to human cloning. Of course, this would cause a great deal of concern in the public. Whether this could be done, or can't be done will become national to international debate.

III. What are "embryonic stem cells" and "somatic stem cells"?

Beginning in 1996, US Congress and the President paid due attention to this adventure in research and application, inviting specialists to give briefing and testimonies. This debate and concern were extended to other developed countries. In that year, President William Clinton, issuing an administrative document, established a *"National Bioethics Advisory Commission"* (NBAC) with Dr. Harold Shapiro, President of Princeton University as the Chairman, with 21 Commissioners, coming from well-known specialists, lawyers, educators, church clergymen and ethicists. The Commission, with guidelines formulated is authorized to study the issue from different angles with far-reaching implications. Then, the Commission shall present recommendation to the President for final decisions.

2001, President George Bush, also with administrative order, puts restriction on the number of stem cell lines (21 cell lines available) and the use of them. The order specifies that "embryonic stem cells (ESC) can't be used for human reproductive cloning; destroying/killing human embryos to obtain stem is un-lawful and is not permitted. There are existing stem cell-lines available and are good enough for lab use these cells for research and future application in curing diseases. Such cell lines could be used for therapeutic use, as permitted and certified. The federal government, through the National Institute of Health, would issue grants for such research and clinical endeavor."

When my Chinese version of this book was under consideration for publishing in 2006, on June 30, the US Senate, under the majority leader Senator Bill Frist, was debating the House Bill H.R.#810, requesting the White House being lenient in the use of cell lines. Pres. Bush vetoed the bill, insisting on its violation of ethical principle. At the same time, NIH was instructed to look for the availability of cell lines available, without going to destroy human embryos.

Over these years, there have been debates in US Congress, and also in the scientific establishments. In 2009, when President Obama came to the presidency, he loosened the funding restriction. He considered that the stem cells are "scientifically worthy projects". But, he maintained the ethical responsibility guidelines, ensuring that couples who donated their embryos were fully informed of other options. He authorized more federal funds, being available for existing lines and somatic cell lines. In April, 2010, NIH published a new guideline. At the same time, NIH approved nine lines that had never before been eligible for federal funding and four long-used lines derived from researchers at Univ. of Wisc., known as H7, H9, H13 and H14

The latest developments in both ethics and scientific accomplishments"

A. In April of 2010, *President Obama appointed the following scholars and individuals to the National Bioethical Panel*:

Raju Kucherlapati, Geneticist, Harvard Medical School

Nelson Michael,   Retro-virologist, Walter Reed Army Inst. Of Research

Daniel Sulmasy, Bioethicist, University of Chicago

Gutmann,   President, Univ. of Penn.;   Chair-person

James Wagner,   President, Emory Univ., Vice Chair

Lonnie Ali, Muhammad Ali Enterprises

Anita Allen, Lawyer/Bioethicist

Barbara Atkinson, Vice Chancellor, Univ. of Kansas Medical Ctr.

Nita Farahany,   Lawyer, Vanderbilt Univ.

Christine Grady,   Nurse/Bioethicist, Nat. Institute of Health

Stephen Hauser, Neurologist, Univ. of Calif., San Francisco

For Chinese Churches in USA and elsewhere, I wrote two articles in English, explaining what are embryonic and somatic stem cells, their use and ethical implications. One article was published in "The Challenger" by Chinese Christian Missions in Petaluma, Calif., under the   title "Stem Cell Research and Cloning: Controversy and Challenge",   Oct-Nov, 2001. My intention was to encourage Chinese churches and Christians to take part in public debate, and making informed decisions.

In 2002, when I was traveling and itinerary ministry in both England and Ireland, both my wife and I had the privilege of visiting Roslin Institute at Edinbough where the sheep Polly was first cloned. On that, Dr. Ian Walnut was traveling elsewhere for lectu.   Dr. John King received us cordially for a visit, explaining the procedures and showing us the lab and equipments used in cloning sheep. Under returning to USA, I wrote the second article on "Clones and Cloning: From Polly to Human?". I strongly advocated that more experiments wee essential before going any further. At the same time, Dr. Walmute and other two fellow-scientists wrote their advisory article in Science, Jan. 17, 2003, strong urged fellow scientists stopping in going to use the imperfect cloning technology in human cloning work.

A. Nobel prize in physiology and medicine, in 2012:

In October, 2012, Nobel Prize Committee announced that the Nobel Prize in Physiology and Medicine was granted to two researchers on induced stem cell in vitro.   Prof.. Shinya Yamanaka of Kyoto University, Japan, and British Biologist, Prof. John Gurdon of Cambridge Univ., England, did in their research work on stem cells. Specifically, Prof. Gurdon transplanted the genetic material from an

intestinal cell of one frog into an egg cell from another. The egg developed into a tadpole, showing that ordinary cells contain the entire genetic instruction manual for the whole organism. His concluded it from his experiments that bio-scientists should be able to derive anyone kind of cell from another, because cells have contained all the same genetic information. For years scientists were hesitant to accept it as valid, though cloning mice had become laboratory mainstays. This consequently led to the first cloning of a mammal, the sheep Dolly at Rosline Institute of Scotland, in 1997. Since then scientists have cloned more than one dozen and half of animals, as stated before in my book, such animals as mice, dogs, cats, pigs, and horse. Multiple attempts have been attempted to clone monkeys have failed.

In 2006-07, Japanese molecular biologist, Prof.. Shinya Yamanaka extended this insight by turning the genetic time-clock back on individual cells from mice and humans. By sprinkling four genes on ordinary skin cells, Yamanaka discovered that such manipulation could revert the genetic clock to an early embryonic stage. This was the so-called "induced embryonic cells" (iPS) which behave much like the stem cells gleaned from human embryos. They could be grown into many other types of tissues, like embryonic cell,

The breakthrough offered hope that someday skin cells could be harvested from a patient, being sent back in time to an embryonic state, and then grown into replacement tissues such as heart muscle or nerve cells. A huge global research effort was working to develop pluro-potent stem cells, which could be used for treatment for heart disease, some form of blindness, Parkinson's disease and many other disorders. Yamanaka's work has been now extended to hundreds of laboratories around the world that scientists are exploiting the techniques to study virtually every other kind of disease. Bio-scientists have been using such transformed cells to study so-called "disease in a disk" made from patients with Alzheimer's, Parkinson's and Huntington's diseases. Research teams have also found shortcuts to turn skin cells directly into muscle fibers and brain neurons.

The first human trials of induced stem cell therapies could begin in 2013. In a press briefing recently, Prof. Yamanaka said that those three diseases present an attractive targets for the first experimental tests.

In its citation, Nobel Committee said that the dual ground-breaking discoveries have completely changed our view of development and cellular specialization. Research fields have been established, and textbooks have been rewritten. By re-programming human cells, scientists have created new opportunities to study diseases and develop methods for diagnosis and treatment. The importance could not be overstated.

Right after the Nobel announcement, again at Kyoto University in Japan, a team of researchers led by stem cell biologist Mitinori Saitou has produced normal mouse pups using oocyes, or immature egg cells, created in vitro from embryonic stem and induced pluripotent stem cells. This achievement was the first for

mammals. The researchers cultured mouse ES and iPS cells in protein cocktails to produce primordial germ cell-liked cells. To get oocytes, researchers mixed these cells with fetal ovarian cells, forming re-constituted ovaries that they grafted onto natural ovaries in female mice. Four weeks later, the primordial germ cell-like cells had developed into oocytes. After in vitro fertilization, the researchers implanted the resulting embryos into surrogate mother, producing normal mouse pups, the term reported their results online Oct. 4, 2012 in Science, AAAS

" It is remarkable that one can produce oocytes capable of sustaining complete development starting with embryonic stem cells," says developmental biologist David Solter of Singapore Institute of Medical Biology who was not involved with the research. Saitou says that with more work, the team may be able to eliminate the grafting step, generating viable oocytes completely in vitro. In addition to shedding light on early developmental processes, the technique could lead to new human fertility treatments if technical challenges and ethical issues can be resolved", says Dr. Solter   (Science, News of the Week, page   24, Oct. 5, 2012, AAAS).

B. Is cloning work defyng Christian doctrine of God's creation?

In 2003 when both my wife and I were in the city of Christchurch of New Zealand for Christian itinerant ministry among Chinese Churches, I spoke on subjects of science and Christian faith。 As usual, at the end there was a question-and-answer period. One visiting scholar from People's Republic of China, was doing something preliminary in nature on this subject. She shared her results the audience. In her experiments, she was able to transfer one piece of nuclear material to another cell. She thought that she was creating something new in her work. Therefore, she proudly announced "*creating*". Other attendants debated it with her as to whether this was creating new thing or simply transferring one fragment of nuclear material to another cell? The audience looked to me for an answer.

Explicitly, I answered her that   this is not a creation, but a transferring of *existing material* to another cell."   It took me several minutes to explain it and clarified it. The audience of that class was mostly university professionals and technicians. They even needed a clarification between creation and lab. manipulation of existing cells with genetic informations. Common citizens with no professional training may likely be in need of more words to clarify the issue.

C. My professional advice to Christians and Christian churches:

At the end of this chapter, I would like to offer my professional advice to Christian churches   and Christians. Clone and cloning technology did create a false impression of creation. Therefore, there has been a debate in our society. and sometime in churches. Cloning experiments with small animals or farm animals are not simple experiments. They can not be done in one single lab, or with one group of specialized individuals. The technical work takes so many different

trainings. To clone human beings is impossible! Up to this date, this is impossible. This is not a simple understaking. Above all, state government and laws do not allow any such attempt.

D. My personal advices are: Also as conclusion.

1)We all have to be aware of the existence of such a cell technology and stem cell manipulations.   Scientific research and its results have far-reaching applcattions and meaning. Consult with professionals, and read professional journals and scientific publications if you could. Be informed of it, and be aware of its ramifications. Then, make informed judgment, and then decision.

2)Carefully discern/ differentiate what is creation and what is making new things with existing materials. On the basis of differences, then we give our reasonable input and our judgment.

3)Clones and cloning offer a great deal of hope to those who suffer from genetic defects and inheritable malady. If there is any valid hope, we would support it with our resources. Yet, much research remains to be done. There is a limit of what we could do. As Christians and churches, we should support valid and meaningful scientific research, with our contributions. We also support laws which prohibit lab experiments which violate our value and faith.

4)We affirm that life begins at conception. To sacrifice embryo for obtaining embryonic stem cells is a violation of human dignity and value. We should exercise our right and privilege of voting for the laws which prohibit cloning humans, even so-called chimeras (human cells mix with animal cells).

5) We should not react irrationally. If we react without much thinking, then we will be labeled as being religious fanatic. We should mention the technological difficulties first, then the laws of the land. Then, the societal and community concerns, the financial burden.   Though the last is not the least, yet we argue on this in the last. That is our Christian moral conviction and our value systems. To kill a living embryo for obtaining stem cells is under any circumstance not right. We oppose it, as the last argument.

Literature Cited

1. Ian Walmut, 2001

> The Second Creation: The Age of Biological Control by the
> Scientists Who Cloned Dolly。 Headline Co. London,

2. Christianity Today, Oct. issue, 2005

> The Stem Cell Debate: Stemming the Embryonic Tide/Profilers Face
> a Scientific and Public Relations, by Stan Guthrie, et al, pp. 60-71

3. Elias Zerhouni, 2003

> Stem Cell Program（in NIH）Science/AAAS Vol. 300 pp#911-916

4. Leon Kass, 2006

> Being Human: Readings from the President's Council on Bioethics,
>
> PCB in Washington.

5. N.Y. Academy of Sciences, Vol. 913, 2000

> Medical Ethics at the Dawn of 21st Century.
>
> Cloning Human Being and the Ethics. Pp#198-217

6. Sambrook, E. F. et al 1989

> Molecular Cloning. Vol. 1，2，3
>
> Cold Spring Biol. Lab. 年. Y.

7. Joseph Pannos, 2006

> Animal Cloning: The Science of Nuclear Transfer. Scientific
> American Book.

8. American Association for the Advancement of Science, April 27, 2012

> Science: A Sponsored Supplement to Science, Regenerative
> Medicine in China, 72 pages, with 71 articles.

Chapter 20
Genes, Genomic, and Therapies

"When something new is revealed about the human genome,

I experience a feeling of awe at the realization that humanity

Knows something only God knew before."

Dr. Francis Collins, Gen. Director, NIH, USA

Introduction

With the announcement of helical structure of DNA and its functions by Crick and Watson in 1953, biology entered the Molecular Biology Era. This was due to the merging of microbiology, genetics, biochemistry and biophysics. Since then, for 40-50 years and, molecular biologists have worked on genomics and synthetic biology, with amazing results. In 2001, the complete DNA sequence of human genome was announced. Progress made was un-precedent in bio-sciences. In 2006, Prof. Horace Judson of Univ. of Calif., in second edition of his book "the Eighth Day of Creation: Makers of the Revolution in Biology", suggested that this is the 8th day of creation. How true it was! Now, they have been working on "genomic medicine", an individualistic approach to human disease, and even synthetic biology.

I. Gene, Genomic Program

A. Historical perspectives:

In early 1950, using bacteria (E. coli, Bac. subtilis, and Pseudomonas spp.) as models, microbiologists devoted themselves to the study on bacterial genetics and its DNA replication. Genes and their functions were identified. Operons and their induction/repression were elucidated (Jacob and Monod et al). Then, hybridization of DNA and its mechanisms were demonstrated (Delbruck, Luria and Hershey). Genetic engineering with its applications opened the way to alter the genetic constitutions of organisms. In the later years of 90, Microbial genes were identified and position ascertained. In 2001, complete sequence of human genome was announced. Nobody could anticipate the such un-precedent speedy progress in half a century. Those who are interested in the subjects and their historical development could consult college textbooks by Prof. Benjamin Lewin of Harvard University, in "Genes XII", vols. I and II, Jones and Bartlett Publisheres, Boston, Mass., 2013)

Due to space constrain I shall take some of the illustrations from Benjamine Lewin's books to illustrate those important concepts and principles, as follows:

1)Major events in the genetic century: (taken from Benjamin Lewin, pp#)

1865 A.D.:	genes as particular factors
1900:	discovery of nucleic acids
1903:	chromosomes are hereditary units
10:	genes lie on chromosomes
13:	chromosomes are linear arrays of genes
27:	mutations are physical changes in genes
31:	recombinations occur by crossing-over
44:	DNA is the genetic material
45:	a gene codes for a protein
51:	final protein sequence
53:	DNA is a double helix
58:	DNA replicates semi-conservatively
59:	Genetic code is a triplet
67:	genetic engineering
77:	Eukaryotic genes are interrupted
77:	DNA can be sequenced
95:	Bacterial genomes sequenes
96:	Other microbes' genomes were sequenced
01:	Human genome sequence completed (2001)
7:	Individualized genomic disease & treatment
8:	minor differences among different races
9:	translation medicine
2010:	synthetic biology

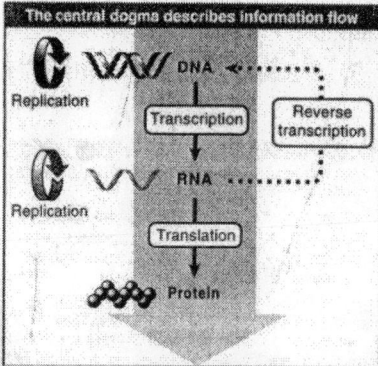

FIGURE 1.16 The central dogma states that information in nucleic acid can be perpetuated or transferred, but the transfer of information into protein is irreversible.

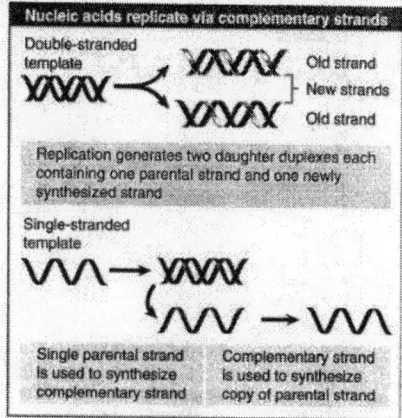

FIGURE 1.17 Double-stranded and single-stranded nucleic acids both replicate by synthesis of complementary strands governed by the rules of base pairing.

Fig. 1. Transcription and translation of genes

(from Bejamin Lewines, 2008)

Sequenced genomes vary from 470 to 30,000 genes			
Species	Genomes (Mb)	Genes	Lethal loci
Mycoplasma genitalium	0.58	470	~300
Rickettsia prowazekii	1.11	834	
Haemophilus influenzae	1.83	1,743	
Methanococcus jannaschi	1.66	1,738	
B. subtilis	4.2	4,100	
E. coli	4.6	4,288	1,800
S. cerevisiae	13.5	6,034	1,090
S. pombe	12.5	4,929	
A. thaliana	119	25,498	
O. sativa (rice)	466	~30,000	
D. melanogaster	165	13,601	3,100
C. elegans	97	18,424	
H. sapiens	3,300	~25,000	

FIGURE 5.2 Genome sizes and gene numbers are known from complete sequences for several organisms. Lethal loci are estimated from genetic data.

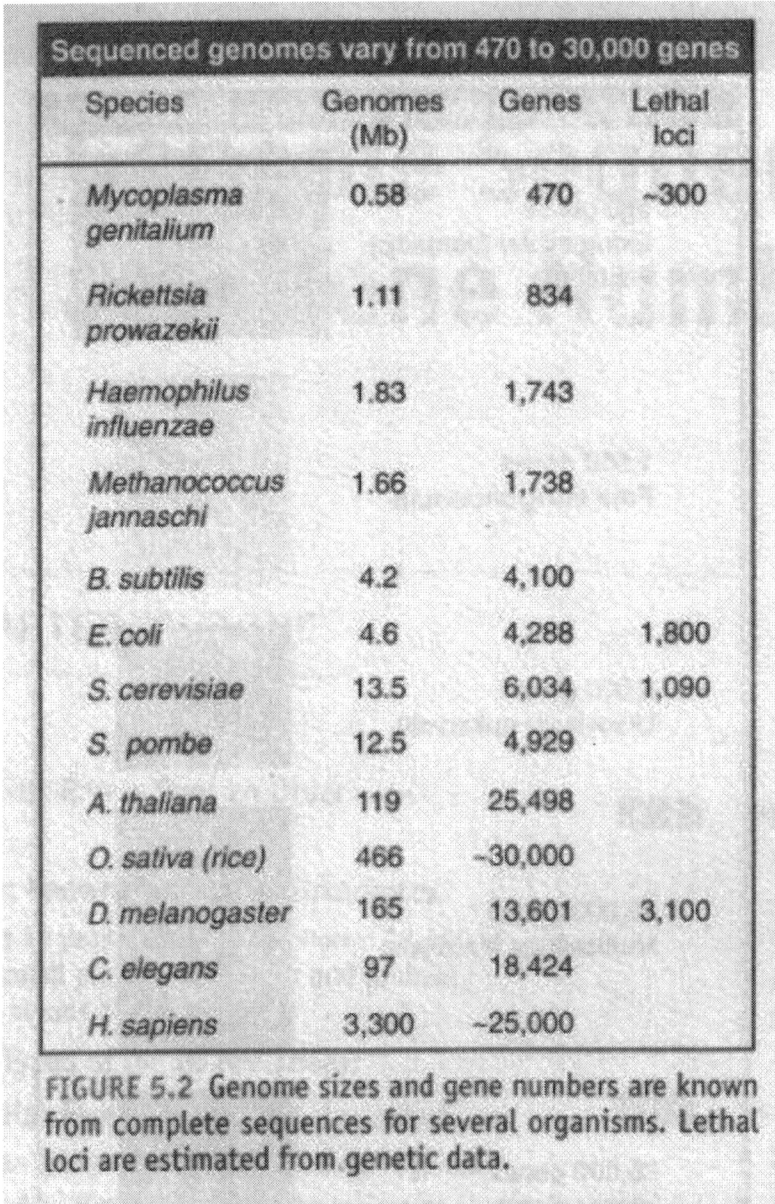

Fig.2   Genomes sequence in different sizes (from Benjamin Lewin, 2008)

FIGURE 9.1 All the triplet codons have meaning: Sixty-one represent amino acids, and three cause termination (STOP).

Fig 3.   Genetic codons (from Benjamin Lewin, 2008)

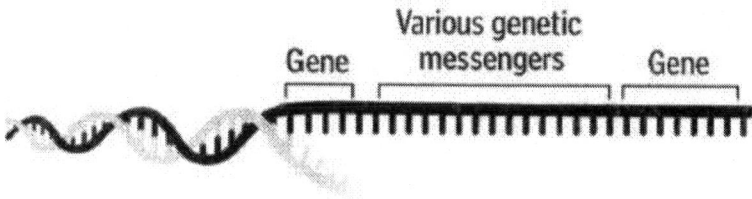

Fig. 4.   Genes are located on upper-stream as well on lower stream.

269

B. Gene and genomes:

In 2006, Science/ AAAS listed the following organisms (as representatives) with their estimated genome size, and genes:

Table l. Genome size: Big and small:estimated genomes of some representative organisms:

Sequenced Organisms	Genome Size	Estimated Genes
Homophiles influenza (bacterium)	1.8 Mbp	1,740
Saccharomyces cerevisiae (yeast)	12.1 Mbp	6,034
Caenorhabiditis elegans(nematode)	100 Mbp	19,099
Arabidopsis thaliana (thalus cress, plant)	160 Mbp	25,000
Drosophia melanogaster (fruit fly)	180 Mbp	13,061
Maus musculus (mouse)	3,000 Mbp	Unknown
Chimpanzee	pending	
Pantroglodytes		
Panpaniscus		
IIomo sapiens (human)	3,500 Mbp	35,000 – 45,000

Takifugu rubripes (Puffer fish)	400 mbp
Oryza sativa (rice)	490 mbp
Allium cepa (onion)	16,400mbp
Podisma pedestris (Mountain grasshopper)	16,500 mbp
Ambystoma tigrinum (tiger)	31,0000mpb
Rana pipiens (Leopard frog)	6,500mbp
Lilium longiglotum (Easter lily)	34,000mbp
Protopterus aethiopicus (marbled lungfish)	130,000,bp

taken from: Science/ AAAS,   291: 1178 ,   Feb 16,   2001

(**www.sciencemeg.org**   )

Looking at the above table, they seem to be that the physical size of organisms is not related to the size genomes or visa versa. So, we scientists could not explain everything in strict materialistic term. Above, all these organisms with similar genome size are not necessarily phylogenetically related. In a way, all these are another mystery!

C. Sequence o human genome, 2001:

In 1990 and thereabout, molecular geneticists felt that the sequencing genomes was a formidable task. It was almost impossible to undertake them by one research institute or even one nation alone. Therefore, in an international conference, they agreed the division of labor among nations.   An international consortium was organized and established as "Genome Bank" or "Bio-Bank". The scientific research results would be centralized as common property, and made it available to those were actively involved in the research endeavor. That very much enhanced the research endeavor worldwide.

One that is worthwhile to mention it, in term of science and Christian faith. In 2001, Prof. *Francis Collins, Dr. J. Craig Venter and their colleagues at NIH* announced the sequence of human genome. This was quite a breakthrough in genomic program, worldwide.

In 2006-2008, Francis Collins, an evangelical Christian scholar, published two books, they are:

1)The language of God: A Scientist Presents Evidence for Belief and

2)The Language of Life. Free Press/Simon & Schuster, Inc., N.Y.

In the following section, I summarize what Dr. Collins has written in his

first book, for reference.

1)31 mbp in human genome   (A=T, C=C)

2)Twenty three pairs of chromosomes in human; 24 pairs in chimpanzee,

3)In addition to functional genes, there are junk DNA, with functions to be elucidated,

4)Up to this point of time, 100,000 genes were known,

5)One gene, by transcription and translation,   to 1 to several proteins,

6)Up to this time, only 2% of total genome was transcribed/translated,

7)20,000 to 25,000 proteins as products have been identified and characterized,

8)*Among different races of human, 99% of their genomes are identical, low level of   genetic diversity).*

In addition, ***Jonathan Pritchard, Univ. of Chicago: Public Library of Science Genetics; National Center for Biotechnology, 2010 confirmed*** what was reported: with following specifics:

a)*Gene KITLG: affects hair, eye and skin pigmentation,*

b)*SLC24A5: affects skin pigmentation, and*

c)*MCIR: affects skin and hair pigmentation.*

9)At Genomic Research of NIH, scientists have been using computer technology, being applied in determining similar sequence of certain stretch of human DNA, to assess whether similar sequence in some other species, they found highly significant match to the genomes of other animals, as shown in the following table, as shown in the following table:

Table 2.   Similar sequences among some species:

	Gene Sequence that codes for protein	Random DNA sequences between genes
Chimpanzee	100%	98%
Dog	99%	52%
Mouse	99%	40%
Chicken	75%	4%

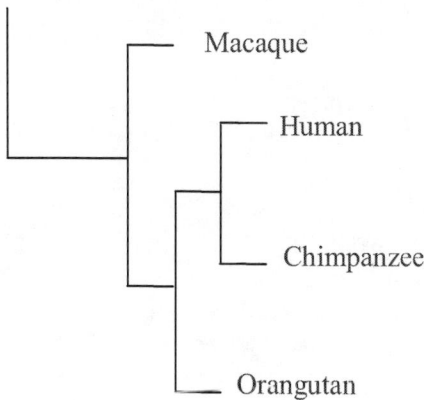

Fig. 1. Tree of life, as given by F. Collins, fig. 18-1, #pp 127

Prof. Collins was Prof. of Human Genetics at Univ. of Michigan, and later on he became the Chairman of the Dept. While he was with the Univ., he attended the Packard Road Baptist Church in Ann Arbor. We met in seminars from time to time, exchanging viewpoints on subjects of common interest.   He is an evangelical Christian, subscribing the school of thought of Theistic Evolution and accepting evolution as the second stage of God's overall plan of creation. On the basis of DNA sequences, he believes that chimpanzees and human beings share the common ancestry. To this point, many of us do not agree. But, we mutually respect one another's views. At the end of the book, he advocates a new term for harmony between science and Christian faith, as "Biologos"   (cf. Chapter 10,

273

pp#197-211). In fact, not too many years later, he established a "Biologos Foundation".

Since then, scientists worldwide have been endeavoring in genomic medicine. In 2009, AAAS announced pioneering program of translation medicine. No body could image that in a matter of 30-40 years, so much advancement in molecular biology could be made.

D. The latest development:

1)One monkey with two different genomes:

Using the nuclear transfer technique (cf. Clones and Cloning), in early 2010, Dr. Shoukhrate Mitalipov et al, at Oregon Health & Science Univ. in Portland, Oregon, published on-line of their lab result in Nature, creating one monkey with nuclear DNA from two monkey mothers. They proposed that they could use this technique to cure birth defect in human!? Others worried about their work be extended. They may not have read the paper written by Ian Walmut. Above all, they might not realize the federal guidelines with respect to going to any higher category of animals.

2)Creating "a cell" from scratch by Dr. J. Craig Venter, in May of 2010:

In genomic research work, at his own Institute, Dr. Craig Venter is well-known as co-sequencer of Prof. Francis Collins, in 2001. In a paper on line, Venter published creating a bacterial "**cell as an artificial copy**" of Mycoplasma mycoides. He, using the nuclear transfer technology, transferred the complete genome to another cell of closely related microbe. The donor genome re-programmed the recipient cell, which went on to replicate and divide. The result was new colonies of Mycoplasma mycoides. This was reported in Science/AAAS Vol. 328, p# 958, May 21, 2010. Yeast geneticist Jef Boeke of Johns Hopkins Univ. School of Medicine considers that Venter's work represents an important technical milestone in the new field of synthetic genomics." In fact, he established the Synthetic Microbiology or Synthetic Biology, as a new field.

That was a great news. Since then, scientists worldwide have been endeavoring in genomic medicine. In 2010, AAAS announced pioneering program of translation medicine. No body could image that in a matter of 30-40 years, such advancement in molecular biology could be made.

II. Gene Therapy and Cell Therapy

1). Gene therapy:

As stated before, when a gene is transcribed, mRNA is formed (in transcription). Then, the mRNA is translated into one or more than protein (in

translation). The expression of this gene through these two processes will be either in the brain or the other organs, specific functions of those proteins will perform either their specific enzymatic function or cellular structural unit. These are normal functions of a gene.

In human population, some individuals, due to genetic defect or being damaged by external factors, were unable to perform these functions. Therefore, there are individuals in our society who lack their inborn genetic capacities. One well-known example is diabetic patient. These individuals either lack the insulin gene or the defect of the insulin gene. Therefore, no insulin or not enough insulin is produced. For treatment, such patients have to receive insulin from time to time. This is a common practice.

As a result of genetic and genomic research, molecular biologists/physicians could treat such patients with gene therapy technology. A brief and comprehensive description of such a technology will be given in the following paragraph.

Insulin gene is isolated and separated from a healthy individual donor (or from cadaver). Such a technology is available. There are "carriers" ("a vehicles", technically "as vectors") available. They are either an attenuated virus (artificially weaken virus) which could infect the patient, yet does not cause a disease (due to weakening or "attenuation"). Or a bacterial plasmid (extra-chromosomal DNA particle) is isolated from bacterium. These carriers, through lab manipulation will carry the "insulin gene" from the donor to the recipient. Then, this transported "insulin gene" will be integrated into the genome of the patient. Therefore, this patient will receive such an insulin gene, acquiring the capacity to produce insulin. The procedure is referred to as gene therapy. Of course, this is a very advanced medical technology. Even so, molecular biologist or gene therapist has to exercise a great deal of precaution and consideration. If any one of the procedure is not correctly done, this will end in disaster. The worst scenario is death of the recipient. Unfortunately, such a scenario did happen. In early 2000, a young man in Penn. died as a consequence of gene therapy. No one could pinpoint the specific failure of the procedure. Therefore, the US Federal Gov., through NIH, prohibited such a practice. A National Advisory Committee was formed to formulate guidelines and oversee such a technology. Much research remains to be done.

2). Cell therapy or cellular product therapy:

Molecular biologists/gene therapists turned their attention to cell therapy or cellular product therapy. Instead, they tried to transfer cells or bone marrow in therapy. This is indeed a step forward and much safer. This is how they do. They take cells which are healthy, containing that defective gene. Then, they transfer the cells from donor to the recipient as therapy. This is much safer technology. Better still is to use bone marrow which contains a number of cells. As you may know that over these years clinicians have been using bone marrow in treating cancer patients and many others. The results have been successful. Once again,

this practice is also guarded by the National Committee, for the right kind of cells and the correct technology.

Another attempt made by molecular biologists and therapists is to gene products of cells, viz. proteins or protein product. This is another open field, right after the report of success with clones and cloning. Scientists have been thinking of using protein products with cloned animals.

With stem cells in therapy, it is considered ever far better. As I discussed it in previous section, there is so much controversy going on in our society. Using somatic stem cells is much better and safer. As I discussed in previous section, somatic stem cells could generate/reproduce only for that organ from which the somatic cells are isolated. The function and regenerative potential is much less than embryonic stem cells.

In conclusion, there are some options for scientists to consider. Each one has its plus and minus. Depending on the success as reported in literature, and so much depending on the judgment of scientists, they make their choice in research and then in clinical application.

III. Personalized medicine and whole-genome sequencing (WGS), and applications:

In 2010, *the human complete genome* was completely sequenced and reported in both scientific journal and public press. DNA sequencing technique was readily made available. This was considered a great stride in genome research, with a great deal of promise for the future. *Personalized medicine* was beginning to appear in medico-scientific journals.

As scientists knew, each human genome contains 200,000 coding sequences (exons) and millions of regulatory elements, defining complex signaling and regulatory network. Any single human individual's genome has about four million sequence variations. Although most of these variants are harmless, some cause disease, predispose people to condition and determine response to treatments. In general, the impact of genetic variants is disproportionate to their frequency. For example, some genetic diseases in newborns are frequently caused by de novo personal variants, which include large DNA deletion or duplications. Sequencing and analysis of human genome's six million base pairs requires extreme accuracy to prevent error. Genomic knowledge is growing exponentially. Thousands of whole human genomes being sequenced around the world (more than 10,000 completed since 2009, and 30,000 expected in 2012). This remarkable progress would increase common attachment of phenotypic information to genotypes, and fast improvement in genome interpretation software.

Concerns and policies of WGS:

WGS is an ultimate genetic test, and it could be ordered for many indications or as a "screening" test. Now, it is important to begin developing policies and recommendations to facilitate clinical adoption of WGS. Regulatory agencies and leading professional societies must work together to provide technical and interpretive standards and guideline for WGS to assure sufficient quality and usability of the date needed for various applications. Reliable specificity and sensitivity statistics should be established for various types of variants and distinct genomic regions. The medical usefulness of diverse genomic elements needs to be established through translational research.

Should WGS results be stored at part of the medical records? How will patients' autonomy and privacy be protected? How can WGS be made affordable for everybody? It is also important to guard against the over-promise of WGS benefits and to work to prevent un-ethical and illegal use of GWS data by others. So far, the US Genetic Information Non-Discrimination Act of 2008 regulates such use in part. But, many more public policy questions will need to be addressed by regulatory or legislative organizations. Both public and physicians in particular should be educated about the benefit and limitations of WGS, as patients will play a vital role in WGS adoptions.

By nature and by its importance, WGS would provide foundational medicine information which is expected to play a critical role in health management and improving physicians' decisions in diagnosis and treatment. In such a case, the complete knowledge of inherited genome variants alone is not sufficient, because it does not take into consideration of genome-specific   impact of environmental and stochastic   factors such as non-inherited cancer-causing mutations.

The availability of WGS provokes many important social and ethical questions, such as informed consent and access to one's own genetic information. In one aspect, we should cherish our personal genome diversity, and celebrate the advances in technology and science that are enabling broader adoption of WGS and that would help people live longer and healthier.

Whole-Genome sequencing (WGS) was already a very powerful research tool to study the molecular basis of thousands of diseases. In addition, medical doctors from at least a dozen large, especially university-related hospitals also use WGS for some of their patients (mostly with idiopathic disease of refractory cancers) but usually as part of a clinical study because only a few laboratories generates WGS in certified laboratory. In some cases, these labs have recently performed sequencing of all of the exons and, if unable to find a genetic cause, have turned to WGS. A more effective approach could be to routinely sequence individuals' entire genome once, preferably early in life, and to continue to use this information to make health-care decisions throughout their life-time. Current WGS technology, in spite of accuracy of only one false single nucleotide

variation per 500 kbp requires improvements for board use in clinical applications. Because the human genome is in fact diploid, it is also critical to determine which variants come from which parent .

To achieve a broad health impact, millions of human genomes will need to be sequenced each year. With accurate projected improvements in sequencing instruments, a rate of over one million WGS tests per year will be reached in this decade. Furthermore, there are continuous cost-efficiency improvements in WGS, and although not achieve yet, for a genome sequence to cost less than $1,000 seems a reachable goal.

The availability of an individual's WGS would provide immediate access to genetic information, and its latest interpretation when needed. This readiness would maximize disease diagnosis, prevention, and treatment, such as cardiac arrest.

As with other genetic tests, genome sequencing is non-invasive, as usually it requires only a small sample of saliva or blood. After sequencing is completed, and the variant data with supporting statistics are stored, an individual's inherited genome can be queried to help answer health questions over a person's life-time. The main goal of WGS an genomic medicine is not only to measure personal propensity to disease but also to determine genome-specific ways of preventing disease and improving treatment.

Conclusion

Molecular biologists have made tremendous contributions in the last 40-50 years. Their reports and results could be used/extended to clinical therapy in treating human diseases. The potentials can not be over-emphasized. All these offer so much for those who suffer from genetic defects and other kinds of diseases. Yet, they are risks and danger involved. Therefore, the Presidents in USA authorized to have national ethical committee established, guiding and overseeing the application of technology. Common citizens should be well informed, so that they could make informed decision and choice. Scientists intend to do their best, offering what they could offer to the society.

As evangelical Christians, (as I offered my professional advice in previous chapter), we should support any meaningful and useful projects, if there is any hope for clinical use. With the information given, we join the others in making informed decision, for the benefit of the society and especially those who suffer from genetic defects.

Literature Cited

1. J. Craig Venter et al, 2001

   The sequence of the human genome.

   Science/AAAS, vol. 291:1304-1351

2. Science/AAAS,   2001

   The Human Genome,   Vol. 291:1177-1303

3. Horace Judson,   1996

   The Eighth Day of Creation: The Makers of the Revolution in Biology.

   Cold Spring Harbor Biol. Lab., N.Y.

4. James D. Watson et al,   5th Ed., 2004

   The Molecular Biology of the Gene

   Pearson Education, N.J.

5. Benjamin   Lewin, 2009,

   Genes VIII

   Oxford Univ. Press, N.Y.

6. B. R. Click and J.J. Pasternack,   1998

   Molecular Biotechnology

7. N. Y. Academy of Sciences,   2002

a) DNA: The Double Helix Perspectives and   Prospectives at 40th Year.

b) Engineering Plants for Commercial Products and Applications. Vol. 792

c)   Medical Ethics at the Dawn of 21st Century, vol.   913

d)   Gene Therapy for Neo-plastic Diseases, vol. 716

Chapter 21
Biblical Exegesis and Hermeneutics in Relation to Science

" Science needs the light of revelation, revelation needs the perspectives of science, both Science and theology are fundamental pursuits.

We must have a spirit of mutual respect and gratitude."

Prof. Dr. Bernard Ramm

Science and theology are two rocks in western civilization and education. Rational research in science has contributed so much to the advancement in our society and technology, especially in the last half of 20th. As given in Chapter 5, Christianity and Christian scholars had so much to do with the birth of modern experimental sciences. Evangelical Christian scholars also made significant contribution in the 20th century, in genomics and other areas. Likely in the 21th millennium they will make ever greater contribution in science. Theology, Christian faith and Church are integral part of western culture. Theology and Christian doctrines not only add new biblical knowledge but also enlighten human mind and energize the spirit. **Genuine Christian faith as expressed faithfully by Christians will eventually express in human life-style and daily behavior in society, and in the world**.

In this chapter, I shall discuss the ways how we interpret the Biblical Scripture and how we apply a particular portion of Scripture in our daily living in home, in community and in society at large; and also in relation to sciences.

A. *Biblical exegesis or hermeneutics*:

Biblical exegesis or hermeneutics is a science, and an art of biblical interpretation. It is a science because it is guided by rational rules and scientific principles within a system. It is an art because the application of the rules and the principles is by personal skill, not a rigid or mechanical imitation. In Christianity, "Sola fidei regula" means that the Holy Bible is the only authoritative book and guide for Christians and the Church and her practices. This is especially true for evangelical Christianity or Protestantism. The almighty God has spoken in the Holy Scripture is the very heart of our Christian faith.

Biblical hermeneutics is by no means an easy task. It takes a great deal of personal training, experience and discipline in working. The Bible, as the revelation of God, was written more than two thousand years ago. To understand it,

to expound it, and to explain it is a formidable task. But, it is attainable with consistent discipline on the part of the one who tries to interpret it. Over these years Christian scholars devoted themselves to the study and interpretation of it, and have written a great deal as literature. So today, in addition to personal devotion and studies, we could consult the writings of the early saints and scholars, for our learning.

There are several important principles we have to bear in mind when we come to interpretation:

1) Historical particularities:

There are something unique and we should give due attention. For example, the writer, using his training, experience and insight tried to convey his message to the readers or listeners. Then, who wrote this book? To whom he was addressing? On what general subject or specific subject? How he said it? What was the style? Under what circumstance he was writing? What he had in mind to explain the subject? Did he use any figure or example? What was his mood in speaking or in writing? Any major doctrines ? What was his teaching or message? All these were historical particularities. It is up to those who study them nowadays to find out.

2) Then, how the writer conveyed his message to the hearers?

Using figures, allegories, with examples? So, there was a literal style used by the writer, or other style?. The speakers who endeavor to expound one book or a chapter, or one section in a chapter, ought to know all these particularities. With all these particularities, they intend to transmit the message to the hearers. In the following section, I shall say more on the literal style.

B. Application is not interpretation:

For any scripture or a paragraph of scripture, or even a chapter of scripture, there is only an interpretation; or one interpretation and one application; or one interpretation with many applications. *Interpretation is one thing, application is another*. Do not be mix them together. Interpretation and application are two entirely different principles. When you lead a Bible study or speak in a church service, always endeavor to find the *interpretation first, then application*.

In a strict sense, there is *only one interpretation*, but t*here are many applications*. Endeavor to find the right/correct interpretation. Under different circumstances, you use the Scripture in a different ways in application. Therefore, there are many applications. Interpretation of Scripture will have applications at the end of any paragraph or a chapter. *To find the right interpretation is what the leader or speaker should endeavor to do. Do not take application or applications as interpretation. This takes a great deal of scholarship*. Often, in the Christian churches, preachers or ministers are not well trained academically

and scholarly, they take the application or many applications as interpretation. Keep in mind, application can not take the place of interpretation. I could not emphasize them strongly enough!

Now, let me come to an application of Scripture. For example, 1 Timothy 3:16 says: "All scripture is God-breathed and is useful for **teaching, rebuking, correcting and training in righteousness**, so that the man of God may be thoroughly equipped for every good work." As you and I could see these verses, there are **four aspects of applications**. Of the four aspects, two of them are directed to Christian daily living, i.e. application in daily living. So application of the Scripture is the second important ingredient. So, how the Christians apply what they have learned or they have been instructed to practice what the Scripture instructs.

C. Principle of immutability and variability:

1)Immutability:

For example, God and his deity, Jesus as Savior, The Bible as the inspired word of God, human and fallen nature, salvation through faith and by grace, one Church. All these are fundamental and basic doctrines. No one could change them.

2)Variability: After interpretation, then you come to application. When you intend to apply this portion of Scripture or just one verse, you could apply it in different circumstances. In other word, application of Scripture verse could vary from one situation to another situation. This is quite different from interpretation.

D. Literal styles:

What literal style did the writers use in writing? Often, writers say things simple and straightforward. Did he use any example or historical incidence or parable to convey the messages? Was there anything hidden that we need to dig into it in order to find out the message? Did he use any metaphor or allegory? Is this prophetic or historical? These are the things we nowadays have to find out in order to find the message conveyed. To the audience in those days the message might be very clear-cut. But to us, it will be quite different. The difference is "then" and "they", and "now" and "we", the meaning and the implication could be quite different. How we today go to interpret them, wc have the following methods:

1. The literal expressions: By and large, there are at least ten different styles as follows:

   a. chop-sui type: a mixture of things, no clear, definite coherent message.

   b. Spiritual and spiritualizing style.

   c. Literal reading and interpretation.

   d. Allegorical method.

e. Parabolic method.

f. Metaphorical method.

G. Typological method.

H. Apologetic method.

I. Polemical method.

J. Topological method.

K. Anagogical method.

L. Historico-culturo-grammatical method.

As shown above, there are so many ways we could interpret a text under consideration. Therefore, the way we consider would determine how we are going to interpret the text. It could vary from individual to individual. It is up to us to exercise our mind and training, using different ways to expose the meaning of it. It is by no means an easy task.

E. Biblical exegesis or hermeneutics in relation to sciences:

The historical incidence of Galileo Galilea by the Roman Catholic Church in the 17th century is something we all remember so well (cf. Chapt. 5). In 1996, Pope John Paul II acknowledged that the mishandling by the Church due to the literal reading of the Scripture of both Old and New. Those of us in both science and in Christian faith have learned the lesson. Literal reading and interpretation have its proper place in biblical hermeneutics. But, using such a method, great care should be exercised. This should not be used often.

Galileo was both a devout Christian and a sincere scientist. He sought earnestly to keep the church, for her own good, from the mistake of making an article of faith out of any disputed, un-settled scientific question, using a questionable scripture. At the same time, he wanted science to be free from the control of theology as well as philosophy. He did not consider the Bible was a science book. ***His famous saying was that***

"God gives us two Books, the Book of Scripture and The Book of Nature.

The former is the Word of God, the latter is the Work of God.

Since God is the author of the two books,

they should not come to contradict each other.

The Bible tells us how to go to heavens, not how the heavens go."

For those who are in one way or another involved in this so-called "Cultural War" in USA, this is something they should keep in their thinking and in their

mind. In Sept. of 2009, in the 150th anniversary celebration of Darwin's Origin of Species, Prof. Ronald Summer of Univ. of Wisconsin used his personally fabricated phrase "anti-evolution movement" the first time on platform. He not only forgot the lesson, but intended to intensify the un-profitable debate. He deliberately choose "Fiat Creationism" or "Scientific Creation" in his talk as the only school of thought, representing Christendom. *It was indeed immoral, and he is anti-scientific*. Yet, many scientists in the audience of that day echoed his sentimental accusation. It was indeed something very regrettable. This is one side of coin. The other side of the coin is so-called "Fundamentalists" in Christian circle who insist that the Bible is a science book. They fought it with no valid reason. Both my wife were sadden with disappointment, and we left the campus of Univ. of Oxford the next day.

Keep this in mind. The Bible was written more than two thousand years ago, with the people's language of those days/that time for the people of that time. That was long before science and experimental science were borne. Indeed, in the Bible there are descriptions of living things and their activities. Therefore, *it is not un-scientific. But it is non-scientific writing because it was written before scientific era*. No effort should be made in searching for scientific facts in the Bible to support moral or religious conviction!

Many Christians whose careers are in the scientific teaching or research do consider that the Bible and science, if they are properly interpreted, give support to each other. *They are complementary*, assisting each other in explanation. For example, they believe that God as the Creator, creating and causing things to grow. The Bible does not tell us explicitly how God Jehovah creates. The Bible is silent on this specific point. Therefore, we Christians could go to sciences, using what sciences have discovered, and proven to be true as supplementary methods of creating things. For example, biochemistry could teach/inform us of the basic constituents, and how they are brought together to form polymers, tissues and cells. Biophysics could assist us to understand how the structures of living things are built together. "*Revelation needs the perspectives of sciences*" is what Prof. Bernard Ramm said in this chapter's quotation. In other word, we strongly believe creation first, then created living things are evolving in a horizontal fashion.

All these indicate that all depends on how we interpret the Scripture, making use of what modern sciences could offer for secondary stage of development and reproduction of living things. In the Literature Cited, I recommend six Christian scholars who strongly recommend *the historic-culturo-grammatic expositorial method of interpretation*. **This is the method I have been using in my Christian ministry over these forty years in churches, in seminaries and in schools**.

Let me conclude this chapter with a quotation of what *Dr. Charles Hummel* given in his book, "*The Galileo Connection: Resolving Conflicts between Science and the Bible*", 1980, IVF Press, Downers Grove, Ill., as a concluding remark on hermeneutics and science:

"Both creation and evolution have varied meanings. It is a mistake to use the terms creationists and evolutionists as if each represents only one concept, or as if they were mutually exclusive positions. Many competent scholars accept both biblical creation and biological evolution. Yet, people are surprised to hear that one can have full confidence in the reliability of the Genesis account of creation, and also use macro-evolution as a scientific theory to correlate known data and guide future research. That set of views, held by Christians of the late 19th century (and also 20th century, as my addition) is common among evangelical Christians in sciences to-day. We should not only recognize the essential difference between the biblical and scientific views of nature, but we also maintain their integrity. In other words,   macro-evolution, like any other scientific theory must be judged on its own merits; its validity is not determined by theological or philosophical convictions. Likewise, a proposed interpretation of the Genesis creation account like other biblical doctrines, must satisfy recognized hermeneutical criteria, and not determined by scientific theories."

I personally agree/subscribe to his *conviction and stand*. Both evangelical Christians and sincere scientists should pay attention to what this quotation says.

Conclusion

Biblical exegesis or hermeneutics is both a science and an art. Therefore, to interpret a paragraph or a chapter of Bible, or using the Bible in public speaking, we should exercise a great deal of care. It requires scholarship and discipline in handling. In principle, for any scriptural verse or paragraph, there is only one interpretation. So, we should aim at discovery of the right interpretation. Yet, there are many applications, depending on circumstance and cases. Both Scripture and Science could be accepted as complementary and supplementary, if being properly handled. In history, we learn a lesson in Galileo's case. Science and Christian faith need not to be in conflict, if each one of the two disciplines remains in her proper sphere.

Chapter 22
A Brief Record of My Lectures on Science and Faith In building "bridges"

"Go, therefore and   make disciples of all the nations; baptizing them in the name of the Father and of the Son and of the Holy Spirit, teaching them to observe all things that I have commanded you; and lo, I am with you always even to the end of the age."

By Jesus Christ, in Matt. 28:18-20

"While Paul was ......in Athens, he was greatly distressed to see that city was full of idols.   So he reasoned with the Jews and God-fearing Greeks......Epicureans and Stoic philosophers began to dispute with him."

By Apostle Paul, Acts 17:16-18

"This world is My Parish"

Rev. John Wesly

Introduction

In 1965, both my wife and I concluded our ministry and professional work (***generally referred to as "tent-making ministry"***) for 7 years in Brazil. With 3 children of ours, we returned to USA. We landed first in Miami. FA, having meetings in American churches, and also relaxing for one week. Then, we flew to N.Y. city where we toured historical sites for 2 weeks. At the same, by invitation I spoke in evangelical American churches. While we were in that city, I was interviewed by Mr. John Smart of "The Missions magazine" of Christian Missions in Many Lands. Then, he wrote an article on our work in Brazil, with the title of ***"Striking Development in Brazil: A 20th Century Example of New Testament Evangelism and Church-Planting"*** for the Missions magazine. Through such a media service, our work in South American were made know to Christian groups in both USA and Canada. Then in the following years I was invited to speak in

many churches in these two countries.

1. Teaching-research work in Michigan:

While we were in Chicago, I was invited to visit Univ. of Mich. (U/M) in Ann Arbor , and Eastern Michigan University (EMU) at Ypsilanti. I was offered an Assistant Professor of Microbiology at EMU, on tenure track. That was indeed the Lord's provision far more and above what we had anticipated. So, with that academic assignment, we settled down in Ann Arbor, MI. People wondered why I accepted the lowest rank of academic teaching-and-research. Yes, I was extremely delighted to accept the offer, with gratitude and humility. I joined the teaching-research faculty in a state university, i. e. EMU. The reason was very simple. While I was in Brazil, I had an appointment with the Brazilian National Research Council (Conselho Nacional de de Pesquisa de Gov. Federal do Brazil), stationing at Instituto Biologico in the Capital City of Sao Paulo). With that assignment, I worked for three-and-half years. I published only three scientific papers.

In 1961, I worked as Assistant Manager of Animal Vaccine Plant of Pfizer Co. for another four years. This was industrial and production work. Working with a group of Brazilian veterinarians and microbiologists, we produced industrially 10 animal viral vaccines, including the foot-and-mouth viral disease of cattle, as the most important one. With this I did not have any extra time for extensive research work.

I fully realized the fact that I was far behind the time in academic scientific endeavor. I decided to take a lower category of professional job, as Assistant Professor of Microbiology, in Michigan. With this, likely I might be able to catch-up in research endeavor. To no one's surprise, with both teaching-and-research, I was promoted to Associate Professor, with tenure, in 1967, two years later. Then, I worked hard in my professional work. In 1972, I was made as Full Professor of microbiology and molecular biology. Also, in 1972, I took my first sabbatical leave of one-year. I was able to go to Massachusetts Institute of Technology for further advancement in research. I was honored with an appointment at the Dept. of Biology at Massachusetts Institute of Technology, working under *Prof. Salvador E. Luria, a Nobel Prize winner of 1969*, on work with bacteriophage genetics. I learned a great deal of molecular biology under his tutorship. The track of promotion was indeed fast. Nothing could make us happier than these. The Lord Savior did grant us his honor in due time.

Of course, while I was teaching-research, I returned to Brazil, in summer months of every yea. My objective was to continue in assisting the church work among the Chinese immigrants. To make a long story short, I have stayed with my teaching-research work for 30 years, quite long time (cf. the following sections).

Teaching-Research work in the People's Republic of China.In 1980 when the diplomatic relations between USA and China was normalized, I and my family

were able to return to the land of my birth for teaching and researching work. The trips took me literally to the four corners of the land. In summer of 1967, I undertook a trip around the world, surveying religious landscape in the world.   In this chapter, I shall briefly summarize my itinerant ministry in these years, dividing it into five time periods:

A.1958-65, in Brazil and Argentina of South America,

B.1965-80, teaching –research in Michigan, USA,

C.1980-2009, visiting professor and work in People's Republic of China,

D.1998-2007,   retirement years in Michigan (somewhat overlapping), and

E.2007-2010, relocating in Maryland, and writing/ministering.

I shall elaborate comprehensively on each of these time periods, in the following:

A.1958-65, in Brazil and Argentina of South American:

In 1957, Univ. of Minn. conferred Ph. D. degree on me. Then, I was on the teaching faculty at Alma Mater, the Lord called me for overseas missionary work. With what I was being taught over these years, I came to the conviction of doing it with dual profession, i. e. professional work and missionary work at the same time. My planning was to engage myself in Christian work while I did my profession in teaching-research. This was generally referred to as "*Tent-Making Professional*" or "*Self-Support Missionary*." (cf. Acts 18:1-4 of the New Testament) in Christendom.

In June of 1958, I arrived in Sao Paulo, Brazil. With my own saving I was able to support myself and my family the first year. Of course, Christian friends in USA sent us of their gifts from time to time, subsidizing my work. The first year was a challenging and busy year. Since this was a new work, it took a great deal of effort and time. I did not seek for any opportunity of professional work.The friends in the Chinese community (population of 10,000 or more), welcome me with their open arms. I spared no effort in making Christ known in this new colony of immigrants. The Brazilian Presbyterian Church in Sao Paulo, through her minister, Rev. Jose Borges dos Santos, invited us to use a beautiful castle known as "Jardim das Oliveiras" (Olivet Garden), as our meeting place. That aided very much physically the pioneer work. The Lord blessed our work with a good measure of success in the year, with a number of people making profession of faith in the Savior Jesus. At the end of first year, ten people were baptized, and a local and indigenous church with eighty some members was on the way being formed. In the early state of church-planting, I was unable to travel far and elsewhere.

Meanwhile, I was trying to associate myself with foreign and American

missionary friends in the area. As a newcomer, I personally did need their advice and assistance. At the same time, I sought to meet with those who were involved in college work. Eventually, I was led to meet with Miss Ruth Siemens who was the Principal of American School in Sao Paulo. She was pioneering the IVF work in Brasil. Her colleagues, Prof. and Mrs. Ross Douglas of Universidade de Sao Paulo also met with me. To my delight, I came to know that they all were tent-makers. We worked together as a team. As a result of it, we had our first annual conference among university students. With thirty some collegians we had a weekend conference on "science and Christian faith". Prof. Douglas spoke specifically on Christian perspective on physics and related issues. I shared with them on my perspective on biology, specifically evolution and creation theories. The response was very enthusiastic and encouraging. So, we repeated it in the next year.

In 1916-62, the Chinese Church was pretty well established, with additional workers. So, with their blessings, I began to look for professional work. Then, the Lord opened the way. Charles Pfizer Co. / International Div., the second largest pharmaceuticals and antibiotics opened another plant for animal vaccines. The Co. was looking for a specialist to head-up the vaccine plant. After a couple of interviews by managerial staffs, I was hired as Assistant Manager of the Vaccine Plant. The charge given to me was to 1) design and build an animal vaccine plant, 2) train technical staffs, and 3) pilot lab work with animal vaccines, and then 4) industrial production. Beginning in 1962, I worked on two jobs at the same time. That was exactly what I had in mind when I first felt the Lord's call for foreign missionary work.

For my training as well for surveying the epidemic situation of the so-called "foot-and-mouth viral disease of cattle and other hoofed animals in South America, I was asked to go to Buenos Aires, Argentina. The International Headquarter of Charles Pfizer in N.Y. had intended to launch this kind of work in South America, the managerial staffs bought a vaccine plant which was owned by Dutch Firm for this very purpose. The animal vaccine plant in that capital city was in operation for a number of years. So, I was asked to go to Argentina for training as well as for international surveying of epidemics. While I was in Buenos Aires Christine with three children of ours was staying in Sao Paulo. So, I had to commute between the two countries on biweekly basis. With the experience in Argentina, I myself designed the plant, and outlined the schedule of industrial production of animal vaccines in Brazil.

Training the professional staff was by no means an easy task. The pilot lab work was even more challenging. Nobody could guarantee how high the potency of the vaccines being produced. So, I myself, working with assistants had to repeat the lab work from time to time, in fact, many times. Eventually, we succeeded. Then, it was up to us to translate the pilot lab work into industrial production. That was even formidable undertaking. All these took a great deal of collaborative work and painstaking efforts on my part as Assistant Manager.

Eventually, we reached our goal! By 1964, the Vaccine Plant produced at least one million doses of vaccines of 5ml each. The product was sold well to meet the demand in the country. In 1965 when I and my family left Brasil for USA, we left behind two accomplished projects. One was the independent and autonomous Chinese Church, the other was the Pfizer's Animal Vaccine Plant.

While I was working in Buenos Aires, I was able to join the IVF group for students' conference. Twice I was speaker on special topics. In summer of 1978 while I returned to Brazil for an extended visit, I attended the foreign missionaries in their summer conference. Three of us were speakers. Prof. John Whitcomb, of Grace Seminary at Winona Lake, IN, ministered on the subject of "Scientific Creationism", Prof. Peter Gromaki of Sidaview College on "Pentecostalism", and I was on "Evolution Theory". Those were something I did not expect.

B. 1965-1980, Univ. teaching-research in Michigan:

The Lord is no debtor to any one who loves Him and serves Him with diligence. The Lord opened the door for me to academic circle in USA. In 1965, I was hired by **Eastern Michigan Univ. (EMU)**, as Assistant Prof. of Microbiology. In a way I did not anticipate I was able to return to academic institution. The good Lord opened the door for which I was very grateful. In 1972, through Prof. Alfred Sussman, Dean of Graduate School and his recommendation, I joined concurrently the research faculty of Dept. of Biological Sciences at **University of Mich.**, as Adjunct Professor.

In those years there was a Christian movement among Chinese students' groups on university campuses. Ann Arbor was no exception. There was a Chinese Bible Study Class (CBSC), operated mostly by students. Without any reservation, both my wife and I casted our lot with them, in the first wcck we were on campus. To make a long story short, in 79, CBSC became a full-fledge church. Three of us, (i.e.: Dr. Li Ai-Kang, Mr. Mao Lai-Chen, and I myself) were recognized as elders of this interdenominational church. That added more responsibility on my shoulder, being charged with both platform ministry and administration. The Lord granted us the privilege of pointing so many Chinese college students and graduates to Christ Jesus as Savior. After a training period in basic doctrines and Christian living, I had the privilege of baptizing them. They were added to the local congregation. In a matter of two to three years, there are more than one hundred and fifty members in local church fellowship. As a general principle, we maintained a very cordial relations with other American evangelical churches in the city. This relationship lasted more than 35 years while we lived in Mich. From time to time whenever I was available, by invitation I traveled quite often. I visited many such Bible classes elsewhere in North America. In addition to sharing with them of my missionary experience in South America, I undertook the subject of *"The Great Commission: Threefold Task"*. In Matt. 28:18-20, the risen Lord commanded his disciples to go, evangelizing and establishing indigenous churches. Knowing my specialty in microbiology and molecular

biology, the church colleagues often asked me to add subjects on bio-science as additional. In those years, evolution versus creation was my principal subject. Since microbes such as viruses and bacteria occupy the borderline between living organisms and non-living ones, I expounded on two theories on biogenesis. i. e. *abiogenesis* (chemical to molecular evolution theory) and biogenesis (creation theory). Those subjects were not exclusively Christian theological questions. They were in essence bioscience questions. For that reason, no one else in academic world could object to my teaching on those subjects.

In 1970 and onward, in metropolitan cities such as N.Y., Washington, D.C. Chicago, San Francisco, Los Angeles, Detroit and Boston and others, interdenominational Chinese Church was organized, and came into existence. In fact, this was again the movement of the Holy Spirit, preparing Chinese professionals for the future.

In early summer of 1979, a Chinese Delegation of Bio-Sciences came from Mainland China, visitin universities and research institutes in the United States of America. Prof. Ming-Chi Wang, Chairman of Bio-Sciences at Fudan Univ. was one of the members. He called on me by long distance while he was in D.C. area. Prof. Wang invited me to visit China, specifically Fudan University in Shanghai. I accepted his invitation. So, I undertook a trip to China in the summer months of that year. On the way to Beijing, I met with my brothers and their families for 10 days in Hunan Prov. Then, I flew to Beijing, the nation's Capital. While in that city, a rare opportunity came to me, meeting the Presidents of the both Academies of Medical Sciences, and of Agric. Sciences. Through their introduction, I was able to meet some high-ranking officials in the Central Government in Beijing. This led to my extensive visits to China in the following 20 some years.

C. 1980-2006, and 2008, 09, as Visiting Professor, teaching-and research work in China:

In 1980 when diplomatic relationship between USA and the *People's Republic of China (PRC)* was normalized, the door was opened for outside visitors. Through previous visit in 1979, both the Ministry of Education (*MOE*) and *Chinese Academy of Agric. Sciences (CAAS)*, extended their invitation to me, returning to China, the land of my birth. In 30 some years of isolation, China was relatively poor in nation's living standard. China was also far behind in scientific endeavors. So, the Government welcomes visitors. They especially extended a hand of welcome to expatriates. It is the fact that they speak the native language. Communication would be far easier. As a policy, the Chinese government could only grant us visitors with official invitation only. In a way that was quite special enough. But, expatriates had to pay their own traveling expenses. Once the visitors were in the country, they would extend the coverage of everything while in China. So, I had to make my own arrangement. Fortunately, with a sabbatical leave of six months granted (with salary paid) by the Univ. in Mich. I was able to return to China. My wife and I traveled together, with our four children. That

was a huge undertaking. Also, that was a rare opportunity for me and the family. This would offer the opportunity to the children in identifying themselves with the Chinese folks. Above all, they could learn the culture, language and family value. Indeed, that was a double blessing.

One week after we arrived in Beijing, under the auspice of CAAS I offered advanced course nationwide, i.e. *Molecular Biology of Animal Viruses*. I used both Chinese and English languages interchangeably in my lectures. They were delighted with these, so that they could learn the science in both languages. This was an additional blessing to the participants. The course was only to faculty and senior research staff, 140 some in number. In fact, many of them heard of molecular biology the first time in their academic life! What a terrible isolation it was to them, for thirty some years! As a result of it, many of these faculty members, and some of them were chairmen of departments, became my close friends. Due to the constraint of space and facilities available, only those associate professors and above, or associate researchers and above, could avail themselves of such an opportunity. Even so, there were more than 140 scholars came. The time was in summer months. The temperature in Beijing in that year was above 85-90 F. There was no air-conditioning in the classrooms or elsewhere. Everyone had to endure the scorching heat. To make me comfortable in lecturing, the staffs bought blocks of ice. The ice blocks were placed behind the lecture lantern. With an electric fans blowing behind, ice blocks were being melted, cold air could blow at me. So, I felt comfortable in lecturing. Chalk board and projector were provided for my use. With handwritings and transparencies projected, I lectured three and half hours with both Chinese and English languages, in the morning of Monday to Friday. Of course, in technical vocabularies and terms, I used English. They were delighted to learn the lessons in both idioms.

The classmates were faculty members and researchers, with a solid foundation in bio-sciences. So all I had to do was to present a comprehensive outline with some details on molecular biology of animal viruses. The afternoon was for lab. method. All these things were relatively new to them. Some of them heard the first time of "molecular biology." The "classmates" listened attentatively, with notes taken. Then, in the evening hours after supper, they compared notes intensively. They worked hard consistently every day. I was told that every night they together reviewed the notes taken. They edited them, and produced a final version of the lecture they had attended on that day. So, on my part, I had to review their final version of lecture. At the end of 4 1/2 weeks' work, they produced a final written text for my review. Immediately after the termination of the course, we are offered to travel, visiting three to four scenic areas or cities, as a kind of payment to my labor. Even on the airplane going to elsewhere, I had to read their manuscript, adding or correcting what they had written down. I worked hard on it. The overall objectives were to produce a written textbook on molecular biology of animal viruses for general use in teaching and in research. They indeed succeeded it with their united efforts. All these indicated how hard they had worked under such stressful conditions in those days.

Through mutual agreement, and also the arrangement made by the senior staffs at CAAS, I toured at least four research institutes in the country. With a travel-guide provided, we toured Harbin and Lanchou Veterinarian Sciences Research Institutes. In addition, two more minor research institutes were also included in itinerary. At each of these places, I was asked to give a couple of talks on current subjects. I was also asked to assist/advise junior staff and graduate students in their research programs. In the early years of modernization, the travels were not easy. Accommodations were poor. Considering their genuine efforts in catching-up, I accepted everything they offered as if they were the best.

Using what we did in 1980 as a format, CAAS repeated the course-offering in 1981. I taught a refreshing course nationwide on "*Molecular Immunology*" in summer months of 1981. Once again, a textbook printed in rough papers, with hand-carving Chinese characters was produced at the end of 5-weeks' lecture. The amazing thing they did was this. Once these faculty and research staff returned to respective institutes, they were asked to repeat what they had learned to junior staffs in their institutes. In turn, these junior staffs would go out to institutes one-level lower, giving the same course to others. Through these repeating process and chain reactions, they passed-on what they had learned quickly and effectively! In a matter of a couple of years, they implemented what they had learned in lectures and in lab exercises at their home institutes! *This was indeed an effective method of transmitting scientific principles in a quick way*!

In 1983, The Beijing Normal University extended their invitation to teach again Molecular Biology of Viruses (in general) for four weeks in the summer months. Of course, the university officially extended their invitation to faculty members in other normal universities in other provinces and capital cities. Altogether, there were 80 some faculty members and senior faculty members. I was asked to use the same format as I had used it before with CAAS in Beijing. So, this was their national efforts to have the scientific principles and methods transmitted quickly. I had no reason of not giving them the materials.   In fact, I enjoyed doing it, and felt I was doing something profitable for the country of my birth.   So far as I could detect them, the results were as good as we had had it before.

After the teaching, the university offered me a travel plan of going to/through the Three Gorges of Yantze River, with everything paid-up by the university. This was their way of "payment" for my time and labor in lectures.

In the summer of 1984, I did not go anywhere. It was because the fact that my wife, Christine had an operation of breast tumor at University of Michigan Hospital, in Ann Arbor. I had to stay home, taking care of my dear life-partner. The operation of lumpectomy was very successful. The tumor only affected a couple of blood vessels, as diagnosed. Christine insisted on having irradiation treatment as well. The Chief of Radialogy Section was a friend of mine. Using irradiation, she treated Christine's left breast, only one, for cure, and also for preventive reason. That was indeed very thoughtful of her in her work of love.

Both Christine and I greatly appreciated her labor and additional efforts. After this, Christine insisted on having chemotherapy as well. This was a tough treatment, on weekly basis. The post-effect was very alarming. But, Christine took it so well, going through the whole course, without much hurt. We thank God for His mercy and grace!

In 1985, CAAS again invited me to offer another advanced course on *"Molecular Genetics"*. This time the course was offered at Harbin Veterinary Sciences Res. Institute (*HVRI*) at Harbin, a city in Manchuria, NE China. The weather was much cooler and pleasant. The participants were members from the research institute itself, and many others institutes as well. In addition to their staff and graduate students, others came from sister institutes. At the end, the officials thought that they have had "enough dosage in molecular biology and its lab. methods". They could take a step further down on the road for modernization. The Ministry of Agric. Sciences which is the superior entity made a decision in establishing an "Institute for Advanced Molecular Research" with funds coming from the Central Gov. We all took part in the inauguration of it. Of course, the officials acknowledged my driving force behind the whole undertaking. Eventually, that Institute became a cutting-edge research unit in the nation. With all these advanced courses in molecular biology over these years, the research endeavor in China, at least veterinary and animal research work, was modernized. It was elevated from traditional to the molecular level. We all were happy with it.

In 1991 when I returned to CAAS on the way to Harbin for another visit, Dr. Wang Yu, Vice President in charge of Foreign Affair, wrote a letter to me. In that letter, he acknowledged, *"with your consistent efforts over these years, our research endeavor has been greatly enriched . It was elevated to the molecular level. Without you and your genuine effort, we were not able to do so. Or it could delay for a number of years. Therefore, we wish to acknowledge it officially in this letter."* At the end, The Ministry of Agric. and Ministry of Education confirmed me an Honorary Professorship. I was delighted to accept it.

The officials in China thought of this format very well and was workable. They decided to adopt it as a general practice. This format was repeated several times. Therefore, I lectured at many other universities in the nation. The trips undertaken covered literally the four corners of the country. In a small but significant way, I contributed what I could do in the modernization drive in China, at least in bio-science. I congratulated on myself of availing of myself the opportunity in time for such an endeavor. How we all had to capture any opportunity which came on our way.

Another side of the coin was this. Over these years, Chinese visiting scholars began to come to universities in USA, for advanced academic studies, leading to either M.S. or Ph.D. degrees. Some of them were so-called "visiting scholars" without degree program. As a result of the modernization drive by the Chinese government, hundreds to thousands came to our shores. The Chinese students' population increased rapidly in all over North America. This offered a great

opportunity to Chinese Christian Churches to evangelize these visitors. Among those who came, a large percentage was in science and related disciplines. So the better way to reach them, in addition to conventional approach with gospel preaching, was to introduce them to the Savior through lectures on science and Christian faith. For that reason, I was invited from time to time by churches for such an effort. Much better result was seen. As a result of consistent efforts made, many of these students did make a profession of faith. With such opportunity available, I produced a set of lecture notes. When time comes, I intend to have it published as a book for the public use. For those who are interested in knowing all these stories, please consult my book entitled in *"My Tent-Making Years"* published by Cosmic Light in Taiwan, Republic of China, in 1995.

After working with the universities in Mich. for 30 some years, I came to a conclusion that I should reach the age of retirement from my teaching-research work. So, I began to phase out my work, both in the university as well at the Chinese Churches. In 1998, I submitted my request to the universities. So, in July of the year I left behind my teaching-research. Both my wife and I myself decide to live in an area where one of our children and family living. As a rule, mother and daughter are getting along much better with other combination. Our daughter, Rebekah as a lawyer has been working with federal government in Washington, D.C. She and her husband, Paul K Martin who was working with the Department of Justice, as Deputy Director of Inspector. Both Rebekah and Paul have their in Bethesda, MD, for quite a number of years. Upon mutual consultation, we decided to move to Maryland. Eventually, we were able to find a suitable home in Potomac, MD. relocated in Potomac, Maryland. We bought our new home at 1117 Fallsmead Way, Potomac, MD 20854-5531, a suburban area of Washington, D.C. It is less than 5 miles away from our daughter Rebekah and her family in Bethesda. Since we came, we have been enjoying tremendously with visits with our three grand-daughters, Anna, Emily and Grace. Once again, with the Lord's guidance, both my wife and I made another right decision. We began to associate ourselves with Chinese Bible Church in the area for Christian fellowship and outreach work.

The last teaching assignment: The last teaching job I had was in 2008. Under the auspices of CAAS, I taught another time of "Molecular Immunology" at the Graduate School in the western district of Beijing. More than 70 graduate students from seven provincial research institutes came. The CAAS-Graduate School provided the accommodation for them on the campus. The class met five times of two-and-half-hours from Monday to Friday. The course lasted more than 5 weeks. As usual, the students are bright and studious. At the beginning, I emphasized again and again that they should not just memorize the fact. With the principles taught, they should exercise their mind in thinking. *As Prof. Albert Einstein once said: " The value of a college education is not the learning of many facts, but the training of the mind to think."*

At the end, a course evaluation was done by the students, with the form of Q

& A prepared by me myself. To my delight, I came to knbow that they all enjoyed the course as taught in an American way. At the end of the course we had a group pictures taken, and also picture of I myself with students coming from different research institutes. We all have a very profitable and enjoyable time together for five weeks.

Then, the officials of the Graduate School of CAAS made arrangement for our tours of visiting three research institutes, including the Special Bio-Medicinal Products' Institute, and Horticultural Research Institute for 3 weeks. As usual, in each of these three places, I was asked to conduct seminars on current subjects to the staff and graduates.

In 2009 when both my wife and I returned to China, I deliberately returned to the campus of CAAS, giving one additional talk of two days on *"The HIV/AIDS Vaccines: Molecular Perspectives"* as supplement to those who had my course in 2008.

Over these years whenever opportunity came, I did speak on "Science and Christian Faith" as a special topics among professionals. I was fully aware of the regulations and restrictions imposed by the government. So, all I did was done within that confine. As a law-abiding citizen, I had no intention of whatsoever in violating the laws of the land. I gave due honor to myself and my profession. Above all, I personally valued the opportunity granted for many years of teaching endeavor in China. I had no intention of abusing the courtesy extended to me and my family.

D. 2008-2010, Christian ministry in USA and overseas:

(overlapping with C.)

I shall divide my overseas trip to two parts. In this section, I shall devote the space of writing my trips in USA. In next section, I shall devote my report on my trips to elsewhere, i.e. other than USA.

Once I retired from teaching/research at universities, I dedicated myself mostly, not exclusively, to Christian ministry in USA and overseas. In the first year and two, my wife and I traveled most confined to SE Asia, i.e. Hong Kong, Singapore, Malaysia, Indonesia, Australia and New Zealand. First, I made contact with churches, Bible Fellowships and Bible Seminaries. At first, I undertook subjects from the Bible, mostly in church and church-planting. Eventually, I intended to go into science and Christian faith. This was one area I do well. No one else could do much and do well in this specific and narrow field.

So, in this section 1) to 6), I shall report on what I did in Christian ministry in SE Asia and Oceania.

1)*Singapore Bible College and Seminary (SBC):*

In Sept. 1998, through the introduction of Mr. Job Wen-Shiew Hu, an alumnus of Nat. Taiwan Univ. , I made my first visit to Singapore Bible College and Seminary (SBC). Singapore is a City-State. In many ways it is a unique city, with high percentage of overseas Chinese. They speak Fu-chian dialect, in addition to a peculiar way of speaking British style of English. Mr. Lee Kuan Yah, a returned legal scholar from Univ. of Cambridge was instrumental to the establish the Republic of Singapore. Rev. Michael Shen, the Principal, made arrangement for me, as Speaker of the Reception to New Students' Week. The subject I undertook was "The Great Commission in the New Century".

In addition, I ministered the Word in a Chinese Church on Sunday. Then, I toured the city before leaving got Malaysia.

2) *Malaysia Bible Seminary (MBS) in Kuala Lumpur:*

The next stop was Kuala Lumpur of Malaysia. This country is predominantly a Moslem nation. The Chinese population amounts to a wee bit less than half of total population. As compared with Singapore, Malaysia is quite different in many ways. As I understand, Chinese Christians are legally restricted in their church services and outreaching activities. As a law-abiding citizen, I followed their tradition and national regulations in conducting the church services, with a free conscience and without fear.

Rev. Chin-Shie Tang, the Principal of Malaysia Bible Seminary (*MBS*) received me cordially for a visit. He arranged for my speaking to the students' body and faculty in devotion hour on Friday. Then, I met with some faculty members. Mr. Jason Lim who was Deputy Director of the Chinese ministry suggested that I should return for another extended visit. He was keenly interested in my science background. He wanted me to conduct a special course on science and Christian faith in the future. I promised to consider this in opportune time.

Then, I was invited to address to a high school student body in the Capital . This high school was a unique and private school, exclusively for overseas Chinese youth, somewhere to 4,000 students. So, I took the subject of *"Challenges to Overseas Youth in the Coming Millennium."* I included practical suggestions for them in society and in business practices. The talk was well received by both faculty and students alike. The Dean, a young lady, encouraged the students to take notes, and put them in daily practices.

Before leaving, I was interviewed by a local Chinese newspaper, *Sing-Chow Daily*. In the interview, I urged the Chinese folks in the country enlarged their horizons in world affairs as well in nation's landscape of religion. The interview was then published in the Daily. Somehow, the Editor –in-Chief, Ms. Siew treated us as friends, wanting us to return for another extended visit.

3) *in Melbourn, Australia:*

Melbourne, Australia was my next stop. Drs. Albert Mau and his wife, Shiao-Ling were Univ. of Mich. alumni. While they were in graduate school, they were associated with the Chinese Bible Study Class. So, we knew them well. They cordially received us for an extended visit. With their arrangement, I spoke in their Chinese Christian Church on *"Perspectives of Sciences and Christian Faith"* for three nights in a row. Happily, the church's meeting hall was filled up to the capacity. Lectures were well received, as never having them before. Of course, we made acquaintance with a number of friends in the church, including the Pastor and his dear wife. Also, I ministered in another Chinese Church on the Lord's Day.

Then, both Albert and Shiao-Ling made arrangement for us to relax in a cottage by the ocean-shore. We enjoyed the quite time together, reminiscing the good old days in Ann Arbor of Michigan.

4)*Massey Univ, in Palmester North, New Zealand,*

New Zealand was our next country for a visit. We arrived in Palmerston North, Prof. and Geoffrey Malcohm as our host family received us cordially. Prof. Malcohm was the former Dean of College of Arts and Sciences at Massey Univ. So, he arranged to have me speaking to the international students' body on campus on Friday night. As agreed, I spoke on "Science and Christian and His Faith". At the end of the service that night, a couple of students made profession publicly.

So, we concluded our extensive visit to SE Asia and Oceania. By way of Honolulu, Hawaii we returned to Potomac, Maryland for a time of rest at home.

E 1999-2004, to England and France: (overlapping with E)

a)Our first trip to England and France:

1)*Christian Family Camp in London*:   In April of 1999, I undertook the trip to London, England. The overall objective was to attend a family camp in the suburban area, being organized by the Chinese Bible Study Groups.   Attending such a camp, I shall get to know a number of the Christian groups and their leaders, and church ministers as well. So, I went. To my delight I found the group relatively large, with more than 300 participants, with 3 speakers. Through group meetings, I came to know the leaders. In turn, they asked me to speak in the afternoon session, sharing our work in Brazil. Also, I took part in a panel discussion. I met Rev.   Chia-Tang Chen,

Pastor of Chinese Christian Church in London. He arranged to have me speaking at weekend seminar on science and Christian faith in his church. I have succeeded more than what I had planned.

2) ***Univ. of Cambridge, and the city itself***: With arrangement made previously, I went to Cambridge where I was cordially received by Edward and Rosa Kwang. Two years ago they came to England from Hong Kong. They were active in both the Chinese Study Class on Univ. of Cambridge campus and Chinese Christian Church in the city. In the weekend, I conducted a series of classes on "Science and Christian Faith", using one of the meeting halls of the Univ. To my surprise, a large number of students and scholars came to the lectures. With transparencies projected, I lectured on i) the birth of modern experimental sciences in 16th to 17th centuries, 2) Christian perspectives on sciences and theology and 3) creation and evolution theories. The interest shown was very encouraging. They asked a number of provoking questions. Of course, I handled them well and to their satisfaction. As usual, the host students offered a potluck dinner at the end of the conference. Through these, I came to know a good number of scholars and students. In the following year or two, we kept a close contact through correspondences.

On Sunday, I spoke in the church service in the morning. Rev. Abe Chung showed me around the city after the service. Then, on Monday he took me to visit the campus of Cambridge. The buildings classic in appearance and in structure were indeed very beautiful and impressive. All the colleges were housed in a large courtyard, classrooms and dorms. As we all know, at Cambridge, they adopt the so-called tutor's system in instruction. Usually, classes are relatively small. The interaction between the Instructor and the students was very cordial and interactive.

3) ***Univ. of Oxford and the city of Oxford***: Rev. Jim-kee Lee of the Chinese Christian Church made arrangement for my visit for the whole

week. So, they expected me to minister on Sunday as well as in weekdays. My host family was a Chinese professional couple. I was able to do a wee bit of sightseeing of the campus. Once again, Oxford is just impressive as what is in Cambridge. In fact, buildings and halls are much more antique and varied. The educational system is very much the same as what I saw in Cambridge. On Wednesday night, I met with some Chinese student and scholars in Bible Study Class. After I presented an outline of the lesson, they responded with questions after questions.

4)*Manchester*: Rev. Chang-Sin Tseng and I met in the family camp while I was in London. He served as Advisor to the organizing committee. So, we agreed that we would meet again in Manchester on my way up to the north. So, I had one weekend meeting in his church, with subjects on science and Christian faith.

5)*Birmingham:* One of the leaders of the family camp was from Birmingham. In fact, he graduated from Fudan University in Shanghai. So, we two had something in common. With his arrangement I made a stopover on Wednesday, leading the Bible Study and sharing my ministry in South America. With this, I concluded my trip to England.

6)*France*: Acrossing the narrow oceanic bay, we arrived at Paris, a beautiful cities. We took the advantage in the city, we toured well-known museums, and historical sites. With the invitation by Overseas Chinese Church, I spoke on the subject of "The Church: Principles and Practices", with special emphasis on local, indigenous elders shepherding the local congregation. The saints greatly appreciated it for such a practical teaching.

So, we concluded our ministry and lectures in both England and France, returning to USA.

b)Our second trip to Europe, 1999-2000:

In 2000, we undertook our second trip to England Europe.

Beginning in this trip, we formulated a travel policy, reducing the time with local churches and their expenses. We decide to stay for a local congregation/church for Friday, Saturday and Sunday when we have meetings and activities. Then, on Monday, Tuesday, Wednesday and Thursday, we shall be on our own, taking a vacation and touring some scenic sites. On Friday, we shall travel to another city where the Chinese church is waiting for our visit and ministry meetings. In other words, we take care of ourselves for four days whereas let the local church congregations have us for the weekend only.

1) We returned for another time to England: We visited and ministered at Chinese Church, with science and Christian faith as our subject with college student groups on Friday and Saturday; and then expository Bible ministry on Sunday, in the following cities:

London,   Cambridge,   Oxford, Manchester, Sheffield,

2) In Paris, France: Once again, we ministered the Word at a Wen-chow dialect Chinese Church, mostly on "The Church: Principles and Practices.",assisting the church-planting work.

3) In Holland: We visited Chinese Christian Church in both Amsterdam and Rotterdam, lecturing on "The Church".

4) In Germany: This was our first visit to Germany. As it is known at that time, there were more than 50,000 Chinese immigrants (more students than merchants) in that country. Since Germany is not a emigrant country, so a large percentage of these folks are short-term students or visitors. Rev. and Mrs. Siegfried Glaw, former missionaries with the China Inland Mission/Overseas Missionary Fellowship, assisted us with the arranging visits and meetings in different cities. Under their advice, we stayed in each city 2-3 days, with lectures specifically targeted at university students only. In two weeks, we visited four university campuses, i.e. Hannover, Hamburg, Tuebigen and Ulm. The response by these students was very encouraging and interesting. In Hamburg, one interesting case happened. One Chinese visiting scholar together with his wife made   decision to become   Christians. We were told that this scholar had made significant contribution to scientific research work, was grand German citizenship. That was quite unique and outstanding

among the Chinese scholars in Germany. That made our trip to Germany much more meaningful.

5)In Czeck's capital city, we stayed for one week. At the weekend meeting I spoke to Chinese students' group.

Then, we concluded our trip to Europe this time.

F. Another trip to Far East and Oceania: 2001-2002

1)At the invitation of China Theological Seminary in Hong Kong, we understook another trip to the Far East. Through the arrangement made by both Rev. Philip Lee and Rev. Thomas Li, I taught a graduate course on science and Christian faith, for two weeks.

2)We also met with friends, Rev. and Mrs. James H. Taylor, III, and visited his office of Medical Professional Services. James gave us an overview of their ministry in SW China.

3)The second time we visited Singapore Bible College and Seminary. Through the arrangement made by Rev. Michael Shen, the Principal, I lectured to both faculty and student body on "Embryonic Stem Cells & Cloning farm animals and Humans in relation to Christian principles of Ethics."

4)Also, the second visit to Malaysia Bible Seminary (MBS) at Kuala Lumpur. Rev. K.M. Kim, and Prof. Jason Lim requested for my intensive lecture on "The Creation Narratives: Five Schools of Thought" to the graduates and senior, for one week. With this lecture, the graduates could see the different interpretations, and would broaden their horizon for future ministry.

5)While we were in K.L., The Singapore Daily Press, working with MBS and Chinese Cultural Society, sponsored a public lecture on "Genetically Modified Foods: Prospective or Peril?" This was well attended. The people objected very much the monopoly by American enterprises on seeds and the price of food products.   The interest in

such a subject by the Malaysians was indeed challenging and interesting.

6) We extended our trip to Oceania. We went to Braesbaum of Australia. The Queensland Bible Institute and College requested for my lecture on "Science and Christian Faith." Taking the advantage in the area, we ministered the Word in Chinese Churches and students' groups on university campus.

7) The next stop was Melbourne, where both Drs. Albert Mau and Shiao-Ning Chen carried on their work with the National Institute of Molecular Biology research work. In the city, there were half a dozen Chinese Churches. On the following week, I spoke at three churches. As shown, the interest shown by Chinese professionals on the subject of science and Christian faith was overwhelming and encouraging.

Both Albert and Shiao-Ning made it possible for four of us spending a weekend together for renewing our Christian fellowship in a beautiful countryside for four days.

8) We paid our second visit to Dr. and Mrs Geoffrey Malcolm, at Palmerston North. Through their arrangement, I spoke at their church on Sunday, and lecture on "Science and Christian Faith" with foreign students at the state university, and courtesy call on "The Christian Foreign Mission Office" of the Christian Brethren Movement.

9) The next step will be in the most beautiful and quiet South Island, and both Albert Mau and Shiao-Ning Chen joined us in this adventure. We rent a car for our journey. The first stop was Christchurch, a city with that unique name, also with a nickname "The Flowering City". The three Chinese Churches in the city united in their efforts, sponsoring a weekend gospel campaign with Bible ministry. Quite a good number of students of both Chinese nationality and foreign languages made profession of faith in the Savior. This indicates the joint effort by churches with open-arms could produce "miracle" in human sense. The South Island is indeed a most beautiful island, with magnificent

mountain range and snow top. The impressive sheep industry on the island is another unique feature. The tip of the island is called "Sound" is so quiet and tranquil, literally you could hear the sound of a drop-needle. Four of us spent a very quite night on board of a boat, it was very enjoyable.

10). Then, we returned to Auckland of the North Island. The Chinese colony is the biggest on the this island country. The Chinese Christian Church had me for a weekend meetings with lecture on science and Christian faith.

Then, we returned to USA by way of Pacific route, with stopover in Hawaii for a week of being our son, Ted and his family on the island.

G. In 2002, a trip to Northern and Eastern Europe: This is our first trip to this part of the world.

1) Stockholm of Sweden: The city is well known for her culture, and also the Assembly Hall of Nobel Foundation. This nation is in a way socialistic, with high tax and excellent social welfare for her citizens. We toured the Assembly Hall and its facilities. In the weekend, the Chinese Christian Church arranged to have me speaking to their services on Friday, Saturday and Sunday as well.

Then, we went to City of Upsala, with so much historical significance for sciences. We visited the Upsala University, where well-known systematist (classification of plants and animals), Prof. Carlos Linne and his Lab, and the gentleman Celsius who first formulated the thermometer with "Celsius degrees". In the Hall of the science building, there is a status of Carl Linne. In his lab., there is his photo and a plaque with the words "Deus Creavit, Linneaeus disposuit" (literally, "God creates, Linne classifies/edited"). We were very much impressed with the caliber of scientists in the early century of natural sciences.

2) Warsaw of Poland: Boarding a sizeable steamship, we Crossed the Baltic Ocean in the whole evening. We landed in a port city of Gdynia

Gdansk, a well-known for its revolution against the totalitarian Communist system by labor leader and forces. We toured the city, seeing some of the historical sites. Then, we took the train to Warsaw, the capital city. We stayed with a Chinese family who lately immigrated to this country. To my surprise, they came to know my birthday by reading my first book, "Our Tent-Making Years.", and celebrated my birthday with a dinner party. Poland remains as a socialistic country, with liberal welfare program for her citizens. There is only one Chinese Church, using a Lutheran Church building for services in Sunday afternoon. In the morning hours, we deliberately attended the Lutheran Church service. To our surprise (or to our least surprise), we found only a dozen citizens attending the service in such a beautiful and elegant church building. After the service, there was a tea for all those attended the service. The Minister invited us to join us going to another city where the massacre of Jewish people (The Holocaust) took place, for a memorial service. Due to the commitment to the Chinese service in the afternoon, we declined the invitation. The Chinese church service was well attended, and I spoke on "The Church, Principles and Practices" for this infant church.

3) Then, we went to Vienna of Austria, the musical capital of the world. The city is indeed beautiful and historical, with magnificent music concert halls. Taking the advantage in such a well-known city, we attended a couple of concerts, listening to symphonies by both Mozart, Beethoven and Caspar, and many others. We enjoyed very much the music events. There is one Chinese Church in the city, with her own small meeting hall. We stayed in a hotel in the neighborhood of the church. To our delight, the music program in the church service was excellent, with beautiful numbers by Chinese students attending those music conservatories in the country.

4) Germany: Taking the train, passing through Belgium, we arrived in Hannover, for our third visit. In two weeks' staying, we visited six

university campuses, including Hannover, Brenen, Clausthal, Aachan, and Bocum-Hagen, with my scheduled lectures on sciences and Christian faith.   By way of Frankfurt, we return to USA.

5)2002, the third trip to England, and the first time to Scotland:

1.The third trip to England, and the first time to Scotland:

In Oct. we undertook the 3rd trip to England.

We visited/lectured/spoke on the university campuses and also Chinese Churches in the following cities (very briefly):

a) Cambridge and the Univ. campus,

b) Oxford and the Univ. campus,

c) Sheffield and the Univ. campus,

d) Manchester and Univ. campus,

As we planned, we stayed one week in each city, speaking on science and Christian faith in weekend, and spoke in church service on Sunday, and then touring the area.

This time, we extended our trip to Scotland, by train.

a) The city of Edinburg, Scotland:

The Chinese Christian Church, composed of students more than anything else met in "Eric Lidden Memorial Church" (named after the well-known track star and missionary to China, Mr. Eric Lidden, with popular movie "Burning chariots "). With their invitation and arrangement, I spoke on science and Christian faith. In addition, I gave one specific lecture on embryonic stem cells and cloning. It was the fact that well-known Roslin Institute where the sheep Dolly and Polly were cloned.

With arrangement made, both Christine and I were able to pay a visit to the Roslin Institute on the weekday. On that day, Dr. Ian Walmut was not available, being on assignment elsewhere. We were cordially received by Dr. John Smith, who conducted a tour of the lab.. and surgical rooms where cloning Polly was done, and the stale where

they were housed. So, we not only saw the cloned sheep, but also touched them with our own hands. Of course, both Dr. Smith and we had exchanged on general principles of cloning and specific steps in producing pharmaceutical products in cloning animals. Upon returning to USA, I wrote two specific articles in English, describing the principles, and ethical implications for Christian public, being published in "The Challengers" by Chinese Christian Missions in Petaluma, Calif.

b)The city of Glassgow: The city itself is indeed very historical, with so many statues and platforms. The Chinese Church conducted its annual welcome service to new students, with me as the speaker. Using science and faith as a launching platform, I shared the gospel message with these students. On Sunday, as usual in my practice, I gave an expository message on the Holy Scripture.

On account of the winter months which were cold in Scotland, we decided to return to USA via England.

H. In 2003, trips in USA and Sao Paulo of Brasil:

1)Trips in USA:

a)To Sao Paulo, Brazil, in April of the year:

The Chinese Christian Church in Sao Paulo, which we had the privilege of founding/establishing it in the 60 was going to celebrate her 40th anniversary. With their invitation, both Christine and I returned to Sao Paulo for two weeks of festival activities and ministry meetings. The 40th Anniversary was indeed a joyful and commemorable service, especially for those old-timers. With gratitude, we reminisced our mutual efforts in cooperation and the blessings bestowed upon us in those old days. In addition, one week of Christian ministry meeting on various subjects was conducted before returning to USA.

b)Trip to Tucson, Arizona: church ministry and touring Grand Canyon: in Feb.

At the invitation of Chinese Christian Church in Tucson, I gave lectures on "Science and Christian faith" to visiting scholars and graduates at the weekend, and ministry on the Church on Sunday.

Taking the advantage of being in Arizona, and by way of Phoenix we toured the Grand Canyon in Yellow Stone National Park. The canyon is indeed magnificent and extraordinary in size and in scenery.

c) To San Diego, Calif., in July 4th weekend:

The Chinese Overseas Mission, through its Executive Board invited me to lecture on "The Creation Narratives: Five Schools of Thought" at their annual conference at July 4th Holiday weekend.

We renewed Christian fellowship with Mr. and Mrs. Wu Yung who were the Founders of the Mission.

d) The Chinese Christian Mission, Inc. in Canada, in Sept.

The Mission had me over to Vancouver, British Colombia for a public forum on "Embryonic Stem Cells and Their Use in Cloning" in the weekend. In the Forum, a medical doctor, a lawyer, and a social worker took part, with me as the principal Speaker on the subject.

e) Trip to Taipei, Taiwan, China, in May:

The China Evangelical Seminary in Taipei, Taiwan invited/arranged me to have a public debate with a Sociologist of the Academia Sinica, Prof. C. S. Wang on "Evolution Theory and Creation Narratives: Should We Make a Choice?" at their Auditorium. As a professor of microbiology and molecular biology for 20 some years I was well prepared for such a task. In every single facet of the evolution theory, I deciphered it in detail, and also differentiated *what are mechanisms and what are principles. We could accept one and reject the other*. Somehow, Prof. Wang took things for granted that he could not give a detailed description and presentation. The conclusion of the debate was very much in my favor. That quite upsets the sociologist, leaving the auditorium with his head down and face-losing. On another day, to the student body as well to the junior

faculty, I gave an analytic presentation on five schools of thought on Christian Creation Narratives.

In December, both Christine and I relocated in Potomac, Maryland, which is only 10 minutes' driving distance from where our daughter Rebekah and her family have been living. With such an arrangement, we two families could care one for another, giving assistance whenever it is needed.

E) 2004-2006: living in new residence, 1117 Fallsmead Way, Potomac, Maryland:

Relocation is quite an undertaking, especially for the wife. It took some time to readjust to the new environment and also a new community. Both my wife and I decide to take "a break" for awhile. I devoted more of my time in writing this book,, "*Science and Christian Faith: Their relationships in Past, Present and Future*", with ministry at large. In April-May we traveled to Shanghai, attending the "Forum on US-China Diplomatic Relations" to which our son Paul Liu as Chairman. While in the city, by invitation, both my wife and I took part in the Centennial Celebration of the Founding Fudan University (in 1980 when China first opened up, as Visiting Prof. I taught molecular biology for 3 months). Also, we took a trip to Manchuria, where I gave a lecture to research staffs and graduates on "Embryonic Stem Cells for Cloning Farming Animals."

While we were in Shanghai, we paid a courtesy visit at "China Protestant Church Office", renewing Christian fellowship. Mr. Jian-Hung Qi, Chairman of the National Committee cordially received us. While I showed him of my manuscript of "Science and Christian Faith", Mr. Qi took a careful reading of the Introduction and the first chapter. Being impressed with the high caliber of these two chapter, Mr. Qi enthusiastically thought that the book was what China needed most. He and his colleague, Rev. Shiao-Fung Xu, the Director of Publication decided to accept the manuscript for publication by their printing press in Shanghai. That was quite an encouragement to me. Upon returning to MD, I decided to add three more chapters. In a matter of six months, I submitted the manuscript to the China Protestant Church Press, for publication.

In turn, The China Protestant Church submitted my manuscript to layers of higher government officials to scrutinize what is presented in the book. The People's Republic of China is a socialistic and totalitarian nation, with strict control of their publication. Though my book is strictly a book of sciences and Christian religious faith, exemption could not be easily granted. It took two years going through these layers of examination and careful scrutiny. Eventually, in early part of 2009, the book was released and approved, going to printing press with 10,000 copies. Luckily, I did not pay any money for the printing. To my delighted, I was given an honorarium of more than US$2,500.00. Without ISBN, the book could only be sold by church bookstore in the country.

F) 2007-2009:

Christine, my wife suffered from arthritis, with terrible pain in her joints. She went through two knee replacement operations, with subsequent physical therapy. Taking a good care of her with all these, I was unable to undertake any travel to foreign countries. So, in more than two years, I stayed home and devoted my time to translating my book into English. In addition I was able to engage in Christian ministry at large in MD and Virginia.

By June of 2009, Christine recovered well from her operations, though she has to *take immunotherapy shots of "humira" once every two weeks*, with additional dietary supplements. So, we were able to resume our travel, at least to Hawaii, and to Shanghai, where our two sons, Ted and Paul and their families resided

In these 3-5 years, the economic-financial downturn worldwide and in USA affected all the nations and their citizens. No one was exempted. Our youngest son, Peter who was working with Neehman Brothers in N.Y. was laid-off. Luckily, Peter went to Shanghai, and found his employment. With that we have more and valid reason in traveling to China.

In Sept. 2008, at the invitation of the Chinese Academy of Agricultural Sciences, we traveled to Beijing, where I taught a graduate course of "Molecular Immunology at the Graduate School, as I mentioned in previous section. Seventy two graduate students coming from fire research institutes were enrolled. The scholastic caliber of these students were amazingly good and high. The course lasted for four and half weeks. At the end of semester, they gave an evaluation of the course itself. To my delight, I found that they all enjoyed so much the latest information presented. With the arrangement made by the Academy, we traveled to Harbin Veterinary Research Institute (one week), Special Pharmacological Products by Animals in Shenyang (one week) and the Horticultural Research Institute at Lao-Ning. By way of Shanghai, we returned to USA.

In Feb. of 2009, once again we attended the "US-China Diplomatic Relation" in Shanghai. We stayed for two weeks. Then, we traveled to Beijing. I met with those graduate students who took the molecular immunology in 2008. Addition to reviewing, I gave a special lecture on "Molecular Vaccine against HIV/AIDS: Strategy and Success".

In that year, the Christian religious landscape in China was changed and amazingly good. There were so many so-called "urban churches" making their appearance in public in different metropolitans. On Sunday, we attended a church service, with more than 800 participants. In addition, I was able to conduct Bible Study Class on the campuses of both Beijing Univ. and Tsing-Hua Univ. To our amazement, the number of students came. The interest shown was encouraging.

In July, we attended the 150th anniversary of the publication of "Origin of

Species" by Charles Darwin on both campuses of Univ. of Cambridge (5th to 11th) and Oxford (15th - 18th). For Cambridge, the theme was "The Impact of Darwinism Worldwide". There were more than 400 scholars coming all over the world. In the morning sessions, there were 2-3 lectures on different aspects on sciences and society at large. Eighty some scholars presented their findings and views, with Q/A followed. For the afternoon, panel discussions were conducted. Of course, there were lively discussion and debate. By and large, scholars focused their presentation with mechanisms for variation in order to survive under adverse conditions. But, when presentation turned to principles and theories of "evolution" or "advancement", then discourse and lively debate were evident. The statistics showed that evolutionists, materialistic to atheists were more than Christian scholars in attendance. Well-known atheists Richard Dawkins and Michael Ruse were there. On 8th, atheist Daniel Bennett (Tufts Univ.) and John Hedley Brooke (well-know Christian scholar of Oxford's Ramsey Ctr. on Science and Religion) had a relatively heated debate on the platform. The gentleman's mannerism in public was very evident, i.e. one was brutal and the other was courteous! The rational why we, evangelical Christian scholars were attending the conference, wanted to know how they presented their evidence, convictions and worldviews. With these we could engage in dialogue in the future. By and large, the atmosphere on Cambridge campus, was friendly, liberal and enjoyable. On Friday, the last day of the Conference, Prof. Martin Rees, together with two Nobel Prize winners on the platform, presented his "*Our final Century*". The conference ended with a warning from an eminent scholar.

The theme for the Oxford Conference (July 15th - 18th) sponsored by the Ramsey Ctr. on Science and Religion" was "The Religious Response to Darwinism.", with 80 some attendants, and a dozen of speakers, representing Moslem, Jewish, Catholic and Protestant in addition to non-religious (a large bulk) scholars. Atheist Ronald Numbers of Univ. of Wisc. was the first speaker on Tuesday. On that day, he monopolized the platform, coining the term "anti-revolutionism" in USA. To our surprise and dismay, the attendants responded un-conditionally. The Protestant's response to Darwinism was wholesale accepting. This showed the science illiteracy among the clergymen in the group. So, we left earlier, with disappointment.Then, both my wife and I spent one week at CCM Christian College at Milton Keynes, with one extension course on "Science and Christian Faith". By way of London, we returned to Maryland, USA.

G) the year of 2010:

As we did in the past, in Feb. we traveled to Shanghai, attending the Forum on US-China Diplomatic Relations. After that, we toured again the scenic West Lake in Zhejiang Prov.

In Oct.-Nov. we returned to Sao Paulo of Brazil, renewing our acquaintance and fellowship with the saints at Chinese Christian Church for four weeks. The

country Brazil was much different from what we knew years ago, with public safety and poverty as two dominant issues in the country. For these reasons, we did not travel to anywhere else.

The remaining months of the years were spent in revising my English version of "Science and Christian Faith", with target publication date in 2011.

(H). 2011: In January, I submitted the complete English version of this book "Science and Christian Faith: Their Relationships in Past, Present and Future" to the Navigators' Press, for their consideration of publishing it.

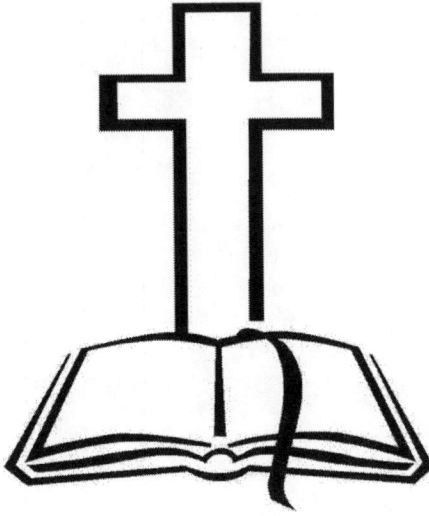

Conclusion

The objectives of our trips worldwide are twofold.   One is to minister the Word of God in Chinese Christian Churches, and Bible Study Classes/Fellowships on university campuses. With God's grace and our consistent effort, we have accomplished what we had intended to accomplish in these years. The other is to present science and Christian faith as search for truth in parallel model. There is no conflict if professionals remain in their respective fields. The conflict is essentially our worldviews. The ultimate objective is to build "intellectual bridges", as I said before in the preface and in other chapters.

The travels with lectures would build intellectual bridges of among scholars and college students, as I had said in my introduction.   As we look back, we are so grateful that we were enabled to do so.

The next job is through printed pages, we shall reach the communities of professionals and Christians, probably those who are interested in our Christian faith. Once we have this printed, it is how to get the book to the hands of those we intend to reach them. This will be our next endeavor.

Chapter 23
Warming Trend in Recent Years

"Science wants to know the mechanism of the universe,
(whereas) religion (wants to know) the meaning (and value).
The two can not be separated."

Prof. Dr. Charles Townes, Nobel Laureate

"Science can address questions about things work and what sequence of events
led to the present circumstances;   religion can address questions about our
relationship with God, and how we should behave toward others.   My scientific
understanding supports my faith. My faith may be non-scientific (I do not say
un-scientific), but it is not irrational! When I examine the orderliness,
understandability, and the beauty of the universe, I am led to the conclusion
that a higher intelligence designed what I see. My scientific appreciation of the
coherence, the delightful simplicity of physics strengthens my faith in God."

By Prof. Dr. William Phillips, Nobel Laureate of 1997

Introduction

In 1876 ***United States of America was borne as a Christian nation,*** with democratic and independent judicial systems. The founding fathers took the lesson from what had happened in the European continent in the early centuries. For religious freedom in worship as the motive, the Puritans migrated to this new continent. Once they founded the new republic, they formulated new constitutions. ***The Constitution clearly declares that a nation under God, with liberty, sacred honor for individual and pursuit of happiness for all of her citizens.*** **"Democracy is the outgrowth of the religious conviction** of the sacredness of every human life. On the religious side, its highest embodiment is the Bible; on the political, the Constitution. As had been said so well," ***The Constitution is the civil   Bible of America.***"[1]

As what was in European continent in early centuries, in USA when a city was designed and built,   it was designed with a Church at the center. Then, in the

neighborhood there would be legal court, post office and railroad station. In higher education, Christian theology occupied the foremost important position in curriculum. The Church was a place where God is worshipped, the Bible will be read, and biblical messages would be preached. The church was also the center for dissemination of biblical Christian truth, and also the center of moral social reform. Clergy was greatly respected in society, not because of their titles, but for the public and religious services they rendered with their education. Christians were the pillars of society, and they were the moving forces for social reform. In 16th – 17th centuries when modern experimental sciences were born in Europe, it was born, owing so much to evangelical scholars and their genuine faith in the Bible. In early centuries, United States of America, Great Britain and some other nations in Europe were regarded as Christian nations, with high moral and social standard. No wonder for many centuries these nations played important role in the world politics and social reform. In USA, Creation narratives by God Jehovah were taught exclusively in schools and in colleges. As one of the democratic foundations, education was the responsibility of the State Government. Many nations around the world were envious of American systems and the way of life.

A. The cause and the tension:

In 1925, evolution theory was taught the first time by a substitute teacher in Dayton City School, Tenn., in the so-called Bible-belt region. That incidence created a big uproar in the public, eventually becoming a nation's news. Unfortunately, that scenario caused those professionals and some citizens a split in thinking and in attitude. Somehow they were seemingly in two camps, creating a gap of misunderstanding. Unfortunately, two American scholars proposed "*War Metaphor*" in their books. Being influenced by such a misnomer, some evolutionists began to have no sympathy to religion. Some of them even became unfriendly to hostile to Christianity. In many ways, they know nothing or very little of what Christianity is, and what they believe. They take the so-called Scientific Creation as if it were the only teaching of the Christian church at large. On the other hand, fundamentalist Christians responded with unfriendly to hostile attitude to scientists and their professions. They generally turn a deaf ear to what the scientists say or what empirical sciences say. This became so-called "*cultural war*" in USA. Evolutionists have moved away from marginal position in the society by and large. In recent years, many of them, due to their trainings and contribution in sciences have occupied strategic and important positions in scientific establishments or media services. In less than sixty years, evolution theory is now being taught exclusively in public schools to the exclusion of creation theory. What a tremendous and tragic change it has been taking place in USA!

Public schools and colleges in USA have become secular more than anything else. So many students were not taught to know what is the philosophy of science. They have little knowledge of what *sciences could accomplish and what sciences can't do. In college curriculum, they are taught in evolution theory, not as a*

bio-science theory, but a bio-philosophy, even a worldview. As years gone by, they have become evolutionists. Many of these evolutionists have occupied strategic positions in both academic world and news media services. They exercise their functions with biased viewpoints. In the last 50 or more years science and technology have made great stride in progress and in contribution. All these enhanced the concept of scientism which is shown in many areas of our society. In addition, the American Civil Liberty Union (ACLU) has taken an anti-Christian stand. In public schools, children of families of faith are often ridiculed. As a result, students majoring in bio-sciences in our nation have been slowly going down, in statistics and in percentages. Above all, the intellectual window of young generation was regrettably shut off, knowing nothing else. No one has ever attempted to estimate how much damage in morality and in creative thinking has been done to our nation and our educational and scientific enterprises.

B. Fundamental educational and epistemological principles:

Fortunately, in recent years, many world-renowned scientists and scholars of faith are annoyed by this sad situation. They do consider *both science and religion as the two rocks of our western civilization and education*. Renowned scholars such as Francis Bacon, Albert Einstein, William Bragg, William Whenell and Alfred Norman Whitehead said/ wrote about the different/specific nature, their methods and different conclusions of the two disciplines. The two disciplines themselves are neutral in nature and in practices. They are the subjects for our genuine research endeavor. The objectives of the two disciplines are different. Therefore scholars use different methods. Their applications are altogether different. Logically, their conclusions are different. They do not contradict to each other, and should not contradict each other. In fact, they are complementary and supplementary. They propose that scholars on both sides ought to have sympathetic attitude to each other. They should understand and appreciate the contributions made in different realms in our society. With this in conviction and in view, they have advocated dialogues between the two groups for mutual understanding and appreciation.. Both disciplines have their importance and their contributions to our knowledge and society.

C. Warming trend in recent years

Beginning in the 60th, and scientific establishment such as US National Academy of Sciences, and AAAS, and some state universities, such as Univ. of Calif., and universities in England such as Cambridge and Oxford, have taken the initiative by sponsoring seminars and workshops on university campuses. With funds made available either by academic societies or philanthropic foundations such as Templeton Foundation, they have sponsored workshops and conferences on campuses or elsewhere. Books of essays given in workshops or seminars have been published. The objective of such meetings is to bring scholars and scientists together for dialogue with open mind, and objective attitude。 All these should

make us being grateful and appreciative. So much has been accomplished. Yet, so much remains to be done.

Due to constraint of space, I shall mention several such workshops and seminars in both USA and England as examples. With such information, it is my prayer and personal efforts, we should promote such dialogue for mutual appreciation and contributions to our society.

1) *In USA:*

    a) ***The American Association for the Advancement of Sciences (AAAS)***, a very large scientific entity, with more than 260 some societies on different disciplines and more than one million of members worldwide, and the publisher of weekly "***Science***" magazine with more one hundred million readers, in 1997 sponsored one workshop in Aug. 15-17, 1997, with the theme of "***Science and God: Can rational inquiry and spiritual conviction be reconciled?***"

More than 360 scholars of different disciplines came and met on the campus of Univ. of Calif. for three days. Subjects under discussion and dialogue include: astronomy, atmospheric sciences, life on other planets, theology and religions, philosophy, neurosciences, and biosciences etc. World renowned scholars such as Sir John H. Stephenson, Arthur Peacocke, John Polkinghorne of Great Britain, and Charles Townes, William Phillips, Francis Collins and Elvin Anderson of USA and many others came to the conference. News media and press reporters were there to cover the event. Then, summaries of essays presented were published in the weekly journal "Science", 1997.

Prof. Charles Townes was the keynote speaker, with theme such as "*Science wants to know the mechanisms of the universe, religion the meaning. The two cannot be separated.*" Dr. Townes is a Prof. of Astrophysics and Astronomy at University of Calif. and a Nobel Laureate. He spoke eloquently on the birth of modern experimental sciences in 16th-17th centuries. That was Christianity in western culture provided for the fertile soil for this historical event. Devout Christians such as Kepler, Cupernicus and Galileo believed God's special revelation and general revelation as shown in this cosmic universe. Owing to their genuine faith in God, they devoted their talent, energy and persistent effort in research with telescope and mathematic calculation, they advocated the sun-centered universe, the first time in history of science. That was the time modern experimental sciences were born. *Galileo was nominated and acclaimed as the Father of Modern Experimental Sciences*.

Profs. Drs. John Houghton, Stephen Hawkings, George Smoot, and Edward Larson endorsed the Big Bang theory as a valid scientific theory, and its being

compatible with the Christian narratives of creation. They are not opposing each other, but being complementary in substances.

b) US National Academy of Sciences made her position very positive with affirmative declaration as

"The US National Academy of Sciences clearly endorses the view that science and religion need not to be in conflict. At the root of this apparent conflict between some religions and evolution is the misunderstanding of the critical difference between the religious and scientific ways of knowing. Religion and science answer different questions about the world. Whether there is a purpose to the universe or a purpose of human existence are not questions for science. Religion and scientific knowledge have played, and will continue to play significant roles in human history."

IV.NY Academy of Sciences: in monthly magazine, Sciences, 1999, issue 34, pp#38-43.

In 1999 USA-NAS published "Science and Creationist: A View from the NAS, 2nd Ed. and in 2008, US-NAS published another "Science, Evolution, and Creationism". The position taken by Nat. Acad. O f Sciences were quite different from what was quoted above.

After reading these two paperbacks, I make the following conclusions. 1. US-NAS fully endorsed the Evolution Theory as a valid bio-scientific theory. No one could deny that. A scientific theory should be taken a scientific theory. In schools, it should be taught as a bio-scientific theory. If it is extended to be a bio-philosophy, even to a worldview, the dispute would come. It is no longer I science domain. Though US-NAS calls it "science, evolution." Above all, we all could differentiate *what are mechanisms*, and *what are theories*. We could agree on mechanisms, and do differ in theories (or conclusion). We all agree on mechanisms such as struggle for existence, survival of the fitted, modification through many years, even centuries. Randomized mutations in a stepwise manner would lead to advanced form of life are something/principles/theories, we question them. Degeneration, even to large scale extinction, is a general rule. Better varieties or species are due to human manipulations by plant geneticists and breeders in the fields or in labs. If it is a worldview, we could call it "scientism", a philosophy or worldview.

Creation is by and large a Christian doctrine, being no longer in the domain in science. In essence, we could call it "creationism", a Christian religious philosophy of worldview. Yet, in creation hypothesis, there are five schools of thought (cf. Chapter 12th of this book). It is true that scientific creation believes

young earth, and less than 10,000 years of human history. It is one of the five schools in Christendom. The Progressive Creation and Theistic Evolution accept evolution theory, and accept it as the second stage of natural development. Intelligent Design is altogether a different approach in both methods (mechanisms and conclusion). It seems that US-NAS singles out Scientific Creation, even Intelligent Design as the one theory that represents what Christian scholars in general believe and accept. This is not true. it is not fair, and not scientific in attitude.

If creation is a philosophy or worldview, then evolution is also a bio-philosophy and worldview. If this is true, in all fairness, we should call both philosophies or worldviews as "Creationism" and "scientism"

In 1999, New York Academy of Sciences (publishing "The Sciences" monthly magazine, carries a series of articles in an annual conference, with the following title, as

"The Odd Couple: Can science and religion live together without driving each other crazy?

More than 500 scholars took part in the conference. They exchange conviction and viewpoints on three questions:

(1) Can the universe described by science also be seen as the creation of the Judeo-Christian God?

(2) Can that God act within the scientific universe? If so, how? And

(3) Can the Christian history with its specific claims about the incarnation of God in the historical person of Jesus of Nazareth, and its premise of resurrection continue to make sense of modern science?

To answer these three questions, scholars of sciences and faith varied. They acknowledged the fact the science and religion are different in disciplines with different methods of searching. Their answers will be different. Answering these three questions are not by sciences. They fall into a different domain, larger than sciences and even philosophies. They are in the domains of worldviews. There is no way to affirm them through scientific inquiry, and also no way to deny them. Answering these questions bigger than ourselves are not up to scientists. They all depend on our philosophies and worldviews.

Following this conference, three participating scholars published their books as follows:

(1) Prof. John Polkinghorne: Belief in God in an Age of Science., Yales Univ. Press.

(2) Prof.J. Wentzel Van Huyssteen: Duet or Duel? Theology and Science in

a Post-Modern World.   Trinity Press International, PA

(3) Prof. Keith Ward: God, Faith & The New Millennium: Christian Belief

in an Age of Sci. Onward, Oxford.

Templeton Foundation was found by Sir John Templeton   of Philadelphia, PA, as a philanthropic   organization. With monetary fund available, the Foundation subsidizes national conference and mutual exchange work. Its aim is to encourage dialogues and workshops by scientists and scholars of faith. Also, the Foundation grants a monetary prize to those who have made significant contribution in these areas. In the years past, scholars such as Ian Barbour, John Polkinghorne,   George Ellis, and Francisco Ayala were conferred with such a honor.

D.   Harvard University Center for Religious Studies.

In 2001, Oct. 21-13, a three-day conference on "*The Quest for Knowledge, Truth and Value in Science and Religion*" was held on the campus. More than 300 scholars of different faith such as Hinduism, Moslem were participants. Scientists in astronomy, physics, atmospheric science, geology, biology, genomics and gene therapy spoke on their disciplines in relation to faith. Prof. Arthur Peacocke was the keynote speaker. The morning sessions were topical. In the afternoon, there were panel discussion. The overall endeavor was to build bridge of mutual understanding and respect.

Prof. William Phillips, Quantum Physicist of Univ. of Maryland, and Institute of Technology and Standard, a Nobel Laureate of 1997 was one of the speakers in morning session. Since he is a well-known evangelical, participants paid special attention to his presentation and in panel discussion. His paper entitled in" *Ordinary Faith and Ordinary Science*" of 12 pages was made available. In his paper and presentation as well, he spoke with a sincere sense of humility and dignity. That is unique among the speakers. I take the liberty of quoting a few paragraphs as follows.

"My scientific understanding supports my faith. My faith may be non-scientific

(I do not say un-scientific), but it is not irrational! When I examine the

orderliness, understandability and the beauty of the universe, I am led to the

conclusion that a higher intelligence designed what I see. My scientific

appreciation of the coherence, the delightful simplicity of physics strengthens

my faith in God.

My favorite song, "in the Garden" by C. Austin Miles, with sweet refrain, "He walks with me, and He talks with me, and He tells me I am His own. And the love we share as we tarry there, none other has ever known" expresses my faith in a personal God who is both the Creator of the universe, and his ultimate concern with welfare of that universe……..I am convinced of the truth of what I believe in God because I can feel God's presence in my life and in the world. Prayer comforts me and helps me to make good choices. If we all (scientists and people of faith alike) are comfortable in surrendering an important part of our lives to something as clearly apart from scientific rationality such as love (not visible but you could feel), then why not faith?

Science can address questions about things work and what sequence of events led to the present circumstances; religion can address questions about our relationship with God, and how we should behave toward others. Science and faith intersect because God wants us to discover as much as possible about the universe He created…….. I believe that scientific research is a deeply religious calling …….. studies of the fine tuning of the universe and the anthropic principle, along with examination of hypothesis about multiple universe and about intrinsic constraints physical laws and constants, may some days give us far more convincing evidence of intelligence behind creation."

On the platform, while Prof. Phillips was singing with the words of "He talks with me and He walks with me, and He tells me that I am his own. And the love we share as we tarry there, none other has ever known" , he sang with hands up and footsteps jumping! He was singing words with his joyful heart and warm feeling! with a genuine sense of praise as his real expression of praise and thanksgiving to God!

That was indeed very impressive. The people in the audience irrespective of having or having no faith were stunned! They all looked at him with a sense of awe. What a brilliant personal testimony in his singing! At the end of his presentation, no body dared to challenge what he had said and sang. Of more than 300 scientists in the auditorium, he was the only Nobel Laureate.

The question-answering session in the afternoon was even more interesting. The panelists asked him specifically whether or not he and his religious faith influences his research undertaking. His answer was:

"When I design an experience in quantum physics, even by myself alone, I design with what I was taught in physics and in its experimentation, exclusively. It is exclusively and entirely on science and scientific principles. My Christian religious faith, though very personal, does not enter into my design at all. With empirical results I obtained, I interpret of them with my training in quantum physics. It is because they are in the domain of science. I do all as a scientist. My religious faith does not have anything to do with them. When I ponder on the paradoxical phenomena as I have so far obtained, I see something so unique and distinctive. They differ greatly from our common observation and experience. I marvel at them! I see the difference! It is at this time when I survey and I ponder on it, I have a sense of awe! Something so different and so amazingly beautiful. Then, I enjoy it with a sense of awe, and I sense it unique. I thank God now I see something only God can design and can show. In other word, it is at the very end of my scientific experiment, I extend my logical conclusion to the area where I could see something only God sees and He can design. It is at this moment, my Christian religious feeling comes in."

Prof. Phillips continued to share something with the panelists. "*Christian religious feeling and concern make me different in my attitude and my decision*. Years ago, while I was invited to join the Manhattan Project, I declined to accept the invitation. Why? It is because I know that the Project has something related to making weapons and their use in war, and in killing people. After a moment of reflection, I declined to accept the invitation. My religious faith does influence me in making my personal decision."

We all see that clear demarcation between science and religion in his logical thinking and reasoning. To many of the people in the audience, no clear distinction is something that causes them being led astray in thinking and in career.

E. Calvin College, Grand Rapids, Michigan. Sept. 20-21, 2001

Calvin College is a Christian Reformed College at Holland, Michigan. The faculty members are known as members of theistic evolution school of thought. The College, the Dept. of Physics invited *Prof. John Polkinghorne of Cambridge Univ. as the speaker*. The theme of the two-days' conference was on "Christian Scholarship in Science and in Religion." In addition to her own faculty and students there were fifty some participants. Prof. Polkinghorne lectured on faith in God in an age of science, and the unity of all knowledge. He also encouraged

Christians to attain higher degree of achievement in scholarship. He is passionate believer in the ultimate unity of knowledge.

F.   Houston, Texas: October 26-28,

Hill Country Institute for Contemporary Christianity, A Symposium of 2012, for Pastors,   Christian leaders, Interested Scientists, and Those pondering the Issues, promoting   a dialogue between faith and science.   A Conversation to Inspire, Equip, and the Unity of the Church,   How Science Supports Christianity and Christianity Explain Sciences.

Participants: Prof. Alister McGrath (King's College, England);   Andy Crouch (Christianity Today),   Ross Hastings (Regent College), Hugh Ross and Fazale Rena (Reasons to Believe), Walter Bradley (Baylor University), Stephen Meyer (Discovery Institute), Deborah Haarsma (Calvin College), John Collins (Covenant Seminary), Darrel Falk (Biologo Foundation), Rob Norris (Fourth Presbyterian Church, MD) and Dinesh D'Souza (Author).

All these scholars and participants are evangelical Christians who consider both Christianity and sciences are mutually explanatory and complementary. Their presentations and discussions covered many facets of these two major disciplines, in a very scholarly and congenial ways. Their presentation and discussions will be published in a book in the future.

G. In England:

Both Univ. of Cambridge and Univ. of Oxford, celebrating the 150th anniversary of the   publication of "Origin of Species", 1859, by Charles Darwin:

(1)Darwin Festival, Univ. of Cambridge: July 5-10   (Monday-Friday, 2009)   "Theme: Darwin's Universal Impact"

More than 400 scientists and scholars took part in this Festival, in five days, with morning talks and debate; and focus on different disciplines in the afternoon sessions.

Abstracts of presentation were printed and given to those participants free.

Speakers (more than 70) dwelt on Darwin's impact on society, health, human nature, belief and modern science. To summarize them is a task impossible. I shall mention only several eminent scholars and their presentation as summaries.

Prof. Richard Dawkins, well-known atheist and former popular-science writer at Cambridge, took the advantage of being one of the programmed speakers claimed that '*Darwin probably did revolutionize the world view of people out in*

324

science more comprehensively than any other scientist'. In his presentation, he outlined "five bridges to evolutionary understanding" which Darwin had attempted to build. My comment is this. As usual, Prof. Dawkins takes something in science as basis on which he launches into his bio-philosophy more than science or any scientific principle (*worldview of people in science more than any other scientist*). People often mistakes that he is delivering something meaningful in science. That is not true in any sense of the word. He is known for anti-Christian philosophy to worldview more than any scientific theory or fact. In this, he is very cunning and skillful. Often, people mistake him as a scientist.

Prof. Denis Alexander, is a Christian gentleman, and Director of Faraday Institute for Science and Religion at Edmond College of Cambridge, spoke on "Is Darwinism incompatible with purpose?" "Genomics, developmental genetics, structural biology and the emergent properties of complex biological systems have all combined to revise our understanding of the evolutionary process. *It will be argued that purpose cannot be derived from the evolutionary narrative.. .. and less plausible the idea that the evolutionary narrative is necessarily purposeless." His latest book entitled in "Creation or Evolution: Do We have to Choose?", 2008 was on display in the hallway*. I bought a copy of it for my reading. Personally, I missed the opportunity of meeting him for a time of sharing our Christian faith on science in relation to bioscience.   Reading his book, I should say that Dr. Alexander subscribes to "the Theistic Evolution", one of the five schools of thought on creation narratives.

Prof.John Hadley Brooks, Director of Ian Ramsey Center of Science and Religion at Oxford spoken on "Darwinism and the survival of religion". He said that

"popular reconstructions of conflict between "creation" and "evolution" are often simplistic, and why religious affiliation and practice continue to survive, despite the intellectual challenge of Darwinism. I suggest that through affirmative, creative responses to Darwin's ideas, religious thinkers have sustained their positions, and opposed their onslaught on Christianity. On the contrary, *Christianity as an intelligent and rational religion will not only survive, but thrive gloriously and worldwide*." Prof. Brooks is a well-known scholar. He has written a good number of books, and also took part in seminars and conferences in Great Britain and elsewhere.

On July 10th, the last morning session deals with *"What Does the Future Holds*? with Prof. Sir Brian Heap as Chairman, a Christian scholar at Cambridge. Renowned scientists such as *Lord Martin Rees, Sir Brian Hoskins, Nobelist, Lord Robert May, President of Royal Society of London* (Chief Scientific Advisor to UK Gov.) were on the panel. This morning session was the most enlightening one. We participants enjoyed it very much their talks. Both Lord Martin Rees and Sir Brian Hoskins spoke on "this world is vulnerable to new and disruptive threat". Indeed, *what does the future holds*? Prof. Lord Martin Rees had written a book, *"Our Final Century"* which is available in the bookstand on

that day. I bought a copy of it. In his book, he discussed increasing world-population , engineered airborne viruses, rogue nano-machines, super-intelligent computers, volcanic super-eruption, major asteroid impact, embittered loners and dissident groups *could threaten humanity*. All these could have un-intended consequences, i. e. "*mutually assured destruction*" (MAD). At the end of his talk, Lord Rees advised on "how to guard (as far as feasible) against the worst risks, while deploying new knowledge optimally for human benefit. *Scientists and technologists, and people of faith have special obligations*. His scholarly presentation and this perspective should strengthen everyone's concern."

The whole conference at Cambridge ends with a genuine advice from such a senior scientist and a statesman of world stature.

(2) "Religious Response to Darwinism, 1859-2009, at Ian Ramsey Center, Univ. of Oxford, July 15-18th, 2009.

Eighty some participants attended the 4-days' conference, with speakers in the morning sessions, and short papers on religious responses in the afternoon. Printed program was made available to participants. Forty eight short summaries were printed, covering a wide range of religious groups of the world. Denominations of Christian groups including Roman Catholic, Lutheran Church, Southern Baptist and Wesleyan Methodist were represented. Prof. Pietro Corsi of Oxford talked on "theologies in Evolution", and Dr. Marwa Elshakry of Harvard Univ., on Exegeses of Evolution: "Muslim responses to Darwin". To my surprise and amazement, all the speakers with religious affiliations, and so-called Christian theological seminaries and churches accepted evolution theory as valid scientific theory. In addition, they have tried to integrate the evolution theory into their theological outlook. All these gave me a great deal of disappointment and frustration! Dennis Hudecki of Univ. of Western Ontario was the only exception. His talk on "Darwinism vs. Intelligent Design, in a religious context" was evangelical in content. He questioned genetic mutations cause harm, not enough time for evolution to happen. That causes a great deal of protest from Jewish rabbis, and modernistic Christians in the audience.

Then, on Thursday, *Prof. Ronald Numbers* of Univ. of Wisconsin, *another well-known atheist from USA*. He took the advantage of being a speaker, he gave a provocative talk on "*Creationism goes Global*", with such a phrase of "*anti-revolutionism movement in USA*", the first time we ever heard of such a misnomer. He opted "the equal-time movement" as his target of ridicule. He used this equal time movement in USA as "anti-revolutionism." To my amazement, the audience which was mostly made of faculty and staff members of Oxford Univ., responded with favoritism. What a disappointment was to those who came with honorable motive. I intended to make comments and ask him some questions, Prof. Numbers deliberately ignored my hand up several times. With frustration and disappointment, we thought that there was no point to continue attending the conference. Therefore, we cut short of our visit, leaving Oxford at much earlier

date.

Over these years, universities in USA and those in England sponsored seminars or workshops from time to time. The overall objectives were to encourage friendly dialogs among scholars of two camps, evolutionism and creationism. The conference at Oxford this year certainly violated that spirit. *It destroyed that "bridge of mutual understanding and appreciation" by these radicalized evolutionists and atheists*. That made many of us very much disappointed.

3). Universities in early years of USA; and new trends in 20th century:

History books tell us that in early years of this new republic of United States of American, theology and training of church clergy were foremost in education. For example, John Harvard himself was a student in Univ. of Cambridge. After he had completed his learning tenure in England, he returned to North America. John Harvard was instrumental to the establishing Harvard Univ., with his name as the name of the university. The first college was the Faculty of Theology, training clergymen for the Protestant Church. Many

other colleges and universities followed the suit. Princeton, Yale, Columbia and Stanford were then established. State Uni. like Univ. of Mich. pursued the same course. The curriculum and teaching in these schools were Christian and evangelical. No wonder that in those years, the church and her corporal activities were lively in the society. At the end of 18th and early 19th centuries, many schools of secular philosophies were gradually introduced, and eventually took over the prominent positions in curriculum. Nowadays, these institutions became secular more than anything else. Biblical Christian evangelical teachings are no longer taught at these institutions. This is indeed a regrettable situation!

One encouraging fact has been that in the second half of last century, there were many centers for science and religion established in state universities and church-affiliated colleges. The objectives of these centers are offering academic programs not only to bring scholars together for dialogue, but also encouraging intersecting study in depth. The Center for Theology and Natural Sciences at Univ. of Calif., on Berkeley campus is a good example. Harvard Univ. has one. Both Univ. of Cambridge (Faraday) and Oxford (Ian Ramsey) also have their centers. Likely, in 21st century more such centers with integrated studies will be forthcoming.

4). Books written by Christian scholars and scientists:

In the last 50 years, many books were written by Christian theologians and scientists on science and Christian faith. They aimed at promoting mutual dialogue, understanding and respect between science and Christianity. Their premises are that the two disciplines are not in any way contradicting to each other.

327

In fact, they are complementary and mutually explanatory. Many of these books are given in Literature Cited of this book. My book is only one of them, in both Chinese language and English language.

Of course, there are many good books written by scientists who in one way or another do not acknowledge having any religious faith. The late Prof. Stephen Jay Gould was pretty well-known among evolutionists. Those who accept theistic evolution do not have quarrel with either creation or evolution. Those who thought creation and evolution as opposing theories are in fact too much simplistic in their thinking and conclusion.

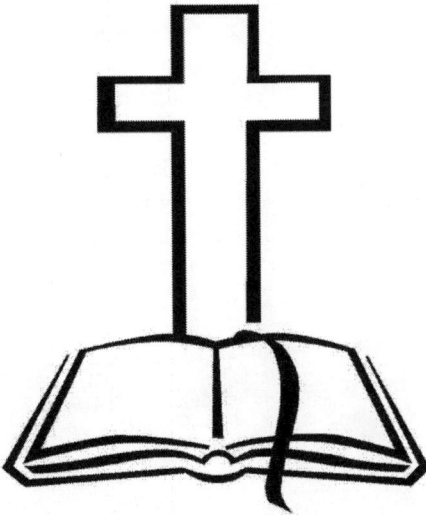

Conclusion

The United States of American (USA) was found as a Christian nation under God. In early years, the population was relatively homogeneous, with Church as the center of social and religious life. The God Jehovah was worshiped, and the Bible was highly esteemed as God's Word. On Sunday, a very high percentage of her citizens went to churches as usual. For two hundred and more years, the nation and her citizens enjoyed the tranquility of life. The other nations and their citizens envied the high standard of living, and the prosperity of the American society. Unfortunately, in 1930 and thereabout, tension arrived. It was due to the fact that in elementary schools the evolution theory was taught at science class. This event generated a great deal of debate in public and "heat" among the American society. The American Civil Liberty Union took part in the debate, lending its support to this new trend. Two American scholars even advocated "The War" metaphor between the evolutionists and Christian creationists. In a matter of four scores of years, evolution theory was taught exclusively at schools, even colleges. What a drastic change it was. The tension became more intensified, "cultural war" was

seen in 50 states of American! Fortunately, historians of sciences, examining the historical background and prevailing conditions, replaced it with "the complexity hypothesis. About the same time, university scholars in this country as well in Europe saw the relationship between sciences and Christian faith in an entirely different light. So, they travel around, having dialogues and conferences on university campuses. They advocated the search for both science and theology is parallel, without conflict. The warming trend has been reinstalled   Now, it is up to those of us who share the same conviction join them in this meaningful undertaking. As Prof. Charles Townes said (cf. the quotation): "*Science wants to know the mechanisms, religion the meaning and value.*" Also, Prof. William Phillips also said more or less along the same line. He said "*my faith is not scientific, yet not un-scientific*". We Christians have our rational." These two scholars are Nobel prize winners. Scientific inquiry and Christian religious search are parallel. They are not in conflict, unless/until we extend our explanations/results beyond our respective domains. Through scientific publications and public lectures they endeavor to generate "light" on the subjects instead of "heat" (terminologies used in physics). In a small way, we should do the same.   In 1954 when I myself came to USA the first time. I was a graduate student at University of Minnesota, in Twin Cities. In those days, evangelical Christians occupied a high percentage of the population. On Sunday, stores were closed, no sport or games were allowed to play. People by and large went to church as a rule of life. Often, we saw Christian parents being well dressed, with their Bible under their arms, taking their children, go to church for worship and hearing a biblical messages. This was a common scene. Crime and public violence were minimal. Newspapers seldom carried any story of crime committed or citizens were murdered. After I had received my graduate degrees, I went to South America as an evangelical missionary and a scientist working with Brazilian National Research Council, and Charles Pfizer Pharmaceutical Company for seven years. When I and my family returned to Minnesota in 1965, social and community conditions were pretty much the same, as I myself saw/experienced seven years ago. Then,

I was employed as professor of microbiology and molecular biology in Michigan for 30 some years. During those years, things in USA were gradually changing, sometimes worse than what we had expected. As years have gone by, national and social conditions in this beloved country of mine has become worse and worse. Of course, there were many factors which contributed this worsening conditions. After all, we evangelical Christians have to bear our responsibilities, and our failure contributed to the worsening conditions in this beloved country of ours, United States of American.

Literature Cited

1. Ian G. Barbour,   1997

    Religion and Science: Historical and Contemporary Issues.

       Harper Collins Co., N. Y.

2. David C. Lindbert and Ronald L. Numbers, 2003

    When Science and Christianity Meet.

       Univ. of Chicago Press, Ill.

3. Gary B. Ferngren, Ed., 2002

    Science and Religion: A Historical Introduction.

       Johns Hopkins Univ. Press, MD

4. Ted Peter and Gaymon Bennett, Ed.,   2003

Bridging Science and Religion.

    Fortress Press, Mpls., Minn.

5. John F. Haught,   1995

    Science and Religion: From Conflict to Conversation.

       Paulist Press, N.Y

6. Robert W. Hanson, Ed.,   1986

    Science and Creation: Geological, Theological & Educational Perceptions.

       AAAS Issues in Science and Technology Series.

       MacMillan Publishing, N.Y.

Chapter 24
Global Climatic Change, and Our Final Century

In 1996 when I was contemplating on writing this book (Chinese version), I thought of having one chapter on global climatic change, an important and upcoming scientific subject of public concern. Somehow, I did not have enough time in doing so. Now, I am translating my book into English, by all means I should endeavor to write it, as additional to the English version.

In this chapter, I shall deal with two subjects, i. e. A). *Global Climatic Change, and* B)."*Our Final Century*" as the warning given by British Astronomer, Prof. Martin Rees when more than 400 scholars and scientists attended conferences on both Cambridge   campus, in 2009.

A). Global Climatic Change: Policy and Chemical Agents:

In 1960-70, under William Clinton's administration, Vice President Al Gore was one of the advocates of controlling greenhouse gas in relation to the climate changes. He strongly urged the federal government as well as industries, specially the auto industry should exercise precautions and adjustment. Those countries in the developing world contributed as much more greenhouse gas; and had the lease control. Consequently, in the last three scores of years, *we witnessed the melting of polar ice sheets, rising temperature of ocean water, tsunami in coastal countries, and devastating storm and un-usual weather with flood worldwide*.

Since 1970 the fact/reality of global warming or climate change has become a most divisive subject in our civilized societies and developing world. The reality of global warming (or climatic change) and our society's response to it represent two different frequent convoluted topics. It is important to separate these two issues so that a reasonable approach may be formulated. It is more so with climate policy. Whether advancing or opposing climate policy or debate, it is important to avoid sensationalism to push one's agenda, only resulting   in greater polarization, distrust and distraction from the real problem. For example, our industrialized society often focuses attention to carbon policy, particularly as it affects energy production and its use. Even with carbon policy, it is not the same thing as climate policy.

Dr. Roger Pielke, Jr., a political scientist specializing in climate guideline, summarizes   the problem into three broad categories as follows:

1.Too often climate policies flow against public opinion.

2. Economic growth is often pitted against climate policy, and

3.Current technology is not sufficient to meet confirmed climate targets.

Since 1970, our understanding of the problem, the use of model in research has offered some good results. Both *global climate model* versus *regional climate model* are used in comparison, yet certainty do not seem to be forthcoming. In the early years it was the *carbon dioxide emission* as man-made, was given so much importance. Without any doubt, carbon dioxide is an important greenhouse gas, and did create a climate change. Yet, stabilizing atmospheric concentration of it does not stop climate change. Research results suggested other agents too. *Agents such as ozone, methane, nitrous oxide, carbon soot, sulfate, nitrate and other aerosols*, along with land use did not receive proper attention. In addition, significant natural climate change has occurred in the past, and will occur in the future with or without human influence. In the early years, all of these agents contributed to the uncertainty in our understanding of the climate system. The shortcoming does not suggest a mandate for action; but they do suggest that responses should be formulated methodically, reasonably and scientifically.

Perhaps greater progress could be made on climate policy if we avoid pitting the environment against the economy. Some advocates for carbon-emission reduction have gone so far as to argue for planned economic recession. Yet, clearly such approach, which would put nations at potential economic disadvantage, is un-likely to be the best policy. Divisive climate change issues have more issues to do with climate policy than the climate change itself.

Pollution control programs, since 1970 have made significant success, reducing pollutants – such as ozone, sulfur dioxide, aerosole, and many other agents . They contributed to the ill-effect of climate change. Carbon dioxide comes from both industrial and agricultural farming animals. Therefore, climate policy should take the followings into consideration, i.e. *a) economic growth, b) current technology and c) climate target and d) scientific research program*.

In early 2013, when our President Obama met with Mr. Xi Ching-Pin of China met in California, both USA and China have agreed on gas cuts of a class of chemicals commonly used in refrigerators and air-conditioners. This is the first key step toward eliminating some of the potent greenhouse gases, such as hydro-fluoro-carbons (HFCs). The chemical group currently accounts for only 2 percent of greenhouse gases. But, consumption is growing exponentially as people in developed countries have grown more wealthy to purchase air conditioners. A global push to get rid of HFCs could potentially reduce the greenhouse gases by the equivalent of 90 gigatons of carbon dioxide by 2050, equal to roughly two years' worth of current global greenhouse gas emission.

Both Obama and Xi said that they would use the framework of the Montreal Protocol, established in 1987 to combat the use of chemicals that were depleting stratospheric ozone. The Montreal Protocol succeeded in phasing out nearly 100

chemicals, but one un-foreseen side-effect was to spur the production of HFCs, which are short-lived and do not damage the ozone but are hundreds to tens of thousands times more potent greenhouse gases than carbon dioxide. Being left unabated, HFCs emissions could grow to 20 percent of carbon dioxide emissions by 2050, a serious climate mitigation concern, the White House said. The United States of America, China and Japan are the largest consumers. "This is a big deal! Obama deserves a lot of credit for this." Said Dr. John Podesta, Chairman of the Center for American Progress, in the federal government. This is really an important achievement. Experts estimate that it could shave 0.5 degree Celsius from the projected increase in global temperatures by the end of this century. "The China-USA Agreement on phasing down HFCs under the Montreal Protocol will provide the single biggest, fastest, cheapest, and secure piece of climate mitigation available to the world through 2020" commented by Durwood Zaelke, President of the Institute for Government & Sustainable Development and a long-time Advocate of fast-action mitigation under the Montreal Protocol.HFCs, un-like other pollutants, are manufactured by humans and not found in nature. In addition, they are being used in insulating foams, solvents, and aerosol products. There are substitute in some applications, such as automobile air conditioners, but many substitutes are not available yet.

Although the issue of HFCs has been on the table for the past several years, the agreement by China to wind down HFCs use came together over the past week (June 2013) as to the two sides prepared for the summit between Obama and Xi. On the Chinese side, the powerful National Development and Reform Commission played a key role while working with the White House and international climate negotiation from the US State Department.

Much work remains to be done. About 30 countries have not agreed to phase down HFCs. But, China, the biggest market, has been considered the key to persuade others to join the meaningful efforts. The fact that China moved in this way have a huge impact on the whole discussion. This also signal a move in China, where an extreme bout of air pollutants in Beijing and other major cities last winter triggered widespread call for action to reverse the tide of governmental degradation.

In 2013, another Advocate for man-made climatic change and its grave threat, came up In U.SA. On April 3rd, 2 013, The Washington Post carries a news report in the Federal Government. ***Dr. James E Hansen*** working with NASA, was one of the first climatologists to speak out about the potential danger of man-made global warming in the 1980s. In 1988, he first told US Congress that man-made greenhouse gases were heating up the planet.. His projections were widely dissected over the years by supporters and skeptics alike. His testimony was one of the first and clearest public statements on global warming. "*It is time to stop waffling so much and say that the evidence is pretty strong that greenhouse effect is here.*" At that time, he offered three scenarios for future temperature increases, depending on how emissions rose. Yet, temperatures haven't risen

quite as sharply as he thought they would. What was that? Many scientists thought that climate sensitivity – basically, the amount that the Earth will warm in response to a doubling of carbon-dioxide in the atmosphere – it was closer to three Celsius (5,45 degree Fahrenheit) than Hansen's early prediction of 4.2 degree Celsius .

However, those 1988 predictions were quite useful. As NASA's Gavin Schmidt has pointed out, Hansen's early – and relatively crude – climate model forecast the future much better than models that assumed no global warming at all. In 2007, Hansen warned that climate scientists were understating the risks of year-level rise. That year, the inter-governmental Panel on Climate Change publicly predicted that sea levels could rise as much as 59 centimeters (23.2 inches) by 2100. Many observers looked at the number and said, "That is all?" But that number was only a partial estimate, and Hansen helped write several papers arguing that scientists weren't properly communicating the full risk of sea-level rise to "scientific reticence." In fact, he noted, data from the distance past suggested that the *ice sheet in Greenland and west Antarctica* could melt quite quickly once they started warming. In the years since many climate scientists now believe that the ice sheets will melt more quickly than previously thought!

For instance, in 2009 , one scientific study predicted accelerate in the decades ahead and reach two to six feet by 2100. Hansen now thinks that international climate change goals aren't ambitious enough. World leaders have aimed to limit global warming to 2 degrees Celsius or less. But in an attention-grabbing 2008 paper, Hansen and his colleagues argued that we should be aiming for 1.5degree Celsius or less. Here is Hansen's logics: For 7,000 years, sea levels have stayed remarkably stable, which has allowed human civilization to develop and prosper. But at plenty of other points in the geological record, *sea-levels rises to a few yards per century are not heard of*. Hansen's research suggests that in the past, it has not taken much to set off this process. Sea levels have been a couple of years higher when the world was only a degree or two Celsius warmer than it is to-day.

Hansen argued that we need to rapidly bring carbon-dioxide level in the air back down below *350 parts per million* (we are currently at about 391 ppm and rising fast). Hansen contents, *the only way to achieve that is for the world to phase out coal use quickly.* That paper led to plenty of debate among scientists. While Hansen's goal was considered politically difficult to achieve, his paper helped give rise to environmental groups, which have pushed for rapid reduction in carbon dioxide emissions. Hansen argued that *a higher carbon tax is the best way to deal with climate change*, rather than the cap-and-trade strategy. Hansen was not an economist. But he waded into economic policy debate by heavily criticizing the mechanisms used by countries in Europe, and in California, in which emission caps are set and companies are allowed to sell available pollution allowances to others. Instead, Hansen said, it would be better to have a simple carbon tax, with the revenue rebated to the public. *Hansen became increasingly*

outspoken in recent years, criticizing former President George W. Bush's climate policies and protesting the Keystone XI pipeline. From his perch at NASA, Hansen often clashed with high-ranging officials in various federal administrations. In 1989, he complained that the Office of Management and Budget was trying to water down his testimony on global warming. But, his relations with the Bush administration were particularly fraught. In 2004, Hansen claimed that NASA Administrator Sean O'Keefe had tried to dissuade him from talking about human influence on the atmosphere. Hansen had also criticized Bush appointees for editing scientific reports to make global warming seem much less. He was especially vocal about the Bush administration's stance that more research was needed before dealing with climate change: *"Delay of another decade, I argue, is a colossal risk."*

During the Obama years, Hansen was arrested while he protested the Keystone XL pipeline, which was waiting White House approval. "We have reached a fork in the road," Hansen said, "and the politicians have to understand we should go down this road of exploiting every fossil fuel we have – tar sands, tar shale, offshore drilling in the Artic –

But the science told us we couldn't do this without creating a situation where our children and grand-children would have no control over the climate system."Hansen was one of the first climatologists who had spoke out about the potential danger of manmade global warming in 1980. *He left NASA, and he became a climate activist in USA*! While his paper was published on Washington Post, he became a nation-wide advocate, with a sign on a stone saying "Climate change: A Matter of Life or Death". It showed how grave it was the situation, and how much attention Obama and his administration should have paid attention to what scientists had said, and what scientific papers they had so far published.

So many other prominent climate scientists had left the government to become full-time activists, realizing the grave scientific climatic situation in USA and our world to-day.

Science/AAAS May 3, 2013, Vol. 340, pages 540 carried another article pertaining to Dr. James Hansen's retirement from NASA, as summarized it as follows: "For decades, American climate scientist James Hansen published important papers on global warming, and shared his data at congressional hearings. He has been arrested five times (cf. photo) in protest against the continued burning o fossil fuels. In 1988, he appeared in the Congress, declaring "the world was warming, that humans were most likely responsible…. And heat waves could increase as a result. In the following years his pronouncement has proven essentially correct as the data came in. Hansen has been ahead on the science for decades and has played a very important role in communicating the science of climate change to the public, and to the US government. In the meantime, he is keeping up his outreach effort, including a book that he was writing. Consequently, in the last three scores of years, we witnessed the melting of polar ice sheets and rising of ocean water, and tsunami in coastal countries In 2013, another

Advocate for man-made climatic change and its grave threat, came up.

In USA, On April 3rd, 2013, The Washington Post carries a news report in the Federal Government. Dr. James E Hansen was one of the first climatologists to speak out about the potential danger of man-made global warming in the 1980s. In 1988, he first told US Congress that man-made greenhouse gases were heating up the planet.. His projections were widely dissected over the years by supporters and skeptics alike. His testimony was one of the first and clearest public statements on global warming. "It is time to stop waffling so much and say that the evidence is pretty strong that greenhouse effect is here," At the time, he offered three scenarios for future temperature increases, depending on how emissions rose. Yet, temperatures haven't risen quite as sharply as he thought they would. What was that? Many scientists thought that climate sensitivity – basically, the amount that the Earth will warm in response to a doubling of carbon-dioxide in the atmosphere – it was closer to three Celsius (5.45 degree Fahrenheit) than Hansen's early prediction of 4.2 degree Celsius . All told, however, those 1988 predictions were quite useful. As NASA's Gavin Schmidt has pointed out, Hansen's early – and relatively crude – climate models forecast the future much better than models that assumed no global warming at all. In 2007, Hansen warned that climate scientists were understating the risks of year-level rise. That year, the inter-governmental Panel on Climate Change publicly predicted that sea levels could rise as much as 59 centimeters (23.2 inches) by 2100.Many observers looked at the number and said, " That is all?" But that number was only a partial estimate, and Hansen helped write several papers arguing that scientists weren't properly communicating the full risk of sea-level rise to "scientific reticence." In fact, he noted, data from the distance past suggested that the ice sheet in Greenland and west Antarctica could melt quite quickly once they started warming. In the years since many climate scientists now believer the ice sheets will melt more quickly than previously thought. For instance, one 2009 study predicted accelerate in the decades ahead and reach two to six feet by 2100. Hansen now thinks that international climate change goals aren't ambitious enough. World leaders have aimed to limit global warming to 2 degrees Celsius or less. But in an attention-grabbing 2008 paper, Hansen and his colleagues argued that we should be aiming for 1.5 degree Celsius or less. Here is Hansen's logics: For 7,000 years, sea levels have stayed remarkably stable, which has allowed human civilization to develop and prosper. But at plenty of other points in the geological record, sea-levels rises to a few yards per century are not heard of. Hansen's research suggests that in the past, it has not taken much to set off this process. Sea levels have been a couple of yars higher when the world was only a degree or two Celsius warmer than it is to-day. As much, Hansen argues, we need to rapidly bring carbon-dioxide level in the air back down below 350 parts per million (we are currently at about 391ppm and rising fast). Hansen contents, the only way to that is for the world to phase out coal use quickly. That paper led to plenty of debate among scientists. While Hansen's goal is considered politically difficult to achieve, his paper helped give rise to environmental groups like 350.org, which have pushed for rapid reduction in carbon dioxide emissions.

Hansen argues that a carbon tax is the best way to deal with climate change, rather than the cap-and-trade strategy. Hansen is not an economist. But he has waded into economic policy debates by heavily criticizing the mechanisms used by Europe and California, in which emission caps are set and companies are allowed to sell available pollution allowances to others. Instead, Hansen says, it would be better to have a simple carbon tax, with the revenue rebated to the public. Hansen has become increasingly outspoken in recent years, criticizing former President George W. Bush's climate policies and protesting the Keystone XI pipeline.From his perch at NASA, Hansen has often clashed with various administrations. In 1989, he complained that the Office of Management and Budget was trying to water down his testimony on global warming. But, his relation with the Bush administration were particularly fraught. In 2004, Hansen claimed that NASA Administrator Sean O'Keefe had tried to dissuade him from talking about human influence on the atmosphere. Hansen has also criticized Bush appointees for editing scientific reports to make global warming seem less dire. He was especially vocal about the Bush administration's stance that more research was needed before dealing with climate change: "Delay of another decade, I argue, is a colossal risk."During the Obama years, Hansen has been arrested while he protested the Keystone XL pipeline, which is waiting White House approval. "We have reached a fork in the road," Hansen has said, "and the politicians have to understand we either go down this road of exploiting every fossil fuel we have – tar sands, tar shale, offshore drilling in the Artic –But the science tells us we can't do this without creating a situation where our children and grand-children will have no control over, which is the climate system."Hansen was one of the first climatologists who spoke out about the potential danger of manmade global warming in 1980. He left NASA, and he became a climate activist in USA. While this paper was published on Washington Post, he became a nation-wide advocate, with a sign on a stone saying "*Climate change: A Matter of Life or Death*". It shows how grave it is the situation, and how much attention Obama and his administration should pay attention to what scientists said and what scientific papers they have so far published. So many other prominent climate scientists have left the government to become full-time activists, realizing the grave scientific situation in our world to-day. Science/AAAS May 3, 2013, Vol. 340, pages 540 carried another article pertaining to Dr. James Hansens retirement from NASA, as I summarized it as follows: "For decades, American climate scientist James Hansen published important papers on global warming, and shared his data at congressional hearings. He has been arrested five times (cf. photo) in protest against the continued burning of fossil fuels. In 1988, he appeared in the Congress, declaring "the world was warming, that humans were most likely responsible.... And heat waves could increase as a result. In the following years his pronouncement has proven essentially correct as the data came in. Hansen has been ahead on the science for decades and has played a very important role in communicating the science of climate change to the public. In the meantime, he is keeping up his outreach effort, including a book that he is writing. If US government does pay due attention to this problem, it would be catastrophic worldwide.

As a consequence of these activities, United States, People's Republic of China, and many other countries have paid much more attention to this universal problem of global climatic change.

B). Darwin Festival on campuses of University of Cambridge in July 5-10; and University of Oxford, in July 15-18, 2009:

The year of 2009 was the 150th year when Charles Darwin published his book of "The Origin of Species". Both Universities of Cambridge and Oxford had one week each of "Darwin Festival" on their campuses. The two universities extended their invitation to those academicians and scientists who are interested in knowing what Darwinism's impact on scholarly learning and scientific research in the world.

Darwin Festival in Cambridge:

On 5th-10th of 2009, more than 400 scholars and concerned scientists coming from the all over the world attended one week of scholarly seminars and discussion. The title of the conference campus of Univ. of Cambridge(July 5th-10th) was Darwin's Universal Impact Printed programs were given to attendants at a charge. The format was by and large like this. In morning session talks given by two to three speakers and then a debate session with 2-4 panelists. In the afternoon, once again with two to three speakers on various subjects, then a panel discussion. Altogether there are 15 sessions, covering various disciplines. Subjects covered in presentation are so diversified, such as adaptation, variation, virus infection and genomics; and so many others. Due to space constraint , I can not cover all of them. Those who are interested, please go the printed program available at the university library.

I only mentioned the session on Friday (10th of July), with renowned scholars on "What Does the Future Hold? The session was chaired by Prof. Sir Brian Heap, Vice President and Foreign Secretary of Royal Society, and a church elder at Cambridge. Speakers include Sir Brian Hoskins, a Nobel laureate, on "the future for the environment on planet earth"; Prof. Lord Robert May of Oxford, President of Royal Society, 2000-2005, on "Cooperation Among Nations in a Crowded World; and Prof. Lord Martin Rees of Cambridge, a world renowned cosmology and astronomy, and Master of Trinity College at Cambridge. Prof. Rees spoke on *Understanding and changing the world beyond 2050*", with his book entitled in "Our Final Century" in hand, and also on the book-table. His lecture was scholarly, emphatic with statistics.

In the following paragraphs, I take the liberty of quoting what he spoke in the session, and what he has written in his booklet, *"Our Final Century: Will Civilization Survive The Twenty-First Century?* By Prof. Martin Rees, The Random House, 2003, 228 pages

In the Preface of his book, Prof. Rees wrote that

"Science is advancing faster than ever, and on a broad front: bio-cyber- and nano-technology all offer exhilarating prospect; so does the exploration of space. But there is a dark side: new science can have unintended consequences. It empowers individuals to perpetrate acts of mega-terror; even innocent errors could be catastrophic. The "downside" from 21st century technology could be graver and more intractable than the threat of nuclear devastation that we have faced for decades. Human-induced pressure on the global environment may endanger higher risk than the age-old hazard of earthquakes, eruptions, and asteroid impact….. If nothing else, I hope to stimulate discussion on how to guard (as far as is feasible) against the worst risks, while deploying new knowledge optimally for human benefit. Scientists and technologists have special obligations. This perspective should strengthen every one's concern, in our interlinked world, to focus public policies on communities who feel aggrieved or are most vulnerable."

"I hope to stimulate discussion on how to guard (as far as is feasible) against the worst risks, while deploying new knowledge optimally for human benefit. Scientists and technologists have special obligations. This perspective should strengthen every one's concern."

Natural disaster and technology shock:

Prof. Rees wrote, "in 21st century we would see more changes than the previous thousand years. Science may alter human being themselves – not just how they live". Then, in the book, he listed the natural disaster, man-made technology shock and   accidents:

1)Natural disaster:

Volcanic super-eruptions, asteroid impact, global warming, hurricanes, earthquakes, floods will be much more and often.

2)Man-induce and man-made threats:

339

a) Atomic bombs, H-bombs, missiles and anti-missiles,

b) Nanotechnology, super-intelligent computers and super-human robots,

c) Biotechnology and bio-threats: more disquieting than nuclear dangers are the potential hazards stemming from microbiology and genetics: With genetic engineering, scientists could produce more virulent strains of: smallpox, foot-and-mouth disease of cattle, anthrax, HIV and ebola, , animal cloning, genetic-modified foods and laboratory errors.

d) Environmental degradation: global warming (with a rise of sea level), poisonous pollution,

e) Population explosion: we need three planets by 2050, in order to support the our life-   style of   the growing population of   8 billions, and

f) Terror nations or groups, religious fanatics, embittered loners, and dissidents

g) Humanity at risk:

" In the 21st century, humanity is more at risk than ever before from misapplication of science. The environmental pressures induced by collective actions could trigger catastrophes more threatening than any natural hazards. Special responsibility lies with scientists themselves: they should be mindful of how their work might be applied, and do all they can to alert the wider public to potential perils. Our primary concerns are naturally with the fate of our present generation, and to reduce the threat to us. Traditional western culture envisages a beginning and an end of our species and our civilization. The theme of this book is that humanity is more at risk than at any earlier phase in its history. The choice may depend on us, in this century."

Summary

Scientists whether you are materialistic, atheistic, as well as theistic scientists, though we differ in many areas, especially in value and moral standard, should take heed to what Prof. Martin Rees presented in both his book and his lecture. He is a Scientist of this age, but a Prophet for the future of mankind.

On March , 2013, Prof. Rees wrote an editorial on *"Denial of Catastrophic Risks" in Science, AAAS, Vol. 339*, page#349. He reiterates his concern and advice to the international community and scientists who are concerned of this "catastrophic risk". He wrote: "some of the scenarios that have been envisaged may indeed be science fiction, but others may be disquieitingly real. *I believe these "extreme risks" deserve more serious study*. Those of us being fortunate enough to live in the developed world fret too much about minor hazards of everyday life: improper air crashes, possible carcinogens in food, low radiation doses, and so forth. But we should be more concerned about events that have not yet happened but which, *if they occur even once, could cause world devastation*.

The main threats to sustain human existence now come from people, not from nature. Ecological shocks that irreversibly degrade the biosphere could be triggered by the un-sustainable demands of a growing world population. Fast-spreading pandemics would cause havoc in the mega-cities of the developing world. Political tensions will probably stem from scarcity of resources, aggravated by the climatic change. Equally worrying are the imponderable downsides of the powerful new cyber-, bio-, and nano-technologies. Indeed, we are entering an era when a few individuals could via error or terror, trigger societal breakdown.

Some threats are well-known. In the 20th century, the downsides of nuclear science loomed large. At any time in the Cold War era, the superpowers could have stumbled toward Armageddon through muddle and miscalculation. The threat of global annihilation involving tens of thousands of hydrogen bombs is thankfully in abeyance, but now there is growing concern that smaller nuclear arsenals might be used in a regional context, or even by terrorists. We can not rule out a geo-political realignment that creates a standoff between new super-powers. So a new generation may face its own "Cuba," and one that could be handled less well or less luckily than was the 1962 crisis.

What are some new concerns stemming from fast-developing 21st-century technologies? Our inter-connected world depends on elaborate networks; electric power grids, air traffic control, international finance, just-in-time delivery, and so forth. Unless these are highly resilient, their manifest benefits could be outweighed by catastrophic (albeit rare) breakdown cascading through the system. Social media could spread psychic contagion from a local crisis, literally at the speed of light. Concern about cyber-attack, by criminals or hostile nations, is rising sharply. Synthetic biology likewise offers huge potential for medicine and agriculture, but in the sci-fi scenario where new organisms can be routinely created, the ecology (and even our species) might not long survive un-scathed.

Should we worry about another sci-fi scenario, in which a network of computer could develop a mind of its own and threaten us all?

Some would dismiss such concern as an exaggerated jeremiads: after all, societies have serviced for millennia, despite storms, earthquakes and pestilence. But these human-induced threats are different – they are newly emergencies , so we have a limited time base for exposure to cope if disaster strikes. That is why a group of natural and social scientists in Cambridge, UK, plans to inaugurate a research program to identify the most genuine of these emergent risks and asset how to enhance resilience against them. True, it is hard to quantify the potential "existential" threats from (for instance) bio- or cyber-technology from artificial intelligence, or from runaway climatic catastrophes. But we should at least stare figuring out what can be left in the si-fi bin(for now) and what has moved beyond the imaginary."

This is what Prof. Martin Rees once again endeavors to make us aware of the coming danger, and how to avoid it if there is a possible through our united efforts.

But, there was disappointing time in the conference, as follows:

The fire was ignited basically by radical evolutionists in their attack on Christian faith. Among the panelists in the afternoon, were *agnostic to atheistic evolutionists Richard Dawkins, Philip Clayton, Michael Ruse, Daniel Dennett; and Ronald Numbers* (he was the only one attended another meeting on the campus on Oxford Univ., one week later). They took the advantage of lecturing/talking, and voicing their public stand against Christian religious faith. Ron Numbers even coined a new term of "Anti-Evolution Movement in USA". This was very much a betrayal to the noble objectives of dialogues held on different campuses over these years. Many of us enjoyed most of it on Cambridge; but we were greatly disappointed by their talks on Oxford campus as their un-justified attempts. The atmosphere was indeed a kind of frustration and sadness.

Chapter 25
Perspectives of Science and Christian Faith in 21st Century

The future course of human history would depend on the decision by scientists and people of faith of this generation as to the proper relationship between science and religion.

Prof. Alfred North Whitehead

In 2000, **Prof. Russell Stannard** of Free University in UK took the lead and Editorship in editing a book entitled in "**God for the 21st Century**", with essays from fifty eminent scholars of 8 countries. The topics were written and divided in eleven parts, as varied as astronomy and cosmology, evolution, genetic engineering, extraterrestrial life, psychology and religious experience, spirituality and medicine, and artificial intelligence. These eminent thinkers and "prophets" discussed science and religion and their interrelationship, for the coming 21st century.

I take the liberty in adopting them in this chapter on prospective for 21st century. They are as follows:

Part One: Origin,

1. The universe as a Home for life,

2. Evolutionary Biology

3. Life in the Universe,

4. Genes and genetic engineering

5. Faith, medicine and well-being

6. The Mind

7. Personhood and the soul

8. Quantum physics and relativity

9. Limitations to science, and

10. Science / Religion dialogue.

I shall summarize what these eminent scholars wrote and discussed, as the core in my presentation.   At the end, I shall add Prof. Martin Rees's talk given at the 150th anniversary of publication of "The Origin of Species" at Cambridge. In a way, Prof. Rees talks about the peril of 21st century.

Part One: Origin:

By Russell Stannard,;   with Ted Burge, Rod Davis and Paul Davis.

In the Preface, Prof. Russell Stannard writes as "Modern science has revolutionized our understating of the world. This much is obvious. But how have these developments impacted on our knowledge of God? And how do we now see human beings fitting into the overall scheme? To find out, Prof. Stannard approached fifty scholars noted for their contributions to the ongoing discussion of the inter-relationships between science and religion (Christianity as my modification). He asked each to write a short essay on some aspects of the way our thinking should be revised in the light of what is known at the dawn of the 21st century. The contributions were not to be scholarly treaties aimed at fellow academicians, but informal writing accessible to a wide readership.

The writers are   drawn from right countries, and represent the Christian Jewish, Islamic and Hindu traditions. Most of them are scientists by profession, but also include are philosophers, theologians and psychologists. The topics range from cosmology, evolution and genetic engineering to extraterrestrial life, the soul, and the current status of the scientific/religious debate. Taken together, these authors present a challenge and enriched understanding of God, and of God's interaction with the world and with ourselves.

Prof. Stannard said, "Much has been written on this topics "Origin" in recent years. Authors strayed beyond confines of their science to venture a few thoughts on how new findings affect traditional ideas about Creator-God. There has been a claim that modern scientific views render worthless of the biblical account of creation. It would be so if the Genesis account were intended as a literal description of our origin."

Dr. Ted Berg's modernized that creation story getting across the same divine truth. The world and where we are, are ultimately dependent for our existence on God. It does so in a way that accords with our modern understanding of cosmology. Rod Davies sees Jodrell Bank radio telescope as his probing into the mystery of early universe as not only a scientific exploration but also an awesome religious quest. The Big Bang and subsequent physical and biological evolution are firmly established beliefs in the minds of nearly all scientists. When set side by side with the story of creation in Genesis, they appear to give a more convincing account of material creation. But, the two accounts have different purposes. The scientific one makes no mention of God. Genesis is primarily concerned with the

divine truth of god and the creation, and God's relation to humankind. Belief in him as Creator and our dependence on him remains firm and un-changed. God said "let there be....And he created the unified forces of physics, with perfect harmony and prescient precision. Out of nothing, and into nothing, God by free decision, set up the spontaneous production of particles, in newborn space and time, producing a silent, seething sphere, infinitesimally small and unimaginably hot. There was onset and evolution, the first stage of creation. Subsequent to this, there are 2nd, 3rd, 4th, 5th, 6th and 7th stages of creation. So, God sent his Son, the Word made flesh, who dwelt among us as Jesus of Nazareth, suffered, died and rose from the dead, and showed his glory, full of grace and truth. That was the beginning of the new creation.

Rod Davies wrote that study of the origin of the universe is both scientific and religious voyage of discovery; scientific because we use the techniques of the scientific methods - exploration and deduction; religious because it contains the element of awe and wonder, and it stimulates questions about purpose and ends. The current scientific view is that the cosmo began with a Big Bang. The universe us expanding from a compact phase of condensed matter since the beginning of time.   Much of my recent scientific effort has been devoted to the search for these week and elusive signals – clues to the secrets of the origin of the universe. The Judeo-Christian reaching out for an understanding of our origin is encapsulated in Genesis: "In the beginning God created the heaven and the earth."

In the New Testament we have the Green philosophical addition, John sums it up in the gospel. The Word or Logos, we have the kernel of what the Christians believe about God the Creator. Having created the world, God is in the world and part of it. In Him we have our being. If we get our minds "around" this philosophical concept, the scientific approach to creation and the religious approach merge.

The anthropic priniciple, which affirms that the universe must have within it those properties which allow life to develop at some stage of its history. "The most n-intelligible thing about the universe is that it is intelligible," said Einstein. In such recent thinking, I begin to see a synthesis of the scientific and religious approach to the wonder and potential of creation.

Dr. Paul Davies said that what happcned before the Big Bang? It is often that science cannot prove the existence of God. Yet, science does have value in theological debate because it gives us new concepts that sometimes make popular notions of God un-tenable. One of these concerns is the nature of time. What God was doing before he created the universe?   The fifth-century theologian St. Augustine solved the problem by proclaiming that the world was made with time and not in time. In other word, time itself is part of God's creation. This is the notion of a timeless Deity. We can see that Augustine was right and popular religion wrong to envisage God as s super being dwells within the stream of time prior to the creation. It means God sustaining   the existence of the universe, and its laws, at all times, from a location outside of space and time.

Paul Davies sees Big Bang as no ordinary exploration; it did not occur at a point of time. Rather, it marked the beginning of time. Many people are disturbed to learn that there could have no God before the Big Bang – because there was no "before". Davies clarifies what it means to think of God as "Creator". Prof. Berg concludes that our belief in God as Creator, and our dependence on Him remain firm and un-changed.

Part Two: The Universe as a Home for Life" (anthropic principle):

By Michael   Poole, Owen Gingerich, Bruce Guiderdoni, Howard Van Till and Gregg Easterbrook.

At first sight, the universe is so vast and hostile, could   it be "a home" for life, satisfying a range of physico-chemico-astronomical conditions, collectively known as *anthropic principle*.

Profs. Michael Pool (King's College) and Owen Gingerich (Harvard University) point out that the universe seems so vast and hostile, yet itself constitutes with ~~there~~ being a purpose behind it, i.e. ~~knockdown~~ knock-down proof   of   a *Designer God.*, having a purpose behind creation.   As Stephen Hawking once said that " if the density of the universe one second after the Big Bang had been greater by one -part -in a -thousand- billion, the universe would have collapsed after ten years. On the other hand, if the density of the universe at that time had been less by the same amount, the universe would have been essentially empty since it was about ten years old." "Without these many details of the physical and chemical world, intelligent life wouldn't exist in our universe. Scientists have given this observation a name, i.e. the *anthropic principle*.   For several decades theists and atheists have been wrangling over the meaning of the anthropic principle. For the theists, the anthropic principle may not be a proof of God's existence, but it is surely a pointer to a creative super-intelligence at work. Fred Hoyle once exclaims, "a super-intelligence was at work." How true it is! Some cosmologists are theists, some are atheists. But they are universally awed by the sweep and grandeur of the cosmos.

Van Till emphasizes that in deep mystery, the gift of self-organization is perhaps best seen as evidence of a creative mind. G. Easterbrook points out that the universe is "pointless" and life "a cosmic joke" is steadily giving way to a more buoyant and meaningful assessment of humanity. Our existence was made possible only by the occurrence of many coincidences. Carl Feit said that "20th century physics not only is compatible with religious thought but actually point to the necessity for the postulate that an Omnipotent and Purposive Creator is running the whole show."

In 1968 when three astronauts, Frank Borman, Jim Lovell and William Anders aboard Apollo 8 were struck by the beauty and frailty of our planet, and also the beauty of it. They read several verses in Genesis 1, seeing distance and difference ~~become~~ between nations vanished. As a consequence, they urged us to

live together peacefully!   The cosmo is not at all hostile to life. Our existence was made possible only by the occurrence of many coincidences as designed by Divine.

A recent survey, reported in Nature, indicates that forty per cent of working scientists have a belief in a personal deity. Carl Feit says that as a professional scientist, I find many of my colleagues are indeed theists. Leading physicists Drs. John Barrow and Paul Davies argue that in 20th century physics not only is compatible with religious thought but actually point to the necessity for the postulate that an Omnipotent and Purposive creator is running the whole show.

Part Three. Evolutionary Biology:

By Arthur Peacocke, Wentzel Van Huyssteen, Barbara Smith-Moran,.

Arthur Peacocke points out that the initial reaction to Darwin's ideas was not negative as popular legend would have us to believe. To-day, we recognize even more clearly that the evolutionary process is an invitation to reflect on our understanding of God's ongoing relationship to the living world. Christianity and science should be seen as complementary – the former giving meaning to the otherwise blind mechanisms of the latter. Huyssteen sees this is leading to rewarding conversations between religion and sciences. Berry said that "science and God, evolution and creation are not alternatives. They are complements. God's work in creation and in evolution can be described exactly the same way. Reason tells us that evolution has taken place in the way Darwin described it, while my faith tells me that God governed the whole process. The New Testament tells us that "through faith we understand that the world was framed by the Word of God so that the things which are seen were made from those which were not seen." It is just as much an act of faith to believe that God did not make the world as it is to believe that he did. Un-believers use faith as much as believers, although in an opposite direction. Christians are entirely happy with the idea that God ha used evolution as his method of creation. Science and God, evolution and creation, are not alternatives. They are complements.

Under the title of "The Disguised Friend: Darwinism and Divinity" Prof. Arthur Peacocke of Oxford University proposes that God is the Continuous Creator. He is all the time creating – through the process of nature which the biologist uncovers. God makes things make themselves. The splendid anorama aaaaaof both cosmic and biological evolution should be a stimulus to worship and awe. Either God is everywhere present in nature, or He is nowhere. It is the interplay of chance and law that allows the matter of the universe to be self-creative of new forms of organization.

Prof. Wentzel van Huyssteen, under the title of "Evolution:the key to knowledge of God" says that evolution by natural selection has traditionally and famously been regarded by many as a foe of Christian theology. Some neo-Darwinians have famously claimed that religion is just an extraneous "virus

of the mind." This position does not take into account the amazing pervasiveness of religion through the ages. Certain Christian theologians are claiming that they are closely related to the evolution of human cognition. On this view, metaphysical and religious beliefs are not at all in conflict with evolution, but are actually make intelligent by evolution.

Prof. Barbara Smith-Moran is a Chairperson of the Episcopal Church Working Group on Science, Technology and Faith, using the title of "The Evolutionary Past and Future of God". She said in the beginning that there are two creation stories, e.g. one in the Creation Narratives, in the Bible, God plays the starring role of Creator "in the beginning". To-day, there is another creation story. The story of evolution that tells us that it happens in a different way. Instead, things took form over billions of years. Evolution is the brainchild of the 19th century scientists Alfred Russell Wallace and Charles Darwin. They see the role of cooperation, not competition alone, as the key to the way evolution works.

Peacocke suggests that if Christian faith is to be intelligible and believable at all to each generation, it must express itself in ways that are consonant with such understandings as the generation has of the world around it. God is the continuous Creator. He is all the time creating – through the processes of nature which the biologists uncovers, God makes things made themselves. The splendid panorama of both cosmic and biological evolution should be a stimulus to our worship, and a sense of awe.

Part Four: Life in the Universe:

By Chris Kaiser, Robert Jastrow, Robert Russell, Willem Dress and Zaki Badawi.

The first question Christopher Kaiser asks, "Are we alone in the cosmos?" Or are there any other living things being out there just waiting to make contact? Any living being with intelligence exists elsewhere? This is not easy to answer. Kaiser writes that good planets are hard to find. Humans are unique. So, why are plants and animals, and humans are able to survive on earth? Most astronomers say that the reason is that we have the moon. The moon is larger enough to raise tides and to make earth's orbit stable. No other planets in the solar system have a moon big enough to do that. Fred Hoyle estimates that a priori probability of life assembling out of inanimate matter to be in ten raised to the one hundred millionth power. Robert Shapiro estimates to be one in 10992. Dress feels the existence of life elsewhere would pose no particular problem for traditional belief in God. Astronomers tell us that giant planets are too cold for water to flow on their surface. They are all made of frozen gases like Jupiter. The smaller planets and moon could be just right size. Can they be stable enough for life? Robert Jastrow says that we may be alone in this universe. Although humans stand at the summit of creation on this planet, in the cosmic order our position is humble.

Part Five: Genes and Genetic Engineering:

By Keith Ward, Elving Anderson, John Habgood, Ted Peters, Celia Deane-Drummond, and Michael Northcott.

This Part Five is the most extensive coverage on science and Christian ethics in life. The ideas discussed are broad and interesting.

Prof. KeithWard   writes as follow: " There is a war between science and religion. At least, there is a group of scientists and philosophers who lose no opportunity to attack belief in God as infantile and incompatible with scientific knowledge. Among the most vocal are a number of neo-Darwinists. They are well-known to many of us. One of them even claims that minds and bodies are anarchistic federation of selfish genes! But, it is not the biology which establishes these claims.   It is rather a dogmatic materialism which interprets the biological evidences in a slanted way. The evidence for God is not objective experience but personal experience. The refusal to count personal experience as evidence is simply a dogma of materialism. For the religious believer, God is not an entity slipped into gaps in the empirical world. God is a spiritual presence, and value who can be sensed in and through all things. Of course, the investigation of nature should tell us something about God – in fact it seems to show how beautiful, intelligent, elegant, and intricate the structure of natural world is, and thereby how intelligent and powerful its Creator is.

How could evolutionary biology throw doubt on this? Only by showing that the evolutionary process is of the blind chance or accident, so that it could not have created by a God for a purpose. For some physicists, there is no such thing as "blind chance" in nature, which is why physicists are rarely as dogmatic as evolutionary biologists. But one main ploy of the neo-Darwinians is to eliminate all signs of purpose from the evolutionary process, by making purposes a by-product of blindly selfish behavior by millions of genes. Genes may indeed be blind, since they have no awareness. But how then can they be called "selfish"? The poetic metaphor of the "selfish gene" is a powerful one, but its defects are greater than its inventor, Richard Dawkins! In his book, he concedes that genes express their selfishness by means of cooperating with other sets of genes – which sounds like what Humpty Dumpty (for whom words can means whatever he wants them to) might mean by "selfishness." The basic fact behind the selfish gene metaphor is that sequences of DNA replicate, and that some sequences replicate efficiently while others do not, largely because of the environmental conditions favoring their survival. The fact behind the "selfish cooperator" metaphor is that the most efficient replicating sequences will often be those which form parts of larger organisms, constructed by the cooperative activity of many sequences of DNA. What the metaphor of selfish gene does is to lead un-suspecting readers to think that persons are by-products of tiny self-serving strings of molecules.

It is better to eliminate the metaphor, and marvel at the truly amazing order

and design of the genetic code, which brings persons into being by incredibly elegant natural processes over many thousands of generations. Genes are neither selfish nor cooperative. But it would not be too difficult to see them as part of an intricate and elegant code written into the amount of structure of matter itself by a supreme Mind, with the purpose of generating responsible and intelligent persons from un-conscious and un-thinking material.

Evolutionary biology is an exciting and mind-expanding subject. It would be sad if it became too closely associated with irrational attacks on a spiritual perception of the world. It promises a better understanding of the rational structure of the world. It promises to expand human responsibility to shape the world toward realizing worthwhile purpose and goal. The goal has been implicit in the universe from the beginning. It would be reasonable to see it as the purpose of the cosmos in the mind of God (by Keith Ward).

Prof. Anderson and Habgood warn against simplistic interpretation, as Prof. Ward points out. The interlocking complexities of the circumstances under which genes operate mean that we are more than our genes. Not only that, the overall picture remains consistent with there being divine purpose. Anderson says that genetic therapies that are directed at genes themselves by enhancing the function of partially defective/deficient genes or by reducing the expression of harmful genes. All these require attention to relevant aspects of life-style. Humans adapt their genes to the environment more than genes adapt to environment. There is the specter of "genetic determinism". That means we are merely the product of our genes. This is indeed theoretically absurd. Do our lives-can be ultimately reduced to the action of genes? Many lines of scientific evidence contract these claims. We can conclude that, while genes are essential for human existence and human behavior. They are by no means sufficient by themselves. The intricate genetic design is fully consistent with a sincere belief in the Creator. We shall never be able to describe adequately humans solely in their genes. Additional modes of understanding, including the spiritual dimension, will continue to be needed in order to complete the picture of what it is to human! All these new challenges will cause us to test our collective humility. There is more to learn, we do not know enough. Results could not be well predicted. He warns that scientists should embark genetic engineering work, especially with higher animals even humans, with a sense of fear and also optimism, but with great care, reversibly whenever possible. Prof. Habgood looks at Richard Dawkins' "selfish genes" as genetic determinism make no sense at all in creatures as complex as we are. We are conscious beings, being open to their environment, and as dependent on social interaction as human beings have always known themselves to be.

The genes are now known to be encoded in the DNA molecule. The Human Genome Project aims to map out all these codes, identifying the function of each. Having done this, it becomes possible to modify their structure, thus giving rise to alternative behavior. Ted Peters raises the question of whether this is desirable or not. Clearly, a strong case can be made for the eradication of diseases arising from

malfunctioning genes. But what of genetic engineering? We must choose – and choose we can; though genetically influenced, we retain our free wills.

Celia Deane-Drummond sees genetic manipulation allowing us to control how a species develops; we can even move genes from one species to another. This offers both promise and risk: We need to proceed cautiously, showing respect for the creature, keeping in mind the whole picture, and remaining alert to our own motive. *Human creativity is a gift from God*. We have here the potential to become co-Creators with God – but only if we act wisely. Further, she says that all great religions have given us a source of wisdom through many centuries. Our desire for knowledge, especially scientific know-how has often blinded us to the need to develop wisdom. In fixing problems we need to look at the whole picture. By wisdom, I mean the ability to have the wisest possible perspectives on life, to see things as a whole. It includes reason but recognize the reason is only part of the story. A theological approach to wisdom becomes the quest for goodness and truth. Then, it is judged by the goodness it promotes for the whole global community. Scientists in the early centuries were well aware of the need to combine their research with their religious insights. Their desire was to work for the common good. Isaac Newton spent much time in the study of theology as in physics. The split between science and religion is a relatively new and modern occurrence over the past several hundred years. We need to reflect on wisdom. Then, we make our wise move.

Michael Northcott talks about the particular contentious issue of the cloning humans. The prospect is raised of genetically engineering a race of perfect super-humans through the creation of "designer babies". Is this what we want? Would it not be better to save our genetic inheritance in its flawed state but being wondrous in diversity?

Part Six: Faith, Medicine and Well-being:

By David Myers, Dale Matthews, Harold Koenig, Herbert Benson and Patricia Myers.

A sense of well-being can be depend on one's state of health. A notable field of research that has opened up in recent years is the scientific   study of the health benefits associated with religious observance. Dale Matthews pointed out that there are more than 300 studies conclusively demonstrating the medical value of religious commitment. In light of this evidence, physicians would do well to encourage patients to continue with, or least consider, authentic religious activities. It has been demonstrated that those who go to church on regular basis is living longer, on average, than those who do not. Harold Koenig puts it, not going to church has the equivalent effect on mortality of smoking one pack of cigarettes per day for 40 years. In addition to physical benefits, religion has been demonstrated to be particularly helpful in regard to mental health. Of course, it remains to be seen whether the association between religion and good health is the

causal one. But either way, the effects cannot be ignored. Herbert Benson and Patricia Myers are led to wonder whether that religious faith could have become incorporated by natural selection in our genes. In our developed countries ~~of the world~~ we have ~~got~~ accustomed to an ever -increasing standard of living. The correlation between income/wealth and happiness is surprisingly weak. The lure of accumulated riches has long held out of the prospect of happiness. Well-being includes physical (material), marital, psychological/mental/ emotional, and spiritual health. It is a total sum of them.

Princeton sociologist Robert Wuthnow found that 89% people felt that our society is too much materialistic. These people thought that they would be happier if they had more money, nicer home and personal home-keeper. Yet, rich people have a higher rate of depression, and divorce is doubled. Movie stars and entertainers use drugs to support their activities, not because they were happier. Many of them end their lives in misery. All purchased is in a vain quest for an elusive joy. No doubt, we all need food, shelter and money. But more of everything does not mean better quality of life. Jesus said that "is not life more important than food and clothing?"

Well-being is a total sum of physical, emotional, marital and spiritual wellness. Medical science and professionals in recent years realize the importance of religious beliefs and practices that have an impact on physical and mental health. People who are married in religious wedding with pledges prove to last much longer, being happier as well. Those who practice more religious involvement, not only have more social contact and support, have much less sickness and earlier recoveries in sickness. In this health-conscious age, patients demand more from medical professionals. They want more compassion and less dispassion. They are more listening and less lecturing. They seek healers of mind and spirit, not just the mechanics of the body. There are reports that people having no religious practices have an effect on mortality equivalent to 40 years of smoking one pack of cigarettes per day! Likewise, some religious beliefs are repressive and controlling, rather than guiding and liberating. Holy healing is an abuse of religious faith. Such cults may instill fear, foster obsessive-compulsive traits. They would lead to close-mindness and prejudice. Good religions have scientific evidence on personal well-being, having positive effect. We need to have faith, love and hope. They have become part of the way to human approaching living. Faith allows us to appreciate the un-seen and not-yet-approved, generating a kind of hope that can't be obtained by reason. Belief in God is natural to humanity, and offers so much blessings. People should be encouraged to consider authentic, autonomous religious activities. Perhaps in 21st century, clinicians will join the clergy to develop new synthesis of scientifically based and religiously meaningful medical practices and cares to help people who suffer, and seek for authentic aid in both body and spirit.

Part Seven: The mind.

By   Dan Blazer, Frazer Watts and Vilayanur Ramachandran.

It is commonly thought that psychological studies are inherently hostile to religious belief. ***Sigmund Freud, an avowed atheist*** originally tried to reduce people to hydraulics, likening them and their mind to a steam engine with pressures contained by valves. Later, he came to accept that neurotic conflicts cannot be reduced to molecules and brain chemistry – he had to engage in"soul talk." For example, the sexual drive is the primary energy for this machine. God is manufactured in the mind of people to contain and control this excess of energy. If God could be eliminated, that energy could be better channeled through mature sexual expression, among other behaviors. Later on, he modified his theory. He recognized that theory was one thing, practice the other.   He listened to people, to their hope, fears, dreams and beliefs. He tried to help them, yet to no avail. Then, he went to the question of brain. He thought that the care of the psyche is the care of the brain. Through medications   he thought that these patients may relieve symptoms. They failed and fell far short of healing the emotion and comforting the soul. In later time, he came to accept that neurotic conflicts could not be reduced to molecules and brain chemistry. Freud himself had to engage in "soul talk". Eventually, he became a "soul doctor". Many of his disciples today renew their interest in the spiritual, and seeking dialogue with theologians. Would Freud turn over in his grave if he knew of this alliance?   Maybe, nobody would think so.

Today, among certain biologists there is once more a drive to try to answer life's ultimate questions solely in term of the physical terms. For example, the care of the psyche is just the care of the brain. But, psychiatrists find – as Freud did before them. This simply does do not the job. Consequently, some of them are expressing renewed interest in the spiritual, as Blazer explains.

Watts asks what can brain science say about religious experience? Psycho-analysts thought of a   "God-spot" in the brain. To their surprise that different parts of the brain are involved in different aspects of religious experience. To people who have faith, a wide variety of   religious experiences bringing a sense of tranquility and purpose that often stay with them for a long time.   life is permeated with the sense of the spiritual. Being so, it is unlikely that scientists will not be able to locate a unique "God spot" in the brain. Buy, how it functions? This is altogether beyond their approach. But, if they did, there would be no reason for concluding that God was not being genuinely revealed through such experiences.

Part Eight: Personhood and the Soul:

By Malcolm Jeeves, John Polkinghorne, Anne Foerst, and Henry Thompson.

In recent years materialistic, even atheistic scientists describe man and woman as a machine, or physical entity with organs, cells and even genes. Artificial intelligence research aims at constructing a machine like human being. Altogether, they thought of human in physical term, paying no attention to the personhood, let along spirit, soul and personhood. Neuroscientist Antonio Damasio contends the distinction between the "brain" and "mind" is an unfortunate cultural inheritance that reflects ignorance of the actual brain and mind relationship. Francis Crick once wrote in his book, "your joy and sorrow are no more than the behavior of a vast   assembly of nerve cells and their associated molecules."

Few neuroscientists any longer believe that humans are composed of two distinct and separate parts, brain and mind, or body and soul. With every neuroscience advance comes further confirmation of the inseparable bond between brain and mind. People of faith continues to speak and sing words that assume that our human nature includes an entity called a soul which interacts with our bodies but leaves at our death. Nobel Laureate John Eccles believes that mind and soul are indeed non-material entities that interacts with the physical body. Dr. Mal Jeeves, as a believer and neuroscientist believes that "I am a unified living being with both physical and mental aspects. The mental dimension of my being is an important as the physical body/brain on which it depends. Over the centuries both Jewish and Christian biblical scholarship reminds us that our "soulishness" can be understood as our relatedness to God, to other humans, and to all the creation. The biblical idea is remarkably similar to neuroscience view that we are psychosomatic unities, not dualistic packages. I am a living being or soul, not a dualistic packages. In this aspect, animals differ from human in "soulishness" in qualitative. Humans have the critical capacities for personal relatedness, complex language, forming theory of mind, historical memory and for contemplating the future. Such highly developed "soulishness"   makes human unique. It confers the capacity for personal relationship with God.

Prof. Polkinghorne thinks that we humans are more than merely materials. When I was hit with a hammer, I am hurt, depending on my body, more than a body alone. We are a kind of package deal, mind and body closely related, not detachable from each other. We should think of it as the system as a whole. Whatever the soul may be, it is surely the "real me". That real me is certainly not the matter of my body. Hebrew scholars in the old days took this package deal full of life. St. Thomas Aquinas thought the same. But, if the "soul" is not a detachable spiritual part, what hope do we have of a destiny beyond death? As Christians we have our hope that death is not the end dependent on our belief in the trustworthiness of God. It makes perfect sense that the pattern that is in me, and re-create those patterns in the world to come. Christians call it resurrection! Such a hope is as credible in this 3rd millennium as it has been in the preceding two thousand years!

Anne Foerst says that it is God's creation of us that assigns value and

personhood to each individual. Since the biblical creation is universal so is the promise is universal

Part Nine: Quantum physics and relativity:

By David Bartholomew, Nancy Abrams, Joel Primack and John Houghton

As a hard science, physics is out to have no paradox. Yet, in quantum physics paradox is common. Light was discovered to have dual nature. Some experiments pointed to its being a wave. Other indicates its being a stream of particles. This is odd. How can something be both a spread-out wave, and at the same time a small localized particle? Paradox has been a feature of Christian theology from earliest time on. For example, Trinity is a good example. He is being God the Father, Son and the Holy Spirit. Each is fully God. Difficult thought it was to see how the apparent contraction is to be reconciled. Any simpler description of God would not do justice to the totality of the evidence. When they come to consider who is Jesus? Then theologians point out that he is fully God and man –omnipotent, omnipresent God and at the same time limited, localized man. Christian theology has many paradoxes, every bit as puzzling as those that have surfaced in quantum physics.

On the other hand, the course of evolution in biology depends crucially on accidents of reproduction. It is over the over the role of chance in evolution that belief in a controlling God has taken a hardest knocks. Literature-popularized writer of Oxford Richard Dawkins see God as un-necessary, chance and accident do it all. If the writer is correct, there appears very little left for any God to do so. After all, in previous battles, science always to have won. Would it not be better to recognize the inevitable and retire gracefully? Retreat would be premature, first, because it is mistaken to suppose that chance is inconsistent with order and purpose. On the contrary, some of life's greatest certainties are built on chance. It seems that uncertainty at one level can lead to another. Sometime, a single event way back in the evolutionary family tree might have played a determining role in whether or not humans would eventually appear on earth. Again, the chance impact of a meteorite cab wipes out whole species – as is believed to have happened to the dinosaurs. Even in such cases, one can still point to a way in which certainty may emerge from uncertainty. Chance may well be a necessary ingredient of the recipe for producing life. From this viewpoint, chance is not an alternative to God, but something one might expect him to know about and use. God does not have to fashion each tiny flower that opens in minute detail. He goes one better and creates a system with the potential for self-creation. One thing we are certain is that intelligent life has appeared in the universe. Does all of this make it any easier to see how God might actually do things, like answer prayer?

In their eagerness to retain the role of God, some Christians have supposed that if we can see no reason for something happening, then God must be directly responsible. The chance at the heart of the atom is then see as one place where

God may be pulling the strings. May be God's way of acting is as mysterious as our own. After all, we really may have little idea of how our own intentions arise and are translated into actions. When we have solved that problem, then we might be better placed to tackle the bigger question of how God does it.

Did Einstein believe in God? Yes or no, it is in a different expression. When astronomer George Smoot announced, in 1992, the discovery of ripple in heat radiation still arriving from Big Bang, Einstein said it was "like seeing the face of God." Another astronomer exclaimed, calling the ripple "*the handwriting of God.*" When Niels Bohr and his associates were developing quantum theory, Einstein first did not accept that the ultimate nature of reality as random. Afterward, after seeing the ultimate nature of reality was randomness, Einstein wrote to Max Born in 1926, "It hardly brings us close to the secrets of the Ancient One. *Einstein* said that "in any case, I am convinced that "*He does not play dice.*" Over the years, physicists were profoundly influenced by the faith of this great man of intelligence who wrote "I am a deeply religious non-believer…. This is somewhat new kind of religion." To Einstein, the concept of a personal God was the main source conflict between science and religion. God was not a father, king, or confidant. Nor was God the source of morality." Then, what kind of God did Einstein believe in?" *Einstein said that "I believe in Spinoza's God who reveals himself in the harmony of all that exists, but not in a God who concerns himself with the fate and actions of human beings."* The rock of Einstein's faith was that the world is rational. Thought it can be proved to be. To Einstein, what made science possible was this faith: causes lead to effects, not by any one's changeable will, but by the operation of natural laws." For him, the great sacrilege was belief in miracle. He was moved by profound reverence for the rationality made manifest in existence. Einstein named this special reverence "cosmic religious feeling. which knows no dogma and no God conceived in man's image. He defined cosmic religious feeling as a "spirit manifested in the laws of the universe – a spirit vastly superior to that of man." He believed that this awareness was the strongest and noble motivation for scientific research, the only creative religious activity of our time." Einstein thinks that why great scientists so often feel drawn to the imagery of God. Those who experience cosmic religious feeling will tend to be more deeply dedicated to their work, and thus likely to become great scientists.

The sacred dimension of science is a subject most scientists today avoid. They may fear mis-understanding and judgment by colleagues. Perhaps they have never really thought through their own ideas. Einstein outspokenness on his religious attitude was rare. Today science is attacked by post-modern philosophers claiming that all truths are relative (a horrendous misuse of Einstein's concept) and by creationists claiming that their metaphor is absolute truth. Under these circumstances, there are good reasons most scientists avoid all possibility of confusion with religion by never using terms suggestive of divinity.

The price we pay is that there is no way to communicate an awesome reality: we are actually answering questions today who very asking used to be a religious

act. The astrophysicists who descried the cosmic ripples as "the hand-writing of God" is a contributor in this chapter. When we interpret the ripple in cosmic background irradiation, we are reading God's journal of the first day.

John Houghton is writing our 4-dimension world of space-time with things we can touch, hear and experience. God is out there in another dimension. If we could find a window into such an extra dimension, that would be something very big indeed. It would create a revolution for us just like Einstein's new time dimension for science. Christianity claims just that. The God out there has entered our world in the person of Jesus. His life is remarkable. So was his death! Even more remarkable is the story of his resurrection from death. The account in New Testament of the Bible describes how he had appeared to his disciple with a new body which could appear and disappear at will. All these could appear just fanciful if it were not that ever since that time people experienced the living person of Jesus. How does this happen? The disciples spoke about a close personal relationship. It is as if they are not just imaging some remote being but experiencing him for real. Because God with the extra dimension is not limited to the dimension of space or time. God has much greater freedom of action than we conceivably know. Hebrews in the Old Testament thought of God as out there and within his people. The prophet Isaiah described God who "dwells in the high and holy place, with him also that is of a contrite and humble spirit. Jesus constantly used pictures and analogies, we call them parables. Scientists especially like to think in term of models. In a world buzzing with scientific and technical language and jargon, metaphor and model from the world of science can help us gain a measure of understanding of other parts of our experience.

Houghton claims that this analogy of God in a fifth dimension, beyond the 4-D world in which we live, really stimulates and stretches our thinking about where God is and how He acts. Just as a 3-D world is solid compared with the flimsy 2-D world of Flatland, so experience which involve God in the extra spiritual dimension can be much more solid and real than the material world we know so well. A message is this that I can bring God into my life and star to experience the fifth dimension now.

Part Ten: Limitations to Science:

By George Ellis, William Stoeger and Robert Hermann.

We all are impressed by the pace of scientific advance, and the way it is transforming our world through technology. Such successes have led certain scientists to adopt a triumphalist stance, claiming their science to be the only sure route to knowledge and understanding. This is known as "scientism". Other modes of investigation (religion, for example) can be dismissed as un-necessary and irrelevant.

George Ellis disagrees. He points out that *valuable though science is, it has its limitations. It is unable to speak meaningfully on subject such as aesthetics*

and ethics, or metaphysical religious issues. Great progress has been made by science in the last century. This underlies the technology that has transformed our lives in various ways. No one could image that a century later we understand the molecular basis of heredity and the genetic coded. The impression given is that we find not limit in the future by science.. This idea is wrong! As our understanding of the universe increases, so does our understanding of the limits on what science will be even able to do. Science and scientific methods have their limits too. *Areas such as love, morality, aesthetics, beauty, the inspiration by symphony, painting, poetry, theatrics,   moral value,   metaphysics and meaning of human existence*. Richter scale could not weigh them, and meter fails to measure them. Love is beyond any way of prove. Another category is metaphysical issues. We all know that gravity exists. But, we can't tell people why it works. The earth pulls the moon at such a long distance, by gravity. That is not an explanation in any fundamental sense. Science can tell you what the laws of physics are, but it cannot tell you why they exist. Science can't tell you why the universe exists. Above all, it cannot tell you whether or not God exist. Yet, you could feel his presence in your life and daily living. These limitations can't be changed by future advance in science; they are fundamental to its nature. We cannot expect to solve ethical or moral or metaphysical issues. Sciences form a valuable part of human life, but it is not the basis for a whole human life. We shall need to study and teach ethics, aesthetics and philosophy and theology as well as science. Those who claim science will supplant any or any of them are indulging in a little fantasy. Be kind to them, but don't take them seriously.

Stoeger writes that scientists often tell us that everything that happens can be explained by processes, regularities and interrelationships described by physics, chemistry and biology. There are no gaps in these laws of nature where God can tinker. Nature looks after itself. If this is true, then God is without a job. First, our daily experience tells us that as humans we can make a difference. We have the will and the freedom to live our lives how we wish. Science has its limitations. Personal and community experiences, such as love, wholeness, truth and beauty, meaning and value take us beyond where science comes to a stop. These personal experiences somehow lead us to believe that there is a God involved in our world and in our lives, at the same time, maintain what the sciences reveal. Scientific knowledge is provisional and incomplete. There is so much for us to learn. The world is much more intricate and mysterious than methods of science can unravel. Science leaves out of its consideration any discussion of the origin of those laws and regularities – why they exist at all, or what meaning or significance they might have. What of questions to do with personal significance and value, of "the spirit", and of what may lie beyond death? They are outside the limits of physics, chemistry, biology and even psychology. God does not act in supposed gaps in the laws of nature, but rather in and through the laws themselves. They are expressions of God's creative activity in nature.

The world of ours functions with regularities, relationships and processes, there are laws that are important to our existence. Yet, they are beyond what

sciences can illuminate. In other word, God acts through all these laws, sustaining all things in existence.

Herrmann expounds the convergence of science and religion. Years ago, popular notion was that science was the only trustworthy path to truth. Now, the situation is quite different. It is no longer people turns for answer. Many of them are huger for deeper meaning. Many of them have to religion and religious truth. Those pioneers in science understood and appreciated the world as God gave it to them showing his wisdom and power. Then, years later, scientists began to believe their methodology, being based upon reason and experimentally verifiable fact. The very success of science led to the gradual separation of science and religion. At 20th century, the pendulum began to swing back. Physicists discovered a basic limitation in the measurement of the particles making up atoms. The upshot of this limitation of measurement was puzzling. Events studied led to know that these particles behaved in a precise mathematical way. The reaction of some scientists was annoyance and disagreement. Finally, Einstein responded with "God does not play dice."

Then, cosmology came to know the "Big Bang", a powerful explosion which seemed to confirm the basic notion found in the first verses of Genesis that the universe originated at some point in the past. On the biological side, the origin of life proved to be quite subtle. There seemed to be a delicate and intricate balance in the structure of the cosmos necessary for the emergence of life. The conditions were so restricted as to be given a name: the anthropic principle. If life came about by purely mechanical, even biochemical means, then it was on the basis of special circumstances. The pursuit of science is like peeling an onion. Each layer removed reveals another layer, and so on. Then, it came a new understanding of the nature of scientific truth. The idea that scientific truth ishas arrived   at without felling or bias, solely based on experimental date, has shown to be a myth. Michael Polanyi, philosopher of science showed that no truth is arrived without the scientist assuming (or having faith in) a particular worldview. Accordingly, even in science, there is no such thing as abstract knowledge; it is always held by some one else as a commitment. So faith component, so important in religion, has its counterpart in science.

Logician Thomas Kuhn described in "The Structure of Scientific Revolutions" that scientific progress was made possible through a series of alternating paradigms. Sociologists went ever so far as to suggest that scientific truth was purely the product of complex social interactions, dependent upon the prevailing "worldview" of those scientists involved.

Then, people began to rethink the importance of religious faith as a valid source of truth and meaning. Some scientists even wrote books about God. They suggested that many new discoveries in science took us well beyond scientific interpretation, reaching instead into the realm of religion. People would conclude that God has placed remarkable signs in heaven, on earth and in us, pointing to religious faith as an equally valid source of truth.

Part Eleven: Science and Religion Dialogue.

By Kitty Ferguson, Martinez Hewlett, Cyril Domb and   Mary Midgley.

As commonly held by some people, science and religion are enemies. Ferguson and Hewlett offer advice to young people that they might usefully engage in science-and-religion dialogue as they likely encounter at college.

It was commonly yet erroneously held view that science and religion were enemies. Many scientists see now that the two enterprises are engaging in new partnership. University science faculties aren't all hotbeds of atheism. Certainly, your will encounter scientific atheists but many scientists believe in God, and many others are agnostics. Why do the atheistic scientists believe no God? The answer is likely to be deeply personal rather than trying to do with science. If they do say science is the root reason, this is sometimes because they grew us with a narrow, impoverished picture of God – one that simply had to give way when science offered a richer view of reality. But some admit that even if the scientific evidence seemed to show that there is a God, they probably wouldn't change their mind. Science is not the atheistic super-weapon that earlier generation thought it was. It doesn't rule out belief – even orthodox belief. Nevertheless, diehards continue brandishing the old weapon, often attacking some caricature of religion that science (and the believers themselves) rule out. They may do this noisily, and with such sarcasm and scorn, but it's hard to remember the gun isn't loaded, Kitty Ferguson wrote.

"Do I have to choose between God and science?" Prof. Martinez Hewlett answer is an emphatically, "no". The reason is "a realistic understanding of both science and theology reveals areas of rich contact, and even of possible confirmation. A critical and realistic view is that each has its separate domain, and method. Yet, there are also point of distinct contact and communication. Science asks questions of physical world that can be answered by elegant instrumental measurements. These yield clues and insights to be used in building our picture of the material universe. But the "what" and "how" queries often lead the investigators to inevitable "why" question. It is here that we find the scientist has no tools to address this kind of question. This is the sphere of philosophers and the theologians. Too often, scientists lacking any theological training are tempted to extend their results far beyond their own area of expertise. They venture to draw conclusion about religious issues. By the same token, philosophers or theologians, walking into my molecular biology lab are tempting to interpret scientific data and critique the theoretical models being used. They should be wary of entering into scientific discussion. They have to have a clear understanding of the current models the scientists use to explain the physical function. Admittedly, such models of nature are tentative, and always subject to revision. At any rate, philosophical to theological reflection and comments should take place within the worldview held by the current culture.

When I talk to my students in the college, I ask them to think critically about the methods they will employ, the models they use, and above all the limitations of both disciplines. He concludes his essay by quoting Albert Einstein, the greatest scientist of this century, saying "religion without science is blind, science without religion is lame." Also, Prof. William Bragg said, "sometimes people ask if religion and science are not opposed to each other. They are! The thumb and fingers of my hand are opposed to one another. It is oppositional so that more things could be grasped!"

Mary Midgley writes in her article that both science and theology are rooted in a sense of wonder! Religion always flows from a sense of awe at something that is greater than ourselves. That is what the science pursues. Scientists often a sense a awe when they see life so wonderful, and cells function with interwoven mechanisms. Increased understanding of biological world increases scientific awe. This is the kind of open-minded intelligence. It is the dogmatic attitude that would set off feuds between the two disciplines.

Pauline Rudd asks the question of what is the meaning of our existence? We all, irrespective of being a scientist or a person of faith, are searching for deeper meaning. For the scientists and people of faith to engage in dialogue is no trivial task. It would take courage, vision, integrity and mutual respect in so doing. For this to happen, we all need to reflect on the current knowledge from our particular disciplines, and then relate this to the innermost need of the human spirit.

Prof. Medhi Golshani of physics Sharif Univ. in Iran asks the question why hasn't the progress of science brought joy and real happiness to human? In fact, in the last several decades, our society has a marked rise in suicide, a feeling of nihilism, drug abuse, and above all conflict between nations. Why? In my view, much of the trouble lies in the philosophical basis underpinning modern science. Originally, science arose in a religious context. Its pioneers saw nature as the handiwork of an all-knowing God. They also saw humankind's role to be stewardship of the earth. But, over the last two centuries, this picture changed. Science in its modern form is silent about God and our responsibilities toward Him and also ourselves, society and the world. The current outlook misses two important facts. First, our world is much richer than empirical science appears to show. Second, to secure our welfare, there has been a sense of responsibility in scientific work as all human actions. We do not expect this responsible attitude to stem from science itself; it must be brought to science! Recent studies reveal that all theories of science are highly colored by philosophical bias or religious conviction. It is in the concept and the theory that would make our science different and valuable. What we need most is to make science theistic. The unity and harmony of this created world help us to reflect on the unity of its Creator.

The emergence of life in this cosmos requires a fine-tuning between 4 basic forces of nature, i.e. gravitation, electrical and two kinds of nuclear force). To have elements (i.e. carbon, nitrogen, oxygen and phosphorus) available, they have made in the interior of stars with proper conditions of temperature, density and so

on. The creation of these necessary conditions, in turn, depends sensitively on the initial stage of our cosmos, and the relative strengths of basic forces. How are we to account for this fine balance between these four forces in nature? The answer is that God deliberately designed the world to be the home for life.

The scientists' worldview affects not only his or her choice of theories, but also the direction which he or she gives to the application of sciences. A theistic outlook urges all scientists to use their knowledge in the service of promoting happiness and welfare of humankind, irrespective of color of skin, creed and races.

This is the end of this inspiring book entitled in "God for the 21st Century" by more than 50 scholars from eight countries. They represent the Christian, Jewish, Islamic and Hindu tradition, under the editorship of Prof. Russell Strannard of Free University, UK; and it is published by John Templeton Foundation Press, Philadelphia, PA; 194 pages, in 2000 A.D.

Allow me to add one more quotation, as concluding remark. Prof. Alfred North Whitehead, renowned educator and philosopher, sais:

"the future course of human history would depend on the decision of this generation as to the proper relations between science and religion – so powerful are religious symbols through which men and women confer meaning on their lives; so powerful the scientific model through which they could manipulate their environment."

Literature Cited

Russell Stannard, 2000, 194 pages

God for the 21st Century

The Author's concluding remarks for the whole book and also the premise:

At the end of this book, let me conclude it with following summary:

The basic premise of this book is that science and Christian faith are two scholastic disciplines. They are neutral in the inherent nature. They do not come into conflict. The conflict would come when professionals interpret their scholarly work no longer in their respective fields. Let sciences be sciences. Let Christianity or Christian faith be religion. Do not make science as a religious subject. By the same token, do not make religion as a science. If we do so, there is no cultural war anywhere in the world.

Let scientists be scientific, objective, open-mind and are willing to understand Christian faith in its proper perspectives. Let Christian scholars also be open-minded, willing to consider science as scientific discipline. Also, keep the domains in our thinking, and in their proper and specific domains. Science is a smaller domain. Philosophy is a bigger domain. Worldview is a even biggest domain among the three. As Scientists, then remain in the domain of science while we present/interpret our scientific and empirical results. Do no tramp to the domain of philosophy. If you do so, likely you would create conflict with others in philosophy. By the same token, when you present your philosophical contemplation, remain in philosophy. Do not contemplate on any implication of your philosophy in science. If you do so, likely you will create conflict. When you talk about/present your religious view, remain as religion. Do not tramp to either philosophy or science (the worst it would be). If we all are faithful to our profession, we should honor our profession. Do not extend one to the other domain, by all means.

Let both sides maintain an attitude of mutual understanding, mutual respect. Then, we all endeavor to make contributions to our scholarly disciplines, and to the society at large.

Both Galileo Galilei and Albert Einstein, as shown in their quotations, said well of these two disciplines. Prof. Martin Rees warns us of this century as our final century! Prof. Alfred North Whitehead said in his book "Science and Modern World": that "Scientific community of scholars should turn its back on their materialistic viewpoint and convictions. Return to an earlier vision in which nature was studied on the assumption that it would reveal evidence of divine purpose", and *"The future course of human history would depend on the decision of this generation of scholars as to the proper relationships between science and religion."* This world is our home! Let us be God's faithful stewards. In science, let us explore and discover new things in this created world. As Christians we are stewards of God's creation. As stewards, we are required to be faithful and diligent in our stewardship.

On March , 2013, Prof. Rees wrote an editorial on "Denial of Catastrophic Risks" in Science, Vol. 339, page#339, reiterates his concern and advice to the

international community and scientists who are concerned of this "catastrophic risk". He wrote: "some of the scenarios that have been envisaged may indeed be science fiction, but others may be disquieitingly real. I believe these "extremerisks" deserve more serious study. Those fortunate enough to live in the developed world fret too much about minor hazards of everyday life: improper air crashes , possible carcinogens in food, low radiation doses, and so forth. But we should be more concerned about events that have not yet happened but which, if they occur even once, could cause world devastation.

The main threats to sustain human existence now come from people, not from nature. Ecological shocks that irreversibly degrade the biosphere could be triggered by the unsustainable demands of a growing world population. Fast-spreading pandemics would cause havoc in the mega-cities of the developing world. Political tensions will probably stem from scarcity of resources, aggravated by the climatic change. Equally worrying are the imponderable downsides of the powerful new cyber-, bio-, and nano-technologies. Indeed, we are entering an era when a few individuals could via error or terror, trigger societal breakdown.

Some threats are well-known. In the 20th century, the downsides of nuclear science loomed large. At any time in the Cold War era, the superpowers could have stumbled toward Armageddon through muddle and miscalculation. The threat of global annihilation involving tens of thousands of hydrogen bombs is thankfully in abeyance, but now there is growing concern that smaller nuclear arsenals might be used in a regional context, or even by terrorists. We can not rule out a geopolitical realignment that creates a standoff between new superpowers. So a new generation may face its own "Cuba," and one that could be handled less well or less luckily than was the 1962 crisis.

What are some new concerns stemming from fast-developing 21st-century technologies? Our inter-connected world depends on elaborate networks; electric power grids, air traffic control, international finance, just-in-time delivery, and so forth. Unless these are highly resilient, their manifest benefits could be outweighed by catastrophic (albeit rare) breakdown cascading through the system. Social media could spread psychic contagion from a local crisis, literally at the speed of light. Concern about cyber-attack , by criminals or hostile nations, is rising sharply. Synthetic biology likewise offers huge potential for medicine and agriculture, but in the sci-fi scenario where new organisms can be routinely created, the ecology (and even our species) might not long survive un-scathed. Should we worry about another sci-fii scenario, in which a network of computer could develop a mind of its own and threaten us all?

Some would dismiss such concern as an exaggerated jeremiads: after all, societies have serviced for millennia, despite storms, earthquakes and pestilence. But these human-induced threats are different – they are newly emergent, so we have a limited time base for exposure to cope if disaster strikes. That is why a group of naturall and social scientists in Cambridge, UK, plans to inaugurate a research program to identify the most genuine of these emergent risks and asset

how to enhance resilience against them. True, it is hard to quantify the potential "existential" threats from (for instance) bio- or cybertechnology from antificial intelligence, or from runaway climatic catastrophes. But we should at least stare figuring out what can be left in the si-fi bin(for now) and what has moved beyond the imaginary."

This is what Prof. Martin Rees once again endeavor to make us aware of the coming danger, and how to avoid it if there is a possible through our united efforts.

The End

Postscript and Acknowledgement

In Chapter 4th, I quoted a number of sayings on science and Christian faith by well-known and prominent scholars. I wish to acknowledge them, and give due credits as theirs. In each chapter, at the beginning of the description, I also gave a couple of quotations. I hope that the quotation would equate well to what is given in each chapter.

Science and Christian Faith

Their Relationships in the Past, Present and Future

作　者／Stephen C. Y. Liu（劉傑垣）
出版者／美商 EHGBooks 微出版公司
發行者／漢世紀數位文化（股）公司
臺灣學人出版網：http://www.TaiwanFellowship.org
地　　址／106 臺北市大安區敦化南路 2 段 1 號 4 樓
電　　話／02-2707-9001 轉 616-617
印　　刷／漢世紀古騰堡®數位出版 POD 雲端科技
出版日期／2013 年 11 月（亞馬遜 Kindle 電子書同步出版）
總經銷／Amazon.com
臺灣銷售網／三民網路書店：http://www.sanmin.com.tw
三民書局復北店
地址／104 臺北市復興北路 386 號
電話／02-2500-6600
三民書局重南店
地址／100 臺北市重慶南路一段 61 號
電話／02-2361-7511
全省金石網路書店：http://www.kingstone.com.tw
定　　價／新臺幣 600 元（美金 20 元／人民幣 120 元）

32090054R00246